GREAT SMOKY &
SHENANDOAH
NATIONAL PARKS

MICHAEL READ
LORETTA CHILCOAT
DAVID LUKAS

LONELY PLANET PUBLICATIONS
Melbourne · Oakland · London

Great Smoky & Shenandoah National Parks
1st edition – March 2005
ISBN 1 74059 937 3

LONELY PLANET OFFICES

Australia
Head Office
Locked Bag 1, Footscray, Victoria 3011
☎ 03 8379 8000, fax 03 8379 8111
talk2us@lonelyplanet.com.au

USA
150 Linden St, Oakland, CA 94607
☎ 510 893 8555, toll free 800 275 8555
fax 510 893 8572, info@lonelyplanet.com

UK
72–82 Rosebery Ave,
Clerkenwell, London EC1R 4RW
☎ 020 7841 9000, fax 020 7841 9001
go@lonelyplanet.co.uk

Published by Lonely Planet Publications Pty Ltd
ABN 36 005 607 983

CONTENTS

THE AUTHORS

MICHAEL READ
**Coordinating Author,
Great Smoky Mountains National Park**

A longtime resident of North Carolina's central piedmont during his formative years, Michael can still switch on that honeyed Southern twang to get out of a jam. An abject failure at the dying art of moonshining, he turned to the stability of clock-punching in 2000, taking a job at Lonely Planet's Oakland office, where he served as senior designer for the award-winning website lonelyplanet.com. In 2003 Michael succumbed once again to a burning case of wanderlust and hit the road as a full-time travel writer. He contributed to Lonely Planet's recent editions of *Mexico* and *USA & Canada on a Shoestring,* and he is a contributing author on the upcoming *Caribbean Islands.*

LORETTA CHILCOAT
**Shenandoah National Park,
Blue Ridge Parkway**

Loretta was born and raised in rural Maryland and spent many camping trips in Shenandoah National Park. Her first hiking experience in the park was a bit of a disaster. Setting off in late afternoon, she and a few friends unwittingly chose one of the most strenuous trails; barely two hours later, they were forced to set up camp quickly because of nightfall. Not only did their tents take in water because they couldn't see the roaring falls a few feet away, but an overnight snowstorm sealed the deal. Luckily, Loretta gave the park, and the beautiful Blue Ridge Parkway, another go – but the next time, she took plenty of maps and warm clothing. A freelance travel writer for more than 10 years, she's lived in Europe, New York City and even a tiny island off the coast of Maine. Firmly planted in Baltimore, she is also a contributing author on Lonely Planet's *USA, Western Europe* and *USA & Canada* on *a Shoestring* guides, and she is the author of the upcoming *Road Trip: Blue Ridge Parkway.*

DAVID LUKAS
Geology, Ecosystem

David has been an avid student of the natural world since the age of five. This same love took him around the world to study animals and ecosystems in Borneo, the Amazon basin and Central America. Now a professional naturalist, David leads natural history tours, conducts biological surveys and writes about natural history. His articles have appeared in many national magazines, and he writes a weekly nature column for the *Los Angeles Times*. His most recent book is *Wild Birds of California*, and he just finished revising the classic guidebook *Sierra Nevada Natural History*. David also contributed to Lonely Planet's *Yosemite National Park*; *Banff, Jasper & Glacier National Parks*; *Grand Canyon National Park*; *Zion & Bryce Canyon National Parks* and the *Costa Rica* guide.

FROM THE AUTHORS

Michael Read Special thanks to commissioning editor Kathleen Munnelly for giving me the nod for this engrossing and truly enjoyable project (and for patiently answering my emails at 2am). To my co-authors, Loretta Chilcoat and David Lukas, thank you for your professionalism, attention to detail and truly excellent work. Gustavus Kundahl lent his considerable expertise and enthusiasm for the Appalachian Trail, mountain music and Cherokee Indians. My beloved iPod and the Clinch Mountain Boys deserve special mention for helping me stay awake during the marathon cross-country drive from California to the Smokies. Much gratitude to Great Smoky Mountains National Park Librarian Annette Hartigan for opening the park's amazing photo library to me. Thanks also to my mother, Jody Read, for tolerating the incursion of her hungry, grown son at her Highlands, North Carolina, home for months on end; to my father, Kenneth 'The Coot' Read, for joining me on a bicycle tour across Cades Cove; and to my Chimney Tops escort, Gerard Granucci. Most of all, thanks to Irene Rietschel for giving me so much to look forward to.

Loretta Chilcoat Many, many thanks to commissioning editor Kathleen Munnelly and to coordinating author Michael Read for the patience and understanding both of them gave to me during write-up. Thanks also to Julia Scott for stellar itinerary assistance, as well as to Aimee Grove, Elly Wells, Frankie Love, Debbie Robinson, Michelle Wilson, Amy Hart, Marcia Greene, Rosemary Chandler, Vicki and Mark Maurer, Mariann Dellerba and the stellar staff at the Shenandoah National Park and Blue Ridge Parkway headquarters. A big thumbs up to my husband, Brad, and the rest of my family for watching three-month old Emaline during my treks and to my travel compatriots, Edith Gans and Maggie West, for additional babysitting on the road and for transcribing my running commentary while driving around hairpin curves.

David Lukas Special thanks to Michael Read for his assistance in tracking down research materials and to Kathleen Munnelly for her gracious feedback on pressing questions.

INTRODUCTION

Without question, the ancient mountains of the southern Appalachians are the most rugged and scenic of the eastern United States. A walk through the woods in the Blue Ridge or Great Smokies will boggle your mind while liberating your senses. Waiting for you are dreamy, hazy-blue mountains receding all the way to the horizon and verdant green forests supporting an almost incomprehensible range of life. Here are some 100 species of native trees – more than in all of northern Europe – and a staggering 1400 species of wildflowers. More than 200 species of birds and 60 of mammals, including a great number of black bears and a burgeoning population of elk, also flourish here in nature's protective embrace. All told, as many as 100,000 higher life forms thrive in the southern Appalachians, yourself included.

Together, Great Smoky and Shenandoah boast well over a thousand miles of trails to beckon hikers ever deeper into the wondrous beauty of the backcountry. The Appalachian Trail – the mother of all footpaths – wends its way through much of this territory. Hiking is just one of the many opportunities that await you. Boisterous streams filled with trout roar down the mountainsides and converge with lazy lowland rivers; anglers rejoice. Numerous waterfalls of almost indescribable beauty spill over moss-covered ledges into misty mountain pools; onlookers swoon with pleasure.

Both Shenandoah and Great Smoky offer mile after mile of enjoyable roadways leading both to major sights and far-flung territories. But for an extended driving tour, the Blue Ridge Parkway takes the prize. Every mile of this beloved American skyway – all 469 of them – entices motorists with something to appreciate, from the simple pleasures of autumn's colorful pageantry to the heart-stopping sight of a mama bear and cub lumbering across the road.

There's a lot of history here, and plenty of opportunities to learn about it. People have occupied these mountains for thousands of years. Centuries before European interlopers began laying claim to these territories, this land was the domain of the Cherokee and Shawnee. When settlers first began supplanting the tribes in the mid-1700s, the Appalachians represented the farthest reaches of the American frontier. The story of how hardscrabble settlers tamed this rugged and isolated wilderness is told by Great Smoky's splendid collection of historic buildings, including restored homesteads, gristmills, churches and schools. In Cherokee, North Carolina, you'll discover the history and legacy of 'the principal people.'

No matter how you choose to explore the parks, you'll uncover the unique personality of each, from the diverse natural and cultural attractions along the Blue Ridge Parkway to the deep forest of Shenandoah to the quintessential hikes and wilderness heritage of Great Smoky. Gateway communities that surround the public lands are destinations in and of themselves. Sample the fudge in Gatlinburg, celebrate the legacy of Dolly Parton in Pigeon Forge or dangle in space from a suspension bridge at Grandfather Mountain. Don't stop there: take in a live bluegrass radio show in Galax or an open-air historical drama in Cherokee, hit the slopes at Wintergreen or Appalachian Ski Mountain or stroll the cosmopolitan boulevards of Asheville. It's your vacation. Seize the day.

USING THIS GUIDEBOOK

With a few tips, you'll be on your way to seeing the sights, finding a great place to stay and choosing activities that suit your proclivities and enthusiasms. With this book as your faithful companion, you'll see the highlights of a park in a day or have a deeper experience over a month. No matter how many times you've visited the Great Smokies or the Blue Ridge, there's always something new to discover.

Even though Great Smoky and the Blue Ridge Parkway are infamous for their car-clogged motorways, it's easy to leave the throngs behind by parking the car and hitting the trail, or by choosing a road less traveled. Armed with this book, you'll discover places where you'll likely encounter nary a soul. Even in Great Smoky's Cades Cove, the most popular destination in America's most popular park, finding tranquility is a simple matter of timing and planning.

A quick flip through the photo highlights will give you an overview of top sightseeing options throughout the parks. If you're looking for ideas on where to go, check out the Itineraries chapter for suggested routes to suit both the flyby traveler and the hiker with two weeks to spare. Want to know just what you can do in the parks? The Activities chapter will leave you spoiled for choice.

For pointers on when to go and what to bring, look in the Planning chapter. The destination chapters provide in-depth coverage of specific parks and gateway towns, including sights, places to stay, where to eat, detailed trail descriptions, driving tours and nearby excursions. And if you're wondering who originally roamed these parts, just how old those mountains are or how a bear spends its winters, the History, Geology and Ecology chapters will satisfy your curiosity.

SOME NOTES ON TERMINOLOGY

In regional parlance, the term 'Shenandoah' might refer to the river or the region at large; for the purposes of this book, it refers specifically to Shenandoah National Park. This book takes similar liberties with the rather long and cumbersome designation 'Great Smoky Mountains National Park.' More often than not, the park is referred to simply as 'Great Smoky.' When the plural form is used (ie 'Great Smokies' or 'The Smokies,'), it refers to the larger mountain range that extends beyond the boundaries of the park.

ORGANIZATION

This book begins with Great Smoky Mountains National Park, the largest and most popular in the region. Next up is Shenandoah National Park, followed by the Blue Ridge Parkway. Although the Blue Ridge Parkway links the two parks, the majority of people travel north to south, both within Shenandoah itself and along the Blue Ridge Parkway, which is why we chose to organize it thusly. If you're traveling north from Great Smoky on your way to Shenandoah, start reading at the end of the Blue Ridge Parkway chapter and work your way backward.

ITINERARIES

Many visitors have only a short time to sample the glorious pleasures of the southern Appalachians, and want to make the most of it. Pity them not: Even a day or two in this mountain paradise is a tonic for the mind and spirit. Luckier still are those with several days or even weeks at their disposal to meander the far-flung corners of the Blue Ridge, sampling the scenery, cuisine and mountain culture all along the way. Ultimately, how you decide to spend your time will be determined by the activities you're interested in pursuing. Here are some suggested itineraries to get you started, ranging from a half day in one park to four weeks of delving into each of them.

Great Smoky Mountains National Park

HALF A DAY

- To beat the crowds, head out early and drive **Cades Cove Loop Rd** (p91) for a gander at historic buildings, wildlife and gentle landscapes.

ONE DAY

Follow the half-day itinerary and then:

- From the trailhead on Cades Cove Loop Rd, enjoy the 5-mile roundtrip hike to **Abrams Falls** (p103), the park's highest-volume waterfall.
- Head to **Townsend** (p148) for quality Southern cooking at a family-style restaurant followed by a good night's rest.

TWO DAYS

Fill the first day with the aforementioned activities and sights.

Day Two

- Visit **Sugarlands Visitor Center** (p84) for the park movie, bookstore browsing and interpretive exhibits.

- From the visitor center, join a ranger-led walk to **Cataract Falls** (p84) or enjoy the nearby **Sugarlands Valley Nature Trail** (p95).
- Drive **Newfound Gap Rd** (p87) from end to end, stopping at **Newfound Gap** and **Mingus Mill**, one of Great Smoky's picturesque water-powered gristmills.
- Visit the fascinating **Mountain Farm Museum** (p86) to learn how settlers cured meats, forged tools and tended their fields and animals.

FOUR DAYS

On the first two days, take in the previously listed sights and activities.

Day Three

- Visit **Clingmans Dome** (p85), the park's highest point, and climb the observation tower for sweeping panoramic views of the Smokies and beyond.
- Park the car and hit the trail! Suggested hikes include **Alum Cave Bluffs** (p97), the quintessential Great Smoky hike, or, for a more demanding ramble, climb **Chimney Tops** (p98), which affords truly spectacular views on both sides of the ridge.

Day Four

- Drive the **Roaring Fork Motor Nature Trail** (p92) to experience old-growth forests and historic homesteads.
- Get your daily waterfall fix on a day hike to either **Grotto Falls** (p96) or **Rainbow Falls** (p96).
- Pack a picnic and river sandals – or perhaps a fly rod – and head to richly forested **Greenbrier Cove** (p87), where the Middle Prong of the Little Pigeon River roars down from the highlands like a river possessed.

ONE WEEK

Combine some of the previously listed activities and sights, then add some of the following into the mix:

- Outfox the cars by bicycling **Cades Cove Loop Rd** (p91) on a Wednesday or Saturday morning.
- Mount a steed and go **horseback riding** (p111) to enjoy the forest from a special vantage point.
- Acquaint yourself with the quiet charms of **Cataloochee** (p87), a former frontier outpost in the park's remote east end. Walk to the **Steve Woody Place** (p104), a fascinating preserved homestead.
- Take a rewarding but challenging overnight backcountry hike to the summit of Mt Le Conte along the **Trillium Gap Trail** (p108) or to the open expanse of **Gregory Bald** (p106).
- Rent an inner tube and float gently down the stream at **Deep Creek** (p116) or the **Townsend Wye** (p90).

Exploring the Smokies

Day One

- Visit America's largest residence, George Vanderbilt's sumptuous **Biltmore Estate** (p234) in Asheville.
- Tour the **Thomas Wolfe Memorial** (p234) and the boardinghouse that provided the setting for *Look Homeward, Angel*.
- Ramble the cosmopolitan boulevards of **Asheville** (p233), which offers a great selection of restaurants and music halls.

Day Two

- Learn about the 'principal people' at the Cherokee Indian Museum and Oconaluftee Indian Village in **Cherokee** (p139). Don't miss an evening performance of the historical drama *Unto These Hills*.

Day Three

- Spend the day enjoying the amazing scenery, sights and activities along Great Smoky's **Newfound Gap Rd** (p87).
- See how settlers eked out a living at the **Mountain Farm Museum** (p86) and **Mingus Mill** (p86).
- Hike on Mt Le Conte to **Alum Cave Bluffs** (p97), one of Great Smoky's best hikes.
- Spend an evening with the fun-loving throng in **Gatlinburg** (p121): grab a meal, tour the aquarium or ride the Sky Lift for a bird's-eye view of town.

Combine some of the previously listed sights and activities.

Day Four

- Hit **Pigeon Forge** (p128) for its popular attractions and shopping opportunities. Ride the coasters at Dollywood, browse the outlet malls for brand-name bargains, catch a dinner theater revue or see Elvis Presley's famous ring at the Elvis Museum.

Day Five

- Return to the park for an exceedingly pleasant tour of **Cades Cove** (p85), a preserved rural valley that epitomizes a bygone era of life in the Smokies.
- Pack a picnic lunch and take the 5-mile roundtrip hike to **Abrams Falls** (p103), the highest-volume waterfall in the park.
- Survey the cove from an overlook on scenic, unpaved **Rich Mountain Rd** (p91).
- Enjoy quality Southern cooking at one of the family-style restaurants in **Townsend** (p148).

Day Six

- Acquaint yourself with the quiet charms of **Cataloochee** (p87), a former frontier outpost in the park's remote east end. Walk to the **Steve Woody Place** (p104), a fascinating preserved homestead.

- Mount a steed and go **horseback riding** (p111) to enjoy the forest from a special vantage point.

TWO WEEKS

Fill the first week with sights and activities from the One Week itinerary. During week two, combine some of the following:

- Get deep into the backcountry on a four-day hike along the **Appalachian Trail** (p108).
- See the inner workings of a mountain on a **guided caving expedition** (p235) near Asheville.
- Relax in the historic mineral baths of **Hot Springs** (p238).
- Get wet and wild on a white-water rafting trip near **Bryson City** (p144) or **Hartford** (p134).
- Drive the **Roaring Fork Motor Nature Trail** (p92) to experience old-growth forests and visit some of the historic homesteads.
- Get your daily waterfall fix on a day hike to either **Grotto Falls** (p96) or **Rainbow Falls** (p96).
- Bring a picnic and river sandals – or perhaps a fly rod – to richly forested **Greenbrier Cove** (p87), where the Middle Prong of the Little Pigeon River roars down from the highlands like a river possessed.
- Board a steam locomotive for a unique tour of the North Carolina mountains on the **Great Smoky Mountains Railroad** (p143).
- Outfox the cars by bicycling **Cades Cove Loop Rd** (p91) on a Wednesday or Saturday morning.
- Take a rewarding but challenging overnight backcountry hike to the summit of Mt Le Conte along the **Trillium Gap Trail** (p108) or to the open expanse of **Gregory Bald** (p106).
- Rent an inner tube and float gently down the stream at **Deep Creek** (p116) or the **Townsend Wye** (p90).

Shenandoah National Park

Directions are easy to follow here – there's only one main drag through the entire park and only four exits/entrances along Skyline Drive's 105-mile length. Without stopping, it's drivable in less than three hours, but you'd be missing the point if you drove straight through.

Visitors should also keep in mind that the two biggest developed areas, Skyland and Big Meadows, are only 10 miles apart, making either a good base for most park activities. To really appreciate Shenandoah's wonders, choose a small section, get out of the car and, for heaven's sake, go take a hike!

ONE DAY

If you only have one day, base yourself near Skyland. Either get an early start and take the scenic route, driving the 41.5 miles down from the Front Royal Entrance, or jump in at the Thornton Gap entrance and drive 9 miles south.

- Spend the morning at **Skyland** (p170), the highest point along Skyline Drive. Choose from two warm-up trails: **Limberlost** (p170) or **The Pinnacles** (p169).
- Grab lunch at **Skyland Lodge** (p184) and enjoy the views through the dining room's floor-to-ceiling windows.
- Take an afternoon **horseback ride** (p182) and enjoy a sunset on the way back.
- Eat at Skyland's taproom and watch a live **clogging performance** (p184).

TWO DAYS

Fill your first day with the previously listed sights and activities, and on Day Two venture out of the park on the following side trips, exiting at Thornton Gap.

Day Two
- Head west on US 211 and visit the famous **Luray Caverns** (p190) for an up close view of stalactites, stalagmites and chilly pools.
- Grab a bite of true Southern grub at the **Farmhouse Restaurant** (p191) before hitting the hay early at **Jordan Hollow Farm** (p190) – you'll want to get up early for the killer breakfasts.

FOUR DAYS

On the first two days, take in the above sights and activities.

Day Three
- Head out on a full-day hike on the **Cedar Run–Whiteoak Canyon Loop** (p175) and enjoy the gorge's six lush waterfalls.
- Spend the night in a rustic cabin at **Big Meadows Lodge** (p183) and wait for the resident bear, who will likely wander by.

Day Four
- Try your hand at **white-water rafting** (p186) or settle in for a more leisurely afternoon of **tubing** (p186) on the Shenandoah River off Skyline Drive.
- Dry off and report for dinner at Jordan Hollow Farm Inn's restored **Farmhouse Restaurant** (p191) in Luray for traditional Southern dishes. For a splurge, sink into one of their sumptuous down beds for a night.

ONE WEEK

For the first half of the week, combine some of the activities and sights listed above. For the rest of the week:

- Take a **hot air balloon ride** (p187) over the Blue Ridge peaks – after all, the road can only take you so high. Or, if you're into extreme sports, go **hang gliding** (p181) from one of the designated launch sites.
- Tour a **winery** (p186) outside Front Royal and sample Virginia's crisp varieties.
- Exit the park at the southern end and spend at least one night in **Staunton**

(p191) at a charming B&B. Take in a Shakespeare performance at the irreverent Blackfriars Playhouse.

- In winter, hit the slopes – or in summer the skate park – at **Massanutten Resort** (p189), near Waynesboro.
- Spend at least one night in a **PATC cabin** (p183) to experience the thrill of 'roughing it' in the backcountry.

Blue Ridge Parkway

The majestic Parkway snakes through two states for 469 miles, so covering all the bases requires a serious two weeks or more. But it's also possible to experience the beauty of the place in as little as a day or two, with select itineraries.

Attractions are sparse along a few stretches, but numerous roads crisscross the Parkway, providing easy access and plenty of opportunities for scenic detours. Drivers should use caution on some access roads in North Carolina, as corkscrew descents are not uncommon.

ONE DAY – VIRGINIA

The unusually named Meadows of Dan area makes a good base from which to explore this section of the Parkway. From Roanoke, either take the Parkway all the way down, or exit at Roanoke Mountain and follow US 221 to Floyd, then take the serpentine Rte 8 back onto the Parkway. From the east, follow US 220 to US 58 westbound, which leads to the Parkway. The driving time between Roanoke and Meadows of Dan is approximately two hours, depending on which route you take.

- Get up early, entering from US 58 (around MP 177), and grab a thick stack of buckwheat pancakes at **Mabry Mill** (p203), the most photographed spot on the Parkway. Afterward, walk off your breakfast on the short trail past living-history demonstrations of ironworking, textile-making and carving.
- Pack a lunch and head for the shaded picnic area at **Rocky Knob** (p203), then stretch your legs on the quick loop trail.
- In the evening, head north, exiting the Parkway at the extremely twisty Rte 8, and stop at the **Floyd Country Store** (p203) for its legendary live bluegrass Friday Night Jamborees. Head back to Meadows of Dan or, if it's too late to make the 20-mile drive (which will take a good 45 minutes to an hour due to the terrain), stay overnight in Floyd.

TWO DAYS – VIRGINIA

Day One

Either use the above itinerary and combine it with Day Two (p25) if you're coming from Bedford, or choose the following and combine it with Day Four of the Four Days – Virginia itinerary:

- Enter the Parkway at Rte 43, heading for the **Peaks of Otter Visitor Center** (p202) and a hike to **Sharp Top Mountain** (p206).
- For less strenuous exploring, detour off the Parkway on Rte 43 east to visit the sobering **National D-Day Monument** (p231) or hit the beach at **Cave Mountain Lake Recreation Area** (p202).

Great Smoky Mountains & Shenandoah National Parks

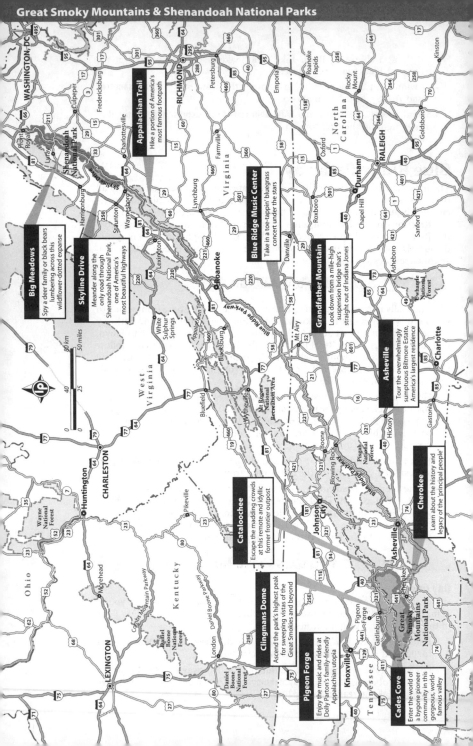

Big Meadows
Spy a deer family or black bears lumbering across this wildflower-dotted expanse

Skyline Drive
Meander along the only road through Shenandoah National Park, one of America's most beautiful highways

Appalachian Trail
Hike a portion of America's most famous footpath

Blue Ridge Music Center
Take in a toe-tappin' bluegrass concert under the stars

Grandfather Mountain
Look down from a mile-high suspension bridge that's straight out of Indiana Jones

Asheville
Tour the overwhelmingly sumptuous Biltmore Estate, America's largest residence

Cherokee
Learn about the history and legacy of the 'principal people'

Cataloochee
Escape the madding crowds at this remote and idyllic former frontier outpost

Clingmans Dome
Ascend the park's highest peak for sweeping vistas of the Great Smokies and beyond

Pigeon Forge
Enjoy the music and rides at Dolly Parton's family-friendly Appalachian utopia

Cades Cove
Enter the world of a bygone pioneer community in this gorgeous, world-famous valley

Great Smoky and Shenandoah National Parks and the Blue Ridge Parkway constitute the most magnificent of Appalachia's protected areas.

GREAT SMOKY, SHENANDOAH & BLUE RIDGE PARKWAY **HIGHLIGHTS**

Like a hummingbird on nectar, you'll soon be lapping up the resplendent beauty of majestic trees, rambunctious creeks and meadows carpeted with the most delicate flowers you've ever seen. As you gaze across primeval mountains shrouded in soft, bluish mist, you'll know that you've arrived in a special place, among precious few left on the planet. Here lie vestiges of past lives, evoked by early settlers' hardscrabble cabins and fertile riverside bottomlands where Cherokee villages once stood. No matter how you choose to explore these magical parks, be it through driving tours, fly-fishing or backcountry hiking, you're sure to thrill at nature's wild splendor.

PIGEON FORGE A violin craftsman displays his talents at Dollywood, Tennessee's top family attraction.

LEE FOSTER

OCONALUFTEE See how early settlers tamed the wilderness at the Mountain Farm Museum.

JOHN ELK III

AUTUMN'S PAGEANTRY The Great Smokies are a leaf peeper's paradise.

CHARLES COOK

JOHN ELK III

CATALOOCHEE Explore the homes of early residents, including the 1903 Caldwell House, in this far-flung mountain outpost.

GREAT SMOKY MOUNTAINS **HIGHLIGHTS**

CHEROKEE Venture beyond the souvenir shops to learn the proud history of the 'Principal People.'

RICHARD I'ANSON

CHARLES COOK

ROARING FORK The 'Place of a Thousand Drips' is just one of many beautiful and accessible waterfalls in Great Smoky.

KAYAKING Take a thrilling ride down the Shenandoah River.

EASTERN BOX TURTLE These land-loving amphibians like to bask in the sun.

SHENANDOAH **HIGHLIGHTS**

WINTER WONDERLAND Enjoy an exhilirating afternoon of cross-country skiing.

SHENANDOAH NATIONAL PARK Sunlight peeks through a lush forest in the heart of the park.

FALL COLOR A patchwork of leaves blankets the ground.

BIG MEADOWS LODGE Curl up by the stone fireplace after a long day of exploring.

BLUE RIDGE PARKWAY This spectacular ribbon of roadway snakes 469 miles along the Appalachian ridge through forests, meadows and farmland.

CARRIAGE RIDES Return to a simpler way of life in the Blue Ridge Mountains.

GROUNDHOG MOUNTAIN View old-fashioned fences and a small cemetery at this observation point.

FLAT TOP MANOR Take in the view from the front porch of this gracious mansion.

LOCAL HARVEST Sample farm-fresh produce grown along the Blue Ridge.

BLUE RIDGE PARKWAY **HIGHLIGHTS**

MABRY MILL Built in 1910, this gristmill is the most photographed sight on the Parkway.

MABRY MILL Powered by water, the restored mill still produces buckwheat flour.

WILDFLOWERS Thickets of vivid wildflowers erupt in spring.

BLUE RIDGE VISTA Admire the view from one of the Parkway's many scenic overlooks.

- Return to the Parkway in the evening for a cozy open campfire at **Peaks of Otter Lodge** (p209).

Day Two

Either spend the day in big-town, small-city Roanoke (see Day Four of the Four Days – Virginia itinerary), or bypass it for points south of Mabry Mill, including the following:

- Keep driving south on the Parkway toward the North Carolina border and explore the rich heritage of mountain music at the **Blue Ridge Music Center** (p204) in historic Galax.
- Try some famous barbecue at **The Smokehouse** (p232).
- Cap the night off by attending a live broadcast of *Blue Ridge Backroads*, an old-time bluegrass radio show, at the **Rex Theater** (p232) in Galax.

FOUR DAYS – VIRGINIA

This four-day journey takes you from Waynesboro to Roanoke.

Day One

- After checking out the **P Buckley Moss Museum** (p194) in Waynesboro, enter the northern section of the Parkway and head to **Wintergreen Resort** (p209) for some R&R.
- Depending on the season, take advantage of the resort's excellent ski and tubing runs or venture south on the Parkway for a warm-weather hike at **White Rock Falls** (p204).
- Regroup back at Wintergreen with a luscious massage in the spa.

Day Two

- Pack a lunch and jump back onto the Parkway at Rte 664, stopping at the **James River Visitor Center** (p201) for a picnic, or just grab a meal at **Otter Creek** (p211).
- Drive south and detour off the Parkway at MP 70, taking an afternoon to enjoy the unusual rock formation at **Natural Bridge** (p229).
- Set up camp at nearby **Cave Mountain Lake Recreation Area** (p202) and toast s'mores beneath the stars.

Day Three

- Linger over a late breakfast at **Peaks of Otter** (p211) and spend the afternoon on the **Fallingwater Cascades Loop** (p205), which winds through part of the George Washington & Jefferson National Forests.
- Pay homage to fallen war heroes at the **National D-Day Memorial** (p231) in Bedford.
- Stay overnight at **Peaks of Otter Lodge** (p209).

Day Four

- Drive south and spend the morning on **Roanoke Mountain** (p230), then take the kids to the **Mill Mountain Zoo** (p231) and/or **Virginia's Explore Park** (p231).
- Head to town for lunch at **Center in the Square** (p230).

- Take an early evening trek back up the mountain for a sunset hike to the glowing landmark **Roanoke Star** (p207). Stay the night in Roanoke.

ONE WEEK – VIRGINIA

Follow the Four Days – Virginia itinerary, adding the following:

Day Five
- Spend the day at **Smith Mountain Lake State Park** (p231) – kids will love splashing around, and everyone will enjoy the relaxed atmosphere.
- In the evening, rest your head in one of the secluded cabins surrounding the lake.

Day Six
- Get up early and drive 50 miles south to **Mabry Mill** (p203) for a thick stack of buckwheat pancakes.
- Afterward, walk off breakfast on the short trail leading past **living-history demonstrations** (p203) of ironworking, textile-making and carving.
- Pack a lunch and head for the shaded picnic area at **Rocky Knob** (p203), then stretch your legs on the quick loop trail.
- In the evening, head north, exiting the Parkway at the extremely twisty Rte 8, and stop at the **Floyd Country Store** (p203) for its legendary live bluegrass Friday Night Jamborees. Stay overnight in Floyd.

Day Seven
- Return to the Parkway and drive south to the **Blue Ridge Music Center** (p204) to learn about the rich heritage of mountain music.
- Follow signs for **Galax** (p231), and spend your day exploring the 'bluegrass capital of the world.'
- Try some famous barbecue at **The Smokehouse** (p232).
- Attend a live broadcast of *Blue Ridge Backroads*, an old-time bluegrass radio show, at the **Rex Theater** (p232) in Galax.

ONE DAY – NORTH CAROLINA

The charming town of Blowing Rock makes a nice base for a Parkway day trip. Blowing Rock intersects the Parkway at MP 292 – take US 321/221 east into town.
- Mosey from the Blowing Rock stables up to Flat Top Manor on a **morning horseback ride** (p224).
- After your ride, drive back up to **Flat Top Manor** (p213) and join a free tour, taking notice of the intricate stained glass windows. Visit the **Parkway Craft Center** inside the manor and pick up a handmade sun-catcher.
- Head south to **Price Lake** (p213) and rent a boat for a relaxing ride.
- Have dinner in the charming town of **Blowing Rock** (p232), take a lakeside stroll and settle into a cozy condo at **Chetola Resort** (p227).

TWO DAYS – NORTH CAROLINA

For the first day, follow the above itinerary.

Day Two

- Head south, crossing the amazing **Linn Cove Viaduct** (p213), and stop at the visitor center to learn the history behind this engineering marvel.
- Stop at **Grandfather Mountain** (p214) and take the winding road to the top. Cross the Mile-High Swinging Bridge and pretend you're Indiana Jones.
- Take an early evening hike to **Linville Falls** (p221), one of the prettiest waterfalls along the Parkway.
- Set up camp at the picturesque **Linville Falls Campground** (p226) and let the burbling stream lull you to sleep.

FOUR DAYS – NORTH CAROLINA

Follow the preceding itinerary for the first two days.

Day Three

- Take a full-morning hike up **Hawksbill Mountain** (p215).
- Head south to the **Museum of North Carolina Minerals** (p216) and learn about the American Revolution on the Overmountain Trail.
- Stop off at **Crabtree Meadows** (p227) for a bite to eat before hiking to spectacular **Crabtree Falls** (p221).
- Spend the night at the peaceful, uncrowded campground at **Crabtree Meadows** (p226).

Day Four

- Drive up to **Mt Mitchell State Park** (p216), the highest point east of the Mississippi. Hike to the observation tower and – if it's a clear day – enjoy the panoramic view of several states.
- Stop at the **Craggy Gardens Visitor Center** (p218) for an excellent photo opportunity, as both sides of the mountain drop off to stunning effect.
- Head south to the **Folk Art Center** (p218) to see the fascinating display of mountain handicrafts. You might even catch a live demonstration of broom-making or quilting in the lobby.

ONE WEEK – NORTH CAROLINA

Follow the itinerary above, adding the following:

Day Five

- Visit America's largest residence, George Vanderbilt's sumptuous **Biltmore Estate** (p234) in Asheville.
- Tour the **Thomas Wolfe Memorial** (p234) and the boardinghouse that provided the setting for *Look Homeward, Angel*.
- Ramble the cosmopolitan boulevards of **Asheville** (p233), which offers a great selection of restaurants and music halls. Stay overnight in a Jazz-Age B&B.

Day Six

- Return to the Parkway and drive south to **Lake Powhatan** (at MP 393, take Rte 191 west; p218). Wander its sandy beaches and, during the hot months, cool off with a dip

- Continue south to **Mt Pisgah** (p218). Admire the view from the observation deck at Mt Pisgah Inn.
- Drive south to **Graveyard Fields** (p223) and hike to three spectacular waterfalls. Or, visit nearby Brevard to rent horses from **Pisgah Forest Stables** (p224).
- Return to **Mt Pisgah Inn** (p226) for dinner; spend the night there or at the campground.

Day Seven
- Head south to **Richland Balsam** (p219), the Parkway's highest point, and stroll the self-guided nature trail.
- Continue on to the **Waterrock Knob Visitor Center** (p219). If you're feeling hardy, hike the strenuous **Waterrock Knob Trail** (p224) up to the top of the knob for a 360-degree view of the Smokies.
- Drive the remainder of the Parkway, taking in the views from **Soco Gap** (p219), **Lickstone Ridge** (p220) and **Big Witch Overlook** (p220).
- Exit the Parkway at its southern end. Follow US 441 into **Cherokee** (p139), where you can learn about the 'principal people' at the Cherokee Indian Museum and Oconaluftee Indian Village. Take in an evening performance of the historical drama *Unto These Hills*. Spend the night in Cherokee.

ONE WEEK ON THE PARKWAY

Though you couldn't possibly see everything the Parkway has to offer in just one week, a seven-day itinerary will show you plenty of sights. A week on the Parkway is the most popular length of time for a visit; in a week you can cover a manageable 67 miles a day.

Day One
- Stop in **Waynesboro** (p194) for groceries before entering the Parkway at the north entrance.
- Drive south, pausing for a stroll along the shore of **Sherando Lake** (p201).
- Stop at the **James River Visitor Center** (p201) for a picnic or grab a meal at **Otter Creek** (p211).
- Continue to the Peaks of Otter and spend the afternoon on the **Fallingwater Cascades Loop** (p205), which winds through part of the George Washington & Jefferson National Forest.
- Stay overnight at the **Peaks of Otter Lodge** (p209).

Day Two
- Start your morning with breakfast at **Peaks of Otter** (p202).
- Drive south to Roanoke Mountain. Take a quick jaunt up the **Roanoke Mountain Summit Trail** (p202) for a dramatic view of Roanoke and Mill Mountain, or treat the kids to **Virginia's Explore Park** (p231).
- Continue on to **Rocky Knob** (p203), where you can spend the night.

Day Three
- Get up early and drive to **Mabry Mill** (p203) for a thick stack of buckwheat pancakes.

- Walk off breakfast on the short trail past **living-history demonstrations** (p203) of ironworking, textile-making and carving.
- Pack a lunch and head for the shaded picnic area at **Rocky Knob** (p203), then stretch your legs on the quick loop trail.
- In the evening, head north, exiting the Parkway at the extremely twisty Rte 8, and stop at the **Floyd Country Store** (p203) for its legendary live bluegrass Friday Night Jamborees. Stay overnight in Floyd.

Day Four
- Return to the Parkway, driving south, and spend the morning at the **Blue Ridge Music Center** (p204) to learn about the rich heritage of mountain music.
- Cross the North Carolina border and stop at **Doughton Park** (p211) for lunch or, if you're not hungry yet, at **EB Jeffress Park** (p212).
- Continue south to **Flat Top Manor** (p213) and join a free tour, taking notice of the intricate stained glass windows. Visit the **Parkway Craft Center** inside the manor and pick up a handmade sun-catcher.
- Have dinner in the charming town of **Blowing Rock** (p232), take a lakeside stroll and settle into a cozy condo at **Chetola Resort** (p227).

Day Five
- Head south, crossing the amazing **Linn Cove Viaduct** (p213), and stop at the visitor center to learn the history behind this engineering marvel.
- Stop at **Grandfather Mountain** (p214) and take the winding road to the summit. Cross the Mile-High Swinging Bridge and pretend you're Indiana Jones.
- Take an early evening hike to **Linville Falls** (p221), one of the prettiest waterfalls along the Parkway.
- Set up camp at picturesque **Linville Falls Campground** (p226) and let the burbling stream lull you to sleep.

Day Six
- Drive south to **Crabtree Meadows** (p227) for a bite to eat before hiking to spectacular Crabtree Falls (p221).
- Stop at the **Craggy Gardens Visitor Center** (p218) for an excellent photo opportunity, as both sides of the mountain drop off to stunning effect.
- Head south to the **Folk Art Center** (p218) to see the fascinating display of mountain handicrafts. You might even catch a live demonstration of broom-making or quilting in the lobby.
- Spend the evening in **Asheville** (p233). Enjoy a good dinner, check out the entertainment options and stay the night in this charming city.

Day Seven
- Return to the Parkway and stop for lunch at **Mt Pisgah** (p218).
- Head south to **Richland Balsam** (p219), the highest point on the Parkway. Take the self-guided nature trail.
- Continue on to the **Waterrock Knob Visitor Center** (p219). If you're feeling hardy, hike the strenuous **Waterrock Knob Trail** (p224) up to the top of the knob for a 360-degree view of the Smokies.

- Drive the remainder of the Parkway, taking in the views from **Soco Gap** (p219), **Lickstone Ridge** (p220) and **Big Witch Overlook** (p220).
- Exit the Parkway at its southern end. Follow US 441 into **Cherokee** (p139), where you can learn about the 'principal people' at the Cherokee Indian Museum and Oconaluftee Indian Village. Don't miss an evening performance of the historical drama *Unto These Hills*. Spend the night in Cherokee.

TWO WEEKS ON THE PARKWAY

This is the ideal timeframe. Follow the one-week itineraries for Virginia and North Carolina for a thorough exploration of all the Parkway has to offer.

Appalachian Adventure

TWO WEEKS

Week One

Spend your first week in and around Great Smoky Mountains National Park.

- On the first day, hit **Pigeon Forge** (p128) for its popular attractions and shopping opportunities. Ride the coasters at Dollywood, browse the outlet malls for brand-name bargains, catch a dinner theater revue or see Elvis Presley's famous ring at the Elvis Museum.
- On the second day, join the fun-loving throng in **Gatlinburg** (p121): grab a meal, see the aquarium or ride the Sky Lift for a bird's-eye view of town.
- In the afternoon, get your first taste of the park's splendid forests on the **Roaring Fork Motor Nature Trail** (p92) or in **Greenbrier** (p87).
- On the third day, head into the park for the movie and exhibits at **Sugarlands Visitor Center** (p84).
- Take Little River Rd to **Cades Cove** (p85) for an exceedingly pleasant tour of the historic and scenic valley.
- In Cades Cove, pack a picnic lunch and embark on the 5-mile round-trip hike to **Abrams Falls** (p103), the park's highest-volume waterfall.
- Enjoy quality Southern cooking at one of the family-style restaurants in **Townsend** (p148).
- On day four, enter the park from Gatlinburg and spend the day enjoying the amazing scenery, sights and activities along **Newfound Gap Rd** (p87).
- Hike on Mt Le Conte to **Alum Cave Bluffs** (p97), one of Great Smoky's best hikes, or take in the view at **Clingmans Dome** (p85), the park's highest point.
- Spend the night at **Smokemont Campground** (p116) or in Cherokee.
- On day five, see how settlers eked out a living at the **Mountain Farm Museum** (p86) and **Mingus Mill** (p86).
- Learn about the 'principal people' at the Cherokee Indian Museum and Oconaluftee Indian Village in **Cherokee** (p139). Make time for an evening performance of the historical drama *Unto These Hills*.

- On day six, acquaint yourself with the quiet charms of **Cataloochee** (p87), a former frontier outpost in the park's remote east end. Walk to the **Steve Woody Place** (p104), a fascinating preserved homestead. Spend the night at **Cataloochee Campground** (p116) or in **Maggie Valley** (p138).
- The next morning, head to the cosmopolitan boulevards of **Asheville** (p233), which offers a great choice of restaurants and nightlife.

Week Two

Spend the first four days of week two along the Blue Ridge Parkway.

- On the first day, head north of Asheville to the **Folk Art Center** (p218) to see the fascinating display of mountain handicrafts. You might even catch a live demonstration of broom-making or quilting in the lobby.
- Drive up to **Mt Mitchell State Park** (p216), the highest point east of the Mississippi. Hike to the observation tower and – if it's a clear day – enjoy the panoramic view of several states.
- Set up camp at picturesque **Linville Falls Campground** (p226) and let the burbling stream lull you to sleep.
- Take an early evening hike to **Linville Falls** (p221), one of the prettiest waterfalls along the Parkway.
- On the second day, stop at **Grandfather Mountain** (p214) and take the winding road to the summit. Cross the Mile-High Swinging Bridge and pretend you're Indiana Jones.
- Have lunch in the charming town of **Blowing Rock** (p232).
- Visit **Flat Top Manor** (213) and join a free tour, taking notice of the intricate stained glass windows. Visit the **Parkway Craft Center** inside the manor and pick up a handmade sun-catcher.
- Explore the rich heritage of mountain music at the **Blue Ridge Music Center** (p204) and in historic **Galax** (p231).
- Continue north to **Rocky Knob** (p203), where you can spend the night.
- On the third day, get up early and head south a few miles to feast on a thick stack of buckwheat pancakes at **Mabry Mill** (p203), the Parkway's most photographed spot. Afterwards, walk off breakfast on the short trail leading past **living-history demonstrations** (p203) of ironworking, textile-making and carving.
- Drive north to Roanoke Mountain. Take a quick jaunt up the **Roanoke Mountain Summit Trail** (p202) for a dramatic view of Roanoke and Mill Mountain, or treat the kids to **Virginia's Explore Park** (p231).
- Drive north and spend the night at **Peaks of Otter Lodge** (p209).
- In the morning, hike the **Fallingwater Cascades Loop** (p205), which winds through part of the George Washington & Jefferson National Forests.
- Stop at the **James River Visitor Center** (p201) for a picnic or grab a meal at **Otter Creek** (p211).
- Set up camp at **Sherando Lake** (p201) or find a bed in **Waynesboro** (p194).

Spend your final three days in and around Shenandoah National Park.

- On the first day, try your hand at **white-water rafting** (p186) or spend a leisurely afternoon **tubing** (p186) the Shenandoah River off Skyline Drive (follow US 211 west for 8 miles, then head north on Rte 340 for 14 miles to Bentonville).

- Dry off and report for dinner at Jordan Hollow Farm Inn's restored **Farmhouse Restaurant** (p191) in Luray, where you can enjoy traditional Southern dishes. For a splurge, sink into one of the inn's sumptuous down beds for a night.

- Spend the night in a rustic cabin at **Big Meadows Lodge** (p183) and wait for the resident bear, who will likely wander by.

- Visit famous **Luray Caverns** (p190) for an up close view of stalactites, stalagmites and subterranean pools.

- Linger over lunch at **Skyland Lodge** (p184) and enjoy the views through the dining room's floor-to-ceiling windows.

- Spend the morning at **Skyland** (p170), the highest point along Skyline Drive. Choose from two pleasant hikes: the **Limberlost Trail** (p170) or a quick stroll along the Appalachian Trail at the **Pinnacles** (p169).

THREE WEEKS

Week One
Spend the first week in and around Great Smoky Mountains National Park, filling your days with the previously listed sights and activities.

Week Two
Spend your second week on and around the Blue Ridge Parkway, hitting the spots from the Two Weeks itinerary. Consider adding the following to your trip:

- In Asheville, take a tour of the sprawling **Biltmore Estate** (p234) and its beautiful gardens. If you're game, visit the **Thomas Wolfe Memorial** (p234).

- See the inner workings of a mountain on a **guided caving expedition** (p235) near Asheville.

- Relax in the historic mineral baths of **Hot Springs** (p238).

- Shop for crafts such as baskets, quilts and pottery from the many talented mountain artists at the **Penland School of Crafts** (p215).

- Do at least one **overnight hike** (p224) in the backcountry and enjoy the solitude.

- Take in a live bluegrass performance in **Galax** (p231), at the **Blue Ridge Music Center** (p204) or at **Altapass Orchard** (p216).

- Pack a lunch and head for the shaded picnic area at **Rocky Knob** (p203), then stretch your legs on the quick loop trail.

- In summer months, cool down on the sandy beaches at **Sherando Lake** (p201), **Cave Mountain Lake** (p202) or **Lake Powhatan** (p218), or let the kids slip down **Sliding Rock** (p225) into a chilly pool.

Week Three
Spend week three in and around Shenandoah National Park. Consider adding the following to the previously listed itineraries:

- At Shenandoah's south end, spend at least a night at one of the charming B&Bs in **Staunton** (p191) and take in a Shakespeare performance at the irreverent Blackfriars Playhouse.

- In winter, hit the slopes – or in summer the skate park – at **Massanutten Resort** (p189), near Waynesboro.
- The road can only take you so high – consider going aloft in a **hot air balloon ride** (p187) over the peaks of the Blue Ridge. Or if you're into extreme sports, try **hang gliding** (p181) from a designated launch site.
- Spend at least one night in a **PATC cabin** (p183) to experience the thrill of 'roughing it' in the backcountry.
- Eat at Skyland's taproom and watch a live **clogging performance** (p184).
- Take an afternoon **horseback ride** (p182) and perhaps enjoy a sunset on the way back.
- Tour a **winery** (p186) in the Luray area and sample Virginia's crisp varietals.
- If you're here in May, enjoy the celebration of **Wildflower Weekend** (p172) at Skyland. In winter, drive to Luray and take part in the **National Audubon Society Annual Christmas Bird Count** (p172).

FOUR WEEKS

Weeks One & Two

Spend the first week in and around Great Smoky Mountains National Park, taking in the previously listed sights. During the second week, consider adding the following to your itinerary:

- Get deep into the backcountry on a four-day hike along the **Appalachian Trail** (p108).
- Outfox the cars by bicycling **Cades Cove Loop Rd** (p91) on a Wednesday or Saturday morning.
- Get wet and wild on a white-water rafting trip near **Bryson City** (p144) or **Hartford** (p134).
- Drive the **Roaring Fork Motor Nature Trail** (p92) to immerse yourself in old-growth forest and visit some of the historic homesteads.
- Get your daily waterfall fix on a day hike to **Grotto Falls** (p96) or **Rainbow Falls** (p96).
- Bring a picnic and river sandals – or perhaps a fly rod – to richly forested **Greenbrier Cove** (p87), where the Middle Prong of the Little Pigeon River roars down from the highlands like a river possessed.
- Take a rewarding but challenging overnight backcountry hike to the summit of Mt Le Conte along the **Trillium Gap Trail** (p108) or to the open expanse of **Gregory Bald** (p106).
- Rent an inner tube and float gently down the stream at **Deep Creek** (p116) or the **Townsend Wye** (p90).

Week Three

Spend your third week on and around the Blue Ridge Parkway. See the Two Weeks and Three Weeks itineraries for the Appalachian Adventure trip.

Week Four

Spend week four in and around Shenandoah National Park. See the Two Weeks and Three Weeks itineraries for the Appalachian Adventure trip.

Mountain Music Sampler

If you love the sweet sounds of a banjo making whoopie with a fiddle, this musical itinerary will expose you to the best toe-tappin', old-time, down-home mountain music of the mighty Blue Ridge. Plan your tour for mid- to late summer, when the festivals are gathering steam and warm evenings lend themselves to happy listening.

- Get into the spirit of things in Townsend with a visit to the **Wood-N-Strings Dulcimer Shop** (p150), where beautiful handmade instruments are on display and local musicians drop by to chew the fat.
- Pay your respects to the reigning queen of country music in Sevierville at the beguiling **Dolly Parton statue** (p133) on the grounds of the Sevier County Courthouse.
- Visit Pigeon Forge's **Dollywood** (p129) and sample some glitzy musical revues and wandering jug bands.
- Enjoy an evening in Cosby at what may very well be the world's only Mexican bluegrass restaurant. **The Front Porch** (p135) showcases rising talent on Friday and Saturday nights.
- Still want more? Hop on over to Maggie Valley and the **Maggie Valley Opry House** (p139), where banjo legend Raymond Fairchild holds court nightly in summer.
- Soak all day, dance funny all night – so it goes at the mid-June **Bluff Mountain Festival** (p239) in Hot Springs.
- Head north to Galax – the 'world capital of old-time mountain music' – for the legendary **Old Fiddler's Convention** (p232), held each August since 1935. Who knew that horsehair stroked across catgut could sound so inviting?
- While in Galax, score tickets to a live Friday night broadcast of *Blue Ridge Backroads*, an old-time bluegrass radio show at the **Rex Theater** (p232).
- A visit to Galax wouldn't be complete without taking in a show at the **Blue Ridge Music Center** (p204), which hosts national string-band acts under the open sky on Saturday evening from June to September.
- By now you've really got a case of the twang. Head north to Floyd for lighting-fast picking on Friday and Saturday at the **Floyd Country Store** (p203). Also in Floyd is the **Jacksonville Center** (p203), where pickers and grinners regularly do their thing in an old barn.
- In late July or early August, Floyd is also home to the eclectic **Floyd-Fest** (p203), where you'll hear everything from progressive bluegrass to whacked-out jam bands.

The Blue Ridge Mountains lend their gentle slopes, lush forests and raging rivers to outdoor enthusiasts of many stripes.

ACTIVITIES

Whether you want to disappear into the backcountry, thrill at the song of the elusive chestnut-sided warbler or let a mighty river rough you up from the safety of a raft, the parks offer seemingly endless possibilities. The activities you choose will largely depend on your temperament, physical ability and interests. Most are offered at every level, from beginner to expert. All you need is a little gumption.

HIKING & BACKPACKING

There's no question about it: The Blue Ridge is a hiker's paradise. Waiting for you are hundreds of miles of trails, from pleasant strolls to arduous weeklong slogs. Whichever path you choose, you'll be rewarded with clean air, crystalline mountain streams and more varieties of plants, critters and trees than you can shake a walking stick at.

There are excellent hikes to choose from in both Great Smoky Mountains and Shenandoah National Parks, as well as along the Blue Ridge Parkway. All three areas have visitor centers that dole out trail maps, information on current conditions and helpful advice. Each also has a national park association that offers specialist guidebooks and maps. See each destination chapter for contact details.

For an overview of recommended hikes, consult the hiking charts in this chapter.

GREAT SMOKY MOUNTAINS NATIONAL PARK

Dust off your boots and lace them tight! Above all other activities in Great Smoky, hiking is the most stirring way to enjoy nature's splendor. More than 850 miles of trails wend their way through the backcountry to every corner of the park. Some follow gorgeous streams or lead to hidden waterfalls; others afford privileged views over the mountain range or offer vistas of wildflowers and groves of gargantuan tulip poplar trees. A few of the longer hikes bestow on the stalwart perambulator all of these features and more.

The hiking opportunities in Great Smoky also include leisurely strolls on **quiet walkways**, short paths that depart from major roads in the park, and

RAINY DAY WOMAN, RAINY DAY MAN

Rain in the Smokies is one thing you can count on – 70 to 90 inches of the stuff falls each year. Visitors are faced with intermittent showers on a nearly daily basis in the spring and early summer, and sometimes a relentless downpour takes hold for days. This makes for green mountains and disgruntled vacationers. Instead of moping, try one of these activities:

✔ Visit the **Museum of the Cherokee Indian** (p140) in Cherokee, North Carolina.

✔ Go **rafting** (p146) – you're bound to get wet anyway.

✔ Head for the **hot springs** (p238) at Hot Springs, North Carolina.

✔ Go **ice-skating** (p123) at Ober Gatlinburg.

✔ Test your rain gear on a short **day hike**.

several **self-guided nature trails**, where you can learn about the Smokies' diverse ecology and folk life.

To really get away from it all, pack your pack and don't look back. Extended overnight hikes will take you to places day hikers can only dream about. By far the most popular route is a segment of the **Appalachian Trail** (p40), which runs for 70 miles along the park's top ridge. Some hearty souls take a week or more to hike the entire route; others leave the trail at the halfway point on Newfound Gap Rd. Backcountry hikers on the AT typically slumber dorm-style in rustic trail shelters. If you're lucky, you might meet a backcountry celebrity in the form of an AT through-hiker. Offer to share your gorp in exchange for a story or two of adventures along the 2174-mile trail, which extends from Georgia to Maine.

Hiking opportunities don't end at the park borders. To the southwest is the **Joyce Kilmer Memorial Forest** (p147), home to some of the biggest and oldest trees in the eastern USA; exceptional day hikes pass through groves of gargantuan, 400-year-old yellow poplars. Flanking the national park to the north and south, the **Cherokee National Forest** (p147) is home to a 150-mile stretch of the Appalachian Trail, as well as many other hiking routes along the scarp of the Blue Ridge.

BLUE RIDGE PARKWAY & SHENANDOAH NATIONAL PARK

With more than 500 miles of hiking trails in Shenandoah National Park alone, and many options along the 469-mile Blue Ridge Parkway, hikers couldn't ask for a more varied palette from which to choose. The AT parallels both Skyline Drive and the Parkway, providing ample opportunities for hikers to trade tales and tips along the way. Outside of the parks, you can follow the presidential twists and turns in the **George Washington & Jefferson National Forests** (p229).

For hikers needing assistance, there's a wheelchair-accessible trail in Shenandoah National Park (see Limberlost Trail, p170).

Difficulty Level

To help you find an appropriate trail, hikes listed within this guide are graded as follows:

- **Easy:** Generally flat and easy to navigate, these trails are occasionally accessible to wheelchairs and suitable for young children.

- **Moderate:** Trails involve some elevation gain but can be hiked by anyone of average fitness.
- **Difficult:** Steep climbs and an overall strenuous endeavor make these trails the territory of the fit only.

Day Hikes

The majority of hikes detailed within this guide are day hikes, taking 45 minutes to eight hours (not including breaks) to complete. See the destination chapters for detailed trail descriptions and information about sights and viewpoints en route.

If it's been awhile since you last hit the trail, err on the side of caution when choosing a hike. If you're truly a novice, start with hikes of 5 miles or less and make sure you've allocated enough time to complete your hike before dark. A person of average fitness and determination travels roughly 1.5 miles per hour.

Always set out with a full bottle of water, rain gear and extra clothing (weather is very unpredictable in the mountains), a hat, sunscreen, bug repellent and a friend. If you're going to be gone for any length of time, carry high-energy snacks and a basic first-aid kit. See Hiking Safety for more details.

Backcountry Hikes

For a wilderness experience that challenges the body and liberates the senses, try an overnight backcountry trail. Hikes vary in length (two days to a week) and difficulty. Detailed hike recommendations are provided in the destination chapters.

As long as you're reasonably fit, well equipped and realistic about your ability, you should have no problem finding an appropriate backcountry trail. However, multiday excursions pose some hazards that should be considered in advance. Injuries, the possibility of getting lost, potentially contaminated drinking water and hypothermia are all pitfalls that can be avoided with proper planning. See Hiking Safety for more details. Close encounters with bears are common enough that it makes good sense to familiarize yourself with the park service's recommendations for traveling through bear country (p39).

As a rule of thumb, most multiday hikers clear roughly 8 miles per day. See Hiking Rules & Permits (p38) for park-specific regulations concerning permits and backcountry camping.

TOP 10 DAY HIKES

✔ **Alum Cave Bluffs** (p97), Great Smoky

✔ **Charlies Bunion** (p100), Great Smoky

✔ **Abrams Falls** (p103) Great Smoky

✔ **Laurel Falls** (p95), Great Smoky

✔ **Andrews Bald** (p102), Great Smoky

✔ **Clingmans Dome** (p101), Great Smoky

✔ **Crabtree Falls** (p221), Blue Ridge Parkway

✔ **Graveyard Fields** (p223), Blue Ridge Parkway

✔ **Hawksbill Summit** (p177), Shenandoah

✔ **Limberlost Trail** (p170), Shenandoah

Hiking Safety

When slipping away from civilization by foot – whether for an afternoon or for several days – safety should always be on your mind. Many a hiker has been caught unprepared for unforeseen circumstances that changed a peaceful walk in the woods into a harrowing misadventure. Here are a few basic rules that will help ensure that your backcountry hike remains the peaceful, rejuvenating experience you envisioned:

- It's extremely important to register when required in the parks and along the Parkway. Always sign your real name and include your itinerary – should an emergency arise and rangers need to contact hikers, they will be armed with correct information, reducing the risk of further problems. Rangers encourage hikers not to go it alone, but if you must, leave an itinerary with someone and pack enough for emergencies...and then some.
- If someone is injured and can't walk, provide warmth and comfort, leave someone with the injured person if possible, note the exact location and circumstances and hike out to get the information to **rescuers** (☎ 911 or 865-436-1230).
- Check the weather forecast and be prepared for changing conditions.
- Don't hike alone, and while on the trail, keep your party together. Let someone at camp know your route and estimated return time.
- Carry rain gear, adequate water, a flashlight or headlamp and a small first-aid kit. Add to that matches in a waterproof container and a whistle to signal rescuers.
- On backcountry hikes, carry detailed topo maps and a compass you know how to use. Follow your progress on the map as you travel and keep a continual fix on your location.
- Avoid wearing cotton. When wet, it will wick out your body heat and put you at risk for hypothermia. Wear and carry clothing made of synthetic fleece or wool. A wet hiker can easily succumb to hypothermia, even in summer.
- Consider the physical limits of your entire group and let the slowest hiker set the pace.
- If you get lost, stay calm. Whatever happens, don't leave the trail.
- Stay clear of all wild animals, particularly bears.
- Deaths and major injuries from falling are not uncommon in this country. Don't put yourself in dangerous situations, and never climb on or near waterfalls!
- Regardless of how crystalline that spring or stream appears, there's no guarantee it's safe to drink. The best defense against illness is to bring drinking water to a roiling boil for one minute. Iodine treatments and filtration systems are also effective but not foolproof.
- Crossing streams can be a dangerous business. In winter and early spring, when water levels are at their highest, it may be necessary to wade.

LEAVE NO TRACE PRINCIPLES

✔ Plan ahead and prepare.

✔ Travel and camp on durable surfaces.

✔ Properly dispose of waste.

✔ Leave what you find.

✔ Minimize campfire impacts.

✔ Respect wildlife.

✔ Be considerate of other visitors.

Hiking Rules & Permits

No matter where you're hiking, stay on the trails – even if it means treading through the mud. Don't attempt to make up lost time by taking shortcuts at switchbacks – this damages the ecosystem and can cause erosion. You might also mar the trail, making it difficult for future hikers to follow. Obey trail closures.

BEAR AWARENESS

The sight of a bear is always a heart-stopping event, even for grizzled, seen-it-all rangers. If you spend considerable time in the southern Appalachians, chances are sooner or later you will see one of these magnificent creatures. Great Smoky Mountains National Park is home to as many as 1800 bears, a density of more than two per square mile, while an estimated 300 to 500 bears roam through Shenandoah. However, this doesn't mean you'll see the animals lining up for ice at the campground – more likely you'll observe them slumbering in trees, shuffling about in blackberry brambles or perhaps even causing a 'bear jam' on the Cades Cove Loop Rd.

Black bears are omnivores that would just as soon gobble up a pawful of grubs, acorns, fruit or roots as a delicious groundhog or deer. Bears generally enter their hibernation dens in October or November, though some may ramble around all winter if the weather is mild. Cubs are born around February, but they don't emerge from the den with their mothers until April or May. A female will tend to her cubs until she's ready to mate again, about every other year.

The most important thing you can do to help keep bears wild and healthy is to secure your food carefully and keep your campsite free of anything that might be of interest to bears. Never feed a bear. Bears that gain a taste for human food or garbage quickly abandon their foraging habits and may have to be relocated or even euthanized. The park service puts it bluntly: To feed a bear is to guarantee its demise.

But what if you encounter a bear on the trail? Above all, keep your distance. Although rare, attacks on humans have occurred, some resulting in serious injury or death. Treat encounters with bears with extreme caution and follow these guidelines:

✔ If you see a bear, remain watchful. Do not approach it. If your presence causes a bear to change its behavior, you're too close. If a bear displays aggressive behavior – making loud noises or running toward you – increase the distance between you and the bear by backing away slowly. The bear will probably do the same. Don't run, lest the bear consider you prey!

✔ If the bear continues to follow you, stand your ground. Talk loudly or shout at it. Try to intimidate the bear, working together with others if possible. Throw nonfood objects or use a stout stick as a deterrent.

✔ If the bear's behavior suggests it's after your food and you are physically attacked, separate yourself from the food and back slowly away. If all else fails, fight back aggressively with any available object.

Report all bear incidents to a park ranger immediately (☎ 865-436-1230).

Though it's tempting to pick a handful of wildflowers on your return hike, think again. It's illegal to disturb natural resources – this includes picking flora, feeding wild animals and tampering with historic structures and fences. Weapons and metal detectors are prohibited at all times. Treat all water from streams and springs before drinking it.

GREAT SMOKY MOUNTAINS NATIONAL PARK

Backcountry camping is allowed only at designated campsites. Some of these are by reservation only; others are set aside strictly for hikers and/or horse campers. **Reservations** (☎ 865-436-1231; ☽ 8am-6pm) for reserved backcountry sites

continued on p45

HIKING THE APPALACHIAN TRAIL

The mighty **Appalachian Trail** is the mother of all footpaths. Running along the spine of the planet's oldest mountain range, it weaves over 2174 miles from Springer Mountain, Georgia, to Mount Katahdin, Maine. It meanders through 14 states, traveling up and down more than 350 mountain peaks above 5000ft, yet it rarely ever leaves the wilderness. The AT (as most users call it) sneaks through one of the world's greatest forests, a dense constellation of fir, oak, maple, spruce, pine, birch, hemlock, ash, cedar and dogwood trees, just to name a few. Often the trees give way to some of the most spectacular vistas imaginable, usually atop the scattered peaks, the highest of which is **Clingmans Dome** (6643ft) in Great Smoky Mountains National Park.

After many years of dreaming, planning and aggressive negotiating – not to mention the massive task of mapping, building and marking the trail – by environmental visionaries and many old school, East Coast hiking clubs, the unequaled Appalachian National Scenic Trail opened for business in 1937. Today the AT is maintained and overseen by the Appalachian Trail Conference (ATC), a nonprofit organization based in Harpers Ferry, West Virginia, which remains the ultimate resource for information on the trail.

TOP 10 UNCLAIMED AT TRAIL NAMES

10. Rainmaker
9. Downwind Skunk
8. Puddles
7. Lyme Lover
6. Bear Bait
5. Possum Drops
4. Tick
3. Bourbon Boy
2. Little Arson Annie
1. Leggy

Each year about 2000 brave, determined and half-loony souls set out to attain the legendary status of an AT through-hiker. Most through-hikers begin from the southern point of Amicalola Falls, Georgia in the early spring. Only 200 or so of these hardy dreamers will stumble out of the impenetrable Maine forests some five months later, looking like Rip Van Winkle on a bender. To become a through-hiker means to overcome an endless scroll of hardships that might include utter exhaustion, hypothermia, malnutrition, giardiasis, Lyme disease, blisters, sprained ankles, debilitating shin splints, sudden lightning strikes, exploding portable stoves, blood-crazed blackflies, mosquitoes, poison ivy, poisonous snakes, marauding bears, angry bobcats, wolves, wild boars, Army Ranger night patrols and simple but dreaded 'falling down.' Falling down can mean anything from tumbling off a high cliff to flopping facedown into a mud puddle under the full weight of your backpack. AT through-hikers are perpetually one small injury away from failure and retreat.

But just as a happy new mother can forget the pain of childbirth, the life-transforming experience of completing the AT erases all accumulated traumas. Through-hikers of the AT are one of America's most precious nature cults. Dedicated and mutually supportive, they're often lifesavers in the face of the AT's fierce elements. And they all have goofy trail nicknames to boot. To name a few mentioned in *Walking the Appalachian Trail* by Larry Luxenberg (an excellent sourcebook): Mountain Laurel, Pooh, Ridgerunner, Sagwagon, Lo-tec, Chasing Autumn, Breeze, Gutless, Sacajawea, Umbrella Lady, the Hobbit, Sweetpea La Foot, Gearhead and the hopeful Lucky, Lucky, Lucky.

If you think you've got the stuff through-hiking dreams are made of, be sure to refer to *The Thru-Hiker's Handbook* by Dan 'Wingfoot' Bruce while plotting your victory march. For a hilarious and informative look at what you might encounter on the AT, check out Bill Bryson's *A Walk in the Woods*. If a paunchy, bear-phobic, middle-aged writer and his inexperienced, doughnut-addicted sidekick can set out to conquer the unforgiving AT, then surely you can too.

The most famous through-hiker is probably **Grandma Gatewood**, who, at age 67, walked into glory and the AT pantheon by completing a through-hike in 1955. In 1964 she became the first person to complete the AT three times. Born in 1887 in a log cabin in Raccoon Creek, Ohio, Gatewood intimately understood the metaphysics of walking. She also was the unwitting pioneer of the light-packing revolution that is now sweeping the backpacking world. Grandma eschewed sleeping bags, tents, backpacks, maps and even hiking boots, preferring to move swiftly and lightly in tennis shoes and a duffel bag filled only with the barest of necessities.

Many stouthearted hikers are derailed and demoralized by gargantuan, leave-nothing-to-chance backpacks that your friendly local 'outdoor specialists' are eager to push. If you want to avoid the relentless misery of a 50lb pack and instead spring along the trail like a well-prepared squirrel, peruse the revolutionary manifesto *Beyond Backpacking: Ray Jardine's Guide to Lightweight Hiking*. Adopting just a few of Ray's hard-earned tactics could mean the difference between completing the AT or bailing out at the first highway.

Of course, it's not necessary to conquer the entire AT in one bold act. Section hikers complete the task piecemeal, selecting times and locations to minimize difficulty. And the vast majority of AT users just drop in for a leisurely stroll, glorying in seemingly endless wilderness while never straying too far from the visitor center snack bar.

If you're sufficiently inspired to take on the mighty AT or just want to dip your toe in the soil and think up a cute trail name for yourself, be sure to consult the **Appalachian Trail Conference** (☎ 304-535-6331; www.appalachian trail.org; PO Box 807, Harpers Ferry WV 25425-0807) and make use of the group's extensive AT knowledge and many publications.

THE SUM TOTAL OF GRANDMA GATEWOOD'S AT HIKING GEAR

Here's all that Grandma Gatewood packed in her homemade denim duffel bag:

✔ sweater
✔ jacket
✔ scarf
✔ light wool jacket to sleep in
✔ plastic curtain for a tent
✔ two plastic 8oz bottles
✔ rain hat
✔ rain cape (also functioned as a ground cloth)
✔ flashlight
✔ Swiss Army knife
✔ teaspoon
✔ tin cup
✔ matches
✔ Band-Aids

✔ Mercurochrome
✔ safety pins
✔ hairpins
✔ needle and thread, buttons
✔ soap
✔ towel

Food
✔ bouillon cubes
✔ chipped beef
✔ raisins
✔ peanuts
✔ powdered milk
✔ salt

NAME	TYPE	LOCATION START	DISTANCE R/T	DURATION R/T	CHALLENGE	ELEVATION CHANGE	FEATURES	FACILITIES	DESCRIPTION	PAGE
Abrams Falls	Day hike	Cades Cove Loop Rd	5 miles	3½ hrs	Moderate	200ft	(icons)	(icons)	One of Great Smoky's prettiest waterfalls.	103
Alum Cave Bluffs	Day hike	Newfound Gap Rd	4.5 miles	3 hrs	Moderate–Difficult	1360ft	(icons)		Quintessential Smoky Mountains hike featuring views, Arch Rock and colorful bluffs.	97
Andrews Bald	Day hike	Clingmans Dome parking area	3.6 miles	2½ hrs	Easy	700ft	(icons)		Spruce fir forest, views and an open bald.	102
Appalachian Trail East	Overnight	Newfound Gap Rd	31.6 miles	4 days	Difficult	4000ft	(icons)	(icons)	A bona fide backcountry adventure along the mother of all footpaths.	108
Cades Cove Nature Trail	Day hike	Cades Cove Loop Rd	0.75 miles	1 hr	Easy	300ft	(icons)		Interpretive nature trail with information on settlers' survival techniques.	102
Charlies Bunion	Day hike	Newfound Gap Rd	8 miles	5½ hrs	Moderate	1000ft	(icons)	(icons)	Trek along the Appalachian Trail with stunning views.	100
Chimney Tops	Day hike	Newfound Gap Rd	4 miles	4 hrs	Difficult	1250ft	(icons)		Challenging hike to a stony outcrop for panoramic views.	98
Clingmans Dome	Day hike	Clingmans Dome parking area	1.5 miles	1 hr	Moderate–Difficult	300ft	(icons)	(icons)	Mile-high hike to park's highest point.	101
Gregory Bald	Overnight	Forge Creek Rd	11.4 miles	2 days	Difficult	2400ft	(icons)	(icons)	Old-growth forest, views from the bald and flame azaleas in June.	106
Grotto Falls	Day hike	Roaring Fork Motor Nature Trail	2.6 miles	2 hrs	Moderate	350ft	(icons)		Views, diverse plant life and a pretty waterfall.	96
Laurel Falls	Day hike	Little River Rd	2.6 miles	1½ hrs	Easy–Moderate	400ft	(icons)	(icons)	Highly accessible paved trail leading to a superb waterfall.	95
Mouse Creek Falls	Day hike	Big Creek Campground	4 miles	3 hrs	Easy	500ft	(icons)		A classic rolling stream, an emerald green swimming hole and a waterfall.	105
Rainbow Falls	Day hike	Roaring Fork Motor Nature Trail	5.6 miles	4 hrs	Difficult	1700ft	(icons)		Strenuous hike through deep forest to a delicate waterfall.	96
Smokemont Loop	Day hike	Smokemont Campground	6.1 miles	4 hrs	Moderate–Difficult	1350ft	(icons)		Lovely streams, plenty of wildflowers and a changing forest.	99
Sugarlands Valley Nature Trail	Day hike	Newfound Gap Rd	0.5 miles	30 min	Easy	None	(icons)	(icons)	Paved loop trail with exhibits and old homesteads.	95
Steve Woody Place	Day hike	Cataloochee Rd	2 miles	1½ hrs	Easy	150ft	(icons)	(icons)	Pretty mountain stream and a preserved homestead.	104
Trillium Gap Trail	Overnight	Roaring Fork Motor Nature Trail	13.4 miles	2 days	Difficult	3100ft	(icons)	(icons)	Ascend Great Smoky's crown jewel peak and sleep on its crest.	108

Legend:

- View
- Great for Families
- Waterfall
- Swimming
- Fishing
- Wildlife Watching
- Restrooms
- Drinking Water
- Picnic Sites
- Ranger Station
- Wheelchair Accessible
- Backcountry Campsite

HIKING IN SHENANDOAH

NAME	TYPE	LOCATION START	DISTANCE R/T	DURATION R/T	CHALLENGE	ELEVATION CHANGE	FEATURES	FACILITIES	DESCRIPTION	PAGE
Blackrock Summit	Day hike	Blackrock Summit parking area	1 mile	1½ hrs	Easy	175ft			Jagged outcrops and one of the best views of Shenandoah Valley.	178
Cedar Run Whiteoak Canyon Loop	Day hike	Hawksbill Gap	8.8 miles	5–6 hrs	Difficult	2495ft			Long, strenuous trail with stunning waterfalls.	175
Compton Peak	Day hike	Compton Gap parking area	2.4 miles	2½ hrs	Easy–Moderate	940ft			Outstanding scenic views and examples of volcanic 'columnar jointings.'	173
Dark Hollow Falls	Day hike	Dark Hollow Falls parking area	1.4 miles	1½ hrs	Moderate–Difficult	440ft			Dramatic falls spilling over a craggy, ancient lava flow.	177
Fox Hollow	Day hike	Dickey Ridge Visitor Center	1.2 miles	1 hrs	Easy	310ft			Quiet trail leading through an old family farmstead.	172
Hawksbill Summit	Day hike	Hawksbill Gap parking area	1.7–2.8 miles	2–3 hrs	Moderate	800ft			Spooky in fog, trail winds up to rare tree species at park's highest point.	177
Limberlost	Day hike	MP 43	1.3 miles	1½ hrs	Easy	negligible			ADA accessible loop through forest and wildflowers.	170
Mt Marshall	Overnight	Jenkins Gap parking area	13.5 miles	2 days	Moderate–Difficult	2450 ft			Explosion of wildflowers in spring and amazing views from a canyon rim.	179
Old Rag Loop	Day hike	Old Rag parking area	7.2 miles	6–7 hrs	Moderate–Difficult	2380ft			A unique landscape of tree canopies, craggy boulders and open cliffs.	174
Riprap	Overnight	Riprap Overlook	9.3 miles	2 days	Moderate–Difficult	2000ft			Picturesque trek through true wilderness.	180
South River Falls	Day hike	South River picnic area	2.2 miles	2–3 hrs	Moderate	850ft			Slightly challenging hike through lush canopies to picture-postcard falls.	178
Stony Man Nature Trail	Day hike	Stony Man Trail parking area	1.4 miles	1½ hrs	Easy	340ft			Rewarding vistas of the park's second-highest peak.	175
Traces	Day hike	Mathews Arm Campground	1.7 miles	1½ hrs	Easy	335ft			Gentle nature trek through a thick oak forest past old settlements.	173

 View
 Restrooms
 Great for Families
 Drinking Water
 Picnic Sites
Waterfall
Swimming
Ranger Station
Fishing
Wheelchair Accessible
Wildlife Watching
Backcountry Campsite

NAME	TYPE	LOCATION START	DISTANCE R/T	DURATION R/T	CHALLENGE	ELEVATION CHANGE	FEATURES	FACILITIES	DESCRIPTION	PAGE
Virginia										
Apple Orchard Falls	Day hike	Sunset Fields Overlook	3.4 miles	3–4 hrs	Difficult	1000ft			Trail passes giant boulders and canopied forest to a multitiered cascade.	205
Fallingwater Cascades Loop	Day hike	Fallingwater Cascades Overlook	1.6 miles	2 hrs	Moderate	260ft			Scenic trek past a series of gentle cascades.	205
Mill Mountain	Day hike	Roanoke Mountain	3 miles	3–4 hrs	Easy–Moderate	670ft			A worthwhile mountaintop jaunt with a glowing neon star as a backdrop.	207
Sharp Top	Day hike	Peaks of Otter Visitor Center	1.6 miles	2–3 hrs	Difficult	1400ft			Popular summit with panoramic vistas.	206
White Rock Falls	Day hike	Slacks Overlook	1.8 miles (one-way)¼	2 hrs	Moderate	840ft			Small but beautiful falls cascading into a clear base pool.	204
North Carolina										
Bluff Mountain	Day hike	Alligator Back Overlook	7.5 miles (one-way)¼	6 hrs	Moderate	320ft			Fairly level trek with 360-degree views.	220
Crabtree Falls Loop	Day hike	Crabtree Falls Visitor Center	2.5 miles	1½–2½ hrs	Difficult	600ft			Rocky trail down stone steps to one of the prettiest waterfalls off the parkway.	221
Linville Gorge	Day hike	Linville Falls Visitor Center	1.4 miles	1–2 hrs	Difficult	1400ft			Challenging yet rewarding trek to a dramatic waterfall.	221
Tanawha Trail	Day hike	Beacon Heights parking area	13.5 miles (one-way)¼	1 day	Easy–Moderate	900ft			Fragile plant ecosystems and unbeatable views.	222
Waterfalls in Graveyard Fields	Day hike	Graveyard Fields Overlook	0.8 miles	45 min	Moderate	340ft			Fun waterfall trail that crosses streams, bridges and a viewing platform.	223
Waterrock –nob	Day hike	Waterrock Knob Visitor Center	0.5 miles	1 hr	Moderate–Difficult	410ft			Short, calorie-crunching climb to the parkway's highest viewing area.	224

Legend

View · Great for Families · Waterfall · Swimming · Fishing · Wildlife Watching

Restrooms · Drinking Water · Snack Shop · Ranger Station · Wheelchair Accessible · Backcountry Campsite

continued from p39

are accepted up to a month in advance. See Backcountry Hikes (p105) in the Great Smoky chapter for more information.

Backcountry permits are required for all overnight trips, but not for day hikes. Permits are available free of charge at most park campgrounds and ranger stations and at Sugarlands and Oconaluftee Visitor Centers (☎ 865-436-1297).

SHENANDOAH NATIONAL PARK & BLUE RIDGE PARKWAY

Permits are required for backcountry camping in Shenandoah. Available from any park entrance station or visitor center, permits are issued between sunrise and an hour before sunset. If possible, apply for one in advance by mail. Write to: Superintendent, Park Headquarters, Attn: Backcountry Camping Permit, 3655 US Hwy 211 East, Luray, VA 22835. Include your name, complete address, start and end dates of your trip, the number in your party and your

PHOTOGRAPHY TIPS

With all that gorgeous scenery, there's never a shortage of subjects to photograph in the parks, but you may be wondering just what camera equipment to bring, and when and how to get the best shots.

✔ Unless you're a professional, the lighter and more compact your equipment, the better; even professionals may want to reassess what is essential. What feels light from the hotel room to the car can become onerous a mile or two up the trail. Tripods can be particularly burdensome; improvise with boulders and backpacks instead.

✔ Take lots of pictures. Don't listen to that inner penny-pincher who tells you that those extra shots are wasteful. Take time with your subject and explore it photographically.

✔ Dusk and dawn are fantastic times to capture the wilderness on film. Focus on objects that the light is reflected on, like mountains, water or clouds, rather than directly photographing the sinking or rising sun.

✔ If the sun goes behind a cloud, don't take that as a signal to put away your camera. Some of the best pictures are taken in soft light; you'll get clean, even colors rather than bleached or drab shots.

✔ Shooting directly into the sunlight can turn your plant, friend or woodchuck into a silhouette. Try to find places where the sun is reflected off some aspect of the landscape, such as snow or granite.

✔ Wildlife poses perhaps the greatest challenge to photographers. Those wide-angle lenses that are great for mountain scenery make distant animals seem even smaller; try to travel with zoom lens capability.

✔ Animals often move quickly, suddenly or constantly – particularly twitching, bobbing birds. One of your best opportunities for taking snapshots of wildlife is from the car window, as animals are generally much less disturbed (and therefore less likely to bolt) than they are if you approach on foot.

✔ You can purchase film at most park visitor centers. For equipment, repairs and one-hour processing, head to Asheville, Gatlinburg or Pigeon Forge.

For further tips, pick up a copy of Lonely Planet's *Travel Photography*.

trip itinerary, including prospective campsites. Day hikers are free to roam without a permit. Campfires are prohibited in the backcountry.

CYCLING & MOUNTAIN BIKING

If you can get away from the roar of traffic and find a road where RVs won't be clipping your elbows, bicycling is a wonderful way to explore the Blue Ridge. Gliding quietly down the road, you'll have excellent opportunities for wildlife viewing, plus the satisfaction of knowing that you're not contributing to the decline of mountain air quality.

Where cars and bicycles must share the road, safety should be a major concern. Wear that helmet, use those rearview mirrors and ride a properly fitted, well-maintained bicycle.

GREAT SMOKY MOUNTAINS NATIONAL PARK

With the exception of the Roaring Fork Motor Nature Trail, bicycles are permitted on most park roads. But be aware that narrow byways, steep inclines and heavy auto traffic make many of the roads ill suited for cyclists.

Cades Cove Loop Rd is the glorious exception. Until 10am on Wednesday and Saturday mornings from mid-May through late September, the 11-mile one-way loop road is closed to vehicular traffic.

Great Smoky Mountains National Park has no mountain biking trails. Bicycles are allowed only on the **Gatlinburg Trail**, the **Oconaluftee River Trail** and the lower **Deep Creek Trail**. Bicycles are prohibited on all other park trails.

Mountain bikers need not mope, however. They can still attain that desirable coating of dust and sweat on several lightly used gravel roads, including two good routes in the Cades Cove area.

Beyond the park borders are the popular and challenging single-track trails of the **Tsali Recreation Area** (p145), north of NC 28 between Fontana and Bryson City in North Carolina.

There are many other splendid mountain biking trails on national forest and recreation lands near Great Smoky National Park. For information, contact the following offices:

Big South Fork National River & Recreation Area (☎ 423-286-7275)
Chattahoochee National Forest (☎ 770-297-3000)
Cherokee National Forest (☎ 423-476-9700)
Mt Rogers National Recreation Area (☎ 800-628-7207)
Nantahala National Forest (☎ 828-257-4200)
Pisgah National Forest (☎ 828-257-4200)
Tsali Recreation Area (☎ 929-479-6431)

BLUE RIDGE PARKWAY & SHENANDOAH NATIONAL PARK

Mountain biking is not allowed in Shenandoah. Road bikers are permitted only on Skyline Drive but not on trails or in campgrounds. Though the scenery is beautiful, bikers need to be aware of tourists in cars, who often swerve while straining for glimpses of the natural beauty. You might be better off trying the more than 900 miles of traffic-free trails and 2000 miles of paved, gravel and dirt roads in the **George Washington & Jefferson National Forests**. Biking is more prevalent along the Parkway, especially in **Pisgah National Forest**. For more detailed information on routes and tours, contact the Blue Ridge Bicycle Club in Asheville, North Carolina (www.blueridgebicycleclub.org), and in Roanoke, Virginia (www.blueridgebicycleclub.com).

HORSEBACK RIDING

It's only natural that you'll want to mount a winsome steed and hit the trail, enjoying a privileged vantage point that only horseback can afford...soon you'll be cantering cross coves and crossing creeks! For many who came before you, riding a horse was the preferred means of transportation through the Blue Ridge.

With 550 miles of hiking trails that accommodate horses, Great Smoky is prized by both serious equestrians and casual backwoods riders alike. Shenandoah's options are more limited; the only place for horesback riding is **Skyland Lodge**. The Blue Ridge Parkway doesn't offer horseback riding from its main drag, though several horse trails crisscross the road and lead past sights (see Flat Top Manor, p213). There's even a bona fide dude ranch in **Burnsville**, with a little city-slicker action for guests only. Those interested in riding should seek out tour companies in surrounding towns such as Blowing Rock and Spruce Pine.

FISHING

For the Cherokee these rugged mountains were the land of plenty: the vast virgin forests were home to elk, bison, black bears and wild turkeys, and the streams were teeming with native brook trout. While much has changed, the good news is that the Blue Ridge remains a fishing paradise unequaled anywhere in the eastern US.

Many of the region's streams originate as springs that burble forth from the backbone of the high mountain ridges. As they tumble down the mountainsides in a series of rushing cascades, they merge to form the wider, slower moving rivers of lower elevations – prime fishing country, all of it.

THEY SHALL BE RELEASED

In relations between fish and people, there are certain rules of etiquette that must be followed. For example, it is considered rude – some might call it cruel – to play a fish until it is utterly exhausted. The finer points of decorum are less obvious, but well-bred anglers come to know them.

While following these guidelines won't persuade a fish to forgive you for catching it, they do demonstrate a sportsmanlike appreciation for the intrinsic dignity of fish.

✔ Common courtesy requires that when you're handling a fish, do so with a wet hand. You mustn't damage that sleek, slimy coat.

✔ You know what they say about a fish out of water. Keep them submerged as much as possible when handling.

✔ Refrain from sticking your fingers in the fish's gills. It embarrasses the fish and may cause damage.

✔ Don't squeeze the fish – they *really* don't like to be squeezed.

✔ Use of barbless hooks is encouraged, and not just by the fish. Remove the hook gently. If necessary, use long-nosed pliers to back out the hook.

✔ If the fish is deeply hooked, cut the line. Do not yank out the hook. It will eventually rust away, like so many hooks that came before.

✔ When releasing your catch, gently hold the fish upright in quiet water facing upstream, moving it slowly back and forth in the water. This lets the disgruntled fish know that its chance has come to swim away.

The mountains provide a wide variety of angling experiences, from remote headwater trout streams to easily accessible, cool-water, smallmouth bass streams. Most waterways remain at or near their carrying capacity of fish and are plum fishing sites throughout the year.

Containing more than 2000 miles of streams within its boundaries, Great Smoky Mountains National Park protects one of the last wild brook trout habitats east of the Mississippi. Known to mountain people as 'brookies,' 'speckled trout' or simply 'spec,' these beautiful fish live in headwaters above 3000ft. They're distinguished by a top fin with wormlike markings and tri-color bottom fins of white, black and orange. Sadly, the brook trout has lost more than 75% of its range in the park due to the introduction of nonnative fish and logging.

As the waterways wend their way down to lower elevations, nonnative rainbow and brown trout assert their dominance. Further downstream, as the forest canopy opens the waters to the sun, the fish community shifts once again to become the domain of smallmouth and rock bass and a motley crew of shiners, minnows, suckers and darters.

A great book on the subject is *The Fly Fisherman's Guide to the Great Smoky Mountains National Park* by H Lea Lawrence.

Fishing Rules & Permits

The practice of low-impact, leave-no-trace fishing is part of an ethic that all outdoor enthusiasts should embrace. Local fishing rules and regulations are not merely suggestions, but rather mandates informed by science, enforced by law and controlled by conservation officers. Regulations such as bag limits and bait prohibitions are meant to protect what are perhaps the most fragile elements of a mountain ecosystem: its streams and rivers. Comply with all laws out of gratitude for nature's bounty.

In Great Smoky, fishing is permitted in most streams year-round, from 30 minutes before official sunrise to 30 minutes after official sunset. To protect threatened fish, certain posted streams are closed to fishing. A Tennessee or North Carolina fishing license, available in towns outside the park, is required. You may keep a combined total of five of the following: rainbow trout, brown trout and smallmouth bass up to 7 inches long. Each fisher is limited to one handheld rod. Only artificial flies or lures with a single hook are permitted. Any typeof fish bait, or for that matter those alluring artificial scents, is strictly *verboten*.

Fishing in Shenandoah and along the Virginia section of the Blue Ridge Parkway is possible year-round, but it's catch-and-release only unless otherwise designated (there are 24 streams in Virginia from which you can take fish home). Single-hook artificial lures are required. Licenses are also required for nonresidents age 12 and older. You can pick up a five-day, nonresident license ($6.50) at the park's waysides or at local sporting goods stores. Daily catch is limited to six trout, and they must be more than 9 inches in length.

RAFTING & BOATING

This is the land of fast water. From almost any trail you can hear it racing down the mountain. It pours over cliffs and roars down gorges. At lower elevations rivers converge and waters rise as they move toward the nearest available ocean. Some flow slow and deep and wide; others charge through the landscape with a force that compels one to wonder whether a dam has ruptured. It's the latter that are of concern to white-water rafters.

Around Great Smoky, the Nantahala, Big Pigeon, Ocoee and French Broad Rivers provide the action for rafting trips. Whether you're an adrenaline junkie who likes it rough or a mother hen whose main concern is keeping

WATER HAZARDS

When you see so many crystalline rivers and streams tumbling down every mountain, it's mighty tempting to don your river sandals and splash around a bit, particularly on a hot day. Before you do, consider the following:

✔ River levels can rise rapidly after a heavy rainfall. A localized thunderstorm dumping rain far upstream on the park's highest peaks can create sudden and unexpected flood conditions in lower elevations. And you might not have felt a single raindrop.

✔ Do not wade in or attempt to cross a rain-swollen stream. Medical assistance for the injured may be many hours away. Supervise children at all times.

✔ Exposure to cold water can quickly lead to hypothermia.

✔ Do not climb on rocks. Over the years several fatalities and innumerable injuries have resulted from people climbing on rocks near waterfalls or along the riverbanks. These rocks are slippery due to mist and algae.

✔ Do not dive or drop into the water. Submerged rocks, trees or debris could be just below the surface.

✔ If you fall in or find yourself accidentally swimming in fast moving water, do not try to stand up. Most drownings result from getting a leg or ankle caught in an underwater rock ledge or between boulders. The force of the water can push you over and hold you under. The standard defensive swimming position in fast-moving water is to lie on your back with your feet pointing downstream and your toes up toward the surface. Always look downstream and prepare to fend of rocks with your feet.

– National Park Service

the baby chicks from going into the drink, you'll have no problem finding a rafting outfitter sensitive to your proclivities. Most of the action centers on the towns of Bryson City, North Carolina, and Hartford, Tennessee.

Nantahala Outdoor Center (☎ 888-662-2199; www.noc.com; 13077 NC 19W) is the grand-daddy of white-water outfitters. Nantahala's main campus, 13 miles west of Bryson City, is a bustling place, with affordable lodging, restaurants, a river store and rafts piled up to the heavens. The staff conduct rafting adventures in the Nantahala gorge, provide kayak instruction and dole out rental craft. NOC also has outposts on the Big Pigeon River, near Hartford, and other area rivers.

At the southern end of the Blue Ridge Parkway near Cherokee, the **Blue Ridge Outing Company** (☎ 800-572-3510; www.raftwithkids.com) specializes in family-friendly raft trips on the Tuckaseigee River; children as young as four years old can go.

More and more folks are traveling with their own watercraft, ready to pull over at a moment's notice to dip a paddle in the water. One of the prettiest lakes for a relaxing paddle is **Lake Calderwood**, on US 129 just beyond the southwest border of Great Smoky. Part of the Cherokee National Forest, this pristine, undeveloped lake has a boat ramp and is well loved by trout fishers.

It can be challenging to find a place along the Blue Ridge Parkway where you can take that canoe or kayak off the roof rack. Boats without motors and/or sails are permitted only on **Price Lake** (MP 295), on the Parkway south of Boone, North Carolina – there's a ramp behind the parking area. Visitors can also rent boats.

River Tubing

Since there are no rivers suitable for rafting within the boundaries of Great Smoky Mountains National Park – and also because it's hella fun – some feckless souls like to park their butts in inner tubes and bounce down the rivers like so many balls in a Japanese pachinko game. Calling **Townsend**, Tennessee the 'tubing capital of the free world' might be a dubious compliment, but try telling that to the chubby kid floating harmlessly down the Little River.

If this sounds like good, cheap fun to you, you'll find plenty of opportunities for tubing in and around Townsend, Gatlinburg and Cherokee.

SWIMMING

With water, water everywhere in Great Smoky, chances are you're probably going to get wet. Crystalline **Fontana Lake** and hundreds of miles of mountain streams beckon on hot summer days.

Near the Blue Ridge Parkway are neighboring state parks and national forests with developed swimming areas, such as the sandy shores of **Sherando Lake**, near MP 13 in the George Washington and Jefferson National Forests. On summer days, kids especially enjoy slipping down **Sliding Rock**, off MP 276.

Although all streams in Great Smoky and Shenandoah are open for unsupervised swimming, there are attendant hazards and dangers – so many, in fact, that the park service does not recommend splashing around in the streams at all. The Blue Ridge Parkway takes it a step further by banning the activity outright, although you'll frequently see people splashing near waterfalls and shallow pools. Before you sneer and call the park service a killjoy, consider the rangers' well-reasoned warnings (see Water Hazards, p49).

HANG GLIDING

Experience the beauty of gorges and peaks from a bald eagle's view. You can hang-glide from three points in Shenandoah National Park. A permit is required in advance; you must have a minimum Hang 3 rating. Contact the park's **Communication Center** (☎ 540-999-3422; Rte 4, Box 348, Luray, VA 22835). Permission from landowners is required in order to hang-glide on private property. You can also hang-glide from two points on the Blue Ridge Parkway (Raven's Roost and Roanoke Mountain), with a permit obtained from a ranger station. Gliders must be rated Hang 3, and Ravens Roost requires a Cliff Launch rating.

Blue Sky Hang Gliding School (☎ 804-241-4324; www.blueskyhg.com; Penn Laird, VA) offers lessons by appointment in the beautiful Shenandoah Valley near Harrisonburg, Virginia, in addition to regularly scheduled lessons at a location near Richmond, Virginia.

SKIING

When the white stuff falls, closing certain stretches of road in Great Smoky, Shenandoah and along the Parkway, snowbirds take full advantage of these deserted roads on skis or snowshoes. Fire roads, certain trails and even Skyline Drive's shoulder also provide a unique means of experiencing these areas during a winter wonderland. Clingmans Dome Rd in Great Smoky, closed to auto traffic from December to March, is a popular cross-country skiing and snowshoeing route. Visitors must bring their own equipment since there are no roadside facilities. Several ski resorts like **Wintergreen**, **Massanutten** and **Chetola** offer more extensive cross-country and downhill skiing, as well as snow-tubing for families.

Downhill skiing – or something resembling it – is also a feature of **Ober Gatlinburg** (☎ 865-436-5423, 800-251-9202 snow report; www.obergatlinburg.com; 1001 Parkway, Gatlinburg, TN), a ski resort and amusement park near the north entrance to Great

Smoky. Experienced skiers may throw up their hands in disgust at the lack of powder or challenging runs, but first-timers and families have a ball. See Gatlinburg (p121) for more information.

BIRD AND WILDLIFE WATCHING

Ever since Hernando de Soto returned to Spain with stories of his expedition through Cherokee territory in 1540, naturalists have celebrated the astonishing biodiversity of the southern Appalachian Mountains. Here, a fortuitous combination of geography and climate has created one of the most diverse ecosystems on the planet. It's impossible to walk through these woods without having close encounters with birds and wildlife. For more information about the ecology of the Blue Ridge, consult the Ecosystem chapter.

Bird-Watching

Great Smoky, with its 800-plus square miles of mostly unbroken forest, is home to more than 240 species of birds. At least 110 species breed here, and more than 60 species are year-round residents. Many others are just passing through, as the Appalachian Mountains are one of the main flyways for eastern migratory birds. Other than a good field guide and a pair of binoculars, you don't need expensive gear to watch and identify them.

Bird-watchers along the Blue Ridge Parkway are similarly giddy, and with good reason: This is prime territory for spotting a great variety of birds. Summer ranger programs in Shenandoah National Park and along the Parkway include guided birding walks – check out the free *Shenandoah Overlook* or *Blue Ridge Parkway Travel Directory* publications for listings and themes.

The bird population of the southern Appalachians includes many celebrities and a few bona fide superstars, including the wild turkey, the Northern saw-whet owl, the red crossbill and the peregrine falcon.

The Great Smoky Mountains Association publishes *Birds of the Smokies*, a basic guide to get you started, available at any park visitor center. Also available is the specialty map *Birds & Birding* ($1).

> ## BIRD LYRICS
>
> Birds are the beat poets of the woods, and many birding enthusiasts can quote them at length. Birding mnemonics combine words and phrases with patterns of bird songs. Popular examples include the following:
>
> ✔ **Barred Owl** Who cooks for you—who cooks for you
>
> ✔ **Eastern Wood-Peewee** Pee-oh-wee, pee-oh-wee, pee-eer
>
> ✔ **Yellow Warbler** Sweet, sweet, I'm so sweet
>
> ✔ **Indigo Bunting** Sweet, sweet, sweeter, sweeter, here, here
>
> ✔ **Yellow-Throated Vireo** Look up...see me?...over here...higher still!
>
> ✔ **White-Breasted Nuthatch** Yank, yank, yank
>
> ✔ **Eastern Towhee** Drink-your-teeeeeeeeeee!
>
>

Wildlife Watching

An eastern box turtle lumbers across the trail to Chimney Tops. By Abrams Creek a white-tailed deer and her speckled fawn pause to fix their eyes on you before leaping into the undergrowth and vanishing. Fireflies flash in synchrony on a warm summer evening near Elkmont. In Cataloochee Valley a 600lb elk grazes in the early morning light, impervious to the guttural chortlings of the wild turkeys that amble by. And what's this? That freshly gouged log is surely the work of Great Smoky's undisputed Grand Pooh-Bah: A black bear has just sharpened its claws. Let's just keep on moving.

Keep your eyes open and your senses sharpened, and the creatures will reveal themselves. It's only a matter of patience and curiosity. Because of the dense foliage that covers these mountains, it's best to start your wildlife-watching safari in open areas like **Cades Cove** and **Cataloochee** in Great Smoky and **Big Meadows** in Shenandoah, where animals such as white-tailed deer, turkeys, bears and woodchucks like to catch some rays. On the unpaved **Balsam Mountain Road** and along the **Roaring Fork Nature Trail**, bears and sometimes red or gray foxes make their presence known. Be particularly alert in the early morning and at dusk, as many animals are most active nocturnally.

It's a little sad, though, when many prime bear-spotting sights are in developed areas like Skyland Lodge and Big Meadows Lodge – the latter location brags about a resident bear who comes out to forage around dinnertime.

In Shenandoah and along the Blue Ridge Parkway, you'll often wonder if you've stumbled into a Far Side cartoon when a great brown bear lumbers into the road ahead and dares you to a staring competition. Open areas like **Big Meadows** and approximately 10 miles of open farmland south of the **Blue Ridge Music Center** are favorite watering holes for deer and hedgehogs.

While it's tempting to offer a bear a Twinkie, feeding wildlife is strictly forbidden. The park service puts it bluntly: feeding a wild animal usually guarantees its demise (see Bear Awareness, p39).

Don't be a stalker. If you approach an animal so closely that it changes its behavior, you're too close. Harassing wildlife is a crime punishable by fine or even imprisonment. As in all matters regarding your privileged enjoyment of these protected lands, tread lightly and let wild things stay wild.

RANGER PROGRAMS

Who is that dapper Dan in the funny hat, and what is he saying about that pile of bear scat on the trail? Why, it's a park ranger giving a nature talk. In Great Smoky and Shenandoah, the National Park Service conducts guided nature and history walks, films, talks and slide shows. In summer multiple events take place every day of the week, ranging from gristmill tours and mountain farm demonstrations to naturalist hikes, hayrides and full-moon strolls.

Rangers wear a lot of hats, so to speak. In a given week they might perform a search and rescue operation, clear hiking trails after a storm, rescue a stranded motorist or participate in an ecosystem restoration or environmental monitoring program. Their ultimate mandate is to keep the parks safe, pristine and accessible to the millions of visitors who come each year.

Many rangers will tell you that their favorite duty is to act as a docent for inquisitive visitors. When someone asks why the seal salamander does pushups on a streamside rock, more often than not a ranger is ready with an answer and a smile. You might even find a ranger's enthusiasm for bear scat contagious.

The parks' quarterly newspapers, *Smokies Guide* and *Shenandoah Overlook*, publish up-to-date calendars of available programs. Pick one up at a visitor center or the larger campgrounds.

CLASSES

The **Great Smoky Mountains Institute at Tremont** (☎ 865-448-6709; www.gsmit.org), a year-round residential environmental education center in the Smokies, offers workshops and programs for everyone from grade-school children to Elderhostel groups and teachers. Programs may include hiking, slide shows on flora and fauna, mountain music, living history lessons and wildlife demonstrations. A fee applies for most programs.

A Walk in the Woods (☎ 865-436-8283; 4413 E Scenic Dr, Gatlinburg, TN) features a wide range of classes and seminars for both learned and budding naturalists, including classes on edible and medicinal plants, primitive skills, compass navigation, backpacking and nature exploration with children, to name but a few.

Arrowmont School of Arts & Crafts (☎ 865-436-5860; www.arrowmont.org; 556 Parkway, Gatlinburg, TN) teaches year-round arts and crafts classes for everyone from the novice to the professional. Weekend classes and longer workshops cover subjects ranging from basketry and woodturning to organic sculpture and metal arts.

Try your hand at creating concrete jewelry or a mouth-blown glass vase at the **Penland School of Crafts** (☎ 828-765-2359; www.penland.org; Penland, NC), located off the Blue Ridge Parkway. The school offers week-long instruction in various mediums like metallurgy, bookmaking and woodworking, in the spirit of keeping handcrafted art forms alive in the mountains.

TOP ACTIVITIES FOR KIDS

✔ Become a **Junior Ranger** at Great Smoky, Shenandoah or along the Blue Ridge Parkway

✔ Take a **ranger-guided walk** in Great Smoky or Shenandoah

✔ See Cades Cove by **hayride** (p114), Great Smoky

✔ Attend **Discovery Camp** (p114) in Great Smoky

✔ Watch millers grind corn and wheat at **Mingus Mill** in Great Smoky

KIDS' ACTIVITIES

The Great Smoky region has so much to offer kids and families that it's no wonder this is one of the most popular family destinations in the country. There are plenty of outdoorsy, educational opportunities in the parks, as well as a host of mindless pleasures to be had in the surrounding towns.

Many of Great Smoky's programs and activities are conceived with kids in mind. Some (such as the summer weekly favorite 'Salmandeeerin' for Kids' outing) find both kids and grownups splashing around in streams and peering beneath logs and rocks. Another popular offering is the junior blacksmithing workshop at the Mountain Farm Museum, where kids make their own dinner bell to take home. Reservations are required for many programs; check the park newspaper *Smokies Guide* for scheduling information.

All three parks offer a **Junior Ranger** program, in which kids fill an activity book with observations and park ranger signatures until they become 'certified' and earn a nifty badge. Booklets are available at most park visitor centers. The program also includes nature hikes, wildlife demonstrations and other hands-on activities to familiarize kids with the outdoors.

The **Great Smoky Mountains Institute at Tremont** (☎ 865-448-6709; www.gsmit.org) offers a variety of summer youth camps in the national park. Camps last from six to 10 days and cost $360 to $730. Fees include meals, lodging and most equipment.

The **Smoky Mountain Field School** (☎ 865-974-0150) hosts weekend workshops, hikes and adventures for adults and families throughout the year. In cooperation with the National Park Service and the University of Tennessee, experts on Smoky Mountain plants, wildlife and history lead the programs. Expect to pay a fee.

If this all sounds, well, too *educational*, placate the kids with a bag of cheese puffs as you head to Cherokee for **Santa's Land** , Townsend for river tubing, Gatlinburg for alpine sliding or Pigeon Forge for a musical revue. Kids with a railroad fixation can choose between the **Tweetsie Railroad** theme park in Blowing Rock and the **Great Smoky Mountains Railroad** in Dillsboro.

Other activities along the way include zoos in Roanoke and Maggie Valley, music jamborees and hayrides in Cades Cove.

Soon you will be swooning on a mountaintop or smooching in a cove, but first you have to plan and pack for your Great Smoky odyssey.

PLANNING THE TRIP

Some folks are content to throw a can of beans into a rucksack and just go; others require weeks of meticulous planning and an exhaustive itinerary. Either way, get ready to have a blast.

Perhaps your plan is to go sky-driving on the crest of the Blue Ridge, all the way from Shenandoah National Park to the Cherokee Indian Reservation in North Carolina. Or maybe you're the type who forsakes four wheels in favor of your own two feet: you'll hike the length of the Appalachian Trail as it zigzags across the skyline. Whatever your intentions, a little well-guided planning and pre-education can only make your journey a better one.

The three parks cover an enormous amount of territory. Unless you are planning an epic road trip of a month or more, it's wiser to concentrate on one park or area rather than trying to see everything. If your visit is going to be very brief, careful planning can be a huge asset; knowing beforehand what you want to do and see, how you're going to get around and where you're going to stay will save a lot of precious time.

Many activities require planning, particularly backcountry hikes, where reservations are often imperative. And if you're interested in a particular tour, fishing trip or climb, reservations can't hurt. If you're on a tight budget or schedule, or if you have your heart set on a certain hotel, book ahead. Reservations are especially advisable in July and August, when the parks receive the majority of their visitors.

Try, nevertheless, not to overplan your trip. A spare hour here or an extra day there will give you the flexibility to enjoy the unexpected – wildlife crossing your path, a burbling mountain stream to laze by or a white-water rafting trip that you suddenly feel inspired to join.

WHEN TO GO

All three parks are open year-round, but your experience will vary a lot depending on the season you visit.

Shenandoah's visitor centers (and most facilities) are only open from early spring through late fall; call ahead for specific dates.

Seasonal Highs & Lows

If you're planning a trip to Great Smoky, call for **daily forecasts** (☎ 865-436-1200 ext 630). In Shenandoah, expect temperatures to be about 10 degrees cooler than in the valley; **weather information** (☎ 540-999-3500; www.nps.gov/shen) is available on the Web or through the park hotline.

SPRING

Springtime really lives up to its reputation in the Smokies. Delicate wildflowers adorn the mountainsides as budding hardwoods promise to transform the landscape into an unbroken swath of green. The bears emerge from their cozy dens, ravenous for breakfast. These events you can count on. Less predictable is the weather: Wild swings in temperature and precipitation levels keep visitors busy putting on and taking off their fleeces. Backcountry hikers should be prepared and dress in layers. The weather can change in a flash.

In Shenandoah, wildflowers burst forth in a multitude of colors and trail conditions rebound quickly from harsh ice and snow.

SUMMER

Come June, the air gets thick enough to drink as humidity increases. Summer afternoons bring claps of thunder and buckets of rain; more often than not, the showers are short-lived. The forests drink it up and grow startlingly vibrant. Hikers will want to follow suit. Temperatures can rise to the 90s and then drop precipitously. If venturing into the backcountry, carry protective rain gear and plenty of water.

Sure, it does get hot in Shenandoah, but the crisp mountain air helps keep that mercury down, and you'll often need a light jacket in the evenings.

FALL

September, October and November are the drier months. Berries ripen on the vine almost as fast as bears can devour them. Brook trout get ready to spawn, and the deciduous foliage puts on its annual costume of blazing color. The days are mild and the nights cool and crisp. Temperatures can dip below freezing at night, and light snows often occur at higher elevations.

September is an ideal time to visit Great Smoky if you don't mind brisk evenings. Crowds have waned, the trees are just starting to get gussied up and the wildlife is too busy fattening up for winter to worry about being observed. Gateway towns remain open, and prices begin to drop.

Fiery reds and blazing oranges fill Shenandoah's spectacular treeline in fall, and leaf-peepers often turn the roads into parking lots. Rangers say that September is the best time to visit, since kids are back at school and bird whistles replace high-pitched squeals on the trails.

WINTER

Winters are relatively mild in the Smokies, but the days are notoriously fickle. One will be springlike, while the next might bring temperatures in the 20s and several inches of snow. The upside is that defoliated trees allow for great mountain vistas, wildlife viewing and very private hikes. This is the time when solitude is easiest to come by in the parks and backcountry. Prices in gateway towns reach their annual low.

Several roads in Great Smoky close for the season, including Clingmans Dome and Parson Branch Rds. Drivers should carry chains and be prepared for winter conditions when traveling through higher elevations.

Winters can be brutal in Shenandoah, with dangerous ice, accumulating snow and lower temperatures than in the valley. Most facilities shut down during this slow period, including visitor centers. But for the adventurous, there's cross-country skiing on closed roads, which offer amazing alpine views.

Coping with the Crowds

If you're visiting a national park to escape the madding crowds, you may find that you were not the only person to have that bright idea. In summer the Blue Ridge Parkway sometimes seems like nothing but a slow-moving parade of cars, buses and RVs. Parking your car in Gatlinburg can be an exercise in futility at any time of year. And Cades Cove is frequently paralyzed by a phenomenon known as a 'bear jam'– you guessed it – a bear on a stroll brings traffic to a standstill as drivers leap from their cars with their cameras.

If this doesn't sound relaxing, take heart. With a little strategizing, you can always find peace and solitude – if you just know where to look. All of the parks have busy areas, but it's easy to predict where crowds will coalesce. Naturally, major sights, gateway towns and the most popular scenic routes and trails will never be havens of quietude on a summer day. Try visiting in the early morning or late afternoon, when the throngs have moved on.

If you're hiking, choose a longer trail rather than a series of short ones. Your chances of losing the masses after the first hour or so are practically guaranteed. Take scenic drives in the early morning, when you're most likely to see wildlife; you'll also avoid the tourist convoys. If you're averse to congested roadways, spread out a map to find alternate roads. For folks willing to spend extra time getting from point A to point B, less-traveled roads venture to less-visited corners of the park that are no less rewarding.

GREAT SMOKY MOUNTAINS NATIONAL PARK

Welcoming more than 10 million visitors each year, Great Smoky Mountains National Park is indisputably well loved. Some might say that it's being loved a little too much. There are two peak seasons in the Smokies: midsummer (June 15 to August 15) and the entire month of October. Weekends in October are especially crowded; expect considerable traffic delays.

Cades Cove Loop Rd, the park's most popular attraction, can be anything but serene. Meanwhile, **Cataloochee**, a former frontier outpost in the isolated eastern edge of the park, remains a delightful secret waiting to be discovered. Accessed via a narrow, winding 11-mile road, Cataloochee offers lush old-growth forests, restored farms and homesteads, and opportunities for thrilling wildlife sightings of elk, wild turkeys and even black bears.

Newfound Gap Rd (US 441) – the sole artery running directly through Great Smoky Mountains National Park – is known as much for its heavy traffic as for its stunning views. A beautiful time to make the drive from Gatlinburg to Cherokee is just before dusk, after many visitors have hightailed it back to civilization. Once you cross Newfound Gap, you'll likely have the road to yourself.

The 16-mile western leg of the **Foothills Pkwy**, which runs from US 321 near Townsend to Chilhowee Lake, is underused and lined with breathtaking views, offering an interesting alternate route to Bryson City and Cherokee. From the parkway's terminus at Chilhowee, you can take the meandering byways US 129 and NC 28 past several picturesque lakes created by Tennessee Valley Authority dams.

Other lightly traveled roads include the gravel **Old NC 284**, which travels north from Cataloochee through deep forest to Big Creek Campground near I-40, and the gravel, one-way **Balsam Mountain Rd**, which travels through deep forest and connects to the Cherokee Indian Reservation.

Some of the more popular campsites, such as Elkmont and Cades Cove, are often filled to capacity during high season. Others, like **Cosby** and **Look Rock**, only fill up on holiday weekends. If you arrive on a July afternoon and hope to camp, consider heading straight to one of these.

SHENANDOAH NATIONAL PARK
The good news: There's only one road through the park, so you can't possibly get lost. The bad news: There's only one road through the park. Naturally, this creates 'great outdoors gridlock,' with only four possible exits along a 105-mile stretch. Oh, the agony of creeping behind a behemoth RV while a gaggle of motorcycles revs their engines in your rearview mirror! This is the scenario in summers and early fall; consider a visit in spring or even winter, when you can enjoy a different perspective and crowds are blessedly few.

The most popular areas are popular for a reason: They're home to the park's only lodging, dining and entertainment facilities. **Skyland** and **Big Meadows** are the twin hubs and house three-fourths of park visitors (others camp). You can't avoid crowds here, though the facilities attempt to make stays more comfortable than cramped, with outdoor amphitheaters, playgrounds, spacious dining halls and onsite trails.

Other heavily trafficked areas along Skyline Drive are the junction of US 211 and Skyline Drive (Thornton Gap Entrance Station); many visitors pass through on the way to the popular town of **Luray** and its world-famous caverns. The southern district, particularly around the tip of **Waynesboro**, tends to attract crowds since it's near the start of the Blue Ridge Parkway.

BLUE RIDGE PARKWAY
With a plethora of access roads, the Parkway does a great job of handling the ebb and flow of tourist seasons. **Mabry Mill** is the Parkway's most recognized and photographed attraction – it's *always* packed and is a particular favorite among older travelers and families with young children, thanks to the hearty, inexpensive food and interactive living-history trail. The Peaks of Otter, Roanoke, Linville Falls, Asheville, Mt Pisgah, Mt Mitchell State Park and Grandfather Mountain are also well-visited sites, but it's well worth bumping elbows to see them.

Want true peace and quiet? A surprisingly underused campground is **Crabtree Falls**, with a spectacular waterfall hike and a tasty snack shop. Most of the drive south of Asheville to Cherokee is also a lovely, less-trafficked journey.

Special Events
Events and festivals may mean more crowds, but they also bring a wealth of activities to enjoy. Consider planning your trip around one of the following. For further information and contact details, see Festivals & Events in the destination chapters.

GREAT SMOKY MOUNTAINS NATIONAL PARK
Old Timers' Day, showcasing mountain music and dancing, takes place at Cades Cove in early May and at Cataloochee in late September. September's **Mountain Life Festival** at Oconaluftee Mountain Farm Museum demonstrates traditional cooking and soap making.

In mid-April, the annual **Spring Wildflower Pilgrimage** includes a week of programs covering natural and cultural history topics. In May, the annual **International Migratory Bird Day** is a must for birders.

Learn how mountain folk used to celebrate the holidays at the **Festival of Christmas Past** in mid-December.

Gatlinburg honors its heritage each May with the annual **Scottish Festival & Games**, which features professional and amateur Highland athletics, children's events and concessionaires selling that perennial favorite, haggis.

Townsend hosts two big annual events to celebrate the region's cultural heritage: the **Spring Festival** in late April and the **Fall Heritage Festival** in late September.

SHENANDOAH NATIONAL PARK

Shenandoah celebrates the arrival of spring in mid-May with **Wildflower Weekend**. Nature lovers enjoy walks, exhibits and slide programs that showcase the park's spring wildflowers.

Where there are wildflowers and birds, there are bound to be butterflies. The **North American Butterfly Association Annual Count** enlists volunteers each July to count butterflies. If you're lucky, you might spot a great spangled fritillary or even a dreamy duskywing.

During **Hoover Days**, observed on the weekend closest to Herbert Hoover's August 10 birthday, the public gets a rare opportunity to tour the buildings at the former president's weekend retreat, Rapidan Camp (formerly known as Camp Hoover).

The **Civilian Conservation Corps Reunion** in September brings together some of the men who built practically everything within sight of Skyline Drive (and the Drive itself, for that matter). Shenandoah National Park was the first to have a CCC camp; it started in 1934 and is the oldest in the country.

The **National Audubon Society Annual Christmas Bird Count**, a century-old holiday tradition, sends folks into the sticks to search for birds in a 15-mile-diameter 'count circle' in Page County. The count provides information about trends in bird behavior, populations and migration.

BLUE RIDGE PARKWAY

The Parkway is well known for its summer music festivals. A new festival, **FloydFest** (☎ 540-745-FEST; www.floydfest.com), held in late July or early August in Floyd, Virginia, showcases acclaimed mountain music and a kaleidoscope of

PETS IN THE PARK

Of *course* you want to bring Miss Pookie to the park. And you wouldn't *dream* of leaving Mister Puddles locked up in the laundry room (lest he live up to his name). For many, a family vacation without the family pet is simply unthinkable.

Pets are allowed in campgrounds, picnic areas, parking areas and along roads (not in lodging rooms, though), but they must be kept on a leash not exceeding 6ft in length at all times in Great Smoky, Shenandoah and along the Blue Ridge Parkway. Owners are responsible for cleaning up after their extended family members.

Pets are only allowed on two short walking paths in Great Smoky: the Gatlinburg and Oconaluftee River Trails. In Shenandoah, all trails but the following nine are canine-friendly: Fox Hollow Nature Trail, Stony Man Nature Trail, Limberlost, Old Rag Ridge, Old Rag Saddle (above Old Rag Shelter), Dark Hollow Falls, Story of the Forest Nature Trail, Bearfence Mountain and the Frazier Discovery Trail.

Pets should not be left unattended in vehicles or RVs, and for Pete's sake, don't leave Pete tied up yowling in the campground. Your neighbors will thank you.

diverse rhythms from African to Zydeco. It's Woodstock with a major twang. Then there's the **Old Fiddler's Convention** (☎ 276-236-8541; www.oldfiddlersconvention. com; individual ticket/season ticket $5-10/30) in early August in Galax, Virginia. This world-class hootenanny draws the best fiddlers in the country to jam with kindred spirits playing the dulcimer, banjo, mouth harp and bull fiddles. The campground ($70/site) hosts players and listeners. What could be better than drifting off on a summer night to a bluegrass lullaby?

GATHERING INFORMATION

A great deal of general information about national parks is available by calling the National Park Service information lines:

Great Smoky Mountains National Park (☎ 865-436-1200; www.nps.gov/grsm)
Shenandoah National Park (☎ 540-999-3500; www.nps.gov/shen)
Blue Ridge Parkway (☎ 828-271-4779 or 828-298-0398 in VA; www.nps.gov/blri)

For information about accommodations in the gateway towns, including lodging and commercial campgrounds, contact the following tourism bureaus:

TENNESSEE
Tennessee Tourism (☎ 615-471-2159; www.tnvacation.com)
Cosby/Newport (☎ 423-623-7201; www.cockecounty.com)
Gatlinburg (☎ 800-267-7088; www.gatlinburg.com)
Pigeon Forge (☎ 800-251-9100; www.mypigeonforge.com)
Sevierville (☎ 865-453-6411; www.seviervillechamber.com)
Townsend (☎ 800-525-6834; www.smokymountains.org)

NORTH CAROLINA
North Carolina Tourism (☎ 800-847-4862; www.visitnc.com)
Asheville (☎ 800-257-1300; www.greatsmokies.com)
Bryson City (☎ 800-867-9246; www.greatsmokies.com)
Cherokee (☎ 800-438-1601; www.cherokee-nc.com)
Fontana (☎ 800-849-2258)
Maggie Valley (☎ 800-624-4431; www.maggievalley.org)

VIRGINIA
Virginia Tourism (☎ 800-847-4882; www.virginia.org)

Suggested Reading

The **Great Smoky Mountains Association** (☎ 888-898-9102; www.smokiesstore.org) publishes informative and helpful books and materials about the park, including maps, self-guided auto tour booklets, and nature, history and activity guides. The inexpensive *Great Smoky Mountains Starter Kit* ($5) includes maps, auto tours and hiking brochures.

HISTORY & FOLKLORE

The Great Smokies once constituted the farthest reaches of the American frontier; the first European settlers to arrive were interlopers on Cherokee land. To learn the history of Native Americans and the 'southern highlanders' is to discover a major chapter in the American story. Several good books tell how these Scotch-Irish, German and French arrivals contended with an untamed, uncharted territory.

First published in 1913, *Our Southern Highlanders* by Horace Kephardt is the definitive tome on life in the primeval wilderness of the southern Appalachians. Kephardt's vigorous prose and lack of sentimentality, along with his adventurous spirit, make for an imminently readable volume that is at once historical, sociological and autobiographical.

Trail of Tears: The Rise & Fall of the Cherokee Nation by John Ehle, a sixth-generation North Carolinian, transcends simplistic explanations of the Cherokee's plight in favor of nuanced historical narrative. The book takes you into the villages of the Cherokee and along the cruel Trail of Tears and ultimately demystifies the 'principal people.'

The Wild East: A Biography of the Great Smoky Mountains by Margaret Lynn Brown explores the complex interactions of social, political and environmental changes in the Great Smoky Mountains during the 19th and 20th centuries. This is no quaint portrait of Appalachia.

Cades Cove: The Life & Death of a Southern Appalachian Community, 1818-1937 by Durwood Dunn is filled with stories of the Civil War, moonshiners and barnburners, plus other true tales of life in a lively mountain community. A specialized history of the larger region can be found in Ted Olson's engaging *Blue Ridge Folklife.*

Folk Medicine in Southern Appalachia by Anthony Cavender is a fascinating look into the historical practice of folk medicine in the southern highlands. Profiles of herbalists, a faith healer and a Native American shaman shed light on the practices of backcountry healers.

Food & Recipes of the Smokies by Rose Houk includes some difficult-to-shop-for recipes (roast coon with sweet potato stuffing, for one) and many indispensable tips and observations ('There's forty-eleven ways to use corn'). While this slim volume may not change the way you cook, it does give telling insight into the settlers' hardscrabble kitchens.

Mountain Spirits by Joseph Earl Dabney is a lively chronicle of vanishing Americana: the moonshine life.

For more information about regional history and the founding of Great Smoky Mountains National Park, consult the History chapter.

ECOLOGY

Natural History of Mt. Le Conte by Kenneth Wise and Ron Peterson profiles Great Smoky's most famous mountain, offering informative descriptions of indigenous plants and wildlife, geologic history and the main trails that have long led humans to the summit.

Everything you ever wanted to know about animals and their scat (plus much more) is in *A Naturalist's Blue Ridge Parkway* by David T Catlin.

Great Smoky Mountains: A Visitor's Companion by George Wuerthner is a colorful field guide to common plants and animals, with longer chapters on history, geology, climate and outdoor activities in the region.

Hollows, Peepers, and Highlanders: An Appalachian Mountain Ecology by George Constantz, published by West Virginia University Press, features a quirky selection of incredibly informative chapters focusing on some of the region's most interesting critters and natural phenomena.

Mountains of the Heart: A Natural History of the Appalachians by Scott Weidensaul, is a solidly written overview of the natural history of the Appalachian Mountains from Newfoundland to Georgia.

Great Smoky Mountains National Park: A Natural History Guide by Rose Houk provides a comprehensive introduction to the species, habitats and natural phenomena unique to the Great Smoky Mountains.

ACTIVITIES

Hiking Great Smoky Mountains National Park by Kevin Adams and *Day Hikes of the Smokies* by Carson Brewer are up-to-date compendiums of popular and little-known hikes in Great Smoky, rated by ability and interest.

The Fly Fisherman's Guide to the Great Smoky Mountains National Park by H Lea Lawrence provides expert guidance for anglers hoping to land a good catch in the trout-fishing capital of the eastern US.

The New Appalachian Trail by Edward B Garvey is the story of the author's famous through-hikes, including his most recent at the age of 75. It's also a practical guide, featuring sections on hike planning, food, equipment, footwear and trail etiquette. *The Thru-Hiker's Handbook* by Dan 'Wingfoot' Bruce is considered by many to be the bible for practical information about hiking the AT. *Walking the Appalachian Trail* by Larry Luxenberg offers fresh insight into the many reasons people decide to walk the trail's 2200 miles from Georgia to Maine. *A Walk in the Woods* by Bill Bryson is a hilarious account of the funnyman's journey along the Appalachian Trail.

The following titles pertain mainly to Shenandoah and the Parkway:

Walking the Blue Ridge by Leonard Atkins details day hikes for all levels. *Best Easy Day Hikes in Shenandoah National Park* by Bert and Jane Gildart is a great cheat-sheet for novice hikers.

Story Behind the Scenery: Blue Ridge Parkway offers an easy introduction to the Parkway, with brilliant photography. *Shenandoah: Views of our National Park* by Hullihen Williams Moore is an evocative journal of black-and-white photos taken along Skyline Drive.

Waterfalls of the Blue Ridge by Nicole Blouin, Steve and Marilou Wier Bordonaro and Kevin Adams is the best, most comprehensive book on Blue Ridge waterfalls. *Hikes to Waterfalls* by Joanne Amberson is exactly that, outlining the best-of-the-best gushers.

Internet Resources

For up-to-the-minute information, the Internet offers a wealth of resources. A good place to begin is at **Lonely Planet** (www.lonelyplanet.com), where you'll find current summaries on the ins and outs of traveling in the area. Also on the site, the Thorn Tree bulletin board allows you to post questions to other travelers (and dispense advice when you get back). You can also scroll through previous questions and answers, bringing up recent tips and ideas.

Next, visit the general websites of the **National Park Service** (www.nps.gov) for an overall look at the way each park operates, plus information on fees, regulations and any current issues. The **Forest Service** (www.southernregion.fs.fed.us) maintains a site providing information on USDA holdings in the southern region. From here you can access information about visiting the Cherokee, Nantahala, Pisgah and other national forests.

The **National Park Camping Reservation Service** (www.reservations.nps.gov) offers online reservations for certain campgrounds in the parks. You can also reserve by **telephone** (☎ 800-365-CAMP).

You may also wish to browse visitor information websites for gateway communities near the parks. They are listed at the beginning of this chapter.

GREAT SMOKY MOUNTAINS NATIONAL PARK

Great Smoky Mountains National Park (www.nps.gov/grsm) The official NPS website for the park.

Go Smokies (www.knoxnews.com/kns/gosmokies) A handy site with lots of news and information about the Smokies, maintained by the *Knoxville News Sentinel*.

All the Smokies (www.allthesmokies.com) Information on services, accommodations and events in Gatlinburg, Pigeon Forge and surrounding communities.

Townsend Vacation & Field Guide (www.smokymountains.org) A guide to the 'quiet side of the Smokies.'

SHENANDOAH NATIONAL PARK

Shenandoah National Park (www.nps.gov/shen) The official NPS website for the park.

Shenandoah National Park Hiking Page (www.shenandoah.national-park.com/hike.htm) Extremely detailed site for all your hiking questions.

BLUE RIDGE PARKWAY
Blue Ridge Parkway (www.nps.gov/blri) The official NPS website for the Parkway.
Blue Ridge Parkway Association (www.blueridgeparkway.org) An online guide to member attractions, lodging and food along the Parkway, including a virtual trip planner.
Bicycling the Blue Ridge Parkway (www.nukefix.org/parkway/parkwaymile.htm) A homegrown website with a detailed, milepost-by-milepost account of the Parkway.

Maps
Free NPS maps are dispensed at visitor centers throughout the parks and along the Parkway, as well as at Shenandoah's entrance stations.

The **Great Smoky Mountains Association** (www.smokiesstore.org) publishes a number of inexpensive specialty maps on topics ranging from auto touring and day hikes to waterfalls and wildflowers.

Sold at most visitor centers, National Geographic/Trails Illustrated maps are strongly recommended for serious hikers. Depicted on each 1:70,000 map are all trails, shelters, campsites and recreational features, plus relevant information on wildlife, history, geology and archaeology. Water-repellent versions are available.

The National Park Service's **Harpers Ferry Center** (www.nps.gov/hfc/carto) offers downloadable, digital versions of maps from the official park brochures, created by the excellent NPS cartographers.

If you love to drive the back roads, consider purchasing a DeLorme state atlas. Each edition collects United States Geological Survey (USGS) quadrangles of a state and includes many recreational, cultural and historical symbols at a scale of roughly 1:2.4 miles.

The USGS publishes two 1:62,500 topographical maps of Great Smoky, one each for the east and west side of the park, and three maps at like scale that cover Shenandoah.

Useful Organizations
The **Friends of the Smokies** (☎ 865-453-2428; www.friendsofthesmokies.org) and the **Great Smoky Mountains Association** (☎ 888-898-910; www.smokiesstore.org/about.htm) are nonprofit groups that work with the National Park Service to maintain the parks and provide educational and research opportunities.

The **Great Smoky Mountains Institute at Tremont** (☎ 865-448-6709; www.gsmit.org) offers a wide range of environmentally minded programs for adults and families, including hikes and backpacking trips, seminars for educators, Elderhostel events, nature photography workshops and events for naturalists, including the popular Spring Awakenings Naturalist Weekend. The University of Tennessee operates the **Smoky Mountains Field School** (☎ 865-974-1000; www.outreach.utk.edu/smoky), which also offers a wide range of courses and seminars in Great Smoky.

The **Shenandoah National Park Association** (www.snpbooks.org) sells books and videotapes that educate visitors about the wonders of the park. The **Potomac Appalachian Trail Club** (PATC; ☎ 703-242-0693; www.patc.net) is a volunteer network of hikers providing hiker-related information about the Appalachian Trail. Since a good portion of the AT parallels Skyline Drive, the PATC offers information on lodging in Virginia and maintains a list of cabins available for rent. The **Carolina Mountain Club** (CMC; www.carolinamtnclub.com) is another network of volunteers who organize hikes and conduct trail maintenance along the way. You don't have to be a member to hike with the club, but yearly membership is $12.

continued on p66

✔ WHAT TO PACK

Pack light. You won't regret it, whether carrying your gear up a mountain, hauling it into the hotel or trying to fit it into the trunk of the car. If you forget something, you can usually purchase it at outdoor equipment stores in Gatlinburg and Pigeon Forge or further afield in Asheville, North Carolina and Luray, Virginia. The following list omits obvious items (such as a tent if you're camping) and instead covers things you might be likely to overlook.

Clothing
Bring layers: mountain weather is notoriously fickle and unpredictable. A fleece sweater and rain protection (light and breathable is best) are necessary year-round. Choose carefully when packing for overnight trips; it's easy to overdo it with unnecessary heavy clothing that consumes precious pack volume. Synthetic, quick-dry clothing is best. Also consider:

✔ long underwear (polypropylene)

✔ hat for sun protection, bandana

✔ wind shell

Footwear
For day hiking, light boots are ideal. For backcountry hiking, sturdy boots are essential, particularly if you're carrying a pack. Thick socks will protect tender feet on those first few days on the trail. Also consider:

✔ waterproof sandals

✔ quick-dry, synthetic hiking socks

Toiletries
This is the other category in which folks often bring too much. Leave that bottle of aftershave or cucumber face mask at home. Consider:

✔ insect repellent

✔ sunscreen

✔ skin lotion

✔ pain reliever

✔ lip balm

✔ nail clippers

✔ glasses, sunglasses

✔ eye drops

✔ cloth for cleaning glasses

Camping Gear
In addition to the obvious, bring:

✔ sleeping pad (light and inflatable; consider ThermaRest brand)

✔ sleeping bag that can withstand the damp (ie, not goose down)
✔ sleeping pillow
✔ stuff sacks
✔ camp chair
✔ extra stove fuel
✔ biodegradable soap and scrubber
✔ headlamp and spare batteries
✔ LED mini flashlight
✔ camp towel
✔ sanitary hand gel/hand wipes
✔ fire-starter or kindling

Hiking
Keep it light, but prepare for emergencies. Think about bringing:
✔ day pack with hydration bag
✔ Swiss Army knife
✔ hiking stick
✔ foot, chafing powder
✔ sanitary trowel
✔ toilet paper
✔ water filter, pump
✔ water bottle
✔ water tablets
✔ emergency kit (pen, whistle, duct tape, string or rope, compass, mirror, lighter, extra boot shoelaces)
✔ mini first-aid kit (tensor bandage for sprains, bandages, disinfectant, tweezers, antibiotic cream, Deep Heat and painkillers)

Other handy items
✔ camp saw
✔ umbrella
✔ resealable bags
✔ playing cards
✔ binoculars
✔ field guides
✔ small pad, pens

continued from p63

Three organizations offer mountains of information about the Parkway: the **Blue Ridge Parkway Association** (www.blueridgeparkway.org), the **Blue Ridge Parkway Foundation** (www.brpfoundation.org) and **Friends of the Blue Ridge Parkway** (www.blueridgefriends.org). All contribute funding and support to the National Park Service.

WHAT'S IT GOING TO COST?

As in life, the price tag for your Blue Ridge vacation can vary dramatically depending on the choices you make. Naturally, if you take the economical route by camping and preparing your own feasts, your outlay of funds will be far less than if you choose to eat prime rib and sleep in a 'chalet' or even a motel. If you're going to set up base in one of the gateway towns, note that vacationing in Gatlinburg is generally more expensive than the typical Cherokee or Townsend holiday.

Where you choose to sleep is the biggest variable in determining how much your vacation will cost. See Accommodations for ballpark price ranges and descriptions of each lodging class.

In general, most restaurants in the region are moderate in price. Haute cuisine has not yet made it to the Smokies, and most people 'round here consider a fancy restaurant to be one with a prime rib buffet. A wide variety of family-style places offer economical menus for kids. Joints that extol the virtues of their pancakes are often the cheapest places to grab a bite.

Your transportation outlay will mainly be determined by how much gas you put in your tank. The distances between attractions can be long, and it is quite possible to burn through a tank of gas each day. Unfortunately, plans for a park shuttle system are still in early developmental phase.

By decree, Great Smoky Mountains National Park has never charged an admission fee, and it remains one of the few national parks in the US to maintain this policy. The Blue Ridge Parkway is also free. In Shenandoah you'll be charged $10 to enter in a passenger vehicle and $5 if you walk; your entry ticket is good for seven days. A yearly pass is available for $20.

Activities can add substantially to your budget, particularly horseback riding ($35), white-water rafting ($40) and attraction entrance fees. Some entrance fees can be expensive; Grandfather Mountain, for instance, charges a whopping $12.

ACCOMMODATIONS

There are no hotels or rental cabins in Great Smoky Mountains National Park except for Le Conte Lodge. The lodge, located on top of Mt Le Conte, is accessible only by trail (the hike is 5 miles minimum, one way). Reservations often must be made a year in advance.

Shenandoah National Park offers three rustic lodges, two of which have restaurants, taprooms, gift shops and playgrounds.

Park service campsites range in price from $12 to $20 per site. Depending on your appetite, you may spend $15 to $40 per day on groceries for each hungry adult. Other daily fees may include firewood (generally $5 per bundle) and ice ($2 to $3 per bag). There's no end of **private campgrounds** offering a variety of options, ranging from $15 for primitive sites to $30 for sites with full hookups.

Motel and hotel prices vary considerably by season. Small, **independent motels** are the most affordable accommodations in the gateway towns. Around Great Smoky, Maggie Valley and Bryson City have some of the cheapest; here you can get a double for as little as $45. Depending on the season, you can usu-

CAMPING RULES

The National Park Service maintains **developed campgrounds** at 10 locations in Great Smoky and four locations in Shenandoah. No more than six people may occupy a campsite. Two tents, or one RV and one tent, are allowed per site. The maximum stay is seven to 14 days, depending on the season. Pets are allowed in campgrounds as long as they are restrained on a leash or otherwise confined at all times. Quiet hours are observed from 10pm to 6am.

Both Great Smoky and Shenandoah maintain **group campgrounds** that accommodate a minimum of eight people, require reservations and are for tents only.

For the most part, campsites are available on a first-come, first-served basis. **Reservations** (☎ 800-365-2267; www.reservations.nps.gov) are accepted at three sites in Great Smoky (Elkmont, Smokemont and Cades Cove) and two in Shenandoah (Big Meadows and Dundo) in summer and fall.

For **backcountry campsites** you are required to obtain a free permit. These are available at most ranger stations and campgrounds. In Great Smoky Mountains National Park, you can also get a permit at the Oconaluftee and Sugarlands Visitor Centers; in Shenandoah, all three visitor centers offer backcountry permits. Anyone staying overnight in the backcountry must camp only in a designated site or shelter. Campers need reservations to stay in any shelter, and 14 tent areas also require reservations. Campers should phone ahead for **reservations** (Great Smoky ☎ 865-436-1231, Shenandoah ☎ 540-999-3500; ☸ 8am-4:30pm Mon-Fri). For general backcountry information, phone the **backcountry office** (Great Smoky ☎ 865-436-1297; Shenandoah ☎ 540-999-3500).

Park campgrounds are located in areas frequented by bears and other wildlife. All food, coolers, utensils, stoves and the like must be stored out of sight in a closed vehicle when not in use. Do not throw food scraps or packaging in fire rings. Feeding wildlife is prohibited.

ally find even cheaper digs at small 'mom and pop' motels, where the quality ranges from quaint to decrepit. These places offer the most variety, and some have family-style suites with full kitchens, often priced as low as $50.

As a major tourism region, the Smokies are peppered with any number of **mid-range chain motels**. You'll find them in and around the gateway towns, with all the predictable amenities and then some (except Internet access, which is just starting to take hold in this www-deprived corner of the US). Prices fluctuate wildly depending on the time of year and day of the week. On high-season weekends you'll pay $70 to $145 for a double at a reputable chain.

Cabins are a great option for families and romantics. Ubiquitous around the parks, many rental cabins are in forest settings, providing stark relief to highway-variety accommodations. During high season, expect to pay $85 to $150 per night for a basic unit. During the low season a two-bedroom cabin can go for a song: as little as $50.

Gatlinburg, Pigeon Forge and Townsend are noted for their **mountain lodges**. These places are sometimes grand in scale, with massive fireplaces in the lobby and full-service amenities. The sky's the limit on what you can pay for the height of luxury, but this accommodation class also includes moderately priced options ($90 to $125 during high season).

With a distinct brand of down-home hospitality, the charming **B&Bs** of Maggie Valley and Bryson City deserve a special mention. These are priced in the $95 to $135 range during high season.

BRINGING THE KIDS

Forget Disneyland. Forget Space Mountain. These don't hold a candle to the mighty Smokies. You couldn't ask for a more family-friendly destination than the accommodating national parks and communities of the Blue Ridge. Waiting for you and your brood are campfires beneath the stars, potential bear sightings, the frivolous pleasures of the gateway towns and heart-pounding activities like rafting, biking and horseback riding – all of which will put smiles on kids' faces.

Friendly park rangers in cool uniforms provide programming specifically geared to younger audiences. Through activities like salamander hunts and wildflower identification, these programs inspire kids to interact more fully with the environment (and are way too much fun to be detected as 'educational').

Involve your kids in the planning for your trip; this can get them excited and interested in activities before they even arrive. Several books can inspire your family's youth activities director. *Time Well Spent: Family Hiking in the Smokies* by Charles Maynard profiles many hikes that are just right for groups with kids. *Talking to Fireflies, Shrinking the Moon: Nature Activities for All Ages* by Edward Duensing enables both kids and adults to unravel the delicious mysteries of the forest. *Sleeping in a Sack: Camping Activities for Kids* by Linda White is a colorful guide with ideas about what kids can expect and suggestions for what they might like to do.

At campgrounds, on trails and at visitor centers, you're bound to meet lots of other families. Parents take these encounters as opportunities to swap tips and empathy, while kids waste no time in enlisting play partners. Campgrounds in particular are amiable places to connect with other travelers.

Consider staying close to amenities; the comfort of an ice cream break can recharge tired youngsters and oldsters after a day on the trail. Most restaurants in and around the parks offer kids' menus. Gatlinburg and environs, in particular, feature plenty of attractions to keep young minds captivated, from the **Aquarium of the Smokies** to the **Ober Gatlinburg** amusement park, with its alpine slide, ice-skating and go-carts.

Most kids will amaze you on the trail, mustering more energy than their folks. Trails that wind through the woods and offer a mix of sights – waterfalls, streams and towering old-growth trees – seem to keep kids interested. Alum Cave Bluffs, Clingmans Dome, Sugarlands Valley Nature Trail and Shenandoah's Limberlost are all great options.

Word to the wise: be particularly cautious with children when crossing streams. Rocks are often deceptively slippery, and the swift current can be a hazard (see p49 for more about stream safety). It's also extremely important to control your children at viewpoints, cliffs and waterfalls with precipitous drop-offs; falling deaths are an annual occurrence.

With good luck, good weather and good kids, you'll have a *great* time. Many families make a tradition of it and return to the Smokies year after year.

HEALTH & SAFETY

In an emergency, dial ☎ 911.

Great Smoky Mountains National Park law enforcement dispatch can be reached at ☎ 865-436-1230. First-aid facilities are available at park headquarters and visitor centers. The nearest full-service hospitals are in Sevierville,

Tennessee, 15 miles north of Gatlinburg; Maryville, Tennessee, 25 miles north of Cades Cove; and Bryson City, North Carolina, 10 miles southeast of Oconaluftee Visitor Center.

For emergencies in Shenandoah National Park and along the Blue Ridge Parkway, call ☎ 800-PARKWATCH or ☎ 800-732-0911. The nearest medical facilities are in Front Royal, Virginia, 2 miles from the north entrance to Skyline Drive and Shenandoah National Park; Staunton, Virginia, 15 miles east of the Rockfish Gap Entrance Station of Shenandoah; Roanoke, Virginia, 5 miles from MP 120 of the Blue Ridge Parkway; and Boone, North Carolina, 8 miles from MP 292 of the Parkway. For contact details, see the Information sections in the destination chapters.

If you're in the backcountry, it's imperative that you be prepared to cope with emergencies until you can reach help. If you're traveling out of your home country, purchase medical insurance before you leave.

Water Purification

You've been hiking up a storm and need to slacken your thirst. Before you dip your cup in the nearest stream, consider the likelihood that the crystalline water may contain harmful microbes like *cryptosporidium* or *Giardia lamblia*. To avoid this fate, bring water to a rolling boil, treat it with water tablets or filter it using a water purification system. These lightweight devices are available at outdoor shops ($35 and up). When selecting a system, choose one that removes both bacteria and protozoa and that has a filtering capacity of 0.5 microns or smaller and a flow rate of at least 1 liter per minute. Note that water tablets do not remove *Giardia*.

Symptoms that you've ingested a bug include diarrhea, bloating and horrifying gas; treatment is by antibiotics. While many campgrounds have clean, safe water, treat all water with suspicion.

Sunburn

Your risk of sunburn increases greatly as you gain elevation, even on cloudy or snowy days. Use sunscreen of SPF 30 or greater, wear a hat and sunglasses and try to avoid hiking at midday.

Dehydration & Heatstroke

Dehydration and heat stroke are common conditions that can be life-threatening if left untreated. Children and people over the age of 60 are particularly susceptible. Both maladies can be prevented with basic precautions: make sure you're taking in more fluid than you're losing, protect yourself from extended sun exposure and try to schedule your physical exertion to avoid the hottest part of the day.

Dehydration occurs when the body loses water content and essential body salts. It can be caused by overexposure to the sun or fever, or by loss of body fluids due to diarrhea or vomiting. Symptoms include dizziness, thirst, less-frequent urination and irritability. In moderate cases, rehydrate by drinking fluids or, better yet, sports drinks containing electrolytes. More severe cases should be regarded as a medical emergency; hospitalization and/or intravenous fluids may be required.

Heat stroke is a severe form of heat illness resulting from long, extreme exposure to the sun. People with heat stroke become unable to lower their body temperatures through normal body functions such as sweating. Symptoms include headache, dizziness, disorientation, seizure, rapid heartbeat, loss of consciousness and/or hallucinations. It is imperative for sufferers to be treated immediately, as heat stroke can cause permanent damage or death. While

continued on p72

ACCESS FOR ALL

The parks of the Blue Ridge are eminently accessible for people with special needs. Many of the major sights can be enjoyed from your vehicle, and parks offer accessible facilities and programs. Accessibility remains a major priority for the National Park Service, and improvements are being made all the time.

If you are a US citizen with a permanent disability, you're eligible for a free **Golden Access Passport**, available at the Sugarlands and Oconaluftee Visitor Centers, as well as at the entrance stations to Shenandoah National Park. With the passport, you won't have to pay an entrance fee at federal areas in the US (note that while Shenandoah charges a fee, admission to Great Smoky is already free).

In Great Smoky, ask for an *Accessibility Guide* at the visitor centers, and check the park newspaper, *Smokies Guide*, for information about special activities and ranger-led programs. Comprehensive accessibility information for Shenandoah National Park and the Blue Ridge Parkway is available online at www.nps.gov/shen and www.nps.gov/blri.

GREAT SMOKY MOUNTAINS NATIONAL PARK

In Great Smoky, temporary parking permits for designated spaces throughout the park are available to qualified visitors at Sugarlands and Oconaluftee visitor centers.

Three Great Smoky campsites accept reservations (May 15 to October 31) for wheelchair-accessible campsites: Cades Cove, Elkmont and Smokemont. These sites have been modified, with extra paving and other enhancements, and are adjacent to accessible bathrooms. Deep Creek and Big Creek also have improved sites, though these are less developed. Call for **updated camping information** (☎ 865-436-1230) and **campsite reservations** (☎ 800-365-2267).

The most accessible amphitheater is at Cades Cove; it is level, and adjacent bathrooms accommodate wheelchairs. The amphitheaters at Elkmont and Smokemont have paved trails, but steep inclines.

You'll find accessible picnic areas with restrooms at Cades Cove, Metcalf Bottoms, Big Creek, Collins Creek and Cosby.

Wheelchair-accessible telephones (no audio amplification) are available at Cades Cove ranger station and the Oconaluftee and Sugarlands Visitor Centers.

Sugarlands & Oconaluftee Visitor Centers

These visitor centers are fully served by ramps and facilities, designated accessible parking spaces, accessible restrooms and a water fountain. Wheelchairs are available for loan.

The park movie at Sugarlands is captioned for hearing-impaired visitors. For visually impaired visitors, an audiocassette guide to the nearby **Sugarlands Valley Nature Trail** (p95) is available for loan at the information desk. Park rangers can provide detailed descriptions of objects in the visitor center exhibit area.

Oconaluftee's walkways and inside floor are made of uneven flagstones, which are not the most conducive to wheelchair travel. There are some designated parking spaces for disabled visitors in the lot, and vehicles can also be temporarily parked in the rear of the building for closer access.

Two attractions near Oconaluftee are wheelchair accessible with assistance. Hard-packed gravel paths run between buildings at the **Mountain Farm Museum** (p86). Most museum buildings can be viewed from the outside via the doorways, and a ramp provides access to the house. Most talks and demonstrations are also accessible to visitors in wheelchairs. A half mile north of the visitor center, **Mingus Mill** (p86) is open seasonally. Accessible restrooms are adjacent to the parking area. A 100-yard paved and packed-gravel trail makes the mill accessible with assistance. A single step grants access to the interior or ground floor of the mill.

Cades Cove

Designated accessible parking spaces are available in the parking lot across from the ranger station. The Cades Cove Campground store and adjacent restrooms are wheelchair accessible.

The historic buildings along **Cades Cove Loop Rd** (p91) are hard to manage in a wheelchair due to the steps and the lack of hard-surface walkways. However, many of the exteriors can be viewed from your vehicle.

The visitor center offers a ramp, designated parking, accessible restrooms and a loaner wheelchair. The trail to **Cable Mill** (p86) and the complex of historic buildings is level and surfaced with hard-packed gravel. The Becky Cable House is accessible via a ramp, and the interior of the mill is also accessible when open.

Trails & Auto Tours

Most trails in Great Smoky are steep and rugged, but there are three excellent paved trails that together provide a stunning overview of what the park has to offer. The **Sugarlands Valley Nature Trail** (p95) is a flat, half-mile trail with unique historic and natural features and interpretive exhibits. A large print brochure and an audiotape tour are available at Sugarlands Visitor Center.

The other two paved trails are steep, and those in wheelchairs will probably require assistance. A self-guided 2.5-mile nature trail climbs to the pretty **Laurel Falls** (p95), and a very steep paved path ascends to the top of the Smokies at **Clingmans Dome** (p85).

A one-hour driving tour of **Newfound Gap Rd** (p87) is available for sale on audio cassette, for sale at visitor centers; you can also pick up road guides and self-guided auto tour booklets for other routes.

SHENANDOAH NATIONAL PARK

Most facilities in Shenandoah are accessible, including dining rooms, picnic areas, lodging and bathrooms, with some requiring assistance. Accessible coin-operated showers are available at the Big Meadows, Lewis Mountain and Loft Mountain Campgrounds. Hearing-impaired visitors can call the **Virginia Relay Center** at ☎ 800-828-1120 (TTD) or ☎ 800-828-1140 (voice) for information on the park. The Dickey Ridge Visitor Center offers a slide show with subtitles.

Limberlost (p170) is the park's only accessible trail. The surface is a crushed greenstone, compatible with wheelchairs and even strollers, and the trail loops around an ancient hemlock forest at a smooth 8% grade.

continued from p69

waiting for help to arrive, get the person with heat stroke out of direct exposure to the sun, remove clothing and gently apply cool water to the skin; follow that with fanning. If possible, apply ice packs to the groin and armpits and have the person lie down in a cool area with his or her feet slightly elevated.

Hypothermia

Hypothermia is an extremely dangerous condition involving a plunge in the body's core temperature. It can kill you. Symptoms may include loss of strength and coordination, followed by mental confusion and irrational behavior.

Hypothermia can happen to anyone in any season. To prevent hypothermia, drink copious amounts of water before and during physical exertion. If hiking, rest along the trail to forestall fatigue and eat high-energy snacks to help your body stay warm. No matter how clear the sky when you start hiking, always carry rain protection to guard against wind, rain and cold temperatures.

To treat hypothermia in its early stages, get the victim out of the wind or rain, replace wet clothing with dry clothing and administer hot liquids (not alcohol) and high-calorie, easily digestible food like granola bars or chocolate. Put the person in a warm sleeping bag and get in with him or her. If possible, position the person near a fire or in a warm (not hot) bath. Do not rub a victim's skin.

Snake Bites

The Great Smokies are home to two poisonous snakes, the **northern copperhead** and the **timber rattlesnake**. The copperhead is notoriously aggressive but rarely causes a fatality because its venom is relatively weak. The timber rattlesnake, on the other hand, is not so aggressive, but has large fangs and potentially deadly venom. Its bite must be treated in a hospital or may prove lethal. Rattlesnakes readily announce their presence with a loud buzzing rattle and are best avoided. They should never be killed, however – within the parks, laws fully protect the animals.

In general, snakes would rather save their venom for a delicious rodent than waste it on you. Hence, snakebite incidents are rare. If you are bitten, play it safe and head for the nearest medical facility. Apply a splint to the extremity if possible. Note that snake venom is especially dangerous to young children – act accordingly.

Backcountry hikers can carry a small kit called a Sawyer Extractor, to be used to suck venom from a snakebite. There's little chance that you'll use it, but it's comforting to have it nonetheless.

Poison Ivy

Every hiker should learn to recognize poison ivy. Watch for the plant's clusters of three large leaves and clumps of small, whitish flowers. Even slight contact can cause severe inflammation and rash. Like us, the Cherokee had no cure for these symptoms. Instead, they tried to build an immunity to the pernicious vine by steaming its leaves for several hours and rubbing the resulting paste into their skin. For modern-day visitors to former Cherokee lands, perhaps it's best just to stick to the trails and avoid brushy areas. Wear a hat, long pants and a long-sleeved shirt. If you think you've brushed against the evil weed, remove and isolate the clothes you wore until you can launder them.

Ticks

The Cherokee pounded bear fat into rootstock and smeared it on their bodies to ward off ticks and other insects. As bear fat is hard to come by these days, chemical insect repellent will have to do. While ticks are not as common here as in other parts of the American South, they do exist. After hiking, give yourself and your clothes a thorough check; if a tick has attached itself to you, remove it with tweezers and then thoroughly wash the area. Seek medical attention if part of the tick remains in your skin. Ticks transmit Lyme disease, but to date no cases of this affliction have been reported in the Smokies.

DANGERS & ANNOYANCES
Theft
Beware the dreaded car clout! Each year these thieves prey on parked vehicles at trailheads and parking areas. As a bear is drawn to honey, the common clout is drawn to purses, cameras and electronic equipment. Thieves' favorite victims are careless motorists who leave valuable objects in plain view in a car. To foil these nefarious burglars, keep your valuables on your person, or at the very least lock them in your trunk *before* you get to the parking area. (Thieves may watch you 'hide' your loot under the blanket in the backseat.) Veteran car clouts are skilled at breaking into locked vehicles.

Bugs & Insects
When it comes to pests, visitors to the Smokies get off relatively easy compared to tourists in other large natural areas with extensive wetlands. The good news is that mosquitoes are rarely a problem. The bad news is the prevalence of aggressive **yellowjacket wasps**. The painful sting from this little hellion can cause local swelling, and for some victims it can lead to dangerous allergic reactions. Those prone to allergies should carry epinephrine kits.

Other annoying bugs include stinging **no-see-ums** (properly known as biting midges, punkies or sand flies), found most often in early summer around lowland streams, and **gnats**, which swarm around your face and dive-bomb your eyes. Try to repel them with nonchemical means as much as possible, by wearing protective clothing and moving around a lot.

Road Hazards
Be careful when traveling through **tunnels** in Virginia and North Carolina. A few of the curvier ones create pitch-black conditions; it's recommended that drivers honk their horns and keep headlights on, while pedestrians and cyclists should use extreme caution, moving their flashlights to alert oncoming traffic.

When driving downhill on snowy or icy roads, use a lower gear instead of riding the brakes. When you do apply brakes, do so gently and smoothly. If you become stuck, don't gun the engine or spin your tires; it only makes matters worse. Instead, rock the car by shifting between forward and reverse gears, and apply gentle pressure to the gas pedal.

Curb your impulse to test your driving skills on the region's winding roads. While it may seem like the perfect time to see what your car's suspension and steering systems are capable of, statistics prove otherwise. Each year an average of 50 road accidents cause serious injury in Great Smoky alone. Drive defensively and be ready for what might be coming from around the next curve.

GETTING THERE
Aside from the Gatlinburg Trolley's limited service, there is no public transportation into the region's parks. Driving, bicycling and walking – or signing on with an organized tour – are the only methods of entering.

Great Smoky Mountains National Park

AIRPLANE

Most visitors fly into Knoxville, Tennessee or Asheville, North Carolina, both of which are served by major airlines. Which one you choose may depend on where you plan to enter the park. Knoxville's **McGhee Tyson Airport** (☎ 865-342-3000; www.tys.org) is the better choice if your primary destinations are Gatlinburg (40 miles) or Townsend (30 miles). Fly into **Asheville Regional Airport** (☎ 828-684-2226; www.flyavl.com) if you plan to enter via Cherokee (51 miles).

BUS

There is no public bus service to the park. However, airport shuttles connect Gatlinburg with Knoxville, as do regional buses (May 1 to October 31).

The City of Gatlinburg provides trolley service from the Gatlinburg Chamber of Commerce building to three destinations in the park: Sugarlands Visitor Center, Laurel Falls Trail and Elkmont Campground.

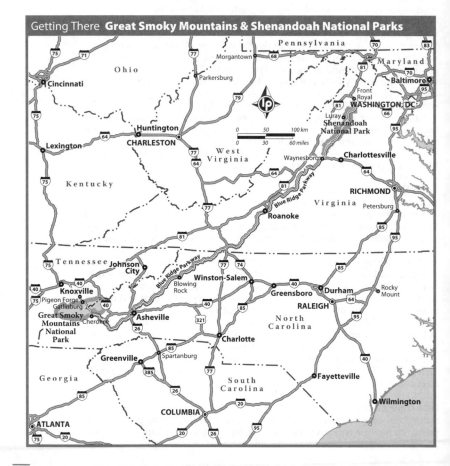

Getting There **Great Smoky Mountains & Shenandoah National Parks**

CAR

The Blue Ridge Parkway connects Shenandoah National Park to the southern entrance of Great Smoky Mountains National Park, near Cherokee. US 441, known in the park as Newfound Gap Rd, cuts across the ridge near the center of the park to connect Gatlinburg with Cherokee.

From the north, take I-40 from Knoxville to US 66; then take US 441 south to Gatlinburg. Park headquarters and the Sugarlands Visitor Center are 2 miles south.

From the south, take US 441 north to Cherokee, North Carolina; then drive 2 miles north to the Oconaluftee Visitor Center.

From the west, take US 129 south to Maryville, Tennessee; then take US 321 north to Townsend and on to the park's west entrance. Drive west about 7 miles through the park to reach Cades Cove Campground.

From the east, take I-40 west from Asheville, North Carolina (40 miles), to US 19, then US 441 to the park's southern entrance near Cherokee.

There are no gas stations or services available in the park. Complete services can be found in Gatlinburg, Townsend and Cherokee.

Car Rental

Car rental agencies have offices in local airports and in Knoxville, Pigeon Forge, Gatlinburg and Asheville.

RV & Camper Rental

Cruise America (☎ 800-327-7799; www.cruiseamerica.com) is one of the country's largest RV rental companies; there's a **branch** (☎ 865-560-9229; Knoxville Car & Truck Rent; 1543 Downtown West Blvd) in Knoxville, 40 miles from the Gatlinburg entrance. Expect to pay at least $1000 for a one-week journey in a small RV, plus additional expenses for gas.

Speed Limits

Although the speed limit occasionally reaches 45mph in the park, more often it is posted as 30mph or lower.

Road Conditions

Newfound Gap Rd (US 441) between the summit and Cherokee is pocked with potholes; drive accordingly. Never cross the center line to avoid rough pavement.

Roads are occasionally closed for extended periods due to flooding or rockslide damage. At the time of writing, **Parson Branch Rd** and **Foothills Pkwy West** were closed for repairs.

OPEN ROADS

The following roads in Great Smoky are only open seasonally:

✔ Balsam Mountain Rd (May 14–Oct 31)

✔ Clingmans Dome Rd (Apr 1–Nov 31)

✔ Forge Creek Rd (Mar 12–Dec 31)

✔ Rich Mountain Rd (Mar 12–Nov 30)

✔ Roaring Fork Motor Nature Trail (Mar 12–Nov 30)

✔ Roundbottom/Straight Fork Rds (Mar 12–Dec 31)

✔ Upper Tremont Rd (Mar 12–Dec 31)

Shenandoah National Park & Blue Ridge Parkway

AIRPLANE

Dulles International Airport (☎ 703-572-2700; www.metwashairports.com/dulles) in Washington DC, is the closest major airport, and that's at least an hour's drive from the park's northern entrance in Front Royal.

Two local airports handle charter and some small-plane commercial flights on US Airways Express. **Charlottesville/Albemarle Airport** (☎ 804-973-8341; www.gocho .com) is 8 miles north of Charlottesville, Virginia on Rte 29, and **Shenandoah Valley Airport** (☎ 540-234-8304; www.flyshd.com) is 18 miles northeast of Staunton.

TRAIN
The closest **AMTRAK** (☎ 800-872-7245; www.amtrak.com) station is in Charlottesville.

BUS
Trailways (☎ 703-691-3052; www.trailways.com)has a station in Waynesboro, just outside the park's southern entrance.

CAR
There are only four vehicle entrances to the park – make a wrong turn and you'll be stuck on Skyline Drive for a long time. Take I-66 East to US 340 South for the (north) Front Royal Entrance Station. For the Thornton Gap (north-central) Entrance, take the Gainesville (Rte 29) exit off I-66 and head south to Warrenton, then take Rte 211 West. For the Swift Run Gap (south-central) Entrance, stay on Rte 29 to Stanardsville, then take Rte 33 West. For the Rockfish (south) Entrance, stay on Rte 29 to Charlottesville and take I-4 West to the entrance.

The Blue Ridge Parkway begins in Waynesboro, at the southern end of Skyline Drive and Shenandoah National Park. Fortunately, there are numerous roads on and off the Parkway, making access for the next 469 miles very easy. From Staunton, take I-64 to Waynesboro, then follow signs north for Skyline Drive or south for the Blue Ridge Parkway. From Roanoke, take US 221/460 North or US 220 South to access the Parkway.

Car Rental
Rental cars are available at local airports and in major cities like Charlottesville, Roanoke, Staunton and Asheville.

RV & Camper Rental
Cruise America (☎ 800-327-7799; www.cruiseamerica.com) is one of the country's largest RV rental companies; there's a **branch** (☎ 540-678-9005; Winchester Auto Rental, 1850 Valley Ave) in Winchester, Virgina, close to the Front Royal Entrance Station. In Harrisonburg, **Shenandoah Valley RV Rentals** (☎ 540-574-3982; 8607 Indian Trail Rd) offers seven-day rentals for $1400 and up. The RV dealer closest to the Blue Ridge Parkway is **Carolina RV Rentals** (☎ 704-377-2303; 2108 Wilkinson Blvd), in Charlotte. **Go RVing** (www.gorving.com) is a great resource for novice RVers.

Speed Limits
The limit in Shenandoah National Park is 35mph; on the Blue Ridge Parkway it's 45mph. Speed limits are strictly enforced, as bears like to lumber across the road, wild turkeys take their time and deer jump out without warning – not to mention the hair-raising, hairpin curves without guardrails and the pitch-black tunnels that easily distract drivers. Be prepared to go significantly slower behind monster RVs and during leaf-peeping season (fall), when it seems as if everyone and their grandma come to watch the colors change.

Road Conditions
Expect crowded highways and byways in fall. At other times of the year the weather wreaks more havoc on the road than do other drivers. Winter driv-

ing can be downright dangerous due to snow and ice. In early spring, look out for wet and often miserable conditions, and be prepared for many foggy days. Call for current driving conditions in **Shenandoah** (☎ 540-999-3500) or on the **Blue Ridge Parkway** (☎ 828-298-0398).

The deepest green forest. The country's most-visited national park. One of the most biologically diverse environments on earth. When describing Great Smoky Mountains National Park, it's only natural to use superlatives.

EXPERIENCING
GREAT SMOKY

The Cherokee called this territory *Shaconage* (shah-con-ah-jey), meaning roughly 'land of the blue smoke.' For millennia, these misty mountains were their primary domain. The Cherokee were supplanted by Scotch-Irish, French and German settlers, a conglomeration that one early settler characterized as 'a heady brew.' In Cades Cove and Cataloochee the historic log homes, churches, mills and schoolhouses of these mountain people still stand with doors wide open. Southern hospitality dictates that visitors are always welcome. As historian Horace Kephart once wrote, 'They die hard, those old ways, in the mountains. Some of them were good ways.'

As is often the case in places of great natural grandeur, human history is trumped by natural history. At about a billion years old, the Smoky Mountains are among the oldest in the world. This ancient land is home to such an astonishing variety of animals and plants that it has been designated an International Biosphere Reserve and a World Heritage Site.

Great Smoky Mountains National Park is eminently accessible, whether you are traveling by car, horse or foot. The most popular sights include the former settlement of Cades Cove, the majestic peaks of Mt Le Conte, the dizzying heights of Clingmans Dome and a wonderful selection of waterfalls, coves and balds. Nearly 10 million people come each year to hike the park's 800 miles of trails, fish its 2000 miles of streams and rivers, drive its nearly 400 miles of paved and unpaved roads or camp at one of more than 1000 developed sites.

With so many visitors, the main arteries and attractions can seem a mite crowded. Studies have shown that 95% of park visitors never venture farther than 100 yards from their cars. It's easy to leave the teeming masses behind by merely parking the beast and stepping into the backcountry. You'll be glad you did.

WHEN YOU ARRIVE

Great Smoky Mountains National Park is open every day year-round. However, Newfound Gap Rd often closes during winter storms, and several others, including Clingmans Dome Rd, close during the winter months.

Unlike other national parks, Great Smoky charges no admission fee, nor will it ever; this proviso was written into the park's original charter as a stipulation for a $5 million Rockefeller family grant.

As there are no fee stations, you will have to stop by a visitor center to pick up a park map and the free park newspaper, *Smokies Guide*.

ORIENTATION

Great Smoky Mountains National Park straddles the North Carolina and Tennessee border, which runs diagonally through the heart of the park, shadowed by the Appalachian Trail (AT). The park encompasses some 521,000 acres and more than 800 square miles. As the crow flies, it is roughly 65 miles wide and 25 miles tall. The north-south **Newfound Gap Rd/Hwy 441** spans from one end of the park to the other, connecting the gateway towns of Gatlinburg, Tennessee on the north-central border and Cherokee, North Carolina on the south-central border.

Unless otherwise noted, all points of interest can be found on the main Great Smoky Map (Map 1) on pp152-3.

Entrances

Great Smoky's most-used entrances lie just outside the gateway towns of **Gatlinburg** and **Cherokee**, at opposite ends of Newfound Gap Rd/Hwy 441. Also heavily used is the Hwy 73 entrance near Townsend, Tennessee, which offers a straight shot to Cades Cove. Less-used entrances, many of which end abruptly at campgrounds or trailheads, include the following:

- **Roaring Fork Motor Nature Trail** from Gatlinburg
- **Rich Mountain Rd** from Hwy 321 near Townsend
- **Happy Valley Rd** from Hwy 129 in the southwestern corner of the park
- **Lakeview Dr** and **Deep Creek Rd** from the Bryson City area
- **Heintooga Ridge Rd** from the Blue Ridge Parkway near Cherokee
- **Cove Creek Rd** and **Old NC 284** on the eastern border
- **Cosby Creek Rd/Hwy 32** near Cosby
- **Greenbrier Rd/Hwy 416** from Hwys 321/73 on the northern border

Main Regions

Great Smoky's regions are differentiated by geographic and historical distinctions. Listed below is a sampling of what specific areas have to offer.

TOP FIVE

✔ Bicycling through the beautiful, historic valley of **Cades Cove** (p85)

✔ Hiking on the mother of all footpaths, the **Appalachian Trail** (p108)

✔ Spending a night on the crest of Mt Le Conte at the hikers-only **Le Conte Lodge** (p117)

✔ Learning how early settlers made ends meet at the **Mountain Farm Museum** (p86)

✔ Spotting bear or wild turkey in bucolic, historic **Cataloochee** (p87)

- **Cades Cove** (Map 2, p154) Located in the western region of the park, this famous cove features a paved loop road with self-guided auto tour, visitor center, restored historic buildings, water-powered gristmill, living-history demonstrations, wildlife viewing and hiking trails.
- **Cataloochee** Near the eastern border in North Carolina, this region features

a self-guided auto tour, historic buildings (including a church and school-house), fishing, hiking trails and horseback riding.

- **Clingmans Dome** At the heart of Great Smoky along the state border, you'll find the park's highest peak, with panoramic views, a paved trail to an observation tower and hiking trails to balds abloom with wildflowers in early summer.
- **Cosby** In the northeastern corner, this little-visited region features waterfalls, hiking trails and solitude.
- **Deep Creek** In the southern lands of Great Smoky west of Cherokee you'll find hikes into the backcountry and to waterfalls, fishing and tubing.
- **Greenbrier** Near Gatlinburg in the north-central part of the park, Greenbrier features early homesites, fishing, swimming and hiking trails.
- **Heintooga-Balsam Mountain** Accessible via the Blue Ridge Parkway, Heintooga Ridge Rd takes you to Heintooga Overlook, Balsam Mountain Rd and high-country hiking trails.
- **Newfound Gap** In central Great Smoky you can access the Appalachian Trail, visit historical markers and take in famous mountain vistas.
- **Oconaluftee** Near Cherokee you'll find a visitor center, the historic Mountain Farm Museum, living-history demonstrations, special events, a water-powered gristmill and access to the Blue Ridge Parkway.
- **Roaring Fork** Beginning in central Gatlinburg, you can set off on a self-guided auto tour, which leads to horseback and hiking trails, historic buildings and waterfalls.
- **Sugarlands** At the north-central entrance to the park is the largest visitor center, which features the park movie, exhibits and a daily roster of ranger-led programs. Nearby is the Sugarlands Valley Nature Trail and the beginning of Newfound Gap Rd (to Cherokee) and Little River Rd (to Townsend and Cades Cove).

Major Roads

Newfound Gap Rd/Hwy 441 is the only thoroughfare that crosses the park. Its northern portal is Gatlinburg, Tennessee (elevation 1340ft), near Sugarlands Visitor Center. It crosses the North Carolina border at Newfound Gap (elevation 5046ft) and then descends to Cherokee, North Carolina (elevation 1200ft), near Oconaluftee Visitor Center.

Little River Rd connects Sugarlands to Townsend and Cades Cove. At the junction with Hwy 73 and the Townsend turnoff, the road changes its name to Laurel Creek Rd for a straight shot to Cades Cove Loop Rd.

The **Roaring Fork Motor Nature Trail** is a popular loop road from Gatlinburg.

Traffic congestion on Newfound Gap Rd and Cades Cove Loop Rd is a given, particularly between July 1 and August 15 and in October. Choosing one of the park's lesser-used roads is a good way to avoid the crowds. These include the following:

Clingmans Dome Rd connects Newfound Gap with the park's highest point (elevation 6643ft) and the observation tower. This road is closed in winter.

Two unpaved, one-way roads connect Cades Cove Loop Rd with the park's northern and southern borders. **Rich Mountain Rd** is a winding road heading north to Townsend, while **Parson Branch Rd** heads south to connect with Hwy 129. Both are closed during the winter.

Heintooga Ridge Rd enters the park from the Blue Ridge Parkway at the southern border of the park and provides access to the one-way, unpaved **Balsam Mountain Rd**.

Gateway Towns

The largest gateway communities are Gatlinburg, Pigeon Forge and Townsend in Tennessee, and Bryson City, Cherokee and Maggie Valley in North Carolina. All offer lodging, dining and shopping opportunities, as well as services such as banking, auto repair and emergency response. See Around Great Smoky (p121) for more information.

INFORMATION

The National Park Service, federal custodian of Great Smoky, oversees all matters pertaining to the operation and protection of the park. **Park headquarters** (☎ 865-436-1200; 107 Park Headquarters Rd) is located just off of Newfound Gap Rd at the Gatlinburg entrance to the park, just before Sugarlands Visitor Center.

Visitor Centers

The park's two main visitor centers are Sugarlands Visitor Center, at the park's northern entrance near Gatlinburg, and Oconaluftee Visitor Center, at the park's southern entrance near Cherokee. The smaller Cades Cove Visitor Center is located on Cades Cove Loop Rd. The Gatlinburg Welcome Center (p122), run jointly by the NPS and the Gatlinburg Department of Tourism, is on Hwy 441, 2 miles north of Gatlinburg. All are open daily year-round except Christmas Day.

Books & Bookstores

The **Great Smoky Mountains Association** (☎ 888-898-9102; www.smokiesstore.org) publishes a wide range of books, maps and guides and distributes individual USGS topographic quad maps. These publications, in addition to a good selection of other books on the region, can be purchased at bookstores in the visitor centers listed above or by placing a phone or Internet order.

Road & Weather Information

The NPS updates road and weather information on its **telephone hotline** (☎ 865-436-1200) on a daily basis. For road information, key in extension 631; the weather forecast is extension 630.

POLICIES & REGULATIONS

Help protect and preserve the park – and yourself – by complying with a few park service regulations.

It's illegal to take or pick anything from the park, from the more obvious things like artifacts and bones to flowers, leaves and rocks. Alcoholic beverages are permitted only in designated camping and picnic areas. Pets must be kept on a leash at all times and are not permitted in public buildings, the backcountry or on trails (with the exception of the Gatlinburg and Oconaluftee River Trails). Fireworks, weapons and hunting are strictly prohibited.

The historic buildings throughout the park are national treasures. They are also covered with graffiti! Defacing preserved buildings is punishable by hefty fines and/or even imprisonment.

Wildlife

The primary goal of the park service's policies and regulations regarding wildlife is to keep the park and all of its denizens wild. Studies have shown that once bears have been exposed to human food, they abandon their natural foraging habits, which seriously compromises their chance of survival. Feeding bears – or even those frisky squirrels – is illegal. Violators are subject to a $5000 fine and/or six months imprisonment.

Moreover, it's illegal to touch, entice, disturb or in any way harass any wild animal. A good rule of thumb is that if your actions cause an animal to change its behavior in any way, you're probably too close.

Food Storage & Garbage Handling

Federal law requires proper food storage. Food, cosmetics and even tooth-paste should be stored in the trunk of your vehicle. If your vehicle lacks a trunk and you must store food in the passenger compartment, be sure to keep it out of sight. Bears have learned to recognize packaged foods, and each year they inflict serious property damage on cars in their single-minded quest for human food.

Garbage must be placed entirely within bearproof garbage cans or dumpsters. Keep a clean camp by removing any food scraps from the ground and on grills and tabletops.

Backpackers must suspend their food and garbage by using either ropes or the cable systems found at all backcountry sites.

Campfires

Campfires are allowed only in fireplaces or established fire rings. Gathering dead and downed wood is permitted, but cutting trees for firewood is strictly prohibited. Firewood can be purchased at Cades Cove, Elkmont and Smokemont campgrounds from March to October.

Backcountry Permits & Regulations

Permits are required for all overnight trips into the backcountry. They are available free of charge at most park campgrounds and ranger stations, at Sugarlands and Oconaluftee Visitor Centers or by calling ☎ 865-436-1297.

See Backcountry Camping (p106) for information on sites and shelters.

Horses

Horses are allowed only on trails specifically designated for equestrian use. Off-trail or cross-country riding is prohibited. Riders may use campsites on designated horse trails; however, some backcountry campsites must be **reserved** (☎ 865-436-1231) in advance.

Fishing

Fishing is allowed from sunrise until sunset year-round. A valid state license from North Carolina or Tennessee, available in gateway communities, is required. Only dry flies with a single hook or artificial lures may be used; the use of natural bait and artificial scents is prohibited. The daily limit is a combined total of five fish. The size limit for rainbow or brown trout and bass is 7 inches. Brook trout must always be released; to possess one is illegal. As part of a trial program, fishing for this protected species is allowed on eight streams within the park; on all other streams it is banned.

Poaching & Foraging

Naturally, the poaching of wild animals is strictly forbidden and punishable by severe penalties. Newer laws make it illegal to forage for wild plants such as ginseng and ramps, a type of wild leek that was once a spring staple for mountain families.

Bicycles & Motorcycles

Bicycles and motorcycles are allowed on campgrounds and paved roads but are strictly prohibited on trails or any road secured by a locked gate. Motorcyclists must wear a helmet. As in so many other places, skateboarding is *verboten* throughout the park.

GETTING AROUND

Most people travel through the park in private vehicles; a stalwart few travel by foot or bicycle. Public transportation in the park is limited to only a few destinations. Tours from Gatlinburg visit many of the major sites.

Car & Motorcycle

Speed limits on most paved roads throughout the park are 30mph. Limits are rarely posted on paved and secondary roads, but rough surfaces and twisting roads mandate a top speed of 20mph in many circumstances. There are no gas or service stations in the park. If you need assistance due to automotive failure on a park road, call the **park dispatch** (☎ 865-436-9171). Complete auto services are available in Cherokee, Townsend, Gatlinburg and Pigeon Forge.

Several park roads are closed in winter; others may close temporarily during inclement weather. If Newfound Gap Rd is subject to a weather-related closure, stop at the nearest visitor center to get information on alternative routes between Tennessee and North Carolina. Passage may be limited to vehicles with tire chains or four-wheel drive.

Cades Cove Loop Rd, Parson Branch Rd, Roaring Fork Motor Nature Trail and Rich Mountain Rd are closed from dusk until dawn.

OPEN ROADS

Several roads in Great Smoky are open only seasonally. They are:

✔ **Balsam Mountain Rd** (🌱 May 14–Oct 31)

✔ **Clingmans Dome Rd** (🌱 Apr 1–Nov 31)

✔ **Forge Creek Rd/Parson Branch Rd** (🌱 Mar 12–Dec 31)

✔ **Rich Mountain Rd** (🌱 Mar 12–Nov 30)

✔ **Roaring Fork Motor Nature Trail** (🌱 Mar 12–Nov 30)

✔ **Roundbottom/Straight Fork Rds** (🌱 Mar 12–Dec 31)

✔ **Upper Tremont Rd** (🌱 Mar 12–Dec 31)

Shuttles

Unfortunately, Great Smoky has not yet moved to emulate the successful public transport systems found in western parks such as Yosemite and Zion. However, from June to October the city of Gatlinburg operates a **trolley** (p128) running between downtown Gatlinburg and the Sugarlands Visitor Center, the Laurel Falls Trail and Elkmont Campground.

Hiker Shuttles

The following services ferry hikers to and from trailheads:

A Walk in the Woods (☎ 865-436-8283; 4413 E Scenic Dr, Gatlinburg, TN)
Mountain Mama's (☎ 828-486-5995; Waterville Rd, Hartford, TN)
Standing Bear Farm (☎ 423-487-0014; 4255 Green Corner Rd, Hartford, TN)
The Hike Inn (☎ 828-479-3677; 3204 Fontana Rd, Fontana, NC)

SIGHTS

One thing's for certain: you'll never be at a loss for things to see or do in Great Smoky Mountains National Park. Breathtaking natural attractions and evocative historic structures beckon from every corner of the park. Rediscover your feet and rekindle your wanderlust on the park's 800 miles of hiking trails: there's a lifetime's worth of hikes to choose from. Pick one and disappear into woods to experience the sweet smell of pine resin and the spongy feel of moss beneath your feet. Misty mountain vistas and dramatic waterfalls are always lovely – and there are plenty of these to go around, to be sure – but

CADES COVE TRAFFIC IMBROGLIO

Cades Cove is the most-visited area in the country's most-visited national park. In 2001 the park service launched a study to propose solutions to Cades Cove's infamous traffic congestion. Due to bumper-to-bumper traffic, during peak season it can take five hours to drive the 11-mile, one-way loop road – longer than it would take to walk! This traffic mess not only aggravates visitors, but also contributes to air pollution in a park already plagued by ozone problems.

With considerable community involvement, the study resulted in several proposed initiatives aimed at solving this awkward problem. One proposal suggests setting up a reservation system that would cap the number of vehicles allowed into the cove at any given time. Another would remove private vehicles from Cades Cove altogether by instigating a no-emissions shuttle service that would make multiple, frequent stops along the loop, allowing visitors to get on and off at their leisure. Whichever remedy the park service settles on, relief is not coming anytime soon. Officials estimate that the earliest implementation of either plan would be in 2007.

many of the best, most memorable park sights are on a smaller scale. Fall to your knees beneath a canopy of trees and go salamander hunting. The sight of an elusive black-chinned red salamander lifting its head to the light is one you'll not soon forget.

Gatlinburg Entrance

After the extreme tourism experience of Gatlinburg, crossing the park boundary into the densely wooded forests is like a cool glass of water. As the park is free, there is no entrance station and you can drive straight into the park. Less than a mile before you reach Sugarlands Visitor Center, Gatlinburg Bypass Rd merges with Newfound Gap Rd/Hwy 441. Shortly thereafter you'll pass the entrance to park headquarters.

SUGARLANDS VISITOR CENTER

Your first stop has got to be this excellent **visitor center** (🕑 8am-7pm in summer, off-season hours vary), which features exhibits, a large bookstore, a free 20-minute film and a well-staffed information desk. During the summer, visitors are welcomed with frequent presentations by rangers, and ranger-led walks to nearby **Cataract Falls** leave from the patio area four times daily between 10am and 4pm. The exhibits provide an informative introduction to the incredible biodiversity of life that abounds in the park, with mounted specimens of the plants and animals you may encounter. Outside the center is a strange, cordoned-off piece of concrete called the 'First Amendment Expression Area;' it's often peopled by folks with strong opinions about park issues such as the future of Cades Cove.

MT LE CONTE

Although you can't reach the top of **Mt Le Conte** (elevation 6593ft) without considerable effort – it's only scalable by foot – it is one of the most familiar sights in the park, visible from practically every viewpoint. Six trails provide access to the peak: Alum Cave (p97), Bullhead, Rainbow Falls (p96), Trillium Gap (p108), Brushy Mountain and the Boulevard. If you can summon the energy to ascend to the peak – and it ain't no stroll – you will be roundly rewarded all along the way with some of the best scenery the park has to offer. Near the summit is **Le Conte Lodge** (☎ 865-429-5704; www.LeConte-lodge .com), the park's only lodging facility.

CLINGMANS DOME ✓

'On top of Old Smoky' is Clingmans Dome (elevation 6643ft), the park's highest peak. At the summit a steep, half-mile paved trail leads to an observation tower offering a 360-degree view of the Smokies and beyond. It can be cold and foggy up here, even when the sun is shining in Sugarlands. From the parking area, trails depart for Andrews Bald (p102), 2 miles away, and Silers Bald, 4 miles west on the Appalachian Trail (AT). To get to the dome, turn off Newfound Gap Rd just south of Newfound Gap and follow the 7-mile Clingmans Dome Rd to the large parking area at the end.

Cades Cove   Map 2, p154

A cove, in Appalachian parlance, means a valley, but Cades Cove is far more than that. Many consider this special place to be a national treasure, thanks to its poignant cultural legacy, telling pioneer architecture and plentiful wildlife. And then there is the landscape itself, lush green fields enveloped by an unbroken expanse of mountains. It's no wonder so many families return year after year.

The first settlers – most of English, Scotch-Irish and Welsh stock – arrived in the 1820s. By 1850 the valley's population had swelled to its peak of 70 households and 451 residents. Today, thanks to the excellent preservation efforts of the NPS, you can still get a vivid sense of life in 19th century Cades Cove through its surviving churches, gristmills and homesteads.

An 11-mile **loop road** encircles the cove; it's open to car traffic from dawn to dusk, except on Wednesdays and Saturdays from mid-May through September, when bicycles (p110) and hikers rule the road until 10am. Pick up the self-guiding auto tour booklet *Cades Cove Tour* from any visitor center to discover more about Cades Cove's attractions and history. *Day Hikes In & Around Cades Cove* ($1.50) is also available.

CADES COVE VISITOR CENTER

Located in the Cable Mill area at the midpoint of Cades Cove Loop Rd, this **visitor center** (☎ 865-436-1200; ☺ 9am-7pm in summer, off-season hours vary) features information, a bookstore and exhibits about pioneer life in the cove. In summer

---

IF YOU ONLY VISIT ONE...

✔ museum, make it the **Mountain Farm Museum** (p86) for its fine collection of historic buildings and fascinating interpretive exhibits on the old ways of farming.

✔ visitor center, make it **Sugarlands** for the park movie, exhibits and ranger-led walks.

✔ historic building, make it **Mingus Mill** (p86), a lovely, water-powered gristmill on a verdant mountain stream.

✔ viewpoint, make it **Clingmans Dome**, the highest point in Great Smoky.

✔ hiking trail, make it **Alum Cave Bluffs** (p97), the quintessential Smokies hike with views, Arch Rock and oddly colored bluffs.

✔ waterfall, make it **Abrams Falls** (p103) for a moderate hike to the perfect site for a waterfall picnic.

✔ festival, make it **Cades Cove Old Timers' Day** (p94) to meet descendants of early settlers and enjoy authentic music and food.

frequent tours of the historic Cable Mill and the Gregg-Cable house start from the visitor center. Other buildings on the site include a blacksmith shop, a cantilever barn, smokehouse and sorghum mill.

CABLE MILL

In order to get bread on the table, early residents of Cades Cove first had to mill their grains and corn. Above all other staples, corn was the most important: Every meal included foods made from cornmeal, including cornbread, mush, hoecakes and spoon bread. Built in the early 1870s by John Cable, Cable Mill was once one of four or five water-powered gristmills to serve Cades Cove's peak population of 700 residents. Powered by Mill Creek, whose waters were routed into the mill via a 235ft flume, Cable Mill features a classic overshot waterwheel. The operation also included a sawmill, providing residents with milled lumber.

TIPTON PLACE

The picturesque Tipton homestead was built by Mexican War veteran 'Colonel Hamp' Tipton in the early 1870s. The grounds include a stately two-floor cabin, blacksmith and carpentry shops and a cantilever barn. As with many other vernacular structures in the park, the doors are open and visitors are free to wander and explore at their leisure.

Cherokee Entrance

Near the gateway town of Cherokee (p139), the primary southern portal into Great Smoky, is an area known as Oconaluftee, once home to the Cherokee. In their language the word means simply 'by the river.' This fertile land has been inhabited for 8000 years, but it wasn't until the 1880s that nonnative settlers put down permanent roots here. Today the area is known for its visitor center, the Mountain Farm Museum and Mingus Mill. A few miles north on Newfound Gap Rd/Hwy 441 is Smokemont Campground (p116).

OCONALUFTEE VISITOR CENTER

Housed in a beautiful old stone and chestnut building, this busy **visitor center** (☎ 865-436-1200) 2 miles north of Cherokee includes the Smokies Discovery Center, where children and families learn about the park's ecosystems and biodiversity through interactive exhibits. A ranger station, accessible restrooms and a bookstore are adjacent to the visitor center. The Oconaluftee River Trail, one of only two in the park that allows leashed pets, leaves from the visitor center and follows the river for 1.5 miles to the boundary of the Cherokee reservation.

MINGUS MILL

In 1886 the Mingus family built this famous **mill** (☯ spring-fall) on their eponymous creek. Today, to the delight of visitors, the turbine-powered mill still grinds wheat and corn much as it always has. The cornmeal pouring into the bag is still warm from the friction caused by the mammoth mill stones, and when in operation the entire building vibrates and hums. A pleasant path enters the woods to follow the 100-yard-long board-walled canal, which delivers water to the mill from Mingus Creek. For a good time that doesn't cost a nickel, toss a couple of leaves into water for an unhurried leaf race.

MOUNTAIN FARM MUSEUM

The excellent **Mountain Farm Museum** and its collection of historic buildings evoke life on a typical farmstead of the late 19th century. Together these structures paint a poignant picture of the mountain people who once eked out their sustenance from this rugged and isolated wilderness. The buildings include a meat house, where a mountain farm's most valuable commodity was butchered, dried and smoked. Other structures are dedicated to chickens, apples, corn, water and blacksmithing. The well-tended garden and old-strain cornfields are beautiful to behold any time of year.

A terrific time to visit is in mid-September for the **Mountain Life Festival** (p94).

Cataloochee Valley

The Cherokee named these lands *Gadalutsi*, which means 'standing up in a row' or 'wave upon wave.' This less-visited former frontier outpost in the park's isolated eastern edge remains a delightful secret waiting to be discovered. Accessed via a narrow, winding 11-mile road, Cataloochee offers lush old-growth forests, restored farms and homesteads and opportunities for thrilling wildlife sightings of elk, wild turkeys and black bears.

Settlers in Cataloochee were drawn by the bountiful reserves of game and fish and fertile bottomlands. Today community buildings such as **Palmer Chapel**, **Beech Grove School** and **Little Cataloochee Church** stand open for visitors to explore.

Facilities include **Cataloochee Campground** (p116), ranger and information stations, restrooms and a **front-country horse camp** (p111). Before making the drive to the valley, pick up the *Cataloochee Auto Tour* brochure (50¢) from any visitor center.

Greenbrier Cove

This wild day-use area 6 miles east of Gatlinburg off Hwy 321 was once one of the most populous communities in the Smokies. Today it's a terrific place to fish, swim or picnic along the gorgeous Middle Prong of the **Little Pigeon River**, or you can hike to some of the most beautiful wildflower spots in the park.

The road into the cove follows the river and offers many places to pull off and enjoy the scenery. At 3.2 miles it forks; the left fork leads to the trailhead for **Old Settlers Trail** and **Ramsey Cascades**, while the right fork passes two picnic areas and dead-ends at a turnaround after 4 miles. At the turnaround, an easy, 1-mile path leads to old homesites, a cemetery and plenty of wildflowers during the spring and early summer.

DRIVING TOURS

Even if you never leave your personal transport bubble, you'll be wowed by the panoramic views, plummeting mountain streams and stately hardwood forests of Great Smoky Mountains National Park. But with so much majesty waving to you from beyond the road's edge, no doubt you'll soon park the car, stretch your legs and do some exploring, as bipeds are wont to do. The following driving tours will show you the best of Great Smoky, whether you stay behind the wheel or venture away from your wheels.

NEWFOUND GAP ROAD
Route: Sugarlands Valley to Oconaluftee Visitor Center
Distance: 29.2 miles one way
Speed Limit: 30mph

Newfound Gap Rd/Hwy 441 begins at Sugarlands Valley, climbs nearly 3000ft to cross Newfound Gap at a lofty elevation of 5048ft, and then descends to

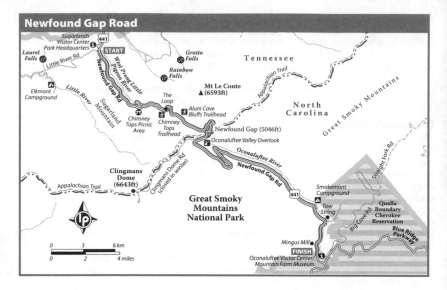

Newfound Gap Road

the Oconaluftee lowlands. Along the way are many turnouts, picnic areas, nature trails, quiet walkways and overlooks – everything that you came for. Pick up the informative *Newfound Gap Road Auto Tour* brochure ($1) at any visitor center.

After 5.6 miles you'll come to the **Chimney Tops Picnic Area**, nestled deep within a cove hardwood forest, one of the few left in the US. The West Prong of the Little Pigeon River passes nearby; its banks provide a delightful place to pick at your trail mix.

Between here and the Chimney Tops Trailhead, at 7.1 miles, you'll have several opportunities to pull over and admire one of the park's best-known geologic features. The Cherokee thought these twin stony outcroppings high on the ridge resembled a pair of antlers, while white settlers characterized them as a pair of stone chimneys. The challenging **Chimney Tops Trail** (p98) leads to the top and truly spectacular views.

At 7.3 miles is a famous patch of road known as **The Loop**. Here the highway passes through a tunnel and crosses over itself, a necessity required by the steep slope.

The trailhead and parking area for one of the park's most popular hikes, **Alum Cave Bluffs** (p97) is at mile 8.8. Over the next 1.5 miles, this stretch of road offers several turnouts for access to the roaring West Prong of the Little Pigeon River.

At 12.2 miles you'll know you've entered the upper elevations of the Smokies as you come to the spruce fir forest that dominates the high mountain slopes. The weather is considerably more prickly up here; on average it's 10 to 15 degrees cooler than in the lowlands, annual rainfall regularly exceeds 80 inches and the wind can be fierce. You'll also see the ill effects of the park's most maligned pest, a tiny nonnative insect called the woolly adelgid. Over a span of just 30 years it has killed more than 70 percent of the park's mature Fraser firs (see 'The Curse of the Wooly Adelgid).

At **Newfound Gap** (mile 12.5) travelers pass from Tennessee into North Carolina and the AT crosses the road. In olden days the road passing over the crest of the Smokies did so at Indian Gap, 1.5 miles west of the current site. When this easier passage was discovered in 1850, it was immediately and permanently dubbed 'Newfound Gap.' Straddling the state line is a monument marking the spot where Franklin D Roosevelt formally dedicated the park in 1940. From here you get your first privileged view into North Carolina.

The turnoff for **Clingmans Dome Rd** is at mile 13.4. Shortly thereafter, at mile 13.9, is a large parking area for the Oconaluftee Valley Overlook, where you will be treated to impressive views into the Oconaluftee River Valley.

Between miles 14.6 and 21.8 are five quiet walkways. These short paths, scattered throughout the park, are excellent places to escape the madding crowds without committing to a longer day hike.

At mile 28.7, **Mingus Mill** (p86) still grinds corn into meal just as it has done for more than a century. The mill is in operation from early spring through fall, though visitors are welcome anytime.

At mile 29.2, the Oconaluftee Visitor Center and **Mountain Farm Museum** (p86) signal the end of the driving tour.

CLINGMANS DOME ROAD
Route: Newfound Gap Rd to Clingmans Dome
Distance: 7 miles one way
Speed Limit: 30mph

This short drive through Great Smoky's high country to the park's highest peak provides several opportunities to learn about regional history and ecology. To the delight of cross-country skiers, the road is closed to cars December through March.

THE CURSE OF THE WOOLLY ADELGID

The park is home to numerous nonnative interlopers, from the odious wild boar to the rapacious kudzu vine, but perhaps the most destructive of all is the woolly adelgid (a-DELL-jid), an aphid-like insect that hitched a ride into the Great Smokies from Europe a century ago. Anyone who drives Clingmans Dome Rd through the once stately forest of red spruce and Fraser fir can see the destruction the adelgid has wrought.

Tragically, over the past 30 years this sap-crazed pest has killed more than 70 percent of the park's mature Fraser firs. The adelgid has infested all Fraser fir stands within the park, threatening the tree with extinction. In 2002 a different form of the dreaded pest was discovered in the park; this one threatens the eastern hemlock, one of the most common – and stately – trees in the park.

Thousands of dollars in donations have allowed park rangers to launch a three-pronged attack on the adelgid. The effort includes spraying infected trees with biodegradable soap, soaking roots with nicotine-based insecticides and releasing predator beetles known for their voracious appetite for – you guessed it – woolly adelgids. In other areas, predator beetles have reduced the adelgid population by 47 to 87 percent.

The University of Tennessee has opened a beetle-raising facility to help meet the urgent need. Beetles cost the park about $1 each. If you'd like to contribute, contact **Friends of the Smokies** (☎ 865-453-2428; friendsofthesmokies.org).

At 1.7 miles is the parking area for **Indian Gap Rd**. Step into the woods to find a trace of road from what was once the major north-south route through the Smoky Mountains. For centuries this had been an Indian trail, but in the 1830s it was widened into a toll road. Traffic of all sorts once passed through here: Indians, explorers, Confederate soldiers, merchants, farmers with livestock herds and families. Until Newfound Gap Rd opened in the 1930s, travelers had no better way to cross the mountains.

The Road Prong Trail follows the road trace from here, descending about 2.4 miles to meet up with the **Chimney Tops Trail** (p98).

The next stop is the **Spruce Fir Nature Trail**. This 0.75-mile loop trail with a self-guiding brochure takes you into a unique but damaged ecosystem found only at the highest elevations of the southern Appalachians. In addition to learning about the plants and animals that survive only at high elevation, you will see first-hand the ghostly skeletons of Fraser firs decimated by the pernicious nonnative woolly adelgid.

From the **Clingmans Dome** (p85) parking area you have several options. You can climb the steep half-mile trail to the observation tower for stunning panoramic views, or hit the trail for **Andrews Bald** (p102), 2 miles away, or **Silers Bald**, 4 miles west on the AT.

LITTLE RIVER ROAD
Route: Sugarlands Visitor Center to entrance of Cades Cove Loop Rd
Distance: 18 miles one way
Speed Limit: 30mph

Formerly an old railroad roadbed serving the timber industry, Little River Rd shadows the snaking Little River to connect Sugarlands Valley with Townsend and Cades Cove. The meandering 18-mile route can take as long as 1½ hours to drive.

A short 3.7 miles from Sugarlands is the trailhead for the paved **Laurel Falls Trail** (p95), one of the most popular hikes in the park.

At 10 miles you'll see a bridge leading to **Metcalf Bottoms Picnic Area**, a large and pretty day-use area on the Little River. Bear sightings are common here. A 1-mile path leads to the delightful **Little Greenbrier School**, a charming, 19th century split-log schoolhouse that also served as a church. Original classroom accoutrements, including desks, benches and a painted blackboard, still line the room.

Another mile and a half down Little River Rd brings you to **The Sinks**, an ominous stretch of white water that once swallowed a derailed logging train whole, according to folklore.

The next major landmark is the **Townsend Wye**, where the West Prong joins Little River and Hwy 73 peels off for Townsend. At this favorite swimming spot you'll find a placid stretch of river with grassy banks. From this point, as you drive into Cades Cove, the road's name changes to Laurel Creek Rd.

Less than a mile past the junction is the opportunity to turn left onto **Tremont Rd**, an uncrowded, 3.2-mile route into an interesting and scenic area of the park that once was home to one of the largest and last logging camps in the Smokies. The *Tremont Logging History Auto Tour* brochure, available at any visitor center, tells the whole story.

The **Great Smoky Mountains Institute at Tremont** (p114), a research facility with a small visitor center and bookstore, is also worth a visit. Two trails provide pleasant river walks with impressive cascades: the **West Prong Trail**, on the right just before the institute, and the **Middle Prong Trail**, at the end of the road.

Some two million people visit **Cades Cove** (p85 and Map 2, p154) each year, most of them via this one-way loop road encircling the valley. Cades Cove has the widest variety of historic buildings of any area in the park, including churches, a gristmill, log houses and cantilever barns.

The cove's wide-open expanses offer some of the best opportunities for wildlife viewing. Bear sightings are fairly common – if one lumbers within sight of the road, traffic comes to a standstill as normally sensible people leap from their cars fumbling with their cameras. You may also hear the peculiar gobbling of wild turkeys or see a multitude of deer, their bobwhite tails sticking straight up in the air as they leap wire fences to cross the road.

The first historic building you'll encounter is a small and picturesque 1820s log home, the **John Oliver Place**. John and Lurany Oliver were the first settlers to establish a homestead in the cove.

A quick succession of churches – the **Primitive Baptist Church**, **Methodist Church** and **Missionary Baptist Church** – give telling insight into the faith of the early settlers. These quiet, Spartan places of worship underscore the central role that religion played in the fabric of the Cades Cove community.

Across from the third church is the turnoff for **Rich Mountain Rd**. After passing another interesting homestead, the **Elijah Oliver Place**, you'll reach the turnoff for the parking area for the popular **Abrams Falls Trail** (p103).

At the halfway point of the loop road are two of Cades Cove's biggest attractions: the **Cades Cove Visitor Center** (p85) and **Cable Mill** (p86).

Just past the **Forge Creek Rd** (p92) turnoff is the **Cades Cove Nature Trail** (p102).

As you begin the last stretch of your Cades Cove tour, you will pass three more restored homesteads: **Dan Lawson Place**, **Tipton Place** (p86) and the **Carter Shields Cabin**.

Traffic congestion continues to be a major issue in Cades Cove, but on Wednesday and Saturday mornings until 10am cars are banned to make way for bicycle and foot traffic.

Buses, trailers and RVs are not permitted. The only restroom facilities on the Loop Rd are at the Cades Cove Visitor Center at Cable Mill. The road is closed from dusk until dawn. Your visit will be greatly enhanced by acquiring the excellent *Cades Cove Auto Tour* brochure *($1)* at any visitor center.

RICH MOUNTAIN ROAD
Route: Cades Cove Loop Rd to park boundary
Distance: 7 miles one way
Speed Limit: 15mph

Across from the Missionary Baptist Church on Cades Cove Loop Rd is the turnoff for Rich Mountain Rd, a one-way gravel road extending to the park boundary and on to Townsend. From 1830 until 1930 Rich Mountain Rd provided the only access into Cades Cove from the north. Keep your eyes peeled for a stand of **shagbark hickory**, a species rarely found in the Smoky Mountains. After 3.4 miles you'll come to a spectacular viewpoint overlooking the cove and the **Primitive Baptist Church** – a favorite spot for photographers.

The road is very narrow at places, and buses, trailers and RVs are not permitted. Rich Mountain Rd is closed from December through mid-March.

FORGE CREEK & PARSON BRANCH ROADS
Route: Cades Cove Visitor Center to Hwy 129
Distance: 8 miles one way
Speed Limit: 15mph

The gravel Forge Creek Rd leads from the Cades Cove Loop Rd to Hwy 129, at the southwestern park border in North Carolina. After 2.3 miles, Parson Branch Rd peels off to the right. At the 5-mile mark are Sams Gap and the trailhead for **Gregory Bald** (p106).

Parson Branch Rd was originally a main artery among a web of roads connecting the smaller coves and hollows with Cades Cove. It runs through an area once called Chestnut Flats, which was a notorious haunt of moonshiners (producers of illegal homemade corn whiskey). Many a shootout took place in these parts over whose moonshine was whose. The nefarious activity continued well into the 20th century – right up until people began to sell out to make room for the national park.

Parson Branch Rd is closed from December through mid-March. Buses, trailers and RVs are not permitted. The road is susceptible to flooding and closes periodically. In September 2004 the rains of Hurricane Ivan caused the road to close until 2005.

ROARING FORK MOTOR NATURE TRAIL
Route: Loop from Gatlinburg
Distance: 6 miles one way
Speed Limit: 15mph

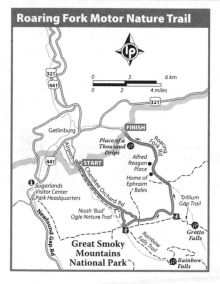

The Roaring Fork area is well loved for its surging streams and waterfalls, glimpses of old-growth forest and its excellent selection of preserved cabins and gristmills.

The loop road begins and ends a short distance from downtown Gatlinburg. From Hwy 441, turn onto Airport Rd at the eighth traffic light. Airport becomes Cherokee Orchard Rd, and the Roaring Fork Motor Nature Trail begins 3 miles later.

The first stop on Cherokee Orchard Rd is the **Noah 'Bud' Ogle Nature Trail**, providing an enjoyable jaunt into a mountain farmstead with a streamside tub mill (an improvised contraption built to crush or grind the family corn) and an ingenious wooden-flume plumbing apparatus.

Immediately following the **Rainbow Falls Trail** (p96) you can either turn around and head back to Gatlinburg or continue on Roaring Fork Rd, a narrow, twisting one-way road. The road follows Roaring Fork, one of the park's most tempestuous and beautiful streams. It passes through an impressive stand of old-growth eastern hemlocks, some of which reach heights of more than 100ft and have trunks stretching as much as 5ft across.

From the Trillium Gap Trail the delicate **Grotto Falls** (p96) can be reached via an easy, short hike through a virgin hemlock forest.

Of considerable historical interest are the hardscrabble cabin at the **Home of Ephraim Bales** and the more comfortable 'saddlebag' house at the **Alfred Reagan Place** (painted with 'all three colors that Sears and Roebuck had'). Reagan was a jack-of-all-trades who served his community as a carpenter, blacksmith and storekeeper.

A wet-weather waterfall called **Place of a Thousand Drips** provides a wonderful conclusion to your explorations.

The Roaring Fork Motor Nature Trail is closed from January to mid-March. Buses, trailers and RVs are not permitted. Pick up the informative *Roaring Fork Auto Tour* brochure (50¢) at any visitor center.

CATALOOCHEE VALLEY
Route: I-40 NC exit 20 to Cataloochee Valley
Distance: 13 miles one way
Speed Limit: 15mph

In many regards **Cataloochee Valley** (p87) is like Cades Cove but without all the people. Like its counterpart to the west, this idyllic valley features glorious mountain scenery surrounding fertile fields, wonderful historic churches, a schoolhouse and homesteads, and excellent opportunities for wildlife viewing. With a peak population of 1200, this was once the largest community within what is now the national park. Perhaps because of the valley's remote location at the end of a gravel road, a mere fraction of Cades Cove's two million annual visitors make the effort to see Cataloochee; if it's solitude you're after, you've found it. Pick up the *Cataloochee Auto Tour* brochure (50¢) at a visitor center or at the valley gate.

To get there, take NC exit 20 from I-40. After 0.2 mile, turn right at the sign and travel 11 miles to the gate. The last 2 miles are on a narrow but well-maintained gravel road following portions of the old **Cataloochee Turnpike**, a former Indian trail that later became an avenue for cattle drovers

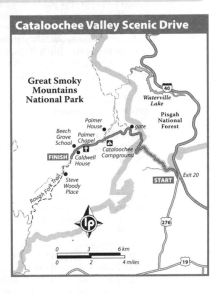

and an inroad for the permanent settlers, who arrived in the 1830s.

A short distance past the gate are **Cataloochee Campground** (p116) and the ranger station, plus a short trail to **Palmer House**, a farmhouse built around 1860 as a 'dogtrot' log cabin. Today it contains a small museum.

Less than a mile down the road is the lovely **Palmer Chapel**. If no one is listening, consider delivering a sermon to the empty pews from the lectern. The open space surrounding the chapel is the site of the annual homecoming celebration, when descendants of Cataloochee residents return to tend the cemeteries, attend services and share a country meal.

Across the road is **Beech Grove School**, an old-timey schoolhouse still outfitted with desks and a dusty blackboard. You can almost hear the shouts of kids on their recess in the sun-dappled fields outside.

Continuing down the road, you'll pass an expansive meadow, a prime place to spot wild turkeys and perhaps even elk.

Who doesn't love to explore a vacant house? You'll get your chance at **Caldwell House** and **Woody House**, where the empty rooms still resonate with the lives once lived here. The latter is accessible via the 1-mile **Rough Fork Trail** (p104).

FESTIVALS & EVENTS

The most popular and perhaps interesting happenings in Great Smoky are the **Old Timers' Day** events, held at Cades Cove in early May and Cataloochee in late September. Former residents, their descendents and others from surrounding areas take part in these colorful, informal events. Mountain music and dancing ensue.

Another well-loved shindig is the annual **Mountain Life Festival** at Oconaluftee's Mountain Farm Museum in mid-September. The centerpiece of this event is a sorghum molasses demonstration, featuring a horse-powered cane mill and a wood-fired cooker. Other activities include hearth cooking and the making of hominy, apple butter, apple cider and soap.

In mid-April the annual weeklong **Spring Wildflower Pilgrimage** features more than 150 programs led by botanists, zoologists, park rangers and other professionals, covering a wide assortment of natural and cultural history topics.

Birders will want to mark their calendars for the second Saturday in May. The annual **International Migratory Bird Day**, which celebrates the incredible journeys of migratory birds between their breeding grounds in North America and wintering grounds in Mexico, Central America and South America, features ranger-led bird walks and a fascinating program of lectures.

The ways of mountain folk are on display at the **Festival of Christmas Past** in mid-December, when artisans, storytellers and musicians show how Christmas was traditionally celebrated in Appalachia.

DAY HIKES

Whether you have an irrepressible urge to climb a mountain or just want to get some fresh air, hiking in Great Smoky Mountains National Park is the single best way to experience the sublime beauty of this singular place. Even if you're only here for a short visit, be sure to include at least one hike in your itinerary. Trails range from flat, easy and short paths to longer, more strenuous endeavors. Many are excellent for families, some are wheelchair accessible, and the majority of trailheads begin from major sights. No matter what your physical ability or endurance level, there's a hike out there for you. Those looking for a multi-day hike should flip to Backcountry Hikes (p105).

In addition to a great number of day hikes, Great Smoky also offers leisurely strolls in the form of quiet walkways, short paths that depart from major roads in the park, and several self-guided nature trails, where you can learn about the diverse ecology and human folk life of the Smokies. Lightly used and easily accessible, these options offer an easy way to enjoy the forest's sublime solitude without having to invest an entire afternoon.

Each visitor center has a bookstore featuring many excellent guidebooks to the park's various hikes. A favorite among day-trippers is *Day Hikes of the Smokies* ($9.95), published by the Great Smoky Mountains Natural History Association. An official trail map ($1) can also be obtained here ($1), or is available for free download (www.nps.gov/grsm/pphtml/maps.html).

The following suggested hikes are some of the most accessible and popular in Great Smoky Mountains National Park.

Around Sugarlands

These hikes are in close proximity to Gatlinburg and Sugarlands Visitor Center.

SUGARLANDS VALLEY NATURE TRAIL
Distance: 0.5 mile round-trip
Duration: 30 minutes
Challenge: Easy
Elevation Change: None

This short, easy trail welcomes everyone – its paved surfaces are ideal for wheelchairs or strollers. An illustrated brochure (50¢), available at the trailhead or any visitor center, provides fascinating information about the old **homesteads** and crumbling **stone walls** you'll encounter. Visually impaired visitors can stop by Sugarlands Visitor Center for a tape player and audiotape that describes trail features.

This nature trail through a burgeoning forest of tulip trees and pines tells the story of the forest's regeneration. A century ago, this river valley on the West Prong of the Little Pigeon River was home to 100 families living in communities with such names as Bullhead, Goober Farm and Forks-of-the-River. The bottomlands were cleared to make room for their fields, churches and schools. By 1920 loggers had cut the hillsides and local farmers had yielded to summertime residents and their simple cottages. When the national park was formed, most of the buildings here were removed, but as you will see, some of their chimneys still stand, even as they are being swallowed by the forest. The trailhead is a half mile south of Sugarlands Visitor Center.

LAUREL FALLS
Distance: 2.6 miles round-trip
Duration: 1½ hours
Challenge: Easy–Moderate
Elevation Change: 400ft

With its close proximity to Gatlinburg and Elkmont Campground, this easy waterfall hike has become so popular that the park service has paved the entire length of the trail to head off the erosion caused by countless pairs of clomping boots. The trailhead on Little River Rd (p90) near Sugarlands is served by the Gatlinburg Trolley (p128). The paved passage is wheelchair accessible with considerable assistance, but curiously the curb at the parking area lacks a ramp and the pavement is uneven toward the end of the hike.

The trail to **Laurel Falls** climbs gently through a forest of oak and pine. At the top, Laurel Branch bursts from a grove of mountain laurel and falls nearly 50ft to collect in a pool that is ideal for soaking your weary gams. From here, the water spills another 40ft to a second pool below.

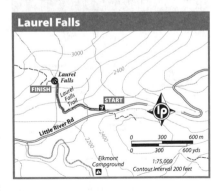

GROTTO FALLS
Distance: 2.6 miles round-trip
Duration: 2 hours
Challenge: Moderate
Elevation Change: 350ft

This lovely hike passes through mature forests supporting old-growth hemlocks to another of Great Smoky's gorgeous waterfalls. The trailhead is on Roaring Fork Motor Nature Trail (p92), 1.7 miles from the start of the one-way road. The parking area may fill up in summer, so get there early in the day.

You will be hiking along **Trillium Gap Trail** (p108), one of the main arteries leading to the summit of Mt Le Conte (6.6 miles from the parking area). The well-maintained trail makes a moderate ascent all the way to the falls. There are a number of easy creek crossings along the way. You might encounter large black-and-white pileated woodpeckers or hear their insistent drumming on the trunks of dead trees. During the spring you might see liverworts or silverbells in bloom or, on warm days, salamanders doing push-ups at the edge of a stream. Most curiously, you could meet a llama pack train carrying food and laundry to Le Conte Lodge – a strange sight indeed, certain to delight children. During the season, llamas make the ascent two or three times a week; if you deem this a must-see, call **Le Conte Lodge** (☎ 865-429-5704) for the current schedule.

Grotto Falls is a favorite subject of photographers. Here, Roaring Fork spills 20ft from an overhanging ledge as the trail passes behind a transparent wall of water. If you're fortunate enough to be at the site when the llama train passes through, you'll return home with the mother of all snapshots.

RAINBOW FALLS
Distance: 5.6 miles round-trip
Duration: 4 hours
Challenge: Difficult
Elevation Change: 1700ft

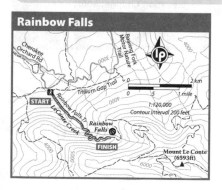

Rainbow Falls

It's hard to imagine that anyone could tire of waterfalls. It is perfectly plausible, however, that one could get tired of *hiking* to waterfalls. Some of the park's most popular falls are the ones that lie near roads or trailheads, easy for anyone to see and enjoy. Alas, Rainbow Falls is not one of them. To see it, one must climb 1700ft in a scant 2.8 miles.

About 100 yards from the parking area on the Roaring Fork Motor Nature Trail, you'll cross Trillium Gap Trail; continue on the Rainbow Falls Trail to climb alongside Le Conte Creek all the way to the falls. The path is absurdly rocky.

After a mile the trail parts company with the creek and heads to the right on a switchback; from here there is a good view back toward Gatlinburg. As the trail heads back to the creek and to another high overlook, you'll find several comfortable rocks for a rest. The next stretch of trail features some huge hemlock trees, including one that naturalists say is among the largest in the park. You will cross a number of small streams and pass a small waterfall

– don't worry, this puny little trickle is not the one you have made so much effort to see!

The long uphill slog is finally rewarded by the sight of misty **Rainbow Falls**, one of the prettiest and most delicate waterfalls in the park. Rivulets of crystalline water spill over an 80ft bluff and then flow through a mossy boulder field in a succession of gentle cascades. It's said that in winter, the entire falls is prone to freeze solid, assuming the shape of an hourglass.

Along Newfound Gap Road

Several of the park's most famous – and consequently most traveled – hiking trails start from Newfound Gap Rd.

ALUM CAVE BLUFFS
Distance: 4.5 miles round-trip
Duration: 3 hours
Challenge: Moderate–Difficult
Elevation Change: 1360ft

The popular Alum Cave Bluffs hike provides a representative sampling of the park's diverse pleasures. Some rate this satisfying hike, which passes through old-growth forest and follows a series of streams as it winds its way up the southern slope of Mt Le Conte, to be the finest the park has to offer. However, the pleasures of the hike must be earned; it's a steady uphill slog all the way from the parking area to the bluffs.

The well-tended trail departs from Newfound Gap Rd at the Alum Cave Bluffs parking area, then shadows the roaring Alum Cave Creek for the first 1.4 miles. After a series of log bridges, it begins to climb through dense Catawba rhododendron

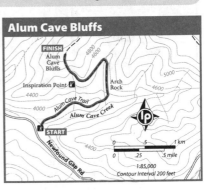

Alum Cave Bluffs

thickets that bloom extravagantly in early June. Keep an eye out for the pygmy shrew scuttling across the forest floor. It is the smallest native mammal in North America.

At **Arch Rock** handcrafted stone steps ascend steeply through the portal of an impressive stone arch that looks like something Frodo was compelled to climb. Beyond this interesting formation the trail crosses the Styx Branch and begins a steep ascent.

The forest gives way to open sky at the next point of interest, a large **heath bald** where mountain laurel and blueberry bushes grow in a dense mass. These areas of vegetation were called 'hells' by the mountain people because they were indeed hellish to cross when there was no trail.

After some huffing and puffing, you'll be repaid for your efforts at a scenic vista called Inspiration Point. After catching your breath and taking in a view of Little Duck Hawk Ridge, hit the trail again for a short climb to **Alum Cave Bluffs**. As it turns out, the name is a misnomer. Waiting for you is not a cave, but rather a rock overhang. Moreover, the rocks contain not alum, but rather sulphur and rare minerals, some not known to occur elsewhere. The dry conditions beneath the overhang create a unique dusting of powder that covers the ground, and colonies of small plants sprout from the rock, including ferns and lichens that vary in color from black to bright neon green. The bluffs are also home to peregrine falcons; it was here that the first recorded nesting of peregrines occurred in the park in 1997 after the successful reintroduction of the raptor in the mid-1980s.

Alum Cave Bluffs are the end of this hike, but if you're game for more delightful punishment, you can continue on to the summit of Mt Le Conte, 2.7 miles up the trail.

CHIMNEY TOPS
Distance: 4 miles round-trip
Duration: 4 hours
Challenge: Difficult
Elevation Change: 1250ft

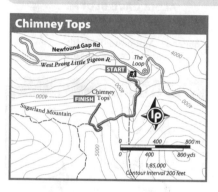

This hike is one of the most popular in the park, due to its short length and easy access from Newfound Gap Rd. The view from the twin peaks of Chimney Tops is nothing short of spectacular. However, before you set out, you should know that this grueling climb could cause a priest to mutter expletives within earshot of children. Moreover, if it's solitude you seek, you probably won't find it on this trail.

The Cherokee called the formations now known as Chimney Tops *Duniskwalguni*, meaning 'forked antlers.' The settlers who came later disagreed; to them, the twin pinnacles of quartzite and slate evoked a pair of chimneys.

From the main parking area on Newfound Gap Rd, you'll descend to cross the **Walker Camp Prong**, a popular river spot with lovely cascades and boulders. As you look downstream, you will see the stream converge with Road Prong, a waterway that you'll cross in short order. After the confluence the waterway becomes known as the West Prong of the Little Pigeon River. After two additional stream crossings via sturdy log bridges, you'll begin to climb in earnest.

About a mile from the trailhead, you'll pass the junction with the Road Prong Trail. Continue to the right. Soon you will leave rhododendron thickets and enter a mixed forest punctuated with giant yellow buckeye trees. In autumn, scan the ground for the trees' shiny, richly colored nuts; carrying one is said to bring good luck.

After a good climb you'll reach a metal culvert crossing the trail. This is a good place to rest up before the arduous ascent to Chimney Tops.

The next half mile of trail climbs steeply with no switchbacks. When you finally reach one, rest with the knowledge that the most physically demanding part of the hike is behind you. From here the trail ascends moderately along Sugarland Mountain. At the next ridge is an opening with a view of Mt Le Conte. After the trail passes along the top of a narrow ridge, you'll get your first view of the **Chimney Tops**.

A sign warns of the dangers of continuing further. If you are hiking with children, it's probably best to turn back, because the passage ahead is treacherous. The rock outcrops can be exceedingly slippery, and if you continue, you may be exposed to high winds or even lightning. Scrambling up the peak requires the use of both hands.

From here you can attempt to climb straight up to the first chimney, or take the alternate route to the right to gain access to the saddle between the peaks. You will enjoy an exceedingly fine panoramic view. To the northeast stand the imposing peaks of **Mt Le Conte** (6593ft), Great Smoky's third-highest mountain; to its right is the narrow ridgeline called **The Boulevard**. Northeast is **Mt Mingus** (5802ft).

Some hikers try to make it to the second hump, but to do so is extremely dangerous. Many serious injuries have occurred here.

SMOKEMONT LOOP
Distance: 6.1 miles round-trip
Duration: 4 hours
Challenge: Moderate–Difficult
Elevation Change: 1350ft

With its formidable ascent and descent, this hike through a pretty mixed-hardwood forest is good for anyone seeking a workout in a beautiful setting. The trailhead is in the D section at the far end of Smokemont Campground. From here, follow the gravel road as it travels alongside Bradley Fork Creek. After about a mile, Chasteen Creek Trail forks to the right (0.1 miles up this trail is Campsite 50, one of the park's most easily accessible backcountry campsites). Continue left along the stream another half mile to the junction with the Smokemont Loop Trail, leading left. You will cross one of the park's longest and bounciest log bridges; at its end the trail turns downstream for a hundred yards or so to a fork. Here you will turn right for a 2-mile ascent along the side of Richland Mountain (avoid the unmarked trail heading straight).

You will pass through a damp mixed-hardwood forest known for its spring and summer wildflowers. At 2.5 miles you'll enter a drier area and enjoy some decent views, including **Newton Bald** to the west.

At 3.4 miles the trail veers sharply to the west, signaling the beginning of a well-earned 2-mile descent through lovely forest scenery. At 5.2 miles you may get a glimpse of **Bradley Cemetery** through the trees to your right. If you'd like to visit the cemetery, avoid the temptation to take one of the unauthorized, eroded trails scuttling down the hillside. Instead, continue about 0.2 mile to the service road, turn right and then right again onto an old road. After about 100 yards, you'll reach a path on the right leading to the cemetery. You'll find some 30-odd weathered graves dating from the late 1800s to 1925.

After you return to the main trail, Smokemont Campground is only a short distance. Once you have entered the campground, walk left on the service road about a half mile to reach the trailhead.

Along the Appalachian Trail
These high-country hikes travel on or near the Appalachian Trail along the crest of the Great Smoky Mountains. For more details on the entire Appalachian Trail, see p40. For a four-day backcountry hike on the Appalachian Trail, see p108.

CHARLIES BUNION
Distance: 8 miles round-trip
Duration: 5½ hours
Challenge: Moderate
Elevation Change: 1000ft

Charlies Bunion was named for an actual bunion on an actual guy named Charlie. This 8-mile round-trip hike from Newfound Gap Rd rewards those who make the effort with spectacular views and a lovely journey through a spruce fir forest. You'll walk the AT the whole way along the border of North Carolina and Tennessee.

These are some very wet mountains – the area gets 7ft of rain each year. Naturally, ferns, lichens, flowers and mosses cover the forest floor. Along the way you'll enjoy privileged views of towering Mt Le Conte. The wide scars on the mountain's north slope are the result of a cataclysmic flash flood in 1951. You'll also see evidence of fir trees that have suffered the destruction wrought by the woolly adelgid. As you look out over the forest, these dead firs stand above the living trees, like stark gray skeletons amid the otherwise lushly forested mountainside.

The hike begins from the parking area at Newfound Gap. The first 3 miles of the hike are a steady uphill slog. At 2.7 miles the trail forks. To the left is the Boulevard Trail to the summit of Mt Le Conte. The AT leading to Charlies Bunion is to the right

For a rewarding 1.5-mile side trip, peel off her for **The Jumpoff**. Take the Boulevard Trail and an immediate right on the narrow Jumpoff Trail angling off to the right. It is steep, rocky and eroded, so be careful. At The Jumpoff, the trail winds along the ridge and takes you to a sheer cliff with soaring views. If you're lucky, you might see a peregrine falcon suspended in space as it rides the rising thermals.

After returning to the AT, you'll soon come across the backcountry shelter

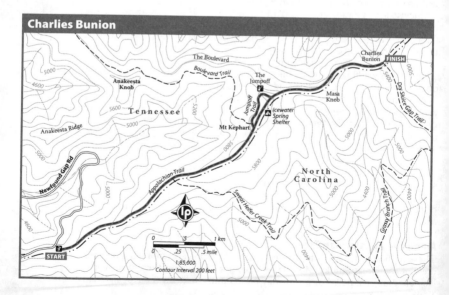

WELCOMING THE ELK

After successful reintroductions of the peregrine falcon and the river otter to Great Smoky, the NPS recently turned its attention to returning elk to the forests and meadows of Cataloochee. It's believed that Carolina's last native elk was killed in the late 1700s. These stately animals weigh an average of 500 to 700lb and have antler spans of up to 5ft in width.

Since 2001, 25 to 30 elk have been released annually by the park service on an experimental basis. The present population is estimated to be in the range of 70 to 80. In 2006 biologists will evaluate the impact elk are having on the park's flora and fauna and on park visitors and neighbors. If the program is deemed a success – and so far the prognosis is good – then the program will be permanently adopted.

at **Icewater Spring**. If you've never seen a backcountry AT shelter, this will be of considerable interest. It's a squat, three-walled rock structure with an open front door and ledges for hikers to sleep on. It's a good place to chew the fat with other hikers. From here it's less than a mile to Charlies Bunion.

You'll walk steadily downhill on a narrow, rocky path before reaching **Charlies Bunion**, a stony outcropping of pinkish rock rising at an angle toward the sky – far more beautiful than any bunion.

CLINGMANS DOME
Distance: 1.5 miles
Duration: 1 hour
Challenge: Moderate–Difficult
Elevation Change: 300ft

At 6643ft, Clingmans Dome is the highest mountain in Great Smoky and the third highest east of the Mississippi. This paved, mile-high trail leads to an observation tower, affording stunning 360-degree views of the Smokies and beyond. To reach the trailhead, turn off Newfound Gap Rd just south of Newfound Gap and follow the 7-mile long Clingmans Dome Rd to the large parking area at the end.

Temperatures on Clingmans Dome can be 10 or more degrees lower than in Gatlinburg or Cherokee. Moreover, biting winds will penetrate flimsy cotton pullovers or windbreakers; prepare for the hike by dressing in layers and donning a cap.

The first section of trail ascends a half mile to the base of the **Clingmans Dome Observation Tower**. You may immediately feel the effects of altitude. Counteract any dizziness or shortness of breath by resting frequently and drinking plenty of water. From here the walkway spirals to the apex of the tower. Some people walk backward up the walkway to lessen the strain on their calves. Those in wheelchairs can be assisted to the top of the tower, but it is very steep and due caution is advised.

The views are spectacular even from the base, but from the top of the tower on a clear day you will be able to see for miles in every direction.

ANDREWS BALD
Distance: 3.6 miles round-trip
Duration: 2½ hours
Challenge: Easy
Elevation Change: 700ft

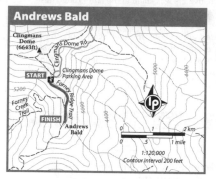

This is an easy hike through a once-verdant spruce fir forest to the most accessible of Great Smoky's balds. The **grassy balds** of the high ridges of the southern Appalachians provide unique ecosystems for plants and animals. It is not known how the balds came into being; some have speculated that these open grassy areas were created by grazing elk or bison.

In the absence of grazing animals, the NPS is working to retain the open character of these special places where oat grass and wildflowers flourish. From late August through mid-September you will very likely find blueberries (that is, if hungry bears haven't harvested them all for themselves). In mid-June flame azaleas and Catawba rhododendron put on a show. October is a wonderful time for autumn leaves.

The trail to Andrews Bald departs from the Clingmans Dome parking area along the Forney Ridge Trail. The first section is a ridiculously steep and rocky descent, but after a half mile you'll enter the spruce fir forest. At 1.2 miles you'll meet the junction with Forney Creek Trail; continue straight. From here it's 0.7 mile to the bald.

On a sunny day the open space of **Andrews Bald** is a delightful place to dance or make love. The views of the mountains receding into the distance are superb. Pack a picnic and a good book and make an afternoon of it.

Cades Cove Area
Map 2, p154

If the traffic congestion in Cades Cove begins to remind you a little too much of home, you'll know it is time to leave your car and set out on foot.

CADES COVE NATURE TRAIL
Distance: 0.75 mile round-trip
Duration: 1 hour
Challenge: Easy
Elevation Change: 300ft

This short, quiet trail passes through a dry pine and oak forest in the heart of Cades Cove. You'll find the trailhead along the Cades Cove Loop Rd (p91), just past the junction with Forge Creek Rd. With the illustrated *Cades Cove Self-Guiding Nature Trail* brochure (50¢) at the trailhead, and with the help of the labels identifying the flora along the trail, you will learn the fascinating story of how hardscrabble settlers in the 1820s utilized these trees and plants to survive and flourish. You may also learn how to identify the most common trees of Great Smoky's lowlands.

The soft wood of the white pine was used to craft basic furniture, while the obliging wood of the yellow poplar, with its broad, straight trunk, was

WATERFALL HIKES

If waterfalls quicken your pulse, you've come to the right place. The following hikes lead to some of the Smokies' best and most accessible waterfalls.

✔ **Abrams Falls** (below) A 5-mile round-trip hike from Cades Cove Loop Rd leads to this photogenic gusher with the largest water volume of any falls in the park.

✔ **Chasteen Creek Falls** This small, graceful waterfall can be reached from Smokemont Campground on a moderate, 4-mile round-trip hike.

✔ **Grotto Falls** (p96) From Roaring Fork Motor Nature Trail, this 2.4-mile round-trip hike through a hemlock forest leads to the only waterfall in the park that you can walk behind.

✔ **Hen Wallow Falls** A 4.4-mile round-trip hike from Cosby Campground leads to this less-visited 45ft waterfall.

✔ **Indian Creek Falls** From Deep Creek Campground, this 1.5-mile round-trip hike leads to a unique fall that slides down 35ft of sloping rock. Along the route is Toms Branch Falls, another beauty.

✔ **Laurel Falls** (p95) From Little River Rd, this easy 2.5-mile round-trip on a paved trail leads to one of the park's most popular falls.

✔ **Rainbow Falls** (p96) From Roaring Fork Motor Nature Trail, this moderately strenuous, 5.5-mile round-trip hike leads to the highest single-plunge waterfall in the park.

✔ **Ramsey Cascades** From Greenbrier, a strenuous 8-mile round-trip hike leads to these magnificent falls that tumble more than 100ft in a spectacular setting.

used to build cabins. The hard wood of the sugar maple came in handy in producing rifle stocks and firewood and in smoking meats for the winter. Pioneers also tapped sugar maple trunks and collected the sap in a bucket; gallons of the stuff were boiled down into a thick, sweet syrup for biscuits and cough medicine. The bark of chestnut oak, high in tannic acids, was used to tan leather. Limber strips of white oak were incorporated in basketry, while the tree's strong and durable timber went into anything from roof shingles to waterwheel shafts. Lichens were use to dye wool yarn.

On this family-friendly trail you'll encounter all of these trees and plants and gain an appreciation for the challenges overcome by the early residents of Cades Cove.

ABRAMS FALLS
Distance: 5 miles round-trip
Duration: 3½ hours
Challenge: Moderate
Elevation Change: 200ft

Abrams Creek and Falls were named after Cherokee Chief Abram, who once lived on the Tennessee River at the mouth of the creek, on land that was later claimed by the manmade Lake Chilhowee.

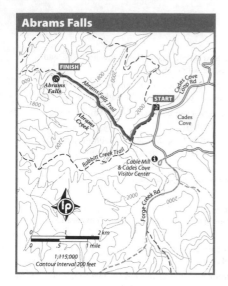

Abrams Falls

The 5-mile day hike to Abrams Falls and back is one of the park's most popular, and for good reason. After following the boisterous creek and its many tributaries, you will arrive at an enormously appealing waterfall that spills into one of the park's largest natural pools. However, the beauty of this place is certainly no secret, and unless it is a gray and rainy day, you can expect to share the experience with scores of others.

You'll find the turnoff for the trailhead 5 miles from the beginning of Cades Cove Loop Rd, just prior to the Cable Mill area. The trail departs from the north end of the parking lot. If the large parking area is full, you should be able to find parking along the entrance road (although this might be a signal to find a less-crowded trail).

Cross the footbridge spanning **Abrams Creek** and turn left to follow the waterway downstream. Although the cumulative elevation loss between here and the falls is only 200ft, the trail rises and dips enough to get your heart pumping. It crosses two pine-covered ridges, where in early spring you might see wildflowers such as trailing arbutus, bleeding hearts or gay-wings.

Abrams Creek is the largest stream completely contained by the national park. By the time it roars over the 20ft ledge at **Abrams Falls**, the creek boasts the highest water volume of any in the park. As is sometimes the case with big gushers, over many centuries the force of the water has carved a bowl-like pool that you may find irresistible. Many people take a well-earned dip in the waters, but be warned that the bottom of the pool is exceedingly slippery. Don't climb on the moss-covered rocks near the falls; this has been the site of many injuries over the years.

The Far East

Great Smoky's eastern region is the most remote and least-visited area in the park. If it's solitude you crave, make a beeline to Cataloochee or Big Creek.

STEVE WOODY PLACE
Distance: 2 miles round-trip
Duration: 1½ hours
Challenge: Easy
Elevation Change: 150ft

In far-flung **Cataloochee** (p87), this short, easy hike leads to the Woody Place, a preserved, early 20th- century homestead open for exploration. Getting to the trailhead is one of the best things about this excursion; you will drive through an exceedingly scenic valley punctuated with historic houses, churches and a schoolhouse. The **Rough Fork Trail** departs from the parking area at the end of Cataloochee Rd and follows an old roadbed, crossing Rough Fork Creek three times on narrow log bridges.

The **Steve Woody Place** is situated in a clearing a mile from the parking area. This handsome house had its roots as a log cabin, but as Woody's family grew to include eight children, he enlarged the home with framed additions, including several bedrooms, porches and a kitchen. As tourists first began to trickle into the valley, Woody, like many of his neighbors, capitalized on this development by stocking the streams on his property with fish and charging fishermen room and board. In this way Woody became emblematic of the changing times in the Smokies, as families shifted from subsistence farming to the economics of tourism.

MOUSE CREEK FALLS

Distance: 4 miles round-trip
Duration: 3 hours
Challenge: Easy
Elevation Change: 500ft

Featuring a swimming hole and a pretty waterfall, this hike will intimately acquaint you with Big Creek, one of the park's most beautiful thundering waterways. Near **Big Creek Campground** (p115), the Big Creek Trail begins at the gate just before the day-use picnic area and continues up an old road built by the Civilian Conservation Corps (CCC) in the 1930s. You'll hike alongside one of those classic roiling mountain streams that Great Smoky Mountains National Park is famous for.

At 1.5 miles, you'll find easy creek access at **Midnight Hole**, a large, deep swimming hole surrounded by rocks suitable for sun worship. As you continue up the trail, you'll reach a good vantage point where you can admire Big Creek's thunderous descent down the mountain. The water is crystal clear; depending on its depth, it may be emerald green or crystalline blue.

At 2 miles you'll reach **Mouse Creek Falls**; watch for a small spur trail on the left. This 35ft waterfall cascades down green moss-covered rocks, hits a ledge and then spills into Big Creek. You couldn't ask for a better picnic spot.

BACKCOUNTRY HIKES

As anyone who has hit the trail with a pack and a map can attest, the pleasures of self-sufficient backcountry camping are beyond compare. To sleep beneath the stars after a delicious dinner of freeze-dried peas and instant banana pudding is a tonic for the body and soul. Backcountry hikes in Great Smoky vary in length (from overnight trips to treks lasting the better part of a month) and in difficulty. As long as you're reasonably fit and realistic about your ability, you'll have no trouble finding a hike. See the Activities chapter for more information about when to go, what to pack and where to camp.

The most complete topographic map of the entire park is published by National Geographic/Trails Illustrated at 1:62,500 ($9.95) and is available at all park visitor centers. Larger-scale USGS maps (1:24,000) sell for $5.95, but you might need several to cover all the areas you want to hike.

Also available at visitor centers, *Hiking Trails of the Smokies* ($18.95) is a complete tome with elevation profiles and historical tidbits on every trail in the park.

Permit Information

Although permits are free, the system is quite strict, and you must obtain a permit before spending the night anywhere in the backcountry. For most sites you can self-register at any ranger station, campground or visitor center. However, some campsites require a reservation (see Backcountry Camping, p106). The reservation office will give you a reservation number to write on your permit.

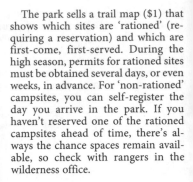

RATIONED CAMPSITES

The following backcountry campsites require reservations from the **backcountry reservation office** ☎ 865-436-1231; 🕒 8am-6pm)

✔	All shelters
✔ 9	Anthony Creek
✔ 10	Ledbetter Ridge
✔ 13	Sheep Pen Gap
✔ 23	Camp Rock
✔ 24	Rough Creek
✔ 29	Otter Creek
✔ 36	Upper Walnut Bottom
✔ 37	Lower Walnut Bottom
✔ 38	Mount Sterling
✔ 47	Enloe Creek
✔ 50	Lower Chasteen Creek
✔ 55	Pole Road
✔ 57	Bryson Place
✔ 61	Bald Creek
✔ 71	CCC Camp
✔ 83	Bone Valley
✔ 113	Birch Spring Gap

The park sells a trail map ($1) that shows which sites are 'rationed' (requiring a reservation) and which are first-come, first-served. During the high season, permits for rationed sites must be obtained several days, or even weeks, in advance. For 'non-rationed' campsites, you can self-register the day you arrive in the park. If you haven't reserved one of the rationed campsites ahead of time, there's always the chance spaces remain available, so check with rangers in the wilderness office.

Backcountry Camping

Anyone staying overnight in the backcountry must camp only in a designated site or shelter. Backcountry sites in Great Smoky Mountains National Park are numbered, while shelters along the AT are named. Backcountry sites also have names, but they are referred to on maps and at the reservation office strictly by number. All sites and shelters are placed near a spring or stream. Springs sometimes run dry, so check ahead with the backcountry office, particularly in dry conditions.

Occasionally the park closes campsites for renovation or due to bear activity. These closures are posted where permits are dispensed, or you can check with the backcountry reservation office.

Reservations (☎ 865-436-1231) are necessary to stay in any shelter; 17 tent areas also require reservations. Questions about the backcountry – but not reservations – are fielded by the **backcountry office** (☎ 865-436-1297).

Backcountry Trails

More than 800 miles of well-marked backcountry trails crisscross these mountains, including 70 miles of the scenic AT. Below are three of the more popular and scenic routes, to give you a taste of what's on offer. All backcountry campsites and shelters listed below have basic cleared sites, tent pads, food-storage cables and access to water.

GREGORY BALD
Distance: 11.4 miles round-trip
Duration: Overnight
Challenge: Difficult
Elevation Change: 2400ft

The hike to Gregory Bald is one of those experiences that is different each time you follow this path. In early spring the trail is flanked with wildflowers, while in June mountain laurel and the Catawba rhododendron's magenta blossoms line the trail. By July, orange and fuchsia azaleas are bursting into bloom. After a hefty climb of 3000ft (900m) in 5.4 miles, you'll be rewarded with not only a nearly 360-degree view, but also a flower-cloaked (in season) bald and a chance at meeting one of the Smokies' black bears over an August crop of mountain blueberry. Fall is also spectacular, since the leaves on all the deciduous trees change color; soon thereafter, the views begin to open up along the ridge as the trees lose their leaf cover. For many, this is the quintessential Smokies hike, which can be done year after year.

Gregory Bald

The park-provided trail map is fine for this well-marked, easy-to-follow route. But if you want more detail, use the National Geographic/Trails Illustrated *Great Smoky Mountains National Park* topographic map, available at visitor centers.

To reach the trailhead, take the Cades Cove Loop Rd from Townsend; at the turnoff for the visitor center and Cable Mill area, go straight onto Forge Creek Rd 2.3 miles until it ends in a small parking area.

The Gregory Ridge Trail begins with a short uphill over a ridge that eventually levels out as it follows Forge Creek. This is a second-growth hemlock forest, and in spring wildflowers carpet the forest floor. The trail crosses the creek several times over footbridges. In June little gray juncos may flit out from their nests on the ground near the trail as you walk by. After the second crossing of Forge Creek a section of old-growth tulip trees appears. After the third crossing, you'll soon see primitive (non-rationed) **campsite 12**. This is your last chance to fill up on water (although this water is from the creek and must be treated).

From here the climbing begins in earnest. The ascent is of a moderate grade and will continue for the next 3 miles, gaining about 2400ft. After about a mile of oak forest, the trail reaches the ridge itself. Mountain laurel is plentiful along this stretch; its white clusters of cup-shaped flowers bloom in June. Beginning at about 4.6 miles, a final, flat stretch offers views to the east. With luck, Spence Field and Thunderhead Mountain will be visible above the field.

At 4.9 miles are Rich Gap and the junction with the Gregory Bald Trail. **Moore Spring** lies about a third of a mile past this point on an unmarked, single-track trail. The side trip to the spring is worthwhile, not only to make use of the water, which wells up beneath a boulder, but also to view the former site of a popular AT shelter when the AT passed this way. The shelter burned down in the 1970s and was not replaced, and since the fire the AT has been rerouted to pass Fontana Lake.

To the right another 0.6 mile from Rich Gap is **Gregory Bald**. The rocky and steepish climb is mercifully short, and soon the bald opens out in all its splendor. If your timing is right (late June), the flame azaleas will be competing for the many bees that buzz around their lovely white, pink, yellow and red blossoms.

From here you can continue on Gregory Bald Trail 0.4 mile to (rationed) **campsite 13**, your home for the night. There's much demand for this site on weekends and weekdays in June, so plan ahead and get that reservation. Consider an early morning return to the bald for sunrise; you'll almost definitely have the place to yourself.

From the bald, the hike returns along the same path.

TRILLIUM GAP TRAIL
Distance: 13.4 miles round-trip
Duration: Overnight
Challenge: Difficult
Elevation Change: 3100ft

This challenging hike takes you behind beautiful Grotto Falls, through old-growth forest and some of the park's finest wildflower areas all the way to the summit of Mt Le Conte. Prearrange lodging at Le Conte Lodge or obtain a reservation to spend the night in the Mt Le Conte Shelter before departing.

The **Grotto Falls** (p96) day hike gives a detailed description of the first 1.3 miles of this hike. The trailhead lies 1.7 miles along the one-way Roaring Fork Motor Nature Trail. The passage to lovely Grotto Falls, which spills from an overhang to allow the path to pass behind, is well maintained and easy.

From the falls the trail turns into a narrow and rocky affair as it starts to ascend in earnest. You'll pass through a verdant mature forest ruled by birches and huge yellow buckeyes. A mile from the falls, great boulders make their appearance. Use caution while crossing the creek through the boulder field, as it is particularly slippery.

Soon you'll begin to see the grassy patches along the trail that signal your arrival at **Trillium Gap**. Here American beech trees dominate, and dense grass blankets the ground. You'll pass the junction with the Brushy Mountain Trail (an excellent 0.8-mile side trip to the summit and back).

From here it is a steep and rocky 3.6-mile ascent to the Le Conte summit. Moss and lichen replace the carpet of grass, and spruce and fir trees come into the mix. The hiking is difficult, but the knowledge that you are approaching the summit of Great Smoky's crown jewel should fill you with a sense of expectation that assuages the difficulty of the climb.

When you finally arrive, **Le Conte Lodge** (p117) will be on the right. If you are lucky enough to have reservations at the lodge, you'll be in heaven. If not, take some time to explore this special place before heading on to your home for the night, the **Mt Le Conte Shelter** (p117), a short distance to the east on The Boulevard. Advance reservations are required for this rationed shelter.

APPALACHIAN TRAIL EAST
Distance: 31.6 miles round-trip
Duration: 4 days
Challenge: Difficult
Elevation Change: 4000ft

The storied **Appalachian Trail** (p40) is an irresistible draw for many hikers. For some it's the only reason they come to the park. Seventy of the AT's 2174 miles pass through the park, and many through-hikers consider these to be the highlight of the entire trail. For the most part, the trail follows the crest of the Great Smoky Mountains, shadowing the shared border between North Carolina and Tennessee.

When hiking at these elevations and distances, it is crucial that you pack for weather that can dip well below freezing. Unless you are truly experienced at cold weather hiking, attempting to make the crossing during the winter months is not recommended. An excellent time to make the trip is in September or October, when traffic on the trails has dissipated somewhat and autumn leaves are at their finest. In October, however, snow should be expected.

Hikers on the AT sleep in backcountry shelters spaced 3 to 8 miles apart; reservations are required (see Backcountry Camping, p106). During the summer, you'll likely need to make the necessary consecutive reservations well in advance.

The following summary should not be used as your sole source of information about the hike; it is meant merely to provide an overview of what to expect along the way. You would do well to photocopy the pertinent sections from *The Thru-Hiker's Handbook* by Dan 'Wingfoot' Bruce, or carry a copy of *Hiking Trails of the Smokies* and the National Geographic/Trails Illustrated map.

This hike takes you from Newfound Gap to the Davenport Gap Shelter at the northeast border of the park. Some stalwart lunatics complete this hike in two days; just smile and wave as they whoosh by. It's far more pleasant to take your time and drink in the scenery like honeyed wine.

If you have two vehicles at your disposal, park one at the Davenport Gap ranger station to use as a shuttle. If you need to procure the services of a commercial shuttle service, try **A Walk in the Woods** (☎ 865-436-8283; 4413 E Scenic Dr, Gatlinburg, TN), **Mountain Mama's** (☎ 828-486-5995; Waterville Rd, Hartford, TN) or **Standing Bear Farm** (☎ 423-487-0014; 4255 Green Corner Rd, Hartford, TN).

Day 1

The first 4 miles of the trail are covered in detail elsewhere in this book; see the **Charlies Bunion** (p100) day hike. From Charlies Bunion continue east on the AT for a half mile to **Dry Sluice Gap Trail**. You'll cross the scenic jagged ridges of **The Sawteeth**. After the cumulative 4-mile climb from Charlies Bunion, the trail veers sharply south and drops along **Laurel Top**, with excellent views along the way. At 8.9 miles you'll reach **Bradley View**, where you can look down on the Bradley Fork watershed. At 10.5 miles you'll head south on Hughes Ridge Trail and hike 0.2 mile farther to **Pecks Corner Shelter** for a good night's sleep.

Day 2

On your second day, return to the AT and begin what is one of the least-traveled stretches of trail in the park. After about a mile of hiking, you'll reach the first point of interest, **Eagle Rocks**, with views of the Middle Prong watershed. After descending from the rocks and climbing across **Mt Sequoyah**, you'll enjoy a lengthy descent before ascending again over **Mt Chapman**. From here it's a relatively short trek to the remote outpost of **Tricorner Knob Shelter**, at the junction of Balsam Mountain Trail. After a taxing but exhilarating 5.3-mile day, you'll be ready for some R&R.

Day 3

Today you will travel 8.4 miles to Cosby Knob Shelter. Eat a good breakfast and head out to pass just below the summit of **Mt Guyot** (6621ft), the park's second-highest peak after Clingmans Dome. After hiking by two good springs, the next mountain you will conquer is **Old Black** (6356ft). Soon after you will enter an open area, passing by a helicopter landing pad. Take a moment to look back at where you've come from, and admire the twin peaks of Mt Guyot and Old Black.

The next several miles provide a welcome descent. You'll pass junctions with the Snake Den Ridge and Camel Gap Trails, then climb 2.5 miles, followed by a downhill cruise to the **Cosby Knob Shelter**.

Day 4
In the morning, don fresh socks if you have them and head down the trail to the junction with Low Gap Trail. From here you'll make your final climb of the hike to the junction with Mt Cammerer Trail. Then it's all downhill or level to trail's end at Davenport Gap. If you deposited a vehicle at the ranger station, turn right on Hwy 284 and walk about a mile to the town of Mount Sterling. Here you will reenter the park and walk 0.2 mile to the ranger station.

OTHER ACTIVITIES

While hiking is certainly one of the most rewarding endeavors in Great Smoky Mountains National Park, you won't want to miss some of its other pleasures. There are empty roads to be biked, fish to be caught and horses to be nuzzled. Anyone with the slightest curiosity about the natural world would be hard-pressed to find a better place to witness the astonishing diversity of life. You can learn a lot at the park's many educational opportunities, including guided walks, evening programs and living-history demonstrations. Kids can become a Junior Ranger or go to summer camp. You'll wonder why you didn't allocate a month or more to your Great Smoky experience.

Cycling

Bicycles are welcome on most park roads, with the exception of the Roaring Fork Motor Nature Trail. However, it is important that you choose your road wisely. Due to steep terrain, narrow byways and heavy car traffic, many park roads are not well suited for safe or enjoyable riding. Great Smoky has no mountain biking trails. Bicycles are allowed only on the **Gatlinburg Trail**, the **Oconaluftee River Trail** and the **Lower Deep Creek Trail**. They are prohibited on all other park trails.

By far the best place for a carefree bicycle tour is **Cades Cove** (p85), particularly when the road is closed to cars (Wednesday and Sunday before 10am from mid-May to late September). The road is also closed to motor vehicle traffic at sunset each evening, and adventurous souls sometimes steal a moonlight ride. These are by far the best times to experience the beauty and history of this singular place. Devoid of the noisy traffic jams that are usually the norm, the cove is a quiet place that more closely resembles its historical roots as a pioneer farming community. As pedal power propels you through the rolling hills past rustic 19th century homesites, you may hear the gobbling of wild turkeys or see a multitude of deer.

All ages can enjoy this safe, pleasant road, although the trip can be a challenge for inexperienced bikers or those with physical limitations, due to its handful of moderate climbs. Drinking water and restrooms are available only at the Cable Mill area, 6 miles into the loop. **Cades Cove Bicycle Rentals** (☎ 865-448-9034; ⏰ 7am-7pm Wed & Sat, 9am-7pm other days mid-May–late Sep), adjacent to the Cades Cove Campground store, rents old-school one-speed bikes with pedal brakes for $4 an hour.

Bicycling the cove will satisfy most folks, but to a serious mountain biker the excursion may seem like little more than an hors d'oeuvre. Luckily, there are several lightly used gravel roads where you can still get that desirable coating of dust and sweat. You'll find two good routes in the Cades Cove area. **Rich Mountain Rd** is a narrow, winding affair that descends from the park's northern border to Cades Cove Loop Rd. If you start at the park border, you will climb 3.3 miles to an excellent view of Cades Cove and then roar down 3.4 miles to the cove. Leading south from a point near the Cades Cove Visitor Center, **Parson Branch Rd** travels through rhododendron tunnels to the Gregory Bald Trailhead (3.3 miles) and then descends to Hwy 129. With some substantial backtracking, it's possible to ride both routes back to back.

AREA BICYCLE SHOPS

The following shops offer everything from equipment sales and repair services to chapped-butt cream:

✔ **Cycle Quest** (☎ 865-429-5558; 3406 Teaster Lane; Pigeon Forge, TN; ☻ 10am-6pm Mon-Sat)

✔ **Shifting Gears** (☎ 865-908-1999; 636 Middle Creek Rd; Sevierville, TN; ☻ 10am-6pm Mon-Fri, 10am-2pm Sat)

The following shops also offer bicycle rentals and tours:

✔ **Bio-Wheels** (☎ 828-236-2453 or 888-881-2453; 76 Biltmore Ave, Asheville, NC; ☻ 10am-6:30pm Mon-Sat, 1-5pm Sun)

✔ **Nantahala Outdoor Center** (☎ 828-488-2446 or 800-232-7238; 13077 Hwy 19W, Bryson City, NC; ☻ 8am-7pm Apr-Aug, 8am-5pm Sep-Mar)

Other lightly used unpaved roads to consider are **Mt Sterling Rd**, which runs 23 miles from Big Creek to Cove Creek near Cataloochee, and **Balsam Mountain Rd**, which connects Balsam Mountain Campground to the Cherokee Indian Reservation. Both are strenuous routes that may require auto shuttles.

Horseback Riding

A staggering – or should we say galloping – 550 miles of the park's hiking trails are open to horses and their humans. Riding is restricted to trails specifically designated for horse use; off-trail or cross-country riding is strictly prohibited. Check the official park trail map to locate authorized trails and bone up on backcountry riding rules and regulations. It's available for $1 at any visitor center, or by download at www.nps.gov/grsm/pphtml/maps.html.

If you've got your own mount, **horse camps** are open April through October. Reservations are required and may be made through the **National Park Reservation Service** ☎ 800-365-2267, code GRE; www.nps.reservations.gov; ☻ 10am-10pm). Record your reservation number – need it when you register at the horse camp.

Five **drive-in horse camps** (☎ 865-436-1230) provide ready access to the park's backcountry horse trails: Cades Cove (Anthony Creek), Big Creek, Cataloochee, Round Bottom and Tow String. Fees are $20 per site, except for Big Creek, which is $25. Fees are not accepted at the horse camp; you must pay for the site when you make your reservation. Each campsite is limited to six people and four horses. Sites vary, but in general you are permitted to have two vehicles and two trailers (horse or camping) at each site. Sites have picnic tables, grills, designated parking spaces, refuse containers, hitch racks and space to pitch a tent or two. Big Creek has flush toilets with cold water. Other horse camps have portable toilets and no drinking water. Water is available for horses either in the campground or at a nearby stream.

Riders may also use **designated campsites** located on trails open to horse use; however, some backcountry campsites must be reserved in advance (see Backcountry Camping, p115). These sites are indicated on the park's trail map.

Not traveling with a horse? Three commercial stables located in or near the park will set you up with a mount, and they offer guided horseback tours from mid-March through late November. Weight limits and age restrictions may apply. Payment is accepted in cash or traveler's checks only.

Located near the entrance of the Cades Cove Loop Rd, the privately run **Cades Cove Riding Stables** (☎ 865-448-6286; 🕘 9am-5pm) leads groups of two to nine people on a 3-mile tour through the foothills (1hr $20). It also operates frequent morning and evening narrated hayrides (1-2hrs $8) and carriage rides (30min $7) in and around Cades Cove.

Smoky Mountain Riding Stables (☎ 865-436-5634; 🕘 9am-5pm) has been an institution since the park was founded. Guided tours of one or two hours pass through beautiful wooded scenery (4/8 miles $20/38). Reservations are required. The stables are 4 miles east of Gatlinburg on Hwy 321.

At the entrance to Smokemont Campground, the smaller **Smokemont Riding Stables** (☎ 828-497-2373; 🕘 9am-4pm) leads a 2 1/2-hour waterfall tour ($48) and a one-hour tour ($20) on forested trails.

Outside the park borders, try one of the following operations:

Next to Heaven Stables (☎ 865-448-9150, 800-407-2231; www.nexttoheaven.com; Hwy 321 near Townsend, TN; 🕘 10am-5pm Mon-Sat) Come here for unguided horse rentals along onsite trails.

Davy Crockett Riding Stables (☎ 865-448-6411; 505 Old Cades Cove Rd, Townsend, TN; 🕘 9am-5pm) Davy Crockett specializes in group trips but also offers guided rides for individuals and families. Overnight pack trips in the Smokies are also available.

Walden Creek Horse Stables (☎ 865-429-0411; www.waldencreekstables.com; 2709 Walden Creek Rd, Pigeon Forge, TN) One- to eight-hour rides on a 500-acre property pass by mountain streams and views. Reservations recommended.

Fontana Riding Stables (☎ 828-298-2211; Hwy 28 at Fontana Dam, near Bryson City, NC; 🕘 seasonally) Two- to four-hour and all-day trips afford grand views of Fontana Dam.

Nantahala National Forest (☎ 828-479-6431) For those traveling with their own horses, these public lands offer miles of trails and stable facilities.

Fishing

The park boasts 2115 miles of streams within its boundaries, and any angler will tell you that it's a fishing paradise. The park protects one of the last wild trout habitats in the eastern US and offers a wide variety of experiences, from remote headwater trout streams to large, cool-water bass streams. Most waterways remain at or near their carrying capacity of fish and provide good fishing action throughout the year. Fishing is permitted from 30 minutes before official sunrise to 30 minutes after official sunset.

Great Smoky has had an active brook trout restoration program since 1987. As part of an evolving conservation methodology, the fishing of brook trout is once again allowed on eight streams within the park, following a lengthy prohibition. That said, you can catch, but you cannot keep – all brook trout must be released (see They Shall Be Released, p47). Having a brook trout in your bag is a big no-no.

Rainbow and brown trout and smallmouth bass up to 7 inches long may be kept, but you cannot keep more than five fish total (in any combination) per day. Rock (or 'red eye') bass are a dime a dozen, and in fact you can keep up to 20.

Fishing is permitted only by the use of one handheld rod (sorry, no dynamite). Only artificial flies or lures with a single hook may be used, so please spare the worms. Use of any type of fish bait or for that matter those alluring artificial scents, is strictly *verboten*.

A dapper conservation officer wearing rubber boots may ask you to produce a valid fishing license or permit from either Tennessee or North Carolina. Either state license is valid throughout the park, and no trout stamp is required. Fishing licenses and permits are not available in the park, but may be purchased in nearby towns. Special permits are required to fish in Gatlinburg and Cherokee.

Detailed information, including a complete list of regulations and a map of fishable park waters, is available at any visitor center or ranger station. For more information, pick up the *Great Smoky Mountains Fishing Regulations* brochure at any visitor center or ranger station.

In neighboring towns are these three excellent fishing outfitters; each sells equipment and provides expert fishing guide service.

Little River Outfitters (☎ 865-448-9459; 7807 E Lamar Alexander Pkwy; Townsend, TN)

Smoky Mountain Angler (☎ 865-436-8746; www.smokymountainangler.com; 376 E Parkway; Gatlinburg, TN)

CCS Fishing Outfitters (☎ 828-497-1555; 626 Tsali Blvd/Hwy 441, Cherokee, NC)

Cross-Country Skiing

While some grumble when roads close due to snow, others find reason to rejoice. Each year, cross-country skiers and snowshoers take full advantage of the several roads that close for the season, and they get downright giddy when others are closed due to a fresh dumping of snow. The average annual snowfall at Newfound Gap is a whopping 69 inches, whereas the park's lower elevations receive an average of only 1 inch four or five times each winter.

The most popular spot for laying tracks on the powder is **Clingmans Dome Rd**, which is conveniently closed December to March. Visitors must bring their own equipment since there are no roadside facilities.

Watching Wildlife

You're going to need some field glasses. You're going to need a field guide. And yes, you're going to need a field (although the forest is just as good). Once these requirements are filled, you need to sit yourself down and wait. With as many as 100,000 higher life forms making their home in Great Smoky, you cannot inhabit a space without sharing it with another living thing, whether it's a fungus, fish, millipede, butterfly, spider or something even more enthralling. Birdsong echoes through every cove and holler, bears lumber across the trail and river otters – after a long absence – have once again taken up residence in select streams.

Anyone can find a fern, but to encounter something furry takes patience and a little know-how. Many animals express their wild natures at night, so keep your eyes peeled early in the morning and at last light. And remember to look up: Many animals pass the day in the trees. Also seek out the wide-open spaces, as in **Cades Cove** or **Cataloochee**, where animals are not as likely to blend into the foliage.

The best places to spot birds are...almost anywhere! The **Roaring Fork Nature Trail**, **Cades Cove Loop Rd** and the trails leaving from **Newfound Gap** are fine places to start your birding odyssey. As you pursue your winged muses through cove and forest, you'll encounter like-minded souls in all corners of the park, burbling effusively about the mnemonic phrasings of the yellow warbler or arguing over whether the cedar waxwing has a pointed, rounded or wedge-shaped tail. Birds of a feather...

Ranger Programs

Great Smoky Mountains National Park is a model for the breadth and depth of its educational programs. On any given day in the summer, rangers conduct guided nature and history walks, films, talks and slide shows. Multiple events are held each day of the week, ranging from gristmill tours and demonstrations to naturalist hikes, hayrides and full-moon strolls.

Evening programs take place at the park's larger campgrounds. Regular season programs begin in early June and continue until October. For spring program schedules, check bulletin board postings or at the visitor centers. Programs include amphitheater slide shows and talks, twilight strolls and Junior Ranger events (see Kids' Activities). **Guided walks** get going in early June. Destinations include homesites, waterfalls and forests.

Living-history demonstrations are also integral to the park's educational programming. You might encounter a blacksmith at Cable Mill pounding out a horseshoe, or a miller at Mingus Mill grinding corn into cornmeal and wheat into flour. The interpreters at Mountain Farm Museum spin wool, weave cloth, forge tools, make sorghum into molasses and perform and explain the daily tasks of mountain people.

Check the park newspaper, *Smokies Guide*, and the biweekly ranger-led program schedule for details on the location and time of programs. Both are available at most campgrounds, ranger stations and visitor centers.

Classes

The **Great Smoky Mountains Institute at Tremont** (☎ 865-448-6709; www.gsmit.org) is a year-round residential environmental education center offering workshops and programs for everyone, from grade-school children to Elderhostel groups and teachers. Programs may include hikes, slide shows on flora and fauna, mountain music, living-history displays and wildlife demonstrations. A recent class catalog included such offerings as nocturnal ecology, photography workshops and a 10-day trek for teens. A fee is charged for most programs.

The **Smoky Mountain Field School** (☎ 865-974-0150; www.outreach.utk.edu/smoky) offers weekend workshops, hikes and adventures for adults and families throughout the year. In cooperation with the NPS and the University of Tennessee, experts on Smoky Mountain plants, wildlife and history lead programs. Tuition is charged.

Kids' Activities

For kids between the ages of five and 12, becoming a **Junior Ranger** truly is as cool as it sounds. Here's how it works: purchase an inexpensive Junior Ranger booklet at a visitor center and have kids complete the fun park-related activities. After a ranger checks their work, they'll receive a cool badge at a campfire ceremony.

Speaking of campfires, on summer evenings at Cades Cove, Elkmont and Smokemont Campgrounds, **storytellers** spin tall tales about early settlers, the Cherokee and ghosts. Check the *Smokies Guide* for more information.

Scattered throughout the park are 10 self-guided **nature trails** with cheerfully illustrated pamphlets filled with fascinating facts and trivia. One with real potential for interesting a kid is the Cades Cove Nature Trail, which tells how early settlers scratched out their sustenance from the forest.

For a great early evening excursion with your family, join the famous **hayrides** ($8; ☼ seasonal) through Cades Cove. Meet at the Cades Cove Riding Stables (p112) at 6pm for a two-hour ride through the valley.

Every summer the Great Smoky Mountains Institute at Tremont conducts **summer camp programs** (www.gsmit.org/Programs/camps.html) for kids ages nine to 17. These range from a day camp for ages six to 10 ($180) to the 10-day Teen High Adventure Trek for ages 13 to 17 ($730).

SLEEPING

Great Smoky Mountains National Park provides varied camping options, but only one place where you can get a room, and you have to hike to the top of a mountain to enjoy this privilege. Consider surrounding towns like

Gatlinburg (p121), Pigeon Forge (p128) and Cherokee (p139) for more lodging options.

Camping

The National Park Service maintains developed campgrounds at 10 locations in the park. Each campground has restrooms with cold running water and flush toilets, but there are no showers or electrical or water hookups in the park. Each individual campsite has a fire grate and picnic table.

During summer and fall, sites at Elkmont, Smokemont and Cades Cove may be **reserved** (☎ 800-365-2267; www.reservations.nps.gov). Reservations are accepted only between May 15 and October 31. Sites may be reserved up to five months in advance. All other campgrounds are first-come, first served.

No more than six people may occupy a campsite. Two tents or an RV and one tent are allowed per site. The maximum stay during summer and fall is seven days; in the off-season it's 14 days. Pets are allowed in campgrounds as long as they are restrained on a leash or otherwise confined at all times. Quiet hours last from 10pm to 6am.

Park campgrounds are located in areas frequented by bears and other wildlife. All food, coolers, utensils, stoves, etc, must be stored out of sight in a closed vehicle when not in use. Do not throw food scraps or packaging in fire rings. Feeding wildlife is prohibited.

For information on backcountry camping, see Backcountry Hikes (p106).

Abrams Creek (campsite $12; Mar-Oct) This small, remote campground on the western edge of the park takes a bit of effort to get to, but you'll be well compensated for your journey. Half of the 16 sites face pretty Abrams Creek; the others are arranged along the edge of the woods. Abrams Creek is a popular fishing spot. From here you can hike to Abrams Falls (5 miles round-trip), one of the park's most isolated and beautiful gushers. RVs are welcome if they're no longer than 12ft. The campground lies 7 miles north of Hwy 129 via Happy Valley Rd.

Balsam Mountain (campsite $14; May-Oct) This small highlands campground is considered by many to be the park's most lovely, thanks to its privileged placement within an 'island' forest of red spruce and Fraser firs. Though the 46 campsites are somewhat small, the upside to this is that it discourages behemoth RVs from roosting (though RVs up to 30ft are allowed). A self-guided nature trail, where you can learn more about this special forest, leaves from the campground. The campground is 8 miles from the Blue Ridge Parkway via Heintooga Ridge Rd. In the morning you can return to Oconaluftee via the one-way gravel Balsam Mountain Rd, which begins its descent to the lowlands at the end of Heintooga Ridge Rd, a short distance from the campground.

Big Creek (campsite $12; Mar-Oct) The smallest of Great Smoky's campgrounds is a walk-in affair used mostly by hikers. RVs are not welcome here. Five of the 12 sites sit beside the cacophonous Big Creek. You must haul your gear from the car a distance of 100 to 300ft. The nearest payphone is at the ranger station, a mile from the campground. The Big Creek Trail provides a great day hike along a fire road to a wonderful swimming spot called Midnight Hole (1.5 miles) and another half mile to Mouse Creek Falls. To get here, take Tennessee exit 451 off I-40, then proceed upstream beside the Pigeon River to the ranger station.

Cades Cove (Map 2, p154; campsite $14-17; open year-round) This campground is always full on summer weekends and during the autumn leaf-peeping season, but there's plenty of room the rest of the year. The 161 sites are shady but situated a mite too close together. In late afternoon the place takes on a downtown feel as everyone hops on bicycles or socializes. In the evenings the Cades Cove amphitheater provides entertainment in the form of ranger programs. A small camp store serves the itinerant camper community, but its offerings are meager. Several hiking trails depart from the campground, and anglers find success in upper Abrams Creek and Forge Creek. RVs up to 35ft are allowed. The campground is 6 miles southwest of the Townsend Wye via Laurel Creek Rd.

Cataloochee (campsite $12; ✆ Mar-Oct) This remote campground in a forest of hemlock and white pine has spacious campsites arranged off a loop road; six of the 27 sites lie along the excellent fishing waters of Cataloochee Creek. The campground fills up on summer evenings. Nearby is the trailhead for the popular 7.4-mile round-trip Boogerman Trail, which loops among old-growth forests and past old homesites. The maximum RV length is 31ft. Take exit 20 off I-40, go west on Hwy 276 to Cove Creek Rd and follow it to Cataloochee Rd.

Cosby (campsite $14; ✆ Mar-Oct) This large, beautifully forested campground is a good alternative to the heavily used Elkmont and Cades Cove sites; it's rarely if ever crowded. Several loops are lined with 157 spacious campsites that afford a remarkable degree of privacy. Bathrooms are conveniently located throughout the grounds. RVs up to 25ft are welcome. Hiking trails leave from every direction; options include the Lower Mt Cammerer Trail to Sutton Ridge Overlook and the Gabes Mountain Trail. The campground lies off Hwy 32 near the Tennessee town of Cosby.

Deep Creek (campsite $14; ✆ Apr-Oct) Near Bryson City, this medium-sized family campground with 108 sites offers a good variety of choices and splendid opportunities for hiking and bird-watching. Section C features creekside tent-only sites; section D, a loop road through the woods, affords more privacy. The waters of Deep Creek give much joy to inner-tubers and anglers. Near the entrance to the campground is the village of Big Creek, with a snack bar and tube rentals. Nearby hikes include Juney Whank Falls (0.6 miles round-trip) and Indian Creek Falls (1.5 miles round-trip). The maximum RV length is 26ft. To get there from the depot in Bryson City, turn right onto Depot St, then left on Ramseur Rd, then immediately right on Deep Creek Rd.

Elkmont (Little River Rd; campsite $14-20; ✆ Mar-Nov) The largest campground in the park and the one closest to Gatlinburg, Elkmont features wooded sites along the Little River. During peak season the 220 sites often fill to capacity by noon. Even though it's larger than Cades Cove Campground, this is a much quieter place. Sections A and B tend to be the most crowded. Nearby hiking trails include the Elkmont Nature Trail, Little River Trail and Jakes Creek Trail. The maximum RV length is 32ft.

Look Rock (Foothills Pkwy W; campsite $14; ✆ May-Oct) Due to its out-of-the-way location, this campsite always has sites available. The 92 sites are fairly small, but chances are you won't have neighbors. Some sites are tucked away in the trees and are quite lovely. Across Foothills Pkwy from the campground is the Look Rock observation tower. RVs no longer than 35ft are allowed. Foothills Pkwy W begins at the intersection of Hwy 321 just north of Townsend.

Smokemont (Newfound Gap Rd; campsite $14-17; ✆ year-round) Near Cherokee, this large and attractive 140-site campground along the wooded banks of the Oconaluftee River is open year-round. Sections B and C feature sunny creekside spots; section F is for RVs (up to 27ft) only. Hiking opportunities include the Smokemont Loop Trail (p99) and a nature trail.

GROUP CAMPING

Seven park campgrounds provide group sites. Each tent-only site accommodates a minimum of eight people, is available seasonally and requires reservations. The maximum length of stay is seven nights. Call the NPS reservation line or hit the web to make **reservations** (☎ 800-365-2267; reservations.nps.gov) for any group campsite. Campsites may be reserved up to five months in advance.

- **Big Creek** (1 site; $40; ⓨ Mar-Oct)
- **Cades Cove** (4 sites; $33-63; ⓨ year-round)
- **Cataloochee** (3 sites; $30; ⓨ Mar-Oct)
- **Cosby** (3 sites; $20; ⓨ Mar-Oct)
- **Deep Creek** (3 sites; $30; ⓨ Apr-Oct)
- **Elkmont** (5 sites; $23-48; ⓨ Mar-Oct)
- **Smokemont** (3 sites; $23-33; ⓨ year-round)

BACKCOUNTRY CAMPING

To stay at a backcountry site, you must obtain a free backcountry permit; many backcountry sites require advance reservations. For more information, see p106.

Park campgrounds are located in areas frequented by bears and other wildlife. All food, coolers, utensils, stoves, etc, must be stored out of sight in a closed vehicle when not in use. Backpackers must suspend their food and garbage by using either ropes or the cable systems found at all backcountry sites. Do not throw food scraps or packaging in fire rings. Feeding wildlife is prohibited.

Lodging

Great Smoky Mountains National Park has only one place where a visitor can sleep overnight in a cozy permanent structure with hot meals. Although you cannot drive there, and the hike to the lodge is more challenging than first-timers often expect, **Le Conte Lodge** (☎ 865-429-5704, fax 865-774-0045; www.lecontelodge.com; summit of Mt Le Conte; mailing address 250 Apple Valley Rd, Sevierville TN 37862) is such a special place that nearly everyone who passes a day or two there makes a solemn vow to return.

Situated at the top of the crown jewel mountain of the Great Smokies, the lodge can accommodate 50 guests per night, housed in rustic cabins or group sleeping lodges. The cabins have upper and lower double bunk beds and sleep two couples or a family of four to five. The lodges accommodate 10 to 13 people each. You'll have to live without electricity or showers; only recently did flush toilets make their first appearance. Old-timey washbasins are standard equipment in the accommodations. Kerosene lamps provide illumination, but definitely pack a flashlight. Leave your laptop down in the valley lest you become the fodder for ridicule.

Hearty all-you-can-eat family-style breakfasts and dinners are served in the lodge dining room; lunch is included for guests staying more than one night.

The lodge is generally open from late March through November. You must book your lodging many months in advance. The lodge begins taking reservations on October 1 for the following year's season. Weekend reservations book first, and the entire season is generally booked by November 1. Reservation cancellations are not uncommon, so if you have no reservation and would like to find space on short notice, try your luck by calling the office; the lodge might be able to accommodate you.

Backpackers who don't want to stay at the lodge (or who don't find any room at the inn) can slumber in a three-sided park service shelter; it's in a small clearing near High Top.

Cabin **rates** (per person adult/child 10 & under $92/74) include meals. The two-bedroom lodges sleeping up to eight people cost $488, with additional fees for up to two extra people (per person $62) and meals (adult/child $31/22). The three-bed-

THE HOUSE THAT JACK BUILT

The first permanent structure on the top of Mt Le Conte was a 15-by-20ft cabin built in 1925 by early park conservationist Paul Adams. It was constructed of notched fir and spruce logs and had one window and door. A drum heater stove in the center of the room provided heat. A passionate naturalist who has been credited with the discovery of new bird species (including the golden crowned kinglet and others considered 'lost' to zoologists), Adams was the first caretaker of the camp that would grow into Le Conte Lodge.

In 1926 Jack Huff and Will Ramsay arrived on the scene and immediately began construction on the first lodge, a 34-by-24ft cabin that was soon christened 'The House That Jack Built.' Thirty-two bunk beds were installed to sleep guests four abreast – fully clothed – with no separate accommodations for men and women. The stove's fire burned through the night, and the windows and doors were kept open regardless of the weather.

Jack Huff and his wife, Pauline, continued to operate the lodge until 1960. Today the lodge is a considerably larger compound that includes several small cabins, a dining hall and recreation hall. Running water is pumped from nearby Basin Spring. Supplies are carried to the top of the mountain three times weekly on the Trillium Gap Trail by llama pack trains; these gentle beasts inherited the job from horses because of the minimal environmental impact that their padded hooves exert on the trails.

room lodges sleeping up to 13 people cost $732, with an additional fee for up to one extra person (per person $60) and meals (adult/child $31/22).

Plan your packing list carefully. The temperature has never reached the 80°F mark atop Mt Le Conte, and when the sun goes down, the temperature drops precipitously. During the summer the nighttime temperature may drop to 40°F; in spring and fall the thermometer may drop into the teens, with snow falling. Bring layered, lightweight clothing and a sweater or jacket, and certainly a poncho or rain gear. Sturdy, broken-in hiking shoes or boots and socks are essential for a comfortable hike up the mountain.

Five trails access the lodge. Approximate hiking times given below assume that the hiker is in good condition and doesn't dawdle along the way. To increase your enjoyment of the trek, give yourself extra time to enjoy the wonders of nature along the way while making sure that you arrive in time to get situated at the lodge before the 6pm dinner hour.

Alum Cave Trail 4.5 miles, four hours (short but steep)
Rainbow Falls Trail 6.7 miles, five hours.
Trillium Gap Trail (p108) 6.7 miles, five hours.
Bullhead Trail 7.2 miles, five hours.
Boulevard Trail 8 miles, six hours.

EATING

Nuts and berries notwithstanding, there's nothing to eat in Great Smoky Mountains National Park, save for guests-only fare at Le Conte Lodge, vending machines at Sugarlands Visitor Center and the meager offerings sold at the Cades Cove Campground store. Campers must bring their own food; see Essentials, opposite, for information about grocery stores. Luckily, there are lots of restaurant options in the surrounding towns. See Around Great Smoky (p121) for listings.

AUTOMOTIVE SERVICES

Auto repair services can be easily found in Gatlinburg, Pigeon Forge, Townsend and Cherokee. The closest offices of the **American Automobile Association** are in Maryville, Tennessee (☎ 865-637-1910; 715 W Lamar Alexander Pkwy; ☽ 8:30am-5pm Mon-Fri), and Asheville, North Carolina (☎ 828-274-2641; 1000 Merrimon Ave; ☽ 8:30am-5pm Mon-Fri).

BOOKS

The **Great Smoky Mountains Association** (☎ 888-898-9102; www.smokiesstore.org) offers a wide range of books, maps and guides, plus individual USGS topographic quad maps.

EMERGENCIES

The **park communications office** (☎ 865-436-9171) can relay emergency messages for park visitors; those who receive emergency messages are listed at visitor centers.
Fire or police emergencies (☎ 911 or 865-436-9171)
Gatlinburg police (☎ 865-436-5181)
Cherokee police (☎ 828-497-4131)

EQUIPMENT

For camping and hiking gear, head to **The Happy Hiker** (☎ 865-436-6000 or 800-445-3701; 905 River Road, Ste 5, Gatlinburg, TN) or **Black Dome Mountain Sports** (☎ 828-251-2001; 140 Tunnel Rd, Asheville, NC). **The Day Hiker** (☎ 865-430-0970; 634 Parkway, Ste 1, Gatlinburg, TN) sells equipment and offers advice tailored specifically for day hikers.

For fishing supplies and expert angling advice, try **Little River Outfitters** (☎ 865-448-9459; 7807 E Lamar Alexander Pkwy, Townsend, TN), **Smoky Mountain Angler** (☎ 865-436-8746; www.smokymountainangler.com; 376 E Parkway, Gatlinburg, TN), and **CCS Fishing Outfitters** (☎ 828-497-1555; 626 Tsali Blvd/Hwy 441, Cherokee, NC).

GROCERIES

Food Lion (☎ 828-497-4737; Hwy 441 Business, Cherokee, NC) has everything you need for your traveler's larder except beer or wine. In Pigeon Forge the modern **Food City** (☎ 865-453-4977; 3625 Parkway) features a complete selection of food, a deli, hard-to-find dry ice, brew and wine.

Townsend's best grocery store, **The Village Market** (☎ 865-448-3010; 7945 Lamar Alexander Pkwy/Hwy 73) has a full deli and decent beer selection.

INTERNET ACCESS

Gatlinburg, Pigeon Forge, Townsend and Cherokee each have public libraries offering free Internet access.

LOST & FOUND

Report lost items and turn in found ones at visitor centers. Also try the **park communications office** (☎ 865-436-9171).

MEDICAL SERVICES

First-aid facilities are available at visitor centers and at park head-quarters. Hospitals can be found in **Sevierville** (Ft Sanders–Sevier Medical Center; ☎ 865-453-7111; Middle Creek Rd, 15 miles north of Gatlin-burg), **Maryville** (Blount Memorial Hospital; ☎ 865-983-7211; Hwy 321, 25 miles north of Cades Cove) and **Bryson City** (Swain County Hospital; ☎ 828-488-2155; 10 miles southeast of Oconaluftee Visitor Center).

MONEY

Gatlinburg, Pigeon Forge, Townsend and Cherokee have 24-hour ATMs and banks with foreign currency exchange. Maggie Valley and Bryson City have ATMs but no exchange services.

POSTAL SERVICE

Visitor centers provide mailboxes but do not sell postage stamps. Post offices can be found in the surrounding towns.

RELIGIOUS SERVICES

Nondenominational Christian worship services are held on Sundays in summer at several park locations. Check the park newspaper, *Smokies Guide*, for more information.

SHOWERS

Park campgrounds do not have showers. Many people freshen up in the nearest stream, while others stop by to shower at commercial campgrounds in outlying gateway communities, including:

Lazy Days (☎ 865-448-6061; $3; 8429 Hwy 73, Townsend, TN)
Alpine Hideaway Campground (☎ 865-428-3285; $3; 251 Spring Valley Rd, Pigeon Forge, TN)
Bradley's Campground (☎ 828-497-6051; $3; Acquoni Rd, Cherokee, NC)

TELEPHONES

There are pay phones at Sugarlands and Oconaluftee Visitor Centers, the larger campgrounds and many ranger stations.

AROUND GREAT SMOKY

Fill up your gas tank and your ice chest and cancel next week's appointments. For now, at least, you're going to take it slow. Waiting for you are raging rivers and gentle streams, empty roads and roadside attractions, mountain music, moonshine and marvelous old country inns. You're in country now.

The towns that surround America's most-visited national park run the gamut from industrial-strength tourist traps to sleepy rural communities hidden in the hills. The Tennessee towns of Gatlinburg, Pigeon Forge and Sevierville – known collectively as 'the tourism corridor' – form a continuous swath of development extending from the park border at Gatlinburg all the way to the French Broad River near I-40. To the east of Gatlinburg is the town of Cosby, self-described as the 'moonshine capital of the world,' and southeast is pleasant Maggie Valley, NC; both communities provide privileged access to less-visited parts of Great Smoky.

South of the park is the Qualla Boundary Cherokee Reservation and the town of Cherokee, the main North Carolina portal to Great Smoky. Here you will discover what happened to the Eastern Band of the Cherokee Indian after the cruel Trail of Tears removed most of the tribe from its ancestral homeland. Surrounding the western side of the park is the region known as 'the quiet side of the Smokies', including beautiful Fontana Lake and Cades Cove's amiable neighbor, Townsend, Tennessee.

THE DUKES LIVE ON

Bo and Luke Duke may be long gone from Hazzard County, cutting albums and performing on Broadway, but *The Dukes of Hazzard* spirit lives on in Gatlinburg. Travelers can't miss the Day-Glo orange paint of the 'General Lee,' parked in front of **Cooter's Place** (☎ 865-430-9909; www.cootersplace.com; 157 Parkway). That's right: Cooter, also known as actor Ben Jones, runs this shrine to all things Dukedom, which doubles as an excellent local bluegrass venue and a front for Cooter's Garage Band. Inside are thousands of photos of the TV cast, plus every imaginable gadget made in the image of Hazzard County: Uncle Jesse salt and pepper shakers, Daisy Duke wind socks, Boss Hogg punching bags, Roscoe P Coltrane beverage coasters and a wide-screen TV playing a constant loop of *Dukes of Hazzard* shows. It's truly a religious experience for anyone who remembers jumping through Mom and Dad's car windows as a kid.

GATLINBURG
Map 4, p155 / ☎ 865 / 3400 / elevation 1340ft

As the old saying goes, people vote with their money. In Gatlinburg you see what they have voted for. Namely: pet fashion accessories. Funnel cakes. Robert Kincaid paintings. Sinister necromancer swords. T-shirts identifying a 'Defender of Freedom.' Gatlinburg is a tourist trap baited with fudge.

The 'Burg,' as it is affectionately called by the folks who return year after year, is well loved by families for its 'mountain village' flavor and seemingly endless opportunities for mindless diversion and frivolous amusement. Gatlinburg is not to everyone's taste, but many folks who initially turn up their noses at the horrors of crass commercialism may come to develop a soft spot for this cornball capital of the South. They become mesmerized by taffy-pulling machines, or find their hearts warming at the sight of craftsmen hand-dipping and carving beautiful candles. Newlyweds stroll in perpetual embrace on the Riverwalk – 10,000 grooms marry 10,000 brides here each year at commercial chapels with names like 'Hillbilly Weddings' or 'Cupid's Chapel of Love.' Before long, even the most resolute grump may crack a smile. That is, if he's not stuck in traffic.

Gatlinburg is a gateway town in the truest sense. Sugarlands, the largest visitor center in Great Smoky Mountains National Park, is close enough to reach by foot. After a pancake breakfast, many people spend their days exploring the park, returning in the evenings to dust off and stroll up and down the main drag wearing expressive T-shirts and brand new flip-flops.

History

The town that came to be known as Gatlinburg was settled in the early 19th century by English, Scotch and Irish immigrants, many of whom were Revolutionary War veterans come to claim title to tracts of land allotted to them here in gratitude for their service. Gatlinburg remained a rural backwater well past 1900. As the timber industry gathered steam, the local economy began to change from one based on subsistence farming to one that participated more fully in the changing economics of the South. The formation of the national park revealed the potentials of tourism, and many of the displaced mountain families moved into town to set up shop as craftsmen, mountain guides and hoteliers. Following World War II, Gatlinburg became a tourist boomtown, forever expanding to meet the requirements of folks hungry for fudge, frivolity and fresh air.

DISHONORED NAMESAKE

Gatlinburg is named for one **Radford Gatlin**, an early settler who came to be so detested that he was eventually banished from the community. A general store merchant, Gatlin was successful in his campaign to cajole his neighbors into naming the place Gatlinburg in exchange for assuming the duties of postmaster.

After years of antagonizing everyone within earshot, Gatlin finally drove his long-suffering fellow townspeople over the edge with his pro-Confederacy views. The county voted 1320 to 1 to remain in the Union, and Gatlin's lone dissenting vote earned him a one-way ticket out of town.

Orientation

Gatlinburg sits on the north-central edge of Great Smoky Mountains National Park, just south of Pigeon Forge on Hwy 441. The West Prong of the Little Pigeon River flows through the middle of town, flanked by the Parkway, Gatlinburg's main drag. Ten numbered traffic lights serve as landmarks.

If you want to avoid the fracas and make a beeline to Great Smoky, the scenic Parkway Bypass peels off Hwy 441 north of town and rejoins the main road at the park border near Sugarlands Visitor Center.

Information

The **Gatlinburg Welcome Center** (☎ 865-436-0519 or 800-568-4748; www.gatlinburg.com; ☺ 8am-6pm Mon-Sat, 9am-5pm Sun) is 2 miles outside town on Hwy 441, on the road to Pigeon Forge. This facility also serves as a visitor center for the national park and includes a bookstore. You'll find two smaller centers on the Parkway at traffic lights 3 and 5. Ask for the historic Gatlinburg walking and driving tour pamphlet.

Parking your car on Gatlinburg's busy streets can be a frustrating exercise. Most folks give up quickly and park for free at either of the town's park-and-ride lots – at the Hwy 441 welcome center on the north end of town, and on

Hwy 321 next to the city hall complex. From there the Gatlinburg Trolley will take you just about anywhere in town. The city also operates a number of other parking lots, including two multilevel garages – one next to the downtown welcome center and the other behind Ripley's Aquarium of the Smokies. These facilities charge hourly fees, but the rates are reasonable, and no matter which you choose, you can easily place yourself close to a trolley stop.

Other resources include the following:

Post office (☎ 865-436-5464; 216 E Parkway; ☷ 9am-5pm Mon-Fri, 9am-1pm Sat)

Anna Porter Public Library (☎ 865-436-5588; 207 Cherokee Orchard Rd; ☷ 9am-5pm Mon & Wed-Fri, 9am-8pm Tue, 9am-1pm Sat) Free Internet access.

Gatlinburg police (☎ 865-436-5181)

Fire, ambulance (☎ 911 or 865-436-5112)

Sights

Gatlinburg's sights are for the most part limited to family-oriented tourist attractions. Most of them are mindless pleasures, and some of them are merely mindless. It is a good idea to park your car and explore the town by foot or via the **Gatlinburg Trolley** (p128). Hours of operation listed are for high season; they are curtailed substantially during the winter months.

WHITE OAK FLATS CEMETERY

Established around 1830, this placid, tree-lined cemetery contains the graves of many of Gatlinburg's early settlers and prominent citizens. You'll find it behind the Village Shops. The oldest section of the graveyard is on the left. The old moss-covered gravestones were called 'gray backs' by the mountain people. If no stone carver was available (or affordable), the deceased were sometimes buried with a beeswax-sealed glass jar containing their name, dates of birth and death, and perhaps a picture.

TSALI MONUMENT

The **Tsali Monument** (377 Parkway) commemorates the martyred Cherokee Indian hero Tsali, who, according to legend, gave his life so that some of his people (now known as the Eastern Band of the Cherokee) might remain in their ancestral Smokies. Although Tsali has no direct connection to the city of Gatlinburg, many of its citizens have Cherokee ancestry and hence a spiritual connection to the man and the legend. Knoxville schoolchildren erected the monument in 1939 to mark the 100th anniversary of Tsali's execution.

CHRISTUS GARDENS

Gatlinburg has one truly unique (some would call it bizarre) roadside attraction, beloved by evangelical Christians and pop culture connoisseurs alike. **Christus Gardens** (☎ 865-436-5155; www.christusgardens.com; 510 River Rd; adult/child 6 & over $10/5; ☷ 8am-8pm) is the quintessential wax museum of the Gospel, with more than 100 biblical figures in starched robes depicting the Bible's greatest hits. Da Vinci's *The Last Supper* gets the 3-D treatment, and the head of Christ – carved from a 6-ton slab of marble – seems to follow your movements as you cross the room. It's a miracle! Also on hand is a fine collection of biblical-era coins.

OBER GATLINBURG

That big green sky-tram ascending from the strip is headed to **Ober Gatlinburg** (☎ 865-436-5423; www.obergatlinburg.com; aerial tramway at Parkway light 9; tramway adult/child $9.50/6.50; ☷ 9am-11pm Mon-Sat, 9am-6pm Sun), Gatlinburg's amusement park and ski resort. While experienced snowbirds will agree that the skiing falls well short of spectacular, the slopes are ideal for first-timers. Summertime attractions include an alpine slide, go-carts and year-round indoor ice-skating (a great option during inclement weather). These diversions are priced separately, but an inclusive pass is available (adult/child $18/14). It's possible to drive up the mountain and pay to park, but the best way to go up is the aerial tramway.

RIPLEY ATTRACTIONS

Ripley Entertainment operates five attractions in Gatlinburg, including the Aquarium of the Smokies. Combo tickets are available for all five attractions (adult/child $52/32).

Impressive in scale and impact, the ostentatious **Ripley's Aquarium of the Smokies** (☎ 865-430-8808; Parkway light 5; adult/child/toddler $18/10/4; ☺ 9am-9pm Sun-Thu; 9am-11pm Fri & Sat) is a real crowd-pleaser. Visitors to the Shark Lagoon step onto a slow-moving walkway through a submerged crystal-clear tunnel on the floor of a million-gallon tank, while dispassionate 11ft sharks and thousands of other sea creatures glide by overhead. Other attractions include a piranha tank, a colorful coral reef and a giant Pacific octopus.

Housed in a large building that appears to have been given a couple of whacks with a wrecking ball, **Ripley's Believe It or Not!** (☎ 865-436-5096; Parkway light 7; adult/child 6 & over $14/8; ☺ 9am-midnight) features thousands of unique and unusual artifacts collected from the far corners of the world. All visitors seem to care about, however, are the shrunken heads.

In addition, Ripley's also operates **Davy Crockett Mini Golf** (☎ 865-430-8851; Parkway light 1), **Haunted Adventure** (☎ 865-436-5096; Parkway light 8) and **Moving Theater** (☎ 865-436-5096; Parkway light 8).

GUINNESS WORLD OF RECORDS MUSEUM

For fans of the superlative, **Guinness World of Records Museum** (☎ 865-436-9100; Baskins Square Mall on Parkway; adult/child 6 & over $10/6; ☺ 9am-11pm) boasts the world's most expensive car, the coolest Batmobile and a mannequin of the world's tallest man. Not to be outdone by Christus Gardens, Guinness also appeals to the faithful with a rendition of Noah's Ark.

GATLINBURG SKY LIFT

For more than 50 years, **Gatlinburg Sky Lift** (☎ 865-436-4307; Parkway light 7; adult/child 3 & over $10/8; ☺ 9am-11pm) has whisked visitors off their feet for a ride up the mountain to an elevation of 1800ft, where gorgeous views of the Smokies are enjoyed by all.

SMOKY MOUNTAIN WINERY

While Tennessee probably doesn't spring to mind when the subject is wine, they've been making the stuff here since before your little brother was born. At **Smoky Mountain Winery** (☎ 865-436-7551; 450 Cherry St; admission free; ☺ 10am-7pm Mon-Sat, 10am-6pm Sun) visitors observe the wine-making process and sample the products, among them a reasonably good cabernet sauvignon. In the same complex is the Smoky Mountain Farms Jelly House, which, disappointingly, is not made of jelly but does sell local treats, including a delicious rhubarb jam to make your teeth ache.

HILLBILLY GOLF

Forget the gorgeous Smokies. We know why you really came: to putt a golf ball through an outhouse. At **Hillbilly Golf** (☎ 865-436-7470; Parkway light 2; adult/child 4 & over $8.50/6.50; ☺ 9am-10pm) an incline railway carries visitors 300ft up to a perch above the town.

Activities & Outfitters

For the fly fisherman, every day is the perfect day for 'wading wet and flirtin' with the brookies'. These anglers are easy to spot, they're the ones standing knee-deep in the Little Pigeon River in the middle of downtown Gatlinburg, flicking a fly while their spouses wait on a park bench, reading. The **Smoky Mountain Angler** (☎ 865-436-8746; www.smokymountainangler.com; 376 E Parkway) is the oldest fly-fishing shop and fishing guide service in Gatlinburg. Well regarded by fly-fishing zealots and newly minted enthusiasts alike for the staff's expert knowledge and infectious passion for the sport, the Angler is also the place to go for gear, including locally hand-tied and commercial flies. A half-day fishing trip for novices begins at $135 and goes up from there.

Go hiking with someone who knows more than you do, and see the forest for the trees. **A Walk in the Woods** (☎ 865-436-8283; www.awalkinthewoods.com; 4413 E Scenic Dr) provides enlightened tours for people who want to experience nature on a deeper, better-informed level. Vesna Plakani and her husband, Erik, are naturalists with vast knowledge of the ecology of the Smokies. In addition to guided walks (2hr/half day/full day $20/35/40) and backpacking trips, they provide trip planning, backpacker shuttle service and camping equipment rental.

Precisely 21ft from the border of Great Smoky Mountains National Park, **The Happy Hiker** (☎ 865-436-6000 or 800-445-3701; 905 River Rd, Ste 5) is Gatlinburg's main hiking and camping supply store. The friendly, knowledgeable staff is up to date on the latest hiking, camping and climbing equipment, and the store stocks major brands of tents, packs, boots and accessories, as well as a large selection of books and maps.

The Day Hiker (☎ 865-430-0970; 634 Parkway, Ste 1) sells equipment and offers advice tailored specifically to day hikers.

Sleeping

Finding lodging in Gatlinburg is rarely a problem: the city boasts nearly 9000 rooms. As is the custom 'round these parts, prices vary according to season, with the highest rates in summer and in October during the height of the leaf-peeping season. Many rooms are furnished to satisfy the desires of honeymooners, but you don't have to be a newlywed to enjoy the luxury of a whirlpool bath. Refrigerators and coffee makers are standard amenities.

BUDGET & CAMPING

Rocky Top Village Inn (☎ 865-436-7826; 311 Historic Nature Trail; s/d/ste $50/55/92; P ⬚ ⬚) Named after the Tennessee state song ('Once I had a girl on Rocky Top, half bear, other half cat...'), this friendly inn two blocks off of Parkway offers basic rooms and a friendly staff of good mountain folks. The rooms are all wheelchair accessible and immaculate, but unfortunately the Rocky Top girl is nowhere in sight.

Roaring Fork Motel & Cottages (☎ 865-436-4385; www.roaringforkmotel.com; 124 Roaring Fork Rd; s/d/cottage $45/55/45-85; P ⬚ ⬚) Near the terminus of the Roaring Fork Motor Nature Trail, this cozy place has an agreeable retro feel to it. Accommodations range from rustic wood-paneled cottages with kitchens to spacious new units. You may not be surprised to learn that the honeymoon cottage ($90) includes a shocking red Jacuzzi.

Sadly, there is no tent-only camping available in Gatlinburg, and those wishing to lay their weary heads on the ground may find themselves aggravated by the bothersome racket of RV generators. The following campgrounds are the quietest, each offering swimming pools, hot showers and clean bathrooms. RV sites all have water and electricity; 'full hookup' sites also include sewer lines and sometimes cable television and high-speed Internet access.

Crazy Horse Campground (☎ 865-436-4434; Hwy 321, 12.5 miles east of Gatlinburg; tent $35, half/full hookup $44/53, cabin primitive/deluxe $94/152; 🖾)

Great Smoky Jellystone Park Camp Resort (☎ 865-487-5534; Hwy 321, 14 miles east of Gatlinburg; off/on stream $20-28/28-38, full hookup $38, cabin primitive/deluxe $65/105; 🖾)

MID-RANGE

Rocky Waters Motor Inn (☎ 865-436-7861; www.rockywatersmotorinn.com; 333 Parkway; d/t $85/95, with kitchen $95, with Jacuzzi $100-144; [P] [🕿] [🖾]) With clean rooms overlooking the river and several configurations to choose from, this older motor lodge provides perhaps the best deal in town for under $100. Options include wood-burning fireplaces, connecting rooms and kitchens. Every room includes a couch, fridge and coffee maker. A single caveat: be on your guard for sudden water temperature fluctuations in the shower.

Bearskin Lodge on the River (☎ 865-430-4330; 849 River Rd; d from $75, ste $150-250; [P] [☒] [🕿] [🖾]) This handsome new hotel, removed from downtown in a quieter part of town, is not fancy but very cozy. The large rooms are decked out in woodsy decor with comfortable beds and they come with refrigerators and coffee makers. Ask for a room in the rear to better enjoy the pleasant sounds of the river. Kids love the 'lazy river' pool, and the regular pool is large and heated for crisp autumn days. The complimentary breakfasts are nothing to write home about, but are they ever?

Fairfield Inn (☎ 864-430-7200; 680 River Rd; s/ste $114/170; [P] [☒] [🕿] [🖾]) This Marriott hotel has bright, spacious rooms with river views and plenty of amenities, including premium cable and gas fireplaces.

Edgewater Hotel (☎ 865-436-4151; 402 River Rd; d/ste $76/185; [P] [☒] [🕿] [🖾]) This place lacks personality but is clean and efficient. The rooms have large windows and pleasant views.

TOP END

Buckhorn Inn (☎ 865-436-4668; www.buckhorninn.com; 2140 Tudor Mountain Rd; d/cottage/guest house $115-130/160/200-300; [P] [🕿]) For more than 60 years, this inn has been charming guests with its romantic ambience and well-appointed rooms. From its flagstone terrace, visitors are treated to a gorgeous, unbroken view of Mt Le Conte's three peaks. The main building has nine sumptuous guestrooms – including a unique 'tree house' room at the top of the inn's original water tower – and an airy dining room serving delicious breakfasts and gourmet dinners. Seven fully furnished cottages with Jacuzzi baths and three stately guesthouses round out the offerings. Weekends and holidays require a two-night stay.

Laurel Springs Lodge Bed & Breakfast (☎ 888-430-9211; www.laurelspringslodge.com; 204 Hill St; r $89-149) A short walk from downtown, this authentic 1930s-era mountain lodge, located on a wooded hillside overlooking the Little Pigeon River, features large country-style breakfasts and five comfortable guest bedrooms with private baths, a rustic great room with a fireplace, and a pleasant outdoor hot tub.

Eating

It's all about pancakes, slabs of meat and country cooking in this town. Portions tend to be American-sized, and prices moderate. Although Sevier County is a dry county, Gatlinburg was granted an exception due to the time-honored loophole known as the grandfather clause. Remember to raise a toast to Grandpaw.

Pancake Pantry (☎ 865-436-4724; 628 Parkway; breakfast $4-9, lunch $6-10; ☺ 7am-4pm) Gatlinburg has a thing for pancakes, and this is the place that started it all. The Pantry's secret is simple: real butter, honest-to-goodness fresh whipped cream and everything made from scratch. At lunch there's gourmet sandwiches with funny names like The Polish Aristocrat; box lunches can be prepared for a meal beneath the trees.

The Peddler (☎ 865-436-2300; 820 River Rd; lunch $5-9, dinner $8-24; ☺ 5pm-close) In a large rustic lodge with exposed timbers and native stone fireplaces, this popular dining spot is the best place in town for a table for two. Diners choose between the lodge and its full menu, including mountain favorites like barbecue ribs and 'moonshine chicken,' and the riverside dining room, with simpler fare that includes steaks and salads. Children's meals are priced at half their age.

Howards Restaurant (☎ 865-436-3600; 976 Parkway; lunch $6-8, dinner $8-23; ☺ 11am-10pm Sun-Thu, 11am-11pm Fri & Sat) This good restaurant is primarily known for its aged Midwestern beef and fresh rainbow trout, but there's also a buzz about the cheesecake: It's fluffy and not too sweet. With a pleasant creekside patio, Howards is a good choice for a languorous meal.

Lineberger's Seafood Company (☎ 865-436-9284; 903 Parkway; dinner $9-22; ☺ 11am-3pm, 5pm-close) Serving quality seafood in the Gatlinburg area for more than 40 years, this restaurant specializes in fresh fish, Alaskan snow crab legs, Angus beef and prime rib. Cocktails are served in the on-site lounge.

Best Italian Café & Pizzeria (☎ 865-430-4090; 968 Parkway; pizza from $11, meals $10-16, ☺ 11am-10pm Sun-Thu, 11am-11pm Fri & Sat) This friendly eatery prepares truly outstanding pizza pies, including a mouthwatering creation called the 'Brazilian Béchamel,' with a rich white sauce, chicken, pineapple, banana peppers, feta and pesto. Also on board are plenty of Italian favorites and really good fresh garlic rolls.

Shopping

Arrowmont School of Arts & Crafts (☎ 865-436-5860; www.arrowmont.org; 556 Parkway; ☺ 8am-4:30pm Mon-Sat) Since 1945, Arrowmont has been at the forefront of the 'cottage craft movement,' an initiative to preserve the production of rustic, handmade items once used by mountain folk in their everyday lives. The effort has enabled mountain craftspeople to make baskets, brooms, quilts, fabrics, furniture and other items at home for sale to an ever-broadening and appreciative audience. The school offers year-round classes in arts and crafts, and five galleries (admission free) display outstanding works. Beautiful handcrafted objects can be purchased at the **Arrowcraft Shop** (☎ 865-436-4604).

Great Smoky Arts & Crafts Community (www.artsandcraftscommunity.com) This 8-mile loop is designated as the Tennessee Heritage Arts & Crafts Trail. Here you'll find any number of artisans selling original collectibles such as candles, baskets, quilts, pottery, folk art and cutout plywood paintings of drunken hillbilly gals wearing naught but their bloomers. It's a pleasant place to spend an afternoon or two, shooting the breeze with the garrulous craftspeople. The trail is on Hwy 321 north, 3 miles from Parkway light 3.

Getting There & Away

Most visitors arrive in the region by car, but traffic congestion in the Smokies can be a real downer, especially along the Great Smoky Mountains Parkway during peak travel seasons. It's worth your while to chart an alternate route: You'll save time and experience less-visited parts of the region.

If you plan to fly into the region, your choices are Knoxville, Tennessee or Asheville, North Carolina, both of which are served by major airlines. See p74 for details.

ALTERNATE DRIVING ROUTES TO GATLINBURG

Unless you're conducting an anthropological study on road rage, consider avoiding the I-40/Hwy 66/Hwy 441 route into Gatlinburg, especially during peak season. Here are alternate routes:

✔ **From the west** Leave I-40 at Hwy 129, near the Knoxville airport. Follow Hwy 129 south to Hwy 321 in Maryville. Travel east on Hwy 321 to Townsend, where you can continue on to Pigeon Forge or enter the park to take the scenic but meandering Little River Rd to Sugarlands Visitor Center near Gatlinburg.

✔ **From the east** Take I-40 west to exit 440 and head south on Hwy 321 through Cosby to Gatlinburg.

✔ **From the south** Take I-85 north to I-985 north to Hwy 23. Take Hwy 23 to Hwy 23/441 through Cherokee, North Carolina and straight through the park to Gatlinburg.

✔ **From the north** Take I-81 south to I-40 east to exit 435 (Newport) and follow Hwy 321 south all the way to Gatlinburg.

Getting Around

The **Gatlinburg Trolley** (☎ 865-436-3897; ☉ summer 8am-midnight, winter 10am-8pm Sun-Thu, 10am-midnight Fri & Sat) picks up and drops passengers at more than 100 locations throughout town and at a number of park locales; look for the Street Trolley signs. Exact fare is required. The trolleys are color-coded by route:

Purple Parkway and Welcome Center (fare 25¢)
Red Upper Loop (fare 25¢)
Yellow Arts & Crafts Community (fare $1)
Gold National Park: Sugarlands Visitor Center, Laurel Falls, Elkmont (fare $2 round-trip)
Pink Dollywood and Pigeon Forge (fare $2 round-trip)
Blue East Parkway and City Hall (fare 25¢)

Pick up a Gatlinburg Trolley route map at the visitor centers or find it within the free *Tennessee Smokies Visitors Guide.*

PIGEON FORGE

Map 5, p156 / ☎ 865 / pop 5100/ elevation 1010ft

Oh, the humanity! On your first lurching procession down Pigeon Forge's main drag, past one hokey miniature golf palace after another, beside countless ostentatious palaces of consumerism, through an endless morass of belching muscle cars and the people who drive them, you may agree that this town is hard to love. Or you may smile serenely and ask, 'What's not to love?'

For those hard-pressed to find a positive aspect to all this commercialism, perhaps the best place to start is Dollywood, a theme park inspired by the tastes and values of the singular Dolly Parton, America's perpetual sweetheart. With its gristmill replica, craft-making demonstrations, exciting rides and ubiquitous music, the place is so damned good-natured and spirited that it's infectious.

Pigeon Forge is also known as a shopping mecca. Here you'll find several outlet malls selling every brand name you've ever heard of, and stores you've never imagined (witness the world's largest teddy bear store).

Orientation

Pigeon Forge is 5 miles north of Gatlinburg and Great Smoky Mountains National Park, 5 miles south of Sevierville and 33 miles southeast of Knoxville. Hwy 441, otherwise known as the Great Smoky Mountains Parkway, is the main thoroughfare; its numbered traffic lights serve as landmarks, often cited in lieu of street addresses. Three interstates run near Pigeon Forge: I-75, I-40 and I-81. They are connected to Pigeon Forge by Hwys 66, 441, 411 and 321.

Information

Pigeon Forge Welcome Center (☎ 865-453-8574 or 800-251-9100; www.mypigeonforge.com; 1950 Parkway; ⊙ 8:30am-5pm Mon-Fri, 9am-5:30pm Sat, 1-5pm Sun)
Pigeon Forge Visitor's Information Center (☎ 865-429-7387; 3107 Parkway, near traffic light 5; ⊙ 8:30am-5pm Mon-Fri, 9am-5:30pm Sat, 1pm-5pm Sun)
Post office (☎ 865-429-2265; 3235 Rena St; ⊙ 8:30am-4:30pm Mon-Fri, 10am-noon Sat)
Pigeon Forge Public Library (☎ 865-429-7490; 2449 Library Dr; ⊙ 9am-6pm Mon, Wed & Fri, 9am-8pm Tue & Thu, 9am-5pm Sat, 1-5pm Sun) The library offers free Internet access.
Pigeon Forge Medical Clinic (☎ 865-453-1924; 3346 Parkway, near traffic light 7)
Pigeon Forge police (☎ 911 or 865-453-9063)
Fire, ambulance (☎ 911 or 865-453-3200)

Sights
DOLLYWOOD

In her bittersweet 'Heartsong,' Dolly Parton sings, 'And now this Smoky Mountain girl has been all around the world / But it makes no difference just how far I roam / I still cling to that place that is so dear to my heart.' Clearly, she's singing about Pigeon Forge, the town that has kept Dolly's career and celebrity alive while many of her contemporaries have faded into obscurity. Her personal theme park **Dollywood** (☎ 865-428-9488; www.dollywood.com; Dollywood Lane; child/senior/adult $33/39/43; ⊙ 9am-8pm high season, closed Jan-Mar) trumps Graceland as Tennessee's most popular tourist attraction.

This wholesome, family-friendly park enthralls kids with its impressive menu of thrill rides – including new arrival Thunderhead, a massive wooden coaster artfully placed between two mountains – and entertains adults with an ongoing series of musical performances and demonstrations by master craftsmen. Other attractions include a large interactive tree house, a museum chronicling Parton's illustrious career, and a bald eagle aviary, among many others. Everywhere you turn there's music, ranging from hokey stage shows to rambling musicians. If you plan to visit the park for more than one day, you'll save money with a season ticket (adult/child $70/57). Consider arriving via the **Pigeon Forge Fun Time Trolley** (p133), as traffic congestion often makes driving to the park a hassle (parking $6). You can deposit your pooch at Doggywood during your visit. Strollers and wheelchairs are available for rent.

On a hot day in the Smokies, the 25-acre water park **Dollywood's Splash Country** (☎ 865-428-9488; 2146 Middle Creek Rd; adult/senior/child $29/27/24; ⊙ 10am-7pm high season, closed Oct-Apr) provides welcome relief to those who enjoy getting flushed through a pipe and dropped into the drink. On the premises are 16 water slides, a 25,000-sq-ft wave pool and the Big Bear Plunge, a white-water rafting adventure ride that takes you banking through dark caverns and crashing through an ominous wall of fog before sending you over a cliff.

MUSEUMS

Outside of Memphis, this shrine to the King can't be beat. At the **Elvis Museum** (☎ 865-428-2001; 2638 Parkway; adult/teen/child $13/9/6; ⊙ 10am-7pm high season) you'll swoon at the sight of Elvis' original TCB ring, featuring a 7-carat diamond enhanced by lighting bolts and his personal logo, 'Taking Care of Business.' Also on view are his personal limousine and honeymoon Caddy, and the world's largest private collection of the King's personal effects (including his royal nasal spray applicator).

The reverent **Carbo's Police Museum** (☎ 865-453-1358; 3311 Parkway; adult/child $8/4; ☯ Apr-Dec) honors the constabulary in all its forms, with a unique collection of authentic police items, including badges, uniforms, billy clubs and confiscated drug paraphernalia. The main draws, however, are items related to Buford Pusser, the sheriff popularized in the *Walking Tall* movies of the 1970s. Pusser, you may recall, was impervious to gunshot and knife wounds and whupped ass until the very end with an iconic axe handle.

To see Buford Pusser's patrol car, you'll have to head to the **Smoky Mountain Car Museum** (☎ 865-453-3433; 2970 Parkway; adult/child $8/4; ☯ Apr-Dec). The collection also includes 007's Aston-Martin, which was featured in *Goldfinger* and *Thunderball*, Al Capone's bulletproof Cadillac and a number of other celebrity cars.

Activities & Outfitters

The **Gatlinburg Golf Course** (☎ 800-231-4128; www.ci.gatlinburg.tn.us; 520 Dollywood Lane) is widely regarded as one of the most dramatic course in the southeast – almost every hole features a gorgeous view of the Smokies. Hole 12, nicknamed 'Sky Hi,' famously drops 200ft from tee to green. Visit the website to learn about lodging partners in order to save substantially on green fees. Without a discount, 18 holes on a Friday or Saturday morning will run you $57. The price is considerably less on weekdays and after 1pm. Juniors and seniors also receive a discount.

After a brief training session, visitors to **Flyaway Indoor Skydiving** (☎ 865-453-7777; 3106 Parkway; single/double flight $25/40; ☯ 12pm-6pm Mon-Fri, 10am-7pm Sat, 10am-5pm Sun) leap into a giant wind silo while wearing billowing super-fly jumpsuits and goggles to float in eerie suspension.

For a gentle excursion down the French Broad, Little Pigeon or the West Prong Rivers, **Mountain View Canoe Rentals** (☎ 865-428-6112; 3048 Parkway; ☯ seasonal) offers guided tours suitable for children ages three and up.

The following outfitters provide gear for outdoor enthusiasts:

The Day Hiker (☎ 865-430-0970; 4676 Parkway) Day hiking gear, books and advice.

Coleman Retail Store (☎ 865-908-3777; 2655 Teaster Lane, Belz Factory Outlet World) Camping equipment and plenty of lanterns.

Cycle Quest (☎ 865-429-5558; 3406 Teaster Lane) Bicycles, gear and service.

Rocky Top Outfitters (☎ 865-429-3474; 3361 Parkway) A fully stocked fly and tackle shop and fishing guide service.

Festivals

The annual three-month **Winterfest** in Pigeon Forge and Gatlinburg celebrates the electric Christmas light. More than seven million of the colorful bulbs adorn the two towns from November to February.

Sleeping

There are scores of lodging choices in Pigeon Forge, ranging from cheap hovels to tacky luxury. Prices vary substantially from season to season and are usually higher on the weekends. Listed here are weekend rates during peak season.

BUDGET & CAMPING

If you're looking for a bargain, be advised that many of the establishments on Parkway with signs that advertise rooms for as little as $15 are not being honest. Once you get inside the office, you'll find the low-end price to be in the $40 range. When challenged, one hotelier had the nerve to explain away the discrepancy with a classic line: 'I'm not lying, the sign is!'

Briarstone Inn (☎ 865-453-4225; 3626 Parkway; d or t $43; P 🏖 🛋) There are plenty of nondescript economic options along Parkway. One dependable choice is this newly remodeled inn near the turnoff for Dollywood. As at similar establishments on Parkway, Jacuzzi rooms are available, and all rooms come with refrigerators and coffee makers.

Due to lack of demand, there are no tent-only campgrounds in Pigeon Forge. Of the several campgrounds catering to RVs, the following are the most pleasant, all offering hot showers, pools and laundry service.

Clabough's Campground ☎ 865-453-0729; 405 Wears Valley Rd; site with/without electricity $34/32; 🛋)

Twin Mountain Outdoor Resort (☎ 800-848-9097; 304 Day Springs Rd; RV $34, tent with/without hookup $24/22; 🛋)

Eagle's Nest Campground (☎ 865-428-5841; 1111 Wears Valley Rd; full hookup $30, tent $24; 🛋)

MID-RANGE

Huckleberry Inn (☎ 800-704-3278; 1754 Sandstone Way; r $110; P 🏖) Very quaint indeed, this beautiful, hand-built log inn dates from 1992. It features three guestrooms furnished with hand-carved furniture and antiques, all with private whirlpool bath. Two rooms feature fireplaces. There are large, screened porches for relaxing and enjoying the complimentary breakfast and majestic views of the Smokies. The entire house can be rented for $300 per night. Pets are welcome.

Wonderland Lodge (☎ 865-428-0779; 3889 Wonderland Way; r $50-88; P) This independent old-timey mountain retreat in Wears Valley between Pigeon Forge and Townsend has no in-room phones or televisions, so forget about calling your broker or watching a rerun of Paris Hilton's *The Simple Life*. Live it for yourself in a rocking chair on the long porch, as crickets and fireflies provide your nightly entertainment. The view of the mountains is superb. The old dining room has been upgraded to a modern restaurant, but otherwise you'll feel like you have stepped back in time.

Guesthouse Inn (☎ 800-695-8284; 219 Emert St; d/ste $70/90; P ✕ 🏖 🖳 🛋) Expect basic, clean accommodations with no surprises (pleasant or otherwise).

Creekstone Inn (☎ 865-453-3557; 4034 River Rd S; ste from $92; P ✕ 🏖 🖳 🛋) In spite of a duck infestation, this well-run hotel overlooking the Little Pigeon River gets high marks for service and amenities. Some of the rooms have private balconies with a privileged view of the river.

TOP END

ResortQuest Mountain Cabins (☎ 865 908-1342; 610 Dollywood Lane; cabin from $180; P 🏖) These individual stand-alone cabins in the foothills surrounding Pigeon Forge provide a perfect romantic getaway for two. Each cabin features a full kitchen, indoor Jacuzzi tub, outdoor hot tub, pool table, fireplace, TV and VCR, balcony and beautiful panoramic views of the surrounding countryside.

There are many rental condos, cabins and chalets in and around Pigeon Forge and Gatlinburg. The following providers are recommended:

A Cabin in the Woods (☎ 800-453-0722; www.acabininthewoods.biz) This spot specializes in honeymoon and family cabins.

Country Oaks Cottages (☎ 866-369-2942; www.countryoaks.com) More than 100 cabins, condos and chalets with one to eight bedrooms are listed.

Pigeon Forge Chalet Rentals (☎ 865-429-4656; www.pigeonforgechalets.com) Choose from a wide selection of chalets.

Michelle's Mountain View Cabins (☎ 865-429-3737; www.mvcabins.com) This family-owned and operated business keeps things personal.

Eating

Pigeon Forge has nearly 100 restaurants; many of these are pancake houses, and many more are chain restaurants. What's missing is a good selection of family-owned eateries so common in other corners of the Smokies.

By county decree the town prohibits the sale of alcoholic beverages in restaurants, but some establishments allow diners to bring their own.

The Old Mill Restaurant (☎ 865-429-3463; 164 Old Mill Ave; meals $6-18; ☺ breakfast, lunch & dinner) This is the place for homemade biscuits and chicken with dumplings. Pigeon Forge's Old Mill – photographed by millions – has been in operation since 1830, grinding thousands of pounds of grain each day with every turn of its giant water-powered wheel. The restaurant features traditional Southern food, much of it made using the mill's own stone-ground products.

La Carreta Authentic Mexican Food (☎ 865-908-6270; 3965 Parkway; dishes $6-10.50; ☺ 11am-10pm Mon-Thu, 11am-10:30pm Fri & Sat, 11am-9pm Sun) This unpretentious restaurant provides welcome relief from Pigeon Forge's corporate restaurant scene. Its excellent combination plates, seafood and grilled meats make this the place to go for authentic south-of-the-border fare.

Bennett's Pit Bar-B-Que (☎ 865-429-2200; 2910 Parkway; dinner $7-19; ☺ breakfast, lunch & dinner) Carnivores are given more reasons to rejoice at this excellent barbecue joint. Here they smoke the ribs, chicken and chopped pork for 14 hours over smoldering hickory wood and slather it all with a toothsome sauce. The gigantic salad bar is definitely worth a visit.

Alamo Steakhouse (☎ 865-908-9998; 3050 Parkway; dinners $8-24; ☺ lunch & dinner) Mammoth Black Angus steaks, chops and chicken are served in this popular restaurant imbued with a Tex-Mex ambience.

Tastebuds Café (☎ 865-428-9781; 1198 Wears Valley Rd; dinner $16-23; ☺ lunch & dinner Tue-Sat) This pleasant restaurant, located away from the Parkway's exasperating crowds, provides a gourmet experience in a relaxed atmosphere. Try an appetizer of shiitake spinach fromage, followed by Chef Jock's scrumptious coconut shrimp – gulf shrimp panfried in a wonderful fresh coconut batter with sweet Mediterranean salsa. Reservations recommended.

If you're looking to restock your camping larder, put together a picnic lunch or throw back a six-pack, head to **Food City** (☎ 865-453-4977; 3625 Parkway).

Entertainment

Pigeon Forge, in an attempt to extract ever more tourist gold, has tried to establish itself as a rival to Branson, Missouri in recent years. This means plenty of theaters showcasing goofy comedy revues and cornball music. While some of the offerings will make your eyes roll back into your head...actually, *all* of them make your eyes roll back into your head. Nonetheless, these shows largely constitute the town's nightlife, such as it is. And if the stars are aligned just so, your gag reflex will give way to your giggle reflex. Following are a few representative offerings.

At **Elwood Smooch's Ole Smoky Hoedown** (☎ 856-428-5600; 2135 Parkway; adult/teen/child $23/12/5; ☺ Mar-Dec) an inductee of the International Clown Hall of Fame gets big laughs with his hillbilly shtick. The show also features 'Blazing Bluegrass and Glorious Gospel' music.

Big teeth and a plastic smile are likely to be the only things you'll remember from the Vegas-inspired 'million-dollar show' **Louise Mandrell in Person!** (☎ 865-453-6263; 2046 Parkway; adult/teen/child $30/17/12; ☺ Mar-Dec).

For something completely different, try **Dolly Parton's Dixie Stampede** (☎ 800-356-1676; 3849 Parkway; adult/child $40/22; ☒ Mar-Dec). This dinner theater extravaganza features 32 horses, showgirls riding ostriches, a buffalo stampede, rope tricks and pig racing. Yes, pig racing. Come hungry – a whole rotisserie chicken will be set before you. Also served is a big slab of pork tenderloin (the managers deny any relationship between the menu and the pig race).

Shopping
According to the tourist bureau, more people come to Pigeon Forge to go shopping than to visit the national park. They flock to the more than 200 factory outlets like dancing bears to genetically modified honey.

Belz Factory Outlet World (☎ 865-453-3503; 2655 Teaster Lane; ☒ 9am-9pm Mon-Sat, 10am-7pm Sun) features 85 famous brand-name outlets.

Tanger Factory Outlet Center (☎ 865-428-7002; 161 E Wears Valley Rd; ☒ 9am-9pm Mon-Sat, 10am-7pm Sat) has 30 outlets, including Liz Claiborne, Samsonite, J Crew and Eddie Bauer.

Getting There & Around
See Gatlinburg (p127) for information about driving and flying to the region.

The **Pigeon Forge Fun Time Trolley** (☎ 865-453-6444; fares 25-50¢; ☒ 8:30am-midnight Apr-Oct, 10am-10pm Nov-Dec, closed Jan-Mar) is a privately run bus service with five routes serving Parkway, Dollywood, Wears Valley, Splash County and the Gatlinburg Welcome Center.

SEVIERVILLE
☎ 865 / pop 11,000 / elevation 900ft

One of Tennessee's oldest towns, Sevierville was named for General John Sevier: Revolutionary War hero, fighter against the Cherokee and the state's first governor. A brilliant tactician, Sevier rose to national prominence in 1780, when he led colonial forces in a rout of the British at Kings Mount, South Carolina, summarily stopping the British southern campaign in its tracks. His memorable Indian war cry – 'Here they are! Come on, boys!' – is the cheerful legacy of what was in fact a grim determination to eradicate the Cherokee completely from eastern Tennessee by whatever means necessary.

Visitors to Sevierville will discover a place infused with personality and quaint Southern charm. One of the historic town's most enduring symbols is the classic white clock tower on the Victorian-era Sevier County Courthouse; it strikes every half hour in the time-honored tradition. You might expect to find a statue of the town's dour namesake and patriarch on the courthouse grounds, but instead you get a bronze statue of hometown girl **Dolly Parton**: barefoot, buxom and looking foxy. She sits coquettishly on a rock holding an acoustic guitar with a butterfly resting on its neck.

Across the street you'll find **Virgil's 50's Restaurant** (☎ 865-453-2782; 109 Bruce St; ☒ 8am-3pm Mon-Fri). Its vinyl booths, meatloaf specials, genuine soda fountain and walls decorated with classic car photos are a winning throwback to the small-town diners of years gone by. Virgil's also doubles as Sevierville's bus station.

Farther down Bruce St is the worthwhile **Sevier County Heritage Museum** (☎ 865-453-4058; 167 E Bruce St; admission free; ☒ noon-5pm Mon-Tue & Thu-Fri), a beguiling small-town museum with a dusty collection that includes quilts, the county's first typewriter and a telephone switchboard operated by a bewigged mannequin. The museum is housed in the handsome old Sevierville post office building, built in 1940 as a WPA project.

Also nearby is the new **Memorial Riverwalk Trail**, a 1-mile path along the west branch of the Little Pigeon River; it features views of the river and the Smokies.

If you want to blend in (or skin a coon), you're going to need a knife. Sevierville boasts one of the best knife stores anywhere: the **Smoky Mountain Knife Works** (☎ 865-453-5871; Hwy 66; ☻ 9am-9pm). Here you'll find more than 5000 varieties of sharp objects suitable for cutting, slicing, paring, carving or impaling, from high-quality pocketknives to ornate swords suitable for Gandalf. Historical exhibits display implements dating back to the 18th century. The store is on Hwy 66, 4 miles south of I-40.

HARTFORD

☎ 423 / pop 800 / elevation 1055ft

Just across the Tennessee border, off I-40 at exit 447, is the tiny town of Hartford. Many thousands of people looking for adventure come here each year for rafting trips on the Big Pigeon River. This pretty, snaking waterway is perfect for mellow float trips (ideal for young children) on its lower waters, and hair-raising white-water thrills on its upper portion. Here you'll find famous Class III and IV rapids with names like Too Late, Vegematic, Razor Blade, After Shave and Lost Guide.

The Big Pigeon is a dam-controlled river, with releases from March through September; at the time of this writing these occurred on Tuesday, Wednesday, Thursday and Saturday. The following outfitters are well regarded for their professional, safe excursions on the Big Pigeon River:

Nantahala Outdoor Center (☎ 423-487-0668; www.noc.com; Hartford Rd; lower river adult/child $36/33, upper river $43)

Smoky Mountain Outdoors (☎ 423-487-5290; Hartford Rd; lower river adult/child $24/30, upper river adult/child $37/34)

5 Rivers Adventures (☎ 888-297-9059; Hartford Rd; lower river adult/child $36/33, upper river adult/child $40/36)

Sleeping & Eating

Foxfire Campground (☎ 423-487-0580; 3541 Hartford Rd; tent site $21, RV site with hookup $26) This pleasant campground offers hot showers and tent sites on the Big Pigeon River, each with a picnic table and fire ring.

Standing Bear Farm (☎ 423-487-0014; 4255 Green Corner Rd; bunk or tent $15; 🖳) Near the AT, this is a lovely sanctuary for hikers and river rats. On an early 20th century farmstead with many original buildings still intact, the accommodations include a rustic bunkhouse and cabin, as well as an authentic teepee. Trail-weary hikers take solace in the hot showers, laundry, free Internet, phone, mail drop and shuttle service. To find this little piece of heaven, take exit 451 off I-40 east. Do not cross the Pigeon River, but rather continue straight past the stop sign and interstate underpass. Green Corner Rd begins after the underpass. Standing Bear Farm is 1 mile up the road on the right.

Mountain Mama's (☎ 828-486-5995; Waterville Rd) This simple country store and eatery is a legendary stop for AT through-hikers. Here you can procure hiker shuttle service and every hiker's primary fetish object: an ice cream bar. To drive there, take the first Tennessee exit off I-40 (or last, depending on which direction you're traveling). Waterville Rd heads back into North Carolina, past Mountain Mama's and on to Big Creek campground in Great Smoky Mountains National Park.

COSBY

☎ 423 / pop 5200 / elevation 1050ft

During and after Prohibition, huge deliveries of sugar rolled into the Cosby area; it was said that 'the sugar comes in dry and goes out shakin'.' So many stories have been circulated about Cocke County's legendary history as the capital of moonshine whiskey that it is difficult to separate fact from fiction. Fortunately, this all becomes irrelevant once you snort a cup of the 'corn.'

In the early 1940s the famous columnist Ernie Pyle came to Cosby to meet some of the moonshiners. He wrote of the experience: 'That day in the moonshining country gave me a new idea of honor. For one thing, most of the moonshiners weren't criminals at all. They were violating a law, of course, but as they said, how else could you make a living up there? And you don't find vicious criminals having genuine respect and friendship for the men who are sending them to the penitentiary right and left.'

Cosby's days as the 'moonshine capital of the world' are long gone, and the town has recently embraced this designation with pride. Today Cosby has a pleasant, small-town feel and offers several lodging options at substantially lower prices than in Gatlinburg or Pigeon Forge. Nearby is the park's second-largest campground, Cosby (p116), with plentiful hiking opportunities. The town also boasts two excellent venues for local bluegrass/mountain music.

Cosby sits on Hwy 321, 25 miles east of Gatlinburg. As you approach from the west, Hwy 321 runs parallel to the park boundary. At the Cosby cross-roads, you can turn right to reach the Cosby Campground and Hwy 32, which follows the curve of the park boundary toward Cataloochee (p87). A left turn brings you into Cosby proper and to Foothills Parkway East.

SLEEPING & EATING

Cosby Creek Cabins (☎ 800-508-8844; 4378 Cosby Hwy/Hwy 321; cabin $95-280; ✗) These cozy cabins feature one to four bedrooms with full baths, well-equipped kitchens, fireplaces and washer and dryer. Naturally, each has a front porch and/or private deck for enjoying the sensual pleasures of the forest and views. There's also a private pond stocked with dinner.

Fox Den Campground (☎ 423-487-3178; Hwy 32S; tent/half/full hookup $20/20/25, r $50; ☎) This peaceful, low-traffic campground also includes an economical, comfortable motel. It's 1 mile south of Hwy 321.

Cub Motel (☎ 423-487-2143; 4344 Cosby Hwy; d $55; P ☎) People like this place for its well-appointed rooms overlooking Big Cosby Creek, its hearty country restaurant and its reasonable rates.

Cub Restaurant (meals $4-12; ☺ breakfast, lunch & dinner) The Cub offers creekside dining and live bluegrass music on weekend evenings.

The Front Porch (☎ 423-487-2875; Hwy 321; dishes $6.50-14; ☺ 5-10:30pm Fri, noon-10:30pm Sat & Sun) Don't deny yourself the experience of a meal at this, perhaps the world's only Mexican bluegrass restaurant. On Friday and Saturday nights, there's real bluegrass music – not the cheap imitation stuff you'll hear in Pigeon Forge – with shows at 7pm and 9pm. On Sunday night during the peak season, come for bluegrass open mic (but don't take the stage unless you know what you're doing!). The menu at this central Cosby spot is filled with traditional Mexican fare, including several vegetarian-friendly options. You are welcome to bring your own hooch for a $1 brown-bagging charge.

Carver's Apple House Restaurant (☎ 423-487-2710; 3460 Cosby Hwy/Hwy 321; breakfast & lunch $4-8, dinner $6-15; ☺ 8am-8pm) This wonderful place, imbued with authentic Smoky Mountain charm, has an agreeable dining room looking out over apple orchards and rolling green hills. You can order apples – in the form of cider, sauce and fritters – with every meal. The menu is filled with country favorites, including sugar-cured ham, high-rise biscuits and gravy. Adjacent is a barn selling well-priced fruits, vegetables, jams and jellies.

continued on p138

THE MOUNTAINS ARE ALIVE WITH

Appalachee is a Choctaw word that means 'people on the other side.' And the people on the other side, in the extreme isolation of their hollers and gaps, developed a pure music, fusing the once disparate sounds of Anglo-Celtic folk, blues, gospel and Western swing. These days, that music is called either bluegrass or mountain music, depending on who you want to argue with.

The grandpaw of bluegrass music was **Bill Monroe**, who pioneered the sound in the late 1940s with the rousing and constantly rotating **Blue Grass Boys**. The Blue Grass Boys were the great factory of modern bluegrass, consistently assembling and releasing such future legends as Lester Flatt (Sparta, Tennessee), Earl Scruggs (Boiling Springs, North Carolina) and Jimmy Martin (Sneedsville, Tennessee).

Musicians Jim Proffitt and Grace Newman, ca 1930.

Bluegrass bands scowl at pianos, drums and electric guitars. They embrace banjos, fiddles, mandolins, down-home acoustic guitars, bass fiddles and dobros.

The bluegrass sound is fast, faster, and ringing with 'high lonesome' vocal harmonies. It's far more evolved and complex than Jed Clampett would let you in on. Like jazz impresarios, great bluegrass players can be recognized immediately by the sound of their pickin'.

Mountain music is mainly the realm of the immortal **Ralph Stanley**. Amid the clamor of bluegrass, he and his Clinch Mountain Boys developed a more traditional sound based on the songs Stanley grew up singing in a holler on Big Spraddle Creek in McClure, Virginia. Stanley's haunting, deep tenor is a national treasure, a must-hear while it's still around.

Though ostensibly uplifting, bluegrass and mountain music often return to a few disturbing and unavoidable themes: hard luck, heartbreak and murder. A classic song that captures all three of these themes is 'Tom Dooley,' best performed by **Doc Watson**, the legendary flat-picker from nearby Deep Gap, North Carolina. The song is about an 1866 murder (committed just a few miles from Watson's home) involving a desperate love quadrangle.

Uncle Joe Quilliams and friends on his farmsted, 1927.

The quadrangle focused on young and handsome Tom Dula, who happened to be the eager love object of two of the most beautiful young ladies in western North Carolina – Laura Foster and Annie Melton. Unfortunately for Tom, Sheriff Grayson had courted both these ladies and was, to say the least, quite displeased. Tom was arrested for killing Laura Foster, though many said it was Annie Melton who stabbed Laura to death.

THE SOUND OF MUSIC

Both Tom and Annie went to trial for the murder, but Tom refused to implicate Annie and as a result was hung by Sheriff Grayson. Annie Melton claimed she was 'too purty' to hang by rope, and the jury agreed. She was released and eventually married Sherriff Grayson. Folks say that only on her deathbed did she tell the truth, and that Grayson was crushed to find out he had lived out his life based on her wicked lie.

Far from the hideous country music circuses of Gatlinburg and Pigeon Forge, Wilkes County, North Carolina hosts bluegrass and mountain music's premier festival, **MerleFest** (☎ 800-343-7857; www.merlefest.org). Named for Doc's beloved son and musical companion, who died tragically and too soon in a tractor accident, MerleFest is a joyous musical and cultural sprawl in Wilkesboro, with multiple stages featuring the best and most interesting performers in contemporary bluegrass and mountain music. The festival is held annually toward the end of April.

You can also hear great bluegrass music along the Blue Ridge Parkway in Floyd County (p203) and Galax (p231).

TOM DOOLEY

– Author unknown

Hang your head, Tom Dooley,
Hang your head and cry;
You killed poor Laurie Foster,
And you know you're bound to die.

You left her by the roadside
Where you begged to be excused;
You left her by the roadside,
Then you hid her clothes and shoes.

Hang your head, Tom Dooley,
Hang your head and cry;
You killed poor Laurie Foster,
And you know you're bound to die.

You took her on the hillside
For to make her your wife;
You took her on the hillside,
And there you took her life.

You dug the grave four feet long
And you dug it three feet deep;
You rolled the cold clay over her
And tromped it with your feet.

Hang your head, Tom Dooley,
Hang your head and cry;
You killed poor Laurie Foster,
And you know you're bound to die.

'Trouble, oh it's trouble
A-rollin' through my breast;
As long as I'm a-livin', boys,
They ain't a-gonna let me rest.

I know they're gonna hang me,
Tomorrow I'll be dead,
Though I never even harmed a hair
On poor little Laurie's head.'

Hang your head, Tom Dooley,
Hang your head and cry;
You killed poor Laurie Foster,
And you know you're bound to die.

'In this world and one more
Then reckon where I'll be;
If it wasn't for Sheriff Grayson,
I'd be in Tennessee.

You can take down my old violin
And play it all you please.
For at this time tomorrow, boys,
It'll be of no use to me.'

Hang your head, Tom Dooley,
Hang your head and cry;
You killed poor Laurie Foster,
And you know you're bound to die.

'At this time tomorrow
Where do you reckon I'll be?
Away down yonder in the holler
Hangin' on a white oak tree.'

Hang your head, Tom Dooley,
Hang your head and cry;
You killed poor Laurie Foster,
And you know you're bound to die.

continued from p135

The Fort (☎ 423-487-2544; 2155 Dark Hollow Rd) For local color (and, if you're smooth, a sip of handcrafted hooch), find your way to this double-wide trailer, said to have been a moonshine dispensary in the not-too-distant past. The ambience, if you can call it that, is one-of-a-kind: Hundreds of $1 bills are stapled to the ceiling (but curiously, no $100 bills). If you ask for the moonshine menu, they'll treat you like the cad you are. The stuff is still served, but it's dispensed strictly on a wink-wink nudge-nudge protocol. Affect a local accent and ask for a 'Short Island Tea' to get the ball rolling. It will come in a paper Coca-Cola cup. One cup of the stuff will make you cross-eyed. To find the place (it's also known as 'Fort Knox'), turn right on Dark Hollow Rd from Hwy 32/Hwy 321, just north of central Cosby, and travel about a mile.

MAGGIE VALLEY

☎ 828 / pop 2900 / elevation 2600ft

On Hwy 19 northeast of Cherokee is the quiet burg Maggie Valley. Although this pretty town has tried mightily to position itself as a resort destination, in truth Maggie remains a country backwater dependent on road traffic to Great Smoky for its livelihood.

Until 2003 Maggie Valley was home to an aged but popular amusement park, Ghost Town in the Sky. With its departure, the town finds itself with a glut of motel rooms and some of the cheapest lodging in the Smokies. The main road through town, Hwy 19/Soco Rd, is lined with hotels, restaurants and other establishments of interest to tourists, but as soon as you leave the thoroughfare, you'll find yourself deep in the country.

SLEEPING & EATING

Lodging prices listed here reflect high-season weekend rates; expect to pay as little as half in low season.

Ed's Motel (☎ 828-926-1879; 6262 Soco Rd/Hwy 19; without/with kitchen $35/45; P) A terrific value, this clean and mellow place includes some units with kitchenettes. One option has two separate bedrooms and the feel of a small apartment.

Abbey Inn Motel (☎ 828-926-1188; 6375 Soco Rd/Hwy 19; d/ste with kitchenette $74/99; P) This classic motor lodge features real retro charm and pleasant grounds with swings and a large picnic area. The rooms are fresh and bright. Pets are welcome for a small additional fee.

Rocky Waters Motel (☎ 828-926-1585; 4898 Soco Rd/Hwy 19; s/d $76/98, cabin $120; P) If you like the idea of waking up to the sound of a burbling brook, consider renting a creekside cabin at this old favorite. Cabins come with kitchenettes and sliding glass doors that open to the creek. There's also a picnic area big enough to accommodate larger groups.

Fireside Cottages (☎ 828-926-1730; 6490 Soco Rd/Hwy 19; cottage $82; P) This quiet lodging option offers pleasant views. Each unit has a full kitchen, two double beds and a queen-size pullout bed, with a total capacity of six guests. Rounding it out are barbecue grills and a nice wooden porch with a swing.

Brooksong B&B (☎ 828-926-5409; www.brooksong.com; 252 Living Waters Lane; r $140-160; P) This new B&B has five rooms, each with Jacuzzi, fireplace and refrigerator. The decor is a little precious, but all fixtures and furnishings are brand spanking new. There's a balcony veranda and a deck overlooking Jonathan Creek. A huge country breakfast is served, with plenty of fresh fruit and sweet-potato pancakes. You'll find Brooksong off Hwy 19/Soco Rd, just inside the western edge of town.

Mountain Joy Cottages (☎ 888-926-1257; www.mountainjoycottages.com; 121 Setzer Cove

Rd; 2-/3-/4-bedroom cottage $149/215/237, romance cottage $154; (P) (X) (R)) Originally the homestead of Maggie Setzer, for whom Maggie Valley is named, this pleasant place offers rustic cabins with modern amenities; each includes a private front porch, fireplace, cable TV and a kitchen. What's more, on the grounds are a stocked trout pond, indoor pool and hot tub. With plenty of open space, weekly rates and a playground, this is a good option for families.

Mountaineer Restaurant (☎ 828-926-1730; 6490 Soco Rd/Hwy 19; breakfast $2.50-5.50, meals $5-15; ⏲ breakfast, lunch & dinner) For three generations this family-run establishment has been a pleasant place to enjoy a big country meal while gazing out the picture windows at the gentle mountain slopes rising from Maggie Valley. The menu features daily specials and huge pork chops, country-fried steak, breaded shrimp and Cajun gumbo. Live entertainment is featured on weekends.

For a little nighttime entertainment, your best bet is the **Maggie Valley Opry House** (☎ 828-648-7941; 3605 Soco Rd/Hwy 19; ⏲ nightly May-Oct), where banjo legend Raymond Fairchild and friends put on a fantastic show of mountain music every night at 8pm.

CHEROKEE

Map 3, p154 / ☎ 828 / pop 25,000 / elevation 1200ft

Maybe it's the Indian 'chief' who poses for photographs with his tip jar near the entrance to the park, or perhaps it's the tribal dancers bedecked in neon-orange jumpsuits on the main drag, but Cherokee is regarded by many to be a tacky tourist trap capitalizing on persistent stereotypes about Native Americans. To be sure there is no shortage of wooden Indians and ersatz Indian 'crafts' for sale, but the town deserves more than a passing glance, and travelers who linger will discover a place that is considerably more complex and rewarding than its reputation suggests. Several worthwhile cultural attractions present the proud heritage of the Cherokee people and tell the sad story of their betrayal through a succession of empty promises and broken treaties.

Of course, to fully appreciate all Cherokee has to offer, one can hardly ignore its lowbrow pleasures. Haul a bag of quarters to the casino or shout out 'bingo!' at a tribal gaming center. Ride the Rudicoaster at Santa's Land and see how St Nick makes ends meet during the summer months. Race a go-cart, saddle up a steed or float merrily down the Oconaluftee River in an inner tube.

History

For centuries leading up to the arrival of outsiders in the Cherokee's domain, the bountiful forests and trout-rich streams of the Great Smokies enabled the tribe to flourish. They called themselves the 'principal people' and believed the Smokies to be the center of the universe. Hernando de Soto and 600 Spanish soldiers arrived on the scene in 1540, searching for gold. For the next 300 years, the Cherokee and the European interlopers perpetuated a bitter cycle of acrimony and bloodshed, with intermittent periods of peaceful relations shattered by the escalating violence of raids and incursions. As the Cherokee came to recognize that they would always be outnumbered and outgunned, they turned to diplomacy as their last chance to retain rights to their ancestral homelands. They signed treaties and were mollified by promises from the US government in exchange for laying down their arms, but time and again the treaties were broken and promises proved empty.

By 1838 common wisdom dictated that the two groups could never live peaceably side by side, and President Andrew Jackson sent troops to the area to round up every Cherokee they could find. More than 15,000 were forced to relocate to Oklahoma along the infamous Trail of Tears; some 4000 would die along the way. More than a thousand escaped this fate and fled into the Smoky Mountains, eventually forming the Eastern Band of the Cherokee. In 1876 their status was finally formalized when the boundaries of the Qualla Boundary Cherokee Reservation were set.

With the advent of the timber industry in the region, during subsequent decades the Cherokee turned to logging to prop up their economy, and the forests that had sustained them for so long were largely denuded. But the opening of Great Smoky Mountains National Park in 1940 changed all that. As hundreds of thousands of visitors began arriving each year, the Cherokee began to try their hand at tourism. The Cherokee Historical Association was organized in 1948 and premiered its outdoor drama, *Unto These Hills*, two years later. In 1952 the association opened the Oconaluftee Indian Village. Today tourism is the primary industry in the Qualla Boundary area, providing jobs for about 65 percent of the local population. The Eastern Band of the Cherokee now numbers nearly 10,000, most of whom live on the reservation.

Orientation

Cherokee is the main North Carolina gateway to the park and the largest town on the 56,000-acre Qualla Boundary Cherokee Reservation. Cherokee's main drag, **Tsali Blvd/Hwy 441**, travels alongside the gentle Oconaluftee River as it flows out of Great Smoky Mountains National Park. South of town, a business spur peels off of Hwy 441 and joins up with a stretch of Hwy 19, passing Harrah's Cherokee Casino and several hotels and campgrounds before rejoining the main road as it enters downtown. As Hwy 441 enters the park, it assumes its second name, Newfound Gap Rd.

Information

The **visitor center** (☎ 828-497-9195 or 800-438-1601; www.cherokee-nc.com; Tsali Blvd/Hwy 441; ☽ 8am-8pm Jun-Aug, 8am-7pm Sep-Oct, 8am-5pm Nov-May) provides local maps and lodging advice.

Talking Leaves Native American Bookstore (☎ 828-497-6044; Hwy 441 at Hwy 19; ☽ 9am-8pm Mon-Sat, 10am-6pm Sun, off-season hours vary) is one of the most comprehensive Native American bookstores east of the Mississippi. The term 'talking leaves' reflects the Cherokee's early regard for written words, particularly those used in broken treaties: When words were no longer of use, they withered and died. The selection includes a wide range of nonfiction books about the Cherokee and other tribes, novels, videos, musical recordings and children's literature. Also of interest are the resources devoted to the Cherokee language and alphabet.

Other local services include the following:

Cherokee Public Library (☎ 828-497-9023; Ginger Lynn Welch Complex, Acquoni Rd; ☽ 8am-5pm Mon-Thu, 8am-4:30pm Fri) Free Internet access.

Post office (☎ 828-497-3891; 671 Tsali Blvd/Hwy 441; ☽ 9am-4:30pm Mon-Fri, 10-11:30am Sat)

Urgent Care Clinic and Pharmacy (☎ 828-497-9036; Hwy 19 next to Harrah's; ☽ 9am-6pm Mon-Fri)

Cherokee Police (☎ 911 or 828-497-6584)

Sights

Don't miss the engrossing **Museum of the Cherokee Indian** (☎ 828-497-3481; www.cherokeemuseum.org; Drama Rd; adult/child $8/5; ☽ 9am-7pm Mon-Sat, 9am-5pm Sun, off-season hours vary) and its impressive interactive exhibits, which wend their way through the stations of Cherokee history from the Woodland and Mississippian Periods to the infamous Trail of Tears. In one display a holographic medicine man explains his herbal remedies over a campfire. Note the examples of written Cherokee language, which is again being taught in local schools. Outside the museum is a giant wooden statue of Sequoyah, the revered genius who invented the Cherokee alphabet. Carved from a single giant California Sequoia log, this work of art single-handedly redeems the wooden Indian.

The **Oconaluftee Indian Village** (☎ 828-497-2111; www.oconalufteevillage.com; Drama Rd; adult/child $13/6; ⊙ 9am-5:30pm May 15-Oct 25) is a replica of an 18th century Cherokee village in a pleasant forest setting. Cherokee guides demonstrate traditional crafts ranging from basket weaving to dugout canoe carving. The grounds include primitive cabins, rustic arbors and a seven-sided council house.

Qualla Arts & Crafts (☎ 828-497-3103; 645 Tsali Blvd/Hwy 441; ⊙ 8am-8pm Jun-Aug, 8am-6pm Sep-Oct, 8am-4:30pm Nov-May) offers authentic Indian handicrafts that are leagues above the tourist schlock sold down the road. Here you'll find ornate rattles made from turtle shells, exquisite carved wooden bowls, baskets and pottery. There is also a good onsite gallery showing a range of contemporary art.

With a cast of 130, the outdoor historical pageant **Unto These Hills** (☎ 866-554-4557; www.untothesehills.com; Mountainside Theatre, Drama Rd; reserved/adult/child $18/16/8; ⊙ nightly except Sun Jun-Aug) dramatizes the history of the Cherokee from the first European contact up to the Trail of Tears. The **ticket office** (⊙ 9am-6:30pm Mon-Sat) is on Tsali Blvd/Hwy 441 near the visitor center.

The town's biggest moneymaker is **Harrah's Cherokee Casino & Hotel** (☎ 828-497-7777; 777 Casino Dr/Hwy 19; ⊙ 24hr). If your idea of a good time is to play video poker (without playing cards or chips), work the slot machines (without coins) and sip free cola (without alcohol), you'll be in heaven. The casino's saving grace might be its three good restaurants: Many folks come here just to eat. You can also spend the night (see Sleeping, p142).

If this all sounds a bit too hygienic, **Tribal Bingo** (☎ 828-497-4320; Hwy 19; $10; ⊙ 7pm Mon-Wed) might restore your faith in gambling. An enterprise of the Eastern Band of the Cherokee, this raucous affair has folks shouting 'bingo!' for pots ranging from $100 to $1500. It's somewhat of a town social affair, and you're likely to hear the Cherokee language spoken as people chat and mutter over their game cards.

There's some gloriously tacky tourist traps in Cherokee and environs, but **Santa's Land Theme Park & Zoo** (☎ 828-497-9191; Hwy 19 east of Cherokee; admission $15; ⊙ 9am-5pm Apr-Oct) gets the prize. You wouldn't think that Santa would be such a big draw in July, but kids love the Rudi-Coaster, train ride and paddleboats. Grownups mostly roll their eyes.

Activities

Cherokee offers several relaxed, family-oriented outdoor activities.

Perfect for a riverside picnic, **Oconaluftee Islands Park** is a serene patch of green in central Cherokee. On the edge of the reservation near the park border, the 200ft **Mingo Falls** makes for a pleasant one-hour day hike. The trailhead is on Big Cove Rd.

Blackrock Outdoor Company (☎ 828-497-4453; Tsali Blvd/Hwy 441) sells camping and hiking supplies, plus a good selection of books and maps. It's across the street from McDonald's.

Saddle up at **Smokemont Riding Stables** (☎ 828-497-2373; 1hr/full day $20/115; ⊙ Apr-Oct), adjacent to Smokemont Campground in Great Smoky Mountains National Park. Among the variety of available horseback tours is a 2½-hour waterfall excursion. All trips begin at 9am.

With 30 miles of streams and three ponds well stocked with trout, it's no wonder that fishing is a popular pastime on the reservation. No state license is needed, but anglers must obtain the $7 Tribal Fishing Permit, available at many Cherokee businesses. Trout season opens the last Saturday of March and ends the last day of February the following year.

CCS Fishing Outfitters (☎ 828-497-1555; 626 Tsali Blvd/Hwy 441; ☒ closed Sun) is a well-stocked fishing supply store.

Sleeping

Cherokee has a good mix of independent motels, predictably comfortable chain hotels and campgrounds. On Hwy 441 south of Cherokee you'll find a number of economical, independent motor lodges. Nearly all places charge considerably higher rates during the high season (generally March to November). High season rates are listed here.

CAMPGROUNDS

The nicest campgrounds are in the national park (p115), but one decent local option is the 40-site **Cherokee Campground & Log Cabins** (☎ 828-497-9838; Hwy 19N at Hwy 441 Business; tent/campsite with hookup/cabin $25/30/85) on Soco Creek. Here you'll find a camp store, hot showers, pleasant cabins and fishing and tubing opportunities.

The pretty **Indian Creek Campground** (☎ 828-497-4361, 1367 Bunches Creek Rd; campsite without/with electricity $22/24, cabin/trailer $40/45), about 8 miles north of town off Big Cove Rd, offers a variety of campsites, including a number of walk-ins. Also available are rustic cabins and fully equipped trailers.

MID-RANGE

Pink Motel (☎ 828-497-3530; 1306 Tsali Blvd/Hwy 441; d $65; P ☒ ☒) This old motel on the main drag has plenty of personality: Its wonderful 50-year-old neon sign features a glimmering fairy, and pink sheets cover the beds. Rooms have coffee makers and back porches with river views.

Pageant Hills Motel (☎ 828-497-4371; 739 Tsali Blvd/Hwy 441; d $51; P ☒) Also sporting a nifty retro neon sign, this economical option stands before an impressive wall of kudzu. The rooms are small but clean.

El Camino Motel (☎ 828-497-3600; Hwys 19/441; weekday/weekend $72/110; P ☒ ☒) Convenient to the casino, this classic motor lodge is a little out of date but friendly and comfortable. Rooms have coffee makers.

Newfound Lodge (☎ 828-497-2746; 1192 Tsali Blvd/Hwy 441; d $88; P ☒ ☒) On the main drag, this place offers large, clean rooms with views and balconies overlooking the river. Rooms are equipped with coffee makers and refrigerators.

TOP END

Harrah's Cherokee Casino & Hotel (☎ 828-497-7777; 777 Casino Dr/Hwy 19; www.harrahs.com; d/ste $149/249; P ☒ ☐ ☒) This place bends over backwards trying to invoke the proud heritage of the Cherokee while milking you for every penny you're worth. Nonetheless, the hotel offers the classiest lodging in town. Guests are indulged with large baths, separate sitting areas and amenities such as hair dryers, coffee makers and humongous in-room television sets.

Hampton Inn (☎ 828-497-3115; www.hamptoncherokee.com; 185 Tsalagi Rd/Hwy 19S; d/t $109/145; P ☒ ☐ ☒) This chain hotel covers all the bases: there's a free breakfast bar, in-room hair dryers, iron and ironing board and wireless, high-speed Internet access, plus connecting rooms, cribs, an outdoor pool and a casino shuttle. What more could we ask for? Perhaps a little personality.

Eating

Cherokee's restaurant scene is, shall we say, a bit underdeveloped. Almost every fast food chain has opened shop in town, and the casino serves the predictable offerings. To escape corporate cuisine, one must look to independently run joints with names like Peter's, Paul's and Grandma's.

Grandma's Pancake and Steak (☎ 828-497-9801; Hwy 441 at Hwy 19; dishes $3-9; ☽ open 7am, closing hours vary) This low-key eatery achieves a certain charm with its checkerboard tablecloths and country-kitsch decor, including 11 presumably empty wasps' nests. But the real reason to come is for the from-scratch biscuits and old-fashioned redeye gravy. Grandma also claims bragging rights for a 'patented' pancake mix, mountain trout and Indian tacos. There's a special menu for kids.

Paul's Diner (☎ 497 2235; 111 Tsali Blvd/Hwy 441; dishes $4-8; ☽ 11am-8pm) Most visitors agree that this bright red roadside joint has the best burgers in town. The rib eye sandwiches and Indian tacos are also quite popular. Folks sit out on the patio or in a cozy dining room festooned with NASCAR posters.

Peter's Pancakes and Waffles (☎ 828-497-5116; 1384 Tsali Blvd/Hwy 441; dishes $5-7; ☽ 7am-2pm) This unpretentious place on the northern edge of town serves fluffy waffles and steak and eggs for breakfast and hearty sandwiches – including a near-perfect Reuben – at lunch.

Prime Sirloin Family Steak House (☎ 828-497-2878; Hwy 19 at Hwy 441 Business; buffet lunch/dinner $7/9; ☽ 11am-9pm Mon-Fri, 11am-10pm Sat) This buffet-style restaurant lays out smoked ham, fried chicken and beef with a wide selection of side dishes. There's also an all-you-can-eat salad and desert bar. Carb-counters beware.

Food Lion (☎ 828-497-4737; Hwy 441 Business; ☽ 24hr) At the Cherokee Crossing shopping center near the southern end of Hwy 441 Business, this large modern grocery store has everything you need for your traveler's larder. Also try the **IGA Reservation Foodliner** (☎ 828-497-8620; Hwy 19 at Soco Rd; ☽ 8am-9pm Mon-Sat). If you're hoping to procure beer or wine, however, you'll have to travel 16 miles to Sylva, as Cherokee is a dry town.

Getting There & Away
To reach Cherokee from the east, take I-40 west from Asheville, then Hwy 19 through Maggie Valley to Cherokee. From the north, take Hwy 441/Newfound Gap Rd through Great Smoky Mountains National Park.

DILLSBORO
☎ 828 / pop 200 / elevation 2036ft
The little town of Dillsboro, on Hwy 441 15 miles south of Cherokee, retains the ambience of a 19th century railroad town. It has always been known not for mining or logging, but rather for arts and crafts.

From its depot in Dillsboro, the historic **Great Smoky Mountains Railroad** (☎ 800-872-4681; diesel excursion child/adult $14-18/28-38, steam excursion child/adult $17-22/35-43) offers a unique journey through the scenic mountains and countryside of western North Carolina along the Murphy Branch Line, established in 1891. Trips depart from Dillsboro and Bryson City and include excursions to the Nantahala Gorge and Tuckasegee River, the Fontana Trestle and Whittier. Special trips include gourmet dinner trains, mystery-theater dinner trains and train and rafting combos from Bryson City.

Dillsboro is also home to one of the most distinguished and oldest inns in the region. The **Jarrett House Inn** (☎ 828-586-0265; www.jarretthouse.com; 100 Haywood St; s/d/t $95/105/110; P ☻), built in 1882, is a handsomely designed building with two floors of wraparound balconies embellished with wrought iron trim. Each room is furnished with period antiques; the only television here is in the lobby. The **Jarrett House Restaurant** (lunch/dinner plates $10/12; ☽ 11:30am-2:30pm & 4:30-7:30pm) has been famous since the days when railroad passengers telegraphed their orders ahead from Balsam depot, 12 miles up the tracks. Restaurant lore states that back in the day, '...the platters of country ham and bowls of redeye gravy kept coming to the tables and caused strong men to weep because they couldn't eat as much as they wanted.'

BRYSON CITY

☎ 828 / pop 8300 / elevation 1740ft

Just west of Cold Mountain, the peak made famous by Charles Frazier's novel and its cinematic adaptation, is the sleepy little mountain community of Bryson City. Sitting on the pretty Tuckasegee River, Bryson City is a peaceful place amid a wealth of natural scenery and outdoor activities. The nearby Nantahala River Gorge is a prime destination for white-water rafting, canoeing and kayaking. The river runs parallel to Hwy 19 southwest of town, from Topton to Wesser.

Activities & Outfitters

Nantahala Outdoor Center Main Campus (☎ 800-232-7238; www.noc.com; 13077 Hwy 19W), 13 miles from Bryson City, is the place that started it all. Since 1972 it's been on the cutting edge in white-water recreation. Today NOC leads rafting and kayaking trips on six area rivers, provides expert instruction and offers lodging (bunk/motel $15/59-72) and dining for outdoor activity enthusiasts of all stripes. There's also a well-stocked store selling outdoor equipment, and a bicycle repair shop.

Other well-established rafting outfitters on the Nantahala Gorge include the following:

Rock-N-Rivers (☎ 828-488-7555; 149 Main St) Rafting, tubing, camping and biking.

Wildwater Ltd Rafting (☎ 800-451-9972; Hwy 19W, 12 miles from Bryson City)

Paddle Inn Rafting (☎ 828-488-9651; 14611 Hwy 19W, 14 miles from Bryson City)

Sleeping

Bryson City has perhaps the highest concentration of lovely old country inns and B&Bs in the Smokies. The best place to pitch a tent near town is at the nearby Deep Creek Campground (p116) in Great Smoky Mountains National Park.

Nantahala Wesser Campground (☎ 828-488-8708; Hwy 74; campsite $18) Eleven miles west of Bryson City, this new and spacious campground is bordered on the east by a trout stream and on the west by beautiful mountain terrain. The wooded campsites are shady and pleasant; families are welcome and large-group accommodations are available.

Historic Calhoun Country Inn (☎ 828-488-1234; www.calhouncountryinn.com; 135 Everett St; r $65-135; ✗ 🐾) This grand old place is smack dab in the middle of town; the well-worn front porch affords a privileged view of the comings and goings on Everett St. Horace Kephart, author of the 1913 regional biography *Our Southern Highlanders*, passed many an evening on this porch late in life in conversation with Granville Calhoun, the inn's namesake and first hotelier. Furnished with period antiques, the 15 rooms feel old in the best way. Family-style meals are served by reservation: the tables are heaped with country ham and chicken, fresh yeast breads, homemade jellies, jams and cobblers, and hand-churned butter. Children are welcome; pets are not. Reservations required.

The Folkestone Inn (☎ 828-488-2730; www.folkestone.com; 101 Folkestone Rd; r $88-148; 🅿 🐾) On a large plot of land near the Deep Creek entrance to the national park, this exceedingly pleasant inn occupies a converted 1920s farmhouse in a grove of mammoth spruce trees. There are 10 guestrooms; some have fireplaces, some have balconies or decks and one room, called 'Boots & Saddles,' welcomes well-behaved pets. The complimentary breakfasts served each morning get high marks for variety and quality.

Cold Springs Country Inn (☎ 828-488-3537; 435 Cold Springs Rd; r $75; ❀) Featuring 10 ground-floor guestrooms with private bathrooms, this amiable country inn isn't as quaint or old as the others, but the price is more economical. It's off Hwy 19, 4 miles west of town.

Hemlock Inn (☎ 828-488-2885; Galbraithe Creek Rd; d/cottage/ste $166/188/172-225; P) This sprawling, full-service mountaintop inn on 52 forested acres is a bit pricey, but the leisurely pace of life here and relative isolation are a big draw for some folks. Bird-watching enthusiasts return year after year for naturalist-led tours and slide lectures, and there are miles of hiking trails on the property. The rooms are comfortable and furnished with country antiques and pieces made by mountain craftspeople. Huge country meals are served family-style in a cozy dining room, and children are welcome. Galbraithe Creek Rd is off Hwy 19, 3 miles northeast of Bryson City.

Eating

Mountain Perks Espresso Bar & Café (☎ 828 488 9561; 9 Depot St; ☾ 7am-3pm Mon-Fri, 9am-3pm Sat) This popular meeting place serves your morning brew, as well as sandwiches, soups, salads and smoothies.

Everett Street Diner (☎ 828-488-9555; 25 Everett St; breakfast or lunch $6-9; ☾ 7am-2pm Mon-Fri) A main street favorite, the diner serves fine country breakfasts and filling lunches.

Soda Pops Fountain (☎ 828-488-5379; 141 Everett St; ☾ 1-9pm Mon-Thu, noon-10pm Sat) This old-timey ice cream shop is the place to be on a summer evening; the sidewalk rocking chairs are filled with happy locals enjoying such concoctions as the Banana Pudding Swirl Freeze. A cool neon ice cream cone sign tempts all passersby out for an evening stroll.

Pasqualino's Italian Restaurant (☎ 828-488-9555; 25 Everett St; lunch $5-8, dinner $13-16; ☾ 11am-close) This breezy restaurant has the feel of a place that's been in business for a while. On the menu are pizzas and Italian favorites, including a particularly good dish simply called 'baked shrimp and scallops.' Kids get their own menu.

SHOPPING

Grampa's Mountain Music (☎ 828-488-5588; Depot St) This mountain music emporium across from the train station sells new and used instruments, including dobros, fiddles, banjos and guitars, as well as a good selection of CDs.

TSALI RECREATION AREA

The popular and challenging single-track **biking trails** of the Tsali Recreation Area provide perhaps the best mountain biking action in the Smokies. Four trails follow the Fontana Lake shoreline and provide gorgeous panoramic views looking north across the water.

The **Tsali Campground** (Nov-Apr/May-Oct $5/15) offers 42 sites with facilities; dispersed forest camping is also permitted free of charge. Trails are reserved for horses on some days; call the **Cheoah Ranger District** (☎ 929-479-6431) for more information. Tsali Recreation Area is accessed via Hwy 28, 5 miles north of Almond.

FONTANA

☎ 828 / pop 100 / elevation 2060ft
At 480ft – the equivalent of a 50-story skyscraper – **Fontana Dam** on the Little Tennessee River is the tallest dam east of the Rocky Mountains. The Tennessee Valley Authority (TVA) began construction in 1942, and due to the urgent need for electric power during World War II, the dam was completed in just 36 months; the finished product had a power-generating capacity of 241

OLYMPIC WHITE WATER

Over millions of years the Ocoee River has carved a deep, meandering channel through the hard mountain rock. From 1912 to 1976, however, this slow process was interrupted when the river's waters were diverted into a wooden flume for use in generating hydroelectric power. The day that the flume was finally condemned and water returned to the long-dry riverbed was a happy one for white-water enthusiasts. These days the water is turned on and off with what must be a mighty lever; it flows 116 days each year on an exact schedule. In a unique arrangement with the electric utilities, outfitters pay $2 per customer to make up for the lost power generation.

In 1996 the world got a glimpse of this raging waterway when the Olympic Canoe & Kayak Slalom competition was held on the Ocoee River. You can view the manmade slalom course and exhibits about the sport at the **Ocoee Whitewater Center** (☎ 423-496-5197; 3970 Hwy 64, Ducktown, TN; ☼ daily Apr-Oct, weekends Nov-Mar). In addition to whitewater action, the center offers a 1-mile wheelchair-accessible hiking trail that crosses a 330ft suspension bridge and circles the center. There are 20 more miles of trails for hikers and mountain bikers, including the Bear Paw and Chestnut Mountain Trails, both of which are loops. A recent addition, the Thunder Rock Express, has received a lot of positive comments from bikers.

The following well-established rafting outfitters lead trips on the Ocoee River:
Ocoee Adventure Center (☎ 888-723-8622; Hwy 64, Ducktown TN)
Wildwater Rafting (☎ 800-451-9972; Hwy 64, Ducktown TN)
Ocoee Rafting Center (☎ 800-251-4800; Hwy 64, Ducktown TN)

megawatts. The 5000 workers who converged at Fontana to construct the dam worked around the clock, seven days a week, in three shifts. A community for these workers and their families was erected in the wilderness, almost overnight. A **visitor center** (☼ 9am-7pm May-Nov) affords an exceptional view of the dam, and visitors can tour the Powerhouse, reached by an incline tram.

Picnic tables and camping accommodations are available in the area. Boaters are served by docks and launch ramps at various sites around the lake. The fishing is superb here; the waters of Fontana Lake are home to rainbow, brown and brook trout, large- and smallmouth bass, walleye, pike, perch, sunfish and crappie.

What was once the construction village is now the **Historic Fontana Village Resort** (☎ 800-849-2258; Hwy 28; campsite without/with hookup $15/20, r $79-149, cabin $59-209; ☼ Mar-Nov; P ☒ ☒), which offers such recreational activities as boating, horseback riding, tennis, basketball and craft making.

The **Appalachian Trail** crosses the top of Fontana Dam. Through-hikers named the nearby trail shelter the 'Fontana Hilton' for the luxurious hot showers available at the TVA visitor center. Hikers can also find satisfaction at the **Hike Inn** (☎ 828-479-3677; 3204 Fontana Rd; lodging $35/45 section hikers/through hikers; P ☒), a small motel dedicated to the needs of hiking enthusiasts. Proprietors Jeff and Nancy Hock are well loved by through- and section-hikers alike for their experience and knowledge of the AT subculture, the local terrain and hiking logistics. In addition to lodging, through-hiker service includes transportation, laundry and a supplies run to Robbinsville. Shuttle service is provided at a rate of roughly $1 per mile, depending on road terrain. Don't miss their personal artifact collection of prehistoric implements from North,

Central and South America. Nancy also makes a delicious picante sauce (pint/quart $3/5). Credit cards are not accepted.

Yellow Branch Cabins (☎ 828-479-4126; 177 Madison Lane, Robbinsville; cabins $165) These three-bedroom, two-bath cabins with full-size kitchens and laundry facilities are great options for families. Less than a mile from Fontana Lake, the cabins sit on a beautiful mountainside lot with breathtaking vistas and abundant wildflowers. From Fontana Village, follow Hwy 28N for 16 miles and turn left on Yellow Branch Rd. You'll find Madison Lane a half mile uphill.

Near Fontana Dam in the far southwest corner of Great Smoky Mountains National Park, **Twentymile Campsite** is near several hiking trails that lead into a wild, roadless region with access to Gregory Bald.

JOYCE KILMER MEMORIAL FOREST

The Joyce Kilmer Memorial Forest was named for the poet responsible for *Trees*, the 1913 poem memorized by millions of schoolchildren and notorious for its flagrant use of mixed metaphors. Think back and perhaps you will remember these immortal lines: 'Upon whose bosom snow has lain / Who intimately lives with rain / Poems are made by fools like me / But only God can make a tree.'

The poem may be bad, but the forest is magnificent. In this remnant of the original Appalachian forest, one gets a sense of the grandeur of the Cherokee's domain prior to the Europeans' arrival. Some of the enormous yellow poplars approach 20ft in circumference, are 100ft or taller and exceed 400 years old. It's said that loggers saved the cutting of this cove for last because they admired the gargantuan trees. Fortunately, the lumber interests went bankrupt before the forest here could be logged, and before the timber industry could regroup, the land was set aside as a protected wilderness.

A 2-mile, figure-8 shaped trail passes through **Poplar Cove**, a living cathedral of some of the East Coast's largest and oldest trees. They rival the Pacific Coast redwoods in size and stature. The forest floor is relatively open because the canopy only allows in a small amount of light. Be prepared to cross several rickety wooden bridges that seem ready to topple into the streams they traverse.

On the road leading to the Joyce Kilmer Memorial Forest parking area, the **Nantahala National Forest Horse Cove Campground** (tent site $10) is beautiful and lightly used, with campsites along the lakeshore and beside a river.

Joyce Kilmer Memorial Forest lies off Hwy 143, 5 miles from its junction with Hwy 28.

CHEROKEE NATIONAL FOREST

The 635,000-acre **Cherokee National Forest** (☎ 423-476-9700; www.southernregion.fs.fed. us/cherokee), the largest tract of public land in Tennessee, flanks Great Smoky Mountains National Park to the north and south; together, the forest and park create a nearly unbroken swath of managed land along the entire eastern border of the state. Although Great Smoky gets most of the attention, the forest's wild terrain at least rivals the park in the beauty of its landscape and the variety of available recreational opportunities. Here you'll find 30 developed campgrounds and picnic areas, 700 miles of trail, hundreds of miles of mountain streams, seven white-water rivers and abundant wildlife. Activities include hiking along the AT, kayaking the raging Ocoee River, touring the back roads and byways by car along the Cherohala Skyway and watching birds and other wildlife.

About 10 percent of the national forest is wilderness; in the northern districts are Big Laurel Branch Wilderness, on Watauga Lake, and Unaka Wilderness. In the southern districts, Little Frog Wilderness lies along a stretch of the Ocoee River and borders the Cohutta Wilderness in Georgia.

FOOTHILLS PARKWAY (WEST & EAST)

The Foothills Parkway is actually two distinct motorways. The 18-mile **western section** connects Townsend with Chilhowee Lake at the southwest corner of the park. The entrance is 6 miles north of Townsend on Hwy 321; from here you'll enjoy 11 miles of stunning vistas of the Smokies skyline before reaching **Look Rock Campground** and the nearby observation tower.

The 6-mile **eastern section** (closed in winter) connects Hwy 32 near Cosby with I-40 and provides access to **Big Creek** (p115) and **Cataloochee** (p87) in Great Smoky Mountains National Park.

Both sections are lightly traveled and provide a good alternative to the heavily used park roads. Each is lined with a number of turnouts affording fine views. If you are lucky enough to be in the region during the turning of the autumn leaves, you couldn't hope to find a better place to enjoy the seasonal colors.

TOWNSEND

☎ 865 / pop 2400 / elevation 945ft

Townsend got its start in 1901 as the headquarters of the Little River Lumber Company, one of the larger logging operations in the Great Smoky Mountains. Thanks to the arrival of the national park, no trees have been felled by loggers since 1938. Since then, Townsend has proclaimed itself to be 'the quiet side of the Smokies.' This designation is a nice way of saying, 'We have very little in common with Pigeon Forge – honest!' But even those who love the artificial turf of Pigeon Forge's miniature golf courses are charmed by Townsend's relaxing pace.

Information

Townsend Visitor Center (☎ 865-448-6134; www.smokymountains.org; 7906 E Lamar Alexander Pkwy; ☺ 9am-6pm) This excellent visitor center sells a good selection of books, including many hard-to-find titles on Appalachian folklore. Also available are two worthwhile brochures: *Shadows of the Past: Townsend Historical Trail* and *Hiking & Biking on the Peaceful Side of the Smokies.*

Townsend hosts two big annual hoedowns celebrating the cultural heritage of the region: the **Spring Festival** in late April and the **Fall Heritage Festival** in late September.

Mary E Tippitt Memorial Library (☎ 865-448-1441; 120 Tiger Dr; ☺ 9am-6pm Mon & Tue, noon-6pm Wed, 9am-5pm Thu & Fri) Free Internet access.

Townsend Post Office (118 Town Square Dr; ☺ 8:30-11:45am & 1-4pm Mon-Fri, 9-11am Sat)

Blount Memorial Hospital (☎ 865-977-4778; 907 E Lamar Alexander Pkwy in Maryville) The nearest full-service hospital is 20 miles northwest.

Townsend police department (☎ 911 or 865-448-6875)

Fire or ambulance (☎ 911)

Sights

The **Tuckaleechee Caverns** (☎ 865-448-2274; 825 Cavern Rd; adult/child $11/5.50; ☺ 9am-6pm) were known to the Cherokee and used as a hiding place. They were opened to the public in 1931 by two friends who had played in the caves together as children, using homemade lamps made from pop bottles and kerosene. The caverns feature several impressive stalagmite formations, including one called 'Toothpick' that is 12ft tall and 6 inches across.

The interesting **Little River Railroad and Lumber Company Museum** (☎ 865-448-2211; Hwy 321; admission free; ☺ 10am-6 Mon-Sat, 1-5pm high season) has a restored locomotive, depot, steam sawmill and a collection of railroad and lumber company artifacts.

Activities & Outfitters

If you're serious about fishing, you won't want to pass up a visit to the world-class fishing emporium **Little River Outfitters** (☎ 865-448-9459; www.littleriveroutfitters. com; 106 Town Square Dr; ☺ 9am-5pm Sun-Thu, 9am-8pm Fri, 9am-6pm Sat). In addition to the best selection of gear, flies and equipment, this place provides expert guides (half/full day $135/155) and a full roster of classes.

Next to Heaven Stables (☎ 864-448-9150; Hwy 321/Wears Valley Rd; ☺ 10am-close Mon-Sat) is one of the few stables in the area to allow riding without the supervision of a guide.

One cool and pleasant way to pass the day is tubing on the Little River. Many tubing outfitters offer shuttle service, but this is the only one called **River Rat** (☎ 865-448-8888; Hwy 321/Wears Valley Rd). Tube rental, including shuttle service, is $12.

Sleeping

Townsend has a wide range of well-priced accommodations, including economical campgrounds and motels, cabins ideal for families and fancy mountain lodges. Listed below are high-season weekend rates; off-season rates are considerably lower.

Lazy Daze Campground (☎ 865-448-6061; 8429 Lamar Alexander Pkwy/Hwy 73; tent site/site with hookup/river site $22/28/31, motel d/t $42/46; cabin $65) Campgrounds like the Lazy Daze – and there are several along Hwy 73 – often provide economical rooms and rustic cabins in addition to camping sites.

Scenic Motel (☎ 865-448-2294; 8254 Lamar Alexander Pkwy/Hwy 73; d $45-54; P ☒ ☒) This economical place with basic rooms is an excellent value but not as scenic as the name implies.

Dock's Motel (☎ 865-448-2234; 8219 Lamar Alexander Pkwy/Hwy 73; d/kitchenette/cabin $55/65/75; P ☒ ☒) The well-priced accommodations include riverfront and creekside cabins and one two-bedroom cabin that sleeps up to ten.

Tuckaleechee Village Motel (☎ 865-448-2267; 7281 Hwy 321/Wears Valley Rd; s/d/kitchenette $59/69/79; P ☒ ☒) This pleasant motel features cottages on the river, with queen-size beds, screened porches and a campfire ring.

Talley Ho Inn (☎ 800-448-2465; 8314 Lamar Alexander Pkwy/Hwy 73; s/d/cottage $55/77/150; P ☒ ☒ ☒) This well-run motel features rooms with balconies or terraces and cottages with complete kitchens that accommodate up to 16 people. Guests receive a 10 percent discount at the Carriage House restaurant next door.

Strawberry Patch Inn (☎ 865-448-6306; 7509 Old Hwy 73; d/ste $89/119; P ☒) This small, friendly inn is comprised of two rustic buildings with large balconies overlooking the Little River – the only inn in town with that amenity. The suites are equipped with full kitchens. Pets are welcome.

Maple Leaf Lodge (☎ 865-448-6000; www.mapleleaflodge.com; 137 Apple Valley Way; lodge r $129-179, 1-/2-bedroom cabin $129-169/139-89; P ☒ ☒) This luxurious lodge has all the amenities you would expect for the price – fluffy bathrobes, king-size beds with log frames, afternoon tea, the works – but the overall effect is perhaps just a bit too sweet, like an excess of Appalachian fudge. Nonetheless, some will find it appealing. The cabins have hot tubs, fireplaces and big, welcoming porches and are generally pleasing. It's a good option for large groups, which receive discounted rates and get run-of-the-house privileges.

Eating

Smokin' Joe's Bar-B-Que (☎ 865-448-3212; 8303 Lamar Alexander Pkwy/Hwy 73; plates $4-8; ☺ 11am-close) Get your fried dill pickles and open-pit barbecue at this simple, clean and welcoming eatery.

Victoria Station (☎ 865-448-6848; 7753 Lamar Alexander Pkwy/Hwy 73; meals $6-16, buffet $7-10; ◷ 8am-9:30pm) This family-friendly place offers casual dining in a pleasant, country-house atmosphere. Good salads and even a veggie burger (a rarity 'round these parts) round out the menu. There's live music on Sunday afternoons.

Back Porch Restaurant (☎ 865-448-6333; 7018 Lamar Alexander Pkwy/Hwy 73; meals $7-15; ◷ 8am-9pm, closed Tue) Housed in a lovely, old-timey cabin, this authentic Southern restaurant features a big wraparound porch and a screened-in porch. If you've been wanting to try wild boar, here's your chance. Back Porch offers a children's menu and nightly specials.

Deadbeat Pete's (☎ 865-448-0900; 7613 Lamar Alexander Pkwy/Hwy 73; meals $7-16; ◷ 11am-10pm Sun-Thu, 11am-11pm Fri & Sat) For something different, this southwestern restaurant has the only huevos rancheros and fajitas in town, not to mention a delicious coyote sandwich (really – it's better than it sounds). Enjoy your meal on an open-air riverfront patio.

Timbers Restaurant (☎ 865-448-6838; 8123 Lamar Alexander Pkwy/Hwy 73; meals $11-19; ◷ 4-10pm) For a more upscale meal, this good family-style restaurant specializes in steaks, prime rib, pasta and seafood.

The Village Market (☎ 865-448-3010; 7945 Lamar Alexander Pkwy/Hwy 73; ◷ 6am-10pm) This large grocery store has a full deli and decent beer selection. For wine or spirits, you'll have to visit Maryville.

Shopping

Wood-N-Strings Dulcimer Shop (☎ 865-448-6647; www.clemmerdulcimer.com; 7645 Lamar Alexander Pkwy/Hwy 73) This very special music store sells handcrafted Appalachian string and hammer dulcimers, ban-jammers and even the occasional bowed psaltery. Even if you're not a musician, step in to hear local musicians trying out the wares or to get the lowdown on upcoming regional musical happenings.

Great Smoky & Shenandoah

MAP SECTION

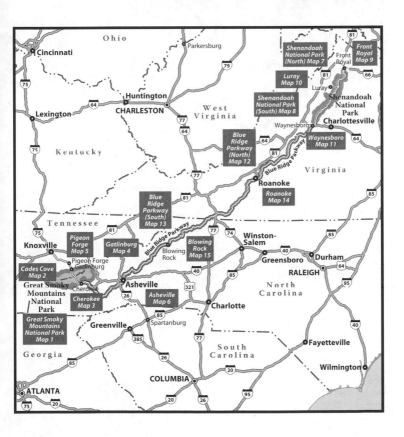

Map 1 **Great Smoky Mountains National Park**

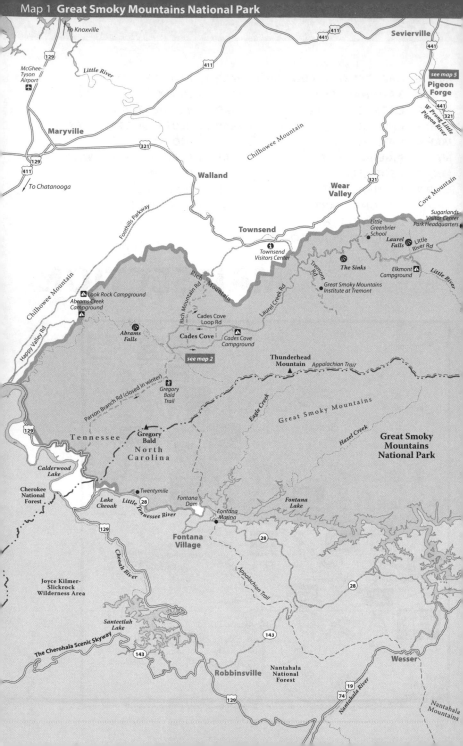

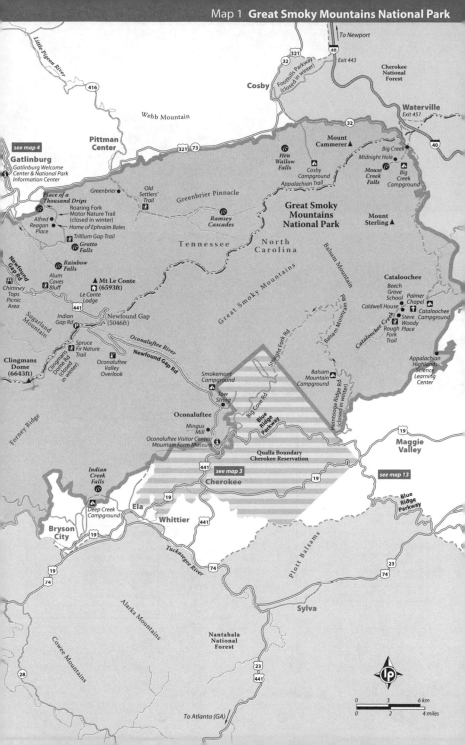

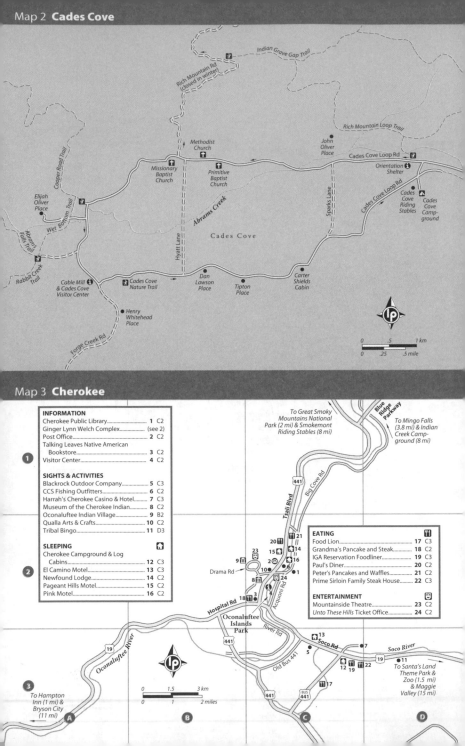

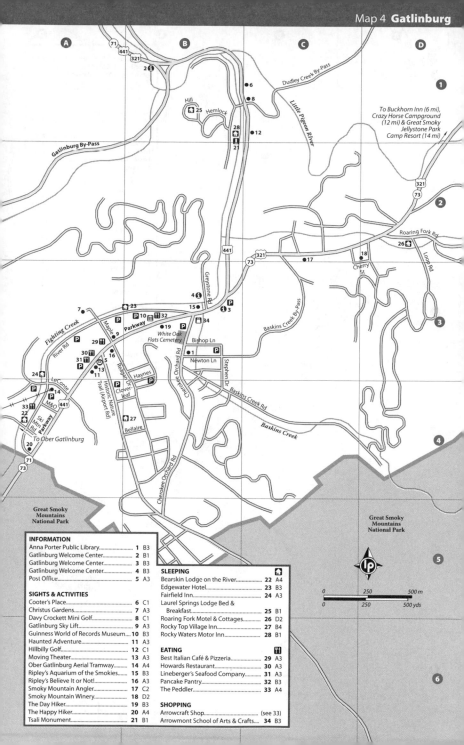

To Buckhorn Inn (6 mi),
Crazy Horse Campground
(12 mi) & Great Smoky
Jellystone Park
Camp Resort (14 mi)

Great Smoky
Mountains
National Park

Great Smoky
Mountains
National Park

| 0 | 250 | 500 m |
| 0 | 250 | 500 yds |

INFORMATION

Anna Porter Public Library	**1** B3
Gatlinburg Welcome Center	**2** B1
Gatlinburg Welcome Center	**3** B3
Gatlinburg Welcome Center	**4** B3
Post Office	**5** A3

SIGHTS & ACTIVITIES

Cooter's Place	**6** C1
Christus Gardens	**7** A3
Davy Crockett Mini Golf	**8** C1
Gatlinburg Sky Lift	**9** A3
Guinness World of Records Museum	**10** B3
Haunted Adventure	**11** A3
Hillbilly Golf	**12** C1
Moving Theater	**13** A3
Ober Gatlinburg Aerial Tramway	**14** A4
Ripley's Aquarium of the Smokies	**15** B3
Ripley's Believe It or Not!	**16** A3
Smoky Mountain Angler	**17** C2
Smoky Mountain Winery	**18** D2
The Day Hiker	**19** B3
The Happy Hiker	**20** A4
Tsali Monument	**21** B1

SLEEPING

Bearskin Lodge on the River	**22** A4
Edgewater Hotel	**23** B3
Fairfield Inn	**24** A3
Laurel Springs Lodge Bed & Breakfast	**25** B1
Roaring Fork Motel & Cottages	**26** D2
Rocky Top Village Inn	**27** B4
Rocky Waters Motor Inn	**28** B1

EATING

Best Italian Café & Pizzeria	**29** A3
Howards Restaurant	**30** A3
Lineberger's Seafood Company	**31** A3
Pancake Pantry	**32** B3
The Peddler	**33** A4

SHOPPING

| Arrowcraft Shop | (see 33) |
| Arrowmont School of Arts & Crafts | **34** B3 |

Map 5 Pigeon Forge

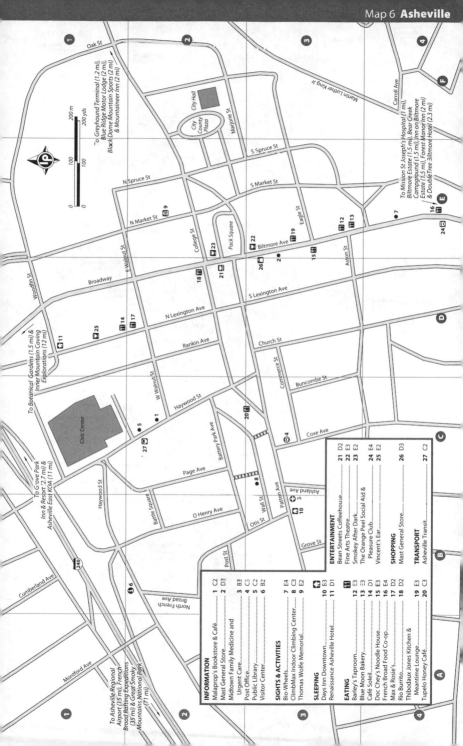

Map 6 **Asheville**

To Greyhound Terminal (1.2 mi),
Blue Ridge Motor Lodge (2 mi),
Black Dome Mountain Sports (2 mi)
& Mountaineer Inn (2 mi)

City County Plaza
City Hall

To Mission St Joseph's Hospital (1 mi),
Biltmore Estate (1.5 mi), Bear Creek
Campground (1.5 mi), Inn on Biltmore
Estate (1.5 mi), Forest Manor Inn (2 mi)
& DoubleTree Biltmore Hotel (2.3 mi)

Martin Luther King Jr
Carroll Ave

Oak St

S Spruce St
S Market St
N Spruce St
N Market St
College St
E Walnut St
Broadway
S Lexington Ave
N Lexington Ave
Rankin Ave
Church St
Commerce St
Buncombe St
Haywood St
W Walnut St
Woodfin St
Majorie St
Pack Square
Biltmore Ave
Eagle St
Aston St

To Botanical Gardens (1.5 mi) &
Inner Mountain Caving
Explorations (12 mi)

Civic Center

To Grove Park
Inn & Resort (2.7 mi) &
Asheville East KOA (11 mi)

Battery Park Ave
Page Ave
Haywood St
Battle Square
O Henry Ave
Otis St
Post St
Grove St
Wall St
Ashland Ave
Patton Ave
Coxe Ave

To Asheville Regional
Airport (15 mi), French
Broad Rafting Expeditions
(35 mi) & Great Smoky
Mountains National Park
(71 mi)

Cumberland Ave
Montford Ave
North French Broad Ave

200 m
200 yds
100
100
0
0

INFORMATION
Malaprop's Bookstore & Café	1 C2
Mast General Store	2 D3
Midtown Family Medicine and Urgent Care	3 B3
Post Office	4 C3
Public Library	5 C2
Visitor Center	6 B2

SIGHTS & ACTIVITIES
Bio-Wheels	7 E4
ClimbMax Indoor Climbing Center	8 C3
Thomas Wolfe Memorial	9 E2

SLEEPING
Days Inn Downtown	10 E3
Renaissance Asheville Hotel	11 D1

EATING
Barley's Taproom	12 E3
Blue Moon Bakery	13 E3
Café Soleil	14 D1
Doc Chey's Noodle House	15 E3
French Broad Food Co-op	16 E4
Max & Rosie's	17 D2
Rio Burrito	18 D2
Thibodaux Jones Kitchen & Meantime Lounge	19 E3
Tupelo Honey Café	20 D1

ENTERTAINMENT
Bean Streets Coffeehouse	21 D2
Fine Arts Theatre	22 E3
Smokey After Dark	23 E2
The Orange Peel Social Aid & Pleasure Club	24 E4
Vincent's Ear	25 E2

SHOPPING
Mast General Store	26 D3

TRANSPORT
Asheville Transit	27 C2

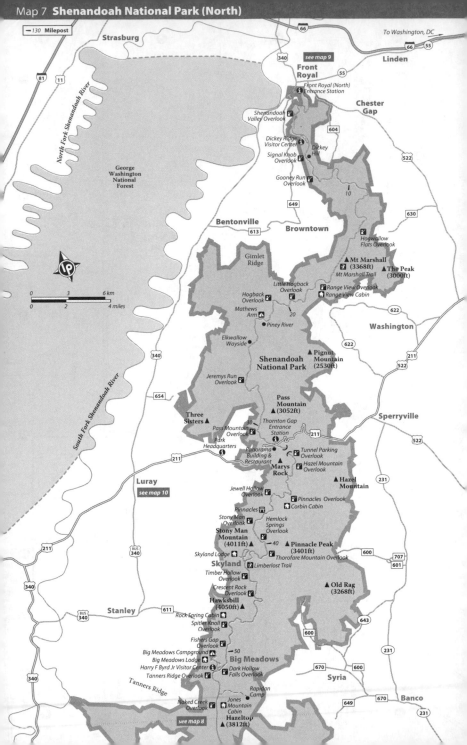

Map 7 Shenandoah National Park (North)

— 130 Milepost

Strasburg

To Washington, DC

81
11

66

340

see map 9

66
55

Linden

Front Royal

North Fork Shenandoah River

Front Royal (North) Entrance Station

55

Chester Gap

Shenandoah Valley Overlook

604

George Washington National Forest

Dickey Ridge Visitor Center

Dickey Hill

Signal Knob Overlook

522

Gooney Run Overlook

10

649

Bentonville

630

613

Browntown

Hogwallow Flats Overlook

Gimlet Ridge

▲ Mt Marshall (3368ft)

▲ The Peak (3000ft)

Mt Marshall Trail

Little Hogback Overlook

Hogback Overlook

Range View Overlook

Range View Cabin

622

Mathews Arm

20

Piney River

Elkwallow Wayside

Shenandoah National Park

▲ Pignut Mountain (2530ft)

622

340

211

522

Jeremys Run Overlook

Pass Mountain ▲ (3052ft)

654

Three Sisters ▲

30

Thornton Gap Entrance Station

Pass Mountain Overlook

Sperryville

Park Headquarters

211

522

Panorama Building & Restaurant

Tunnel Parking Overlook

Marys Rock

Hazel Mountain Overlook

Luray

see map 10

Jewell Hollow Overlook

▲ Hazel Mountain

231

Pinnacles Overlook

Pinnacles

Corbin Cabin

Stony Man Overlook

Hemlock Springs Overlook

Stony Man Mountain (4011ft) ▲

40

211

BUS 340

▲ Pinnacle Peak (3401ft)

600

707

Skyland Lodge

Thorofare Mountain Overlook

601

Skyland

Limberlost Trail

340

Timber Hollow Overlook

▲ Old Rag (3268ft)

Crescent Rock Overlook

Hawksbill (4050ft) ▲

Stanley

611

Rock Spring Cabin

643

Spitler Knoll Overlook

Fishers Gap Overlook

600

231

Big Meadows Campground

50

Big Meadows Lodge

Big Meadows

Harry F Byrd Jr Visitor Center

Dark Hollow Falls Overlook

670

600

Syria

Tanners Ridge Overlook

Tanners Ridge

Rapidan Camp

Naked Creek Overlook

Jones Mountain Cabin

Banco

340

see map 8

Hazeltop ▲ (3812ft)

649

670

231

Map 8 **Shenandoah National Park (South)**

see map 7

— 130 Milepost

▲ Hazeltop
(3812ft)

Grindstone
Mountain
(2850ft) ▲

*The Point
Overlook*

Shenandoah

▲ Bush Mountain
(3527ft)

▲ Bluff
Mountain

615

662

Green
Mountain
(2149ft) ▲

759

Lewis Mountain Lodge
Lewis Mountain
Campground

609

340

*The Oaks
Overlook*

607

759

Piney ▲
Mountain
(1975ft)

Pocosin
Cabin
60

▲ Lewis
Mountain

Kirtley
Mountain
(2593ft) ▲

665

759

Huckleberry ▲
Mountain
(2158ft)

Elkton

623

623

*South River
Overlook*
South River

624

▲ Saddleback
Mountain
(3375ft)

230

*Swift Run Gap
Entrance Station*

340

33

McGaheysville

649

*Swift Run
Overlook*

▲ Hightop
(3587ft)

Stanardsville

33

810

*Eaton Hollow
Overlook*

70

*Bacon Hollow
Overlook*

Rocky
Mount
(2740ft) ▲

▲ Flattop
(3050ft)

*Two Mile Run
Overlook*
*Brown Mountain
Overlook*

Loft Mountain Campground
Loft Mountain Overlook

Brokenback
Mountain
(1750ft) ▲

*Rockytop
Overlook*

*Ivy
Creek
Overlook*

Doyles River Cabin

Nortonsville

Port
Republic

340

Loft Mountain
Wayside

80

County Line
Mountain
(1980ft)

664

*Big Run
Overlook*

659

Loft Mountain
Information
Center

810

663

Grottoes

Doyles River Overlook

Shenandoah
National Park

Dundo Group
Campground

*Blackrock
Summit*

Trayfoot ▲
Mountain
(3374ft)

*Trayfoot
Mountain
Overlook*

Rip Rap Trail

90

*Riprap
Overlook*

*Moormans
River
Overlook*

*Crimora Lake
Overlook*

614

Turk
Mountain
(2960ft) ▲

810

*Sawmill Run
Overlook*

29

619

250

Charlottesville

611

*Calf Mountain
Overlook*

100

64

254

*McCormick
Gap
Overlook*

Crozet

Scott ▲
Mountain
(2760ft)

250

29

Waynesboro

see map 11

250

340

Alton

64

*Rockfish Gap (South)
Entrance Station*

South Fork Shenandoah River

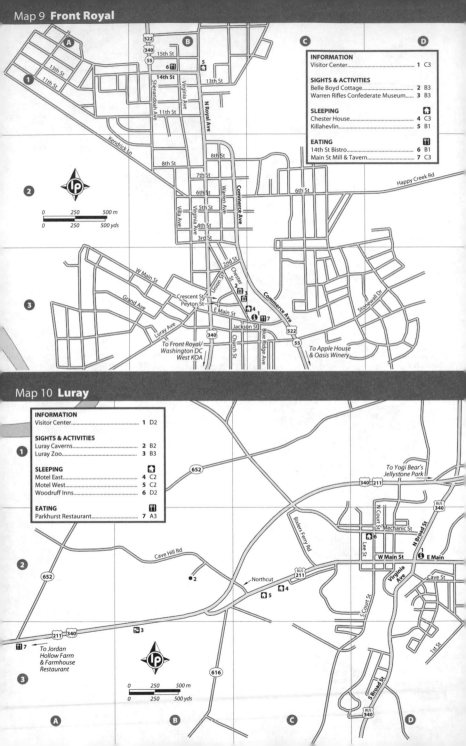

Map 9 Front Royal

Map 10 Luray

Map 11 **Waynesboro**

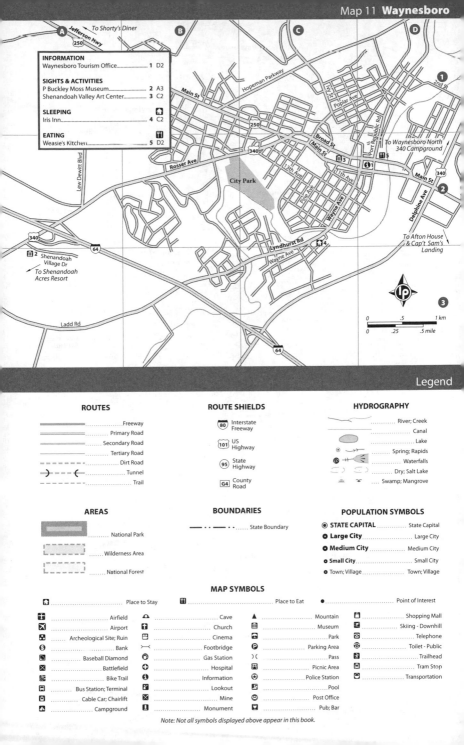

INFORMATION
Waynesboro Tourism Office.................... **1** D2

SIGHTS & ACTIVITIES
P Buckley Moss Museum........................ **2** A3
Shenandoah Valley Art Center............... **3** C2

SLEEPING
Iris Inn.. **4** C2

EATING
Weasie's Kitchen.................................... **5** D2

Legend

ROUTES

............Freeway
..........Primary Road
..........Secondary Road
..........Tertiary Road
..........Dirt Road
..........Tunnel
..........Trail

ROUTE SHIELDS

80 Interstate Freeway
101 US Highway
95 State Highway
G4 County Road

HYDROGRAPHY

............River; Creek
..........Canal
..........Lake
..........Spring; Rapids
..........Waterfalls
..........Dry; Salt Lake
..........Swamp; Mangrove

AREAS

..........National Park
..........Wilderness Area
..........National Forest

BOUNDARIES

..........State Boundary

POPULATION SYMBOLS

◉ **STATE CAPITAL** .... State Capital
◒ **Large City** .... Large City
◓ **Medium City** .... Medium City
◔ **Small City** .... Small City
◦ Town; Village .... Town; Village

MAP SYMBOLS

⌂ .... Place to Stay
🍴 .... Place to Eat
● .... Point of Interest

🕀 .... Airfield
✈ .... Airport
⚒ .... Archeological Site; Ruin
$ .... Bank
◆ .... Baseball Diamond
✕ .... Battlefield
🚲 .... Bike Trail
🚌 .... Bus Station; Terminal
🚡 .... Cable Car; Chairlift
▲ .... Campground

⌂ .... Cave
✝ .... Church
🎬 .... Cinema
⤙ .... Footbridge
⊙ .... Gas Station
✚ .... Hospital
ℹ .... Information
📷 .... Lookout
✕ .... Mine
❚ .... Monument

▲ .... Mountain
🏛 .... Museum
🏞 .... Park
Ⓟ .... Parking Area
)(..................... Pass
🎪 .... Picnic Area
⊛ .... Police Station
🏊 .... Pool
⊗ .... Post Office
🍺 .... Pub; Bar

🏬 .... Shopping Mall
⛷ .... Skiing - Downhill
☎ .... Telephone
🚻 .... Toilet - Public
🚩 .... Trailhead
🚊 .... Tram Stop
🚉 .... Transportation

Note: Not all symbols displayed above appear in this book.

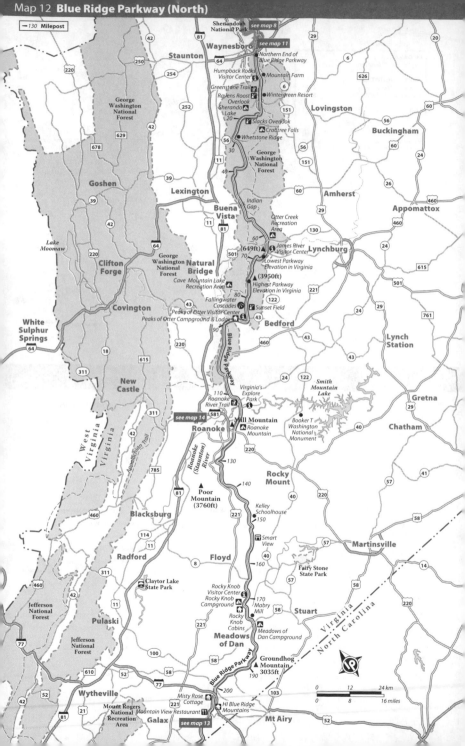

Map 13 **Blue Ridge Parkway (South)**

← 130 Milepost

VP

see map 12

0   12   24 km
0   8   16 miles

Galax   210
Blue Ridge Music Center
89
Cumberland Knob Visitor Center
220

614
81
149
21
Jefferson National Forest
16
91
42
Marion
Independence
221
Stone Mountain Overlook
Devil's Garden Overlook 240
Stone Mountain State Park
Bluffs Lodge
Brinegar Cabin
Doughton Park

Jonesville
421
601

Mount Rogers (5729ft)
762
Grayson Highlands State Park
River House Inn
88
58
91
250

77
421

Abingdon
58
West Jefferson
221
Raccoon Holler Campground
260 Jumpinoff Rock
Wilkesboro

Northwest Trading Post
Cascades Overlook
EB Jeffress Park
280
Daniel Boone's Trace

Statesville
64

81
421
Bristol
19
Boone
421
see map 15
Blowing Rock
Appalachian Ski Mountain
16
18
64
Lenoir
Conover
321

Cherokee National Forest
67
Appalachian Trail
321
Moses H Cone Memorial Park
Julian Price Memorial Park
Beacon Heights Overlook
Boone Fork Overlook
Grandfather Mtn (5890ft)
Price Lake Campground
Pisgah National Forest

Hickory
321

19E
Elizabethton
Johnson City
23
321
261
Linville
19E
221
Linn Cove Viaduct
Brown Mountain Lights (2587ft)
Morganton

Cherokee National Forest
310
Linville Falls Visitor Center
Linville Falls Campground
Hawksbill Mountain (4020ft)

81
Erwin
67
19W
Penland School of Crafts
Spruce Pine
226
Museum of North Carolina Minerals
Linville Falls
Bear Den Campground
Altapass Orchard
Linville Caverns
18

19E
Crabtree Falls Visitor Center
Crabtree Meadows Campground
221
126
Marion
Shelby
226

19
Mt Mitchell (6684ft)
Mt Mitchell State Park
350
40
Old Fort
221
Forest City
74

360
Mt Mitchell State Park Campground
Black Mountain
74

63
23
Craggy Gardens Visitor Center
370
Parkway Headquarters
ALT 74
9
9
64
North Carolina
South Carolina
221
85

Folk Art Center
Asheville
see map 6
Biltmore Estate
Skyland
26
Columbus
26
11
29

40
Canton
Lake Powhatan Recreation Area
400
Hendersonville
25
64
11
Spartanburg
26

Great Smoky Mountains National Park
276
276
Mt Pisgah (5721ft)
Mt Pisgah Campground
Mt Pisgah Inn
410
Sliding Rock
Brevard
390
Taylors
29
85

see map 1
Waterrock Knob Visitor Center
Soco Gap
23
Highest Point on Parkway (6047ft)
Graveyard Fields Overlook
430
Looking Glass Rock Overlook
Devils Courthouse
276
25
Greenville
26
385

441
Big Witch Gap Overlook
Lickstone Ridge Overlook
see map 3
74
Richland Balsam
Nantahala National Forest
178
64

Southern End of Parkway
Cherokee   **Sylva**

Jefferson National Forest
130
614

Virginia
North Carolina

Tennessee

Cherokee National Forest

Sugarloaf Mountain (4579ft)

Cherokee National Forest
Pisgah National Forest

Map 14 **Roanoke**

Map 15 **Blowing Rock**

Shenandoah National Park enchants with its fairytale setting – a lush forest with majestic mountains that pop up between scores of breathtaking overlooks.

EXPERIENCING
SHENANDOAH

The spectacular 105-mile Skyline Drive is the lifeblood of the park, running through its heart and climbing from 600ft to more than 4000ft. Numerous trails sprout from this main artery, providing visitors with many opportunities to dip into the great outdoors.

First proposed as a park in 1926, this stretch of the Blue Ridge Mountains was set aside to provide a peaceful refuge for nearby urban populations. It took 10 years for the people who had lived here to relocate, and in 1936 President Roosevelt dedicated the park, naming it Shenandoah. It was considered a novel experiment to take an over-logged and overgrazed area and allow it to return to its natural state.

The experiment worked. Former cropland and pasture have become wild forest once again, complete with a healthy population of black bears, deer, bobcats, turkeys and 200 species of birds. The park now impresses more than one million annual visitors, who find a landscape substantially similar to what the early settlers discovered.

Some say that *Shenandoah* means 'daughter of the stars'; others translate it as 'river of high mountains.' Whatever interpretation, the park deserves any such beautiful appellation.

WHEN YOU ARRIVE

Most visitors enter the park by car, but pedestrians and bicyclists are also admitted for a fee at certain entrances. Fees for individuals (including bicycles)/vehicles are $5/10 and are good for seven days. Travelers can also purchase a Shenandoah Annual Pass for $20. Families traveling together pay $10. A great value for national park fans, the annual **National Parks Pass** costs $50 and can be purchased at any US national park or online at www.nationalparks.org. Entrance to the park is free on August 25 – the anniversary of the founding of the National Park Service (NPS).

Though the park is open year-round, visitor centers and other facilities are only open from early April through late November. Portions of Skyline Drive also close from dusk until dawn during hunting season and in inclement weather. Though the road doesn't close for fog, it can be a treacherous journey through the misty mountains, so extra precaution is necessary.

Entrance stations give out a great map and a general information sheet about the park, including its mile markers, but it's advised to hit one of the visitor centers for more information.

ORIENTATION
Entrances
Vehicles access the park from four entrances. The **Front Royal (North) Entrance** is accessible via I-66 east to US 340 south. To access the **Thornton Gap (North-Central) Entrance** from the east, take the Gainesville (US 29) exit off I-66 and head south to Warrenton, then take US 211 west to the park; from the west, take US 211 east from Luray. Enter the **Swift Run Gap (South-Central) Entrance** from the east by staying on US 29 to Stanardsville, then taking US 33 west; from the west, follow US 33 east from Elkton. The **Rockfish Gap (South) Entrance** can be reached from the east by staying on US 29 to Charlottesville and taking I-64 west; if you're coming from the west, take US 250 east from Waynesboro.

There are also several pedestrian entrances. Old Rag, Berry Hollow, Weakley Hollow, Lower Whiteoak Canyon, and Little Devils Stairs are among the high-use areas accessible by pedestrians and bicyclists.

Major Roads
The famous and spectacularly scenic **Skyline Drive** is the only road through the park. Twisting like a loose ribbon, it weaves along the top of the Blue Ridge Mountains for 105 miles, ending at the North Entrance of the Blue Ridge Parkway. Concrete mileposts (referenced in this book as MP) on either side of the road indicate location and serve as reference points.

Visitor Service Hubs
The Civil War–era town of **Front Royal** lies just outside the north entrance. Though small, it has an excellent **visitor center** (414 E Main St) with great maps and extremely knowledgeable staff. There's also a small grocery store, gas station and several historic B&Bs.

West of the Thornton Gap Entrance, **Luray** (p190) is best known for its caverns. At the crossroads of US 340 and US 211, it has gas stations, a supermarket and a Wal-Mart for supplies.

In the southern region, the small towns of **Elkton** and **Stanardsville** (both along US 33) and **Waynesboro** (p194; off US 250) offer few amenities, while **Charlottesville** (at the crossroads of US 29 and US 250) and **Staunton** (p191) are major hubs with all modern conveniences.

INFORMATION
Shenandoah National Park Headquarters (☎ 540-999-3500; 3655 US 211E, Luray, VA 22835) is not open to the public, but you can contact this office for park information.

There are three main visitor centers in the park. **Dickey Ridge Visitor Center** (☎ 540-635-3566; MP 4.6; ☼ 8:30am-5pm May-Oct) is closest to the northern park entrance. In the heart of the park is the **Harry F Byrd Jr Visitor Center** (☎ 540-999-3283; MP 51; ☼ 8:30-5pm Apr-Oct). Both places have exhibits on flora and fauna, pamphlets, weather information, ranger-led activities and exhibits. The third visitor center is **Loft Mountain Information Center** (MP 79.5), along the southern portion of Skyline Drive. There are additional ranger stations at **Piney River** (MP 22.1) and **Simmons Gap** (MP 73.2) and a private center at Rockfish Gap, outside the park on US 211, as well as others scattered throughout the park.

All operate from about mid-April to October and provide restrooms, first aid, publications for sale and backcountry permits. They're also starting points for many ranger-led hikes and programs.

Park publications include the free *Shenandoah Overlook*, as well as the 'Park Guide' and 'Exploring Shenandoah National Park' booklets (both $2). Aramark, the park concessionaire, provides the free 'Shenandoah: Your Complete Guide to the Park.'

Rangers recommend that visitors bring all necessities with them, as there are few stores inside the park. However, if travelers find themselves in need of an **ATM**, they're located at the Skyland Lodge registration building (MP 47.1) and Big Meadows wayside (MP 51.2).

Maps

The Potomac Appalachian Trail Club (PATC) produces three excellent maps at 1:62,500 that cover the entire park, since the AT parallels Skyline Drive for its entire length. These are available for $5 each at all visitor centers or from the **PATC** (☎ 703-242-0693). National Geographic/Trails Illustrated publishes a map for the entire park ($10), but the scale is 1:100,000.

If you're inclined to hike with GPS, go to **TrailRegistry** (www.trailregistry.com) and download trail maps and GPS directions. It's free but you have to register, and they're always looking for contributors to add to their trail database. Another very useful website is **TopoZone** (www.topozone.com) for printing out your own topo maps before you go.

POLICIES & REGULATIONS
Food Storage

There are hungry animals out there, and if you don't want them nosing around your campsite, follow park regulations for food storage. Campers should store all food in a park-approved bearproof canister or use a storage pole – provided at backcountry camp huts – to hang food at least 10ft off the ground and 4ft from a tree trunk.

TOP FIVE

✔ Launching a hang glider at **Dickey Hill** (p181) and soaring above the trees

✔ Learning about hemlock forests, peregrine falcons and even a dormant volcano on a **ranger-led hike** (p182)

✔ Enjoying solitude at the crest of the **Stony Man Nature Trail** (p175)

✔ Trekking some of the 101 miles of the **Appalachian Trail** (p179) that weave through the park

✔ Testing your endurance in the backcountry on an overnight hike along **Rip Rap Trail** (p180).

Campfires

Under no circumstances are backcountry campfires allowed – campers must use a camp stove or bring no-cook food. Otherwise, fires are permitted only in designated campfire pits.

Wilderness Permits & Regulations

Permits are issued for certain hikes in the park due to overcrowding, especially on weekends. These trails include Old Rag, Weakley Hollow, Whiteoak Canyon and Little Devils Stairs. Fees are $5/10 per adult/family. Annual park passes are honored at these trailheads.

Fishing

All park streams and tributaries are open for catch-and-release fishing unless designated as 'open for harvest,' in which case you may enjoy your fish dinner. About 30 streams stocked with brook trout are open for fishing from the third Saturday in March until mid-October. You must use artificial lures with a single hook only, and the limit is five trout per day (each fish must be at least 8 inches long). Anglers ages 16 and over (12 and older for nonresidents) must have a valid license ($6.50 for five consecutive days), which can be purchased at Panorama Restaurant, the Big Meadows and Loft Mountain waysides or from sporting goods stores outside the park.

GETTING AROUND

Greyhound/Trailways (☎ 800-229-9424; www.greyhound.com) provides bus service ($38) from Washington, DC to Waynesboro on the park's south end; buses run every morning. There are no buses or trains to Front Royal at the north end of the park. You could try **Plaza Cab** (☎ 540-622-8020) in Front Royal or **City Cab** (☎ 540-886-3471) in Waynesboro for transportation into the park. A bicycle or car is essential here; hitchhiking is difficult and risky.

Car & Bicycle

There are no bus, taxi or shuttle services through the park, so cars and bicycles are the only means of transportation. There has been talk about organizing hiker shuttles between Skyland Lodge and Big Meadows, though by press time no such system was in place.

Speed limits are 35mph through the park for cars and bicycles, and bikes are only permitted on paved roads. Cycling or mountain biking on backcountry trails and fire roads is not allowed. Normal cycling rules apply along Skyline Drive – use correct lighting at night, travel in single file and keep to the right.

It's highly recommended that travelers fuel up before heading into the park. In season there are only three wayside gas stations inside the park, at Elkwallow (MP 24.1), Big Meadows (MP 51) and Loft Mountain (MP 79.5).

Organized Tours

Visitors interested in group tours of the Shenandoah Valley should contact **Wayfaring Travelers** (☎ 410-666-7456; 27 Sunnyview Dr, Phoenix, MD 21131), which organizes two-week trips.

SKYLINE DRIVE

Completed in 1939, the 105-mile Skyline Drive runs along the spine of the Blue Ridge and then continues as the Blue Ridge Parkway all the way to the Smoky Mountains.

There are commercial ventures along Skyline Drive, but the park feels old-fashioned. Most buildings date from the 1930s, when the CCC (Civilian Conservation Corps) provided the labor to build the many rest stops, visitor centers, campgrounds and two grand lodges.

Many trails off Skyline Drive lay hidden at the end of an overlook or just beyond a parking area.

Dickey Ridge Visitor Center (MP 4.6) — Map 7, p158

Dickey Ridge originally operated as a 'wild' dining hall in 1908, with cabins for rent surrounding the hall. However, it closed during World War II and didn't reopen until 1958, when it became a **visitor center** (☎ 540-635-3566; ☾ 8:30am-5pm May 30-Oct 4). Now it's one of the park's two main information centers and contains a little bit of everything you'll need to get you started on your trip along Skyline Drive, including a slide show, exhibits, rest rooms and water.

Gooney Run Overlook (MP 6.8)

Sugar Tree Creek wasn't so sweet for one four-legged friend. Legend has it that Lord Fairfax used to hunt nearby with his beloved pooch Gooney. Unfortunately, Gooney drowned during one hunting expedition. Fairfax renamed what was called Sugar Tree Creek in his dog's honor.

Overlooking the white-water rapids that share its name, Gooney Run was a key marching point for General Stonewall Jackson during the Civil War. From this vantage point you can see the snaky outline of the South Fork of the Shenandoah River and the undulating peaks of the Massanutten Range.

Hogwallow Flats Overlook (MP 13.8)

Map 7, p158

From this overlook you'll be able to see Flint Hill, one of the towns that was designated for resettlement of residents displaced when the National Park Service bought their land. The valley you're peering into is mostly Rappahanock County; the park encloses about one-fifth of the county's land. Note the absence of any urban areas in the valley – locals like their views of the ranges sans light pollution. The Virginia Piedmont is also visible, stretching 70 miles to the coastal plain. Less than a mile south (MP 14.2), a grassy parking area indicates where the AT (Appalachian Trail) crosses the road.

Range View Overlook (MP 17.1)

Map 7, p158

Like an encyclopedic illustration of mountains and ranges, this impressive vista takes in a 14-mile stretch of peaks ranging from Stony Man's craggy face to the Blue Ridge and Massanutten and reaching even as far as the Alleghenies on exceptionally clear days. The radio tower is an easy marker for Hogback Mountain, and a piece of Skyline Drive pokes out at the Mt Marshall overlook point.

Elkwallow Wayside (MP 24.1)

Map 7, p158

Recharge and fuel up (in season only) here. Enjoy three square meals on an open-air patio at the small restaurant or stock up on supplies in the camp store. You'll find rest rooms, water and a pay phone on-site, plus a large picnic area with fireplaces, a comfort station and access to the AT.

Jeremys Run Overlook (MP 26.4)

Map 7, p158

George Washington probably slept here when he surveyed the Fort Valley enclave, nestled in the heart of the Shenandoah Valley and the Massanutten. Gentle cascades punctuate this lovely stream, known for its deep, clear pools and unusual, green-wall rock formations. The moderate-to-strenuous trail dips to a semi-level stretch between two tall, steep rock walls, with numerous stream crossings where water can reach up to your knees. Access the trail via the Elkwallow Gap picnic area (MP 24.2).

Thornton Gap Entrance Station (MP 31.5)

Map 7, p158

US 211 crosses here, offering access to Sperryville.

Pinnacles & Pinnacle Peak Overlook (MP 36.7)

Map 7, p158

Here's a cute little picnic area with comfort stations, fireplaces and water fountains for use during the warm months. In winter you'll find a frost-free faucet and pit toilets behind the comfort stations. From the second parking lot, there's also a very quick hike (20 minutes) along the AT down to a sweeping overlook of Hogback Mountain and Mt Marshall.

You can see the same view from a longer, 2.1-mile hike along very rocky terrain that leaves from the **Jewell Hollow Overlook** (MP 36.4), a little farther north. Look for the access trail from the parking lot, find the AT marker and head right. When you eventually come down from the second summit along the trail, be extremely cautious, as there's a 'dead man's drop' over sheer rock face next to the viewing area.

Hemlock Springs Overlook (MP 39.7) Map 7, p158

From this overlook you can spy the crannies of Nicholson Hollow and a spiked ridge of hemlocks. The spring below was developed to provide running water for a fountain, as well as bathrooms for the Stony Man Overlook.

Skyland (MP 41.7) Map 7, p158

Naturalist George Freeman Pollock envisioned a lofty summer resort where wealthy city folks (who had come to spend the hot months in the clear air of the high mountains) would be toted around in sightseeing wagons and fed elaborate meals as they observed nature. He got it. Skyland Lodge opened in 1890; over the years it grew to incorporate about 15 historic buildings and nature sites. Today it marks the highest point on Skyline Drive and one of the park's primary tourist facilities. Visitors can tour those same 15 sites Pollock created, as well as enjoy horseback rides, ranger activities and evening programs at the lodge (see Sleeping, p182).

A CCC museum dedicated to the many volunteers who built Skyline Drive is scheduled to open in 2006 at the Panorama Building, a deer's sprint off the drive at the Thornton Gap Entrance Station (MP 31.5).

Limberlost Trail (MP 43) Map 7, p158

The park's only wheelchair-accessible path (even compatible with strollers – trust us) loops around an old hemlock forest, as well as some of the oldest red spruces in the park (one tree is estimated to be 250 years old). Unfortunately, the Limberlost Forest and its hemlock trees are in danger from the pesky hemlock woolly adelgid, which has had a devastating impact on the hemlock needles.

The trail wanders across a wooden bridge, and trailside wooden benches offer frequent opportunities to contemplate nature. Toward the end, uprooted trees and clearings mark the destruction that Tropical Storm Fran caused in 1996 (the trail wasn't opened until 1997). The name *Limberlost* came from a favorite novel of George Pollock, Skyland's owner. His wife, Addie, started the preservation drive in this area by purchasing 100 trees, and George took the area's name from the *Girl of the Limberlost* by Gene Stratton Porter.

Crescent Rock Overlook (MP 44.4) Map 7, p158

The commanding peaks of the Massanutten Range, Hawksbill Mountain and Naked Top stretch across the Shenandoah Valley like a panoramic photograph. From the parking lot at this overlook, there are two piece-of-cake leg-stretchers to other spectacular viewpoints: **Bettys Rock** (550 yards), on the right, and **Crescent Rock** (100 yards), to the left. Time your trek for dusk to see some serene deer.

Hawksbill Mountain (MP 45.6) Map 7, p158

The highest peak in the park (4050ft) is also a well-known nesting area for peregrine falcons. An observation tower at the end of this trail (see Day Hikes, p177) makes a long-lasting impression of the park's wondrous beauty.

Big Meadows (MP 51.9) Map 7, p158

There's no doubt you've reached Big Meadows when the trees disappear and the land becomes an open meadow. It's one of the more fascinating landscapes in the park, rife with deer families creeping out at dusk. It's also one of three facilities connected by trails (the others are the **Harry F Byrd Jr Visitor Center**, at MP 51, and the **Big Meadows wayside**, at MP 51.3). The spacious visitor center houses an exhibit on the landscape and history of Shenandoah, as well as a plethora of books, maps and even mountain music. Grab a bite to eat at the wayside coffee shop before gassing up (check out the old-timey fuel pump controls). There's also a small camp store that stocks minimal supplies and a gift shop where you can shop for the folks back home.

If you're really curious about the weather at Big Meadows, modern technology brings it to you live. Watch real-time scenes on the Big Meadows web cam (www.instacam.com; choose Virginia and then Shenandoah National Park).

See Sleeping for information on the campground and picnic area.

Swift Run Gap (MP 67.2) Map 8, p159

Not only are the views of the Massanutten ski resort and High Top summit impressive, but the fine handicraft of the CCC is visible in the creative rock wall in front of you.

At Swift Run Gap you'll also find the junction with US 33 (which travels to Harrisonburg, p188), a park ranger station and the beginning of the southern section of the park. South of this point Skyline Drive becomes just a little wilder before hitting the even taller mountains along the Blue Ridge Parkway.

Loft Mountain (MP 79.5) Map 8, p159

The landscape of Loft Mountain ranges from bucolic grassland to challenging hills and is home to a zoo-like variety of wildlife, especially deer and bears. Unfortunately, Tropical Storm Fran damaged many trees in 1996, and the damage is still evident in backcountry areas despite the park's commendable restoration drive. Here you'll find a wayside, camp store, gas station, picnic area and campground that's much less crowded and more secluded than Big Meadows. The visitor center is comprehensive, with a wide-ranging assortment of publications, from first-person narratives to Appalachian cookbooks.

A 2.7-mile nature hike loops around the northeast summit of Loft Mountain and makes for an enjoyable family excursion. Getting to the trailhead takes a bit of doing, however. Park at the Loft Mountain wayside lot and walk north on Skyline Drive. After passing the Patterson Ridge Trail on the left, look for a dirt road on the right. Take that road past the PATC maintenance building to a junction with the AT, turn right and start your ascent through the trees.

> **PICNIC TIME**
>
> These perfect picnic spots offer a grand vista to complement any meal:
>
> Dickey Ridge MP 4.6
> Elkwallow MP 24.1
> Pinnacles MP 36.7
> Big Meadows MP 51.9
> Lewis Mountain MP 57.5
> South River MP 62.8
> Loft Mountain MP 79.5

Moormans River Overlook (MP 87.4) Map 8, p159

A devastating flood hit this area in 1995, dumping more than 30 inches of rain in a 24-hour period and causing massive mudslides that completely swept entire sections of forest down the mountainside. The park aggressively began reforestation efforts, but the damage is still apparent even today. A strenuous 9.4-mile trail (with a 900ft elevation gain) departs from the Blackrock Gap

EXPERIENCING SHENANDOAH

parking area (about 5 miles north of the overlook), and it's highly advised to leave a car at the endpoint at Jarman Gap.

Rockfish Gap (MP 105.4)
Map 8, p159

The rather bland junction of Rockfish Gap, I-64 and US 250 marks the end (or beginning, depending on where you're coming from) of Skyline Drive. Waynesboro is 4 miles west, while Staunton lies about 15 miles east. The drive runs smack into the Blue Ridge Parkway, also run by the NPS, and the Humpback Rocks Visitor Center (p200) is 5 miles south of the Rockfish Gap Entrance Station.

FESTIVALS & EVENTS

One of the prettiest festivals is **Wildflower Weekend** in mid-May, when the park sponsors various programs celebrating the arrival of spring. Walks, exhibits and slide programs showcase the park's spring wildflowers. In July the **North American Butterfly Association Annual Count** aims to identify and track new and existing species of these beautiful fliers. **Hoover Days**, celebrated on the weekend closest to President Herbert Hoover's August 10 birthday, allows visitors to see inside the buildings of the former president's weekend White House, Rapidan Camp (formerly known as Camp Hoover). Buses leave from the Byrd Visitor Center at Big Meadows.

The CCC pretty much built everything within sight of Skyline Drive, and since Shenandoah was the first national park to include a CCC camp, the park hosts an annual **CCC Reunion** at Skyland every September. First held in 1934, the reunion is the oldest in the country, and everyone is welcome to attend.

In winter, snowbirds of the human species gather for the **National Audubon Society Annual Christmas Bird Count**, a holiday tradition started by the society more than 100 years ago. Volunteers spend a chilly day staking out a designated counting area and searching for their favorite tweeters.

DAY HIKES

With more than 500 hikes in Shenandoah National Park, the biggest challenge is figuring out which ones to explore.

FOX HOLLOW (MP 4.6)
Distance: 1.2-mile loop
Duration: 75 minutes
Challenge: Easy
Elevation Change: 310ft

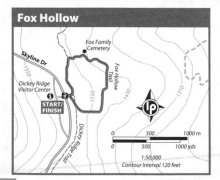

This is a nice, kid-friendly trail that offers a good introduction to how the forests of the Shenandoah area have repopulated themselves and covered what used to be abundant farmland. It's also home to a colorful assortment of **birds** like the hairy woodpecker, Carolina chickadee and American goldfinch.

Start at the Dickey Ridge Visitor Center and cross the street. You'll soon run into the Dickey Ridge Trail. Turn left and proceed about 0.2 mile until you meet up with the Fox Hollow Trail. Continue walking alongside a stone wall that used to mark the Fox family property. After turning right, you'll soon descend to a hollow with a small, crumbly cemetery. This is the **Fox Family Cemetery**, named for the family who worked a farmstead on this land (patriarch Thomas Fox built a surprisingly large seven-room home here).

Past the cemetery you'll alternate between forest and farmland – be on the lookout for **pickerel frogs**, which flourish in the spring. You may notice that one section of this trail looks pretty worn, and that's because a portion used to be an old Fox family road that linked their home to the nearby town of Front Royal. The end of the trail turns sharply upward and pops out into a clearing. You'll see a sign for the Snead Farm Loop Trail – if you want to extend your hike, this loop is a mild, 1.4-mile trek through apple orchards past an old barn.

COMPTON PEAK (MP 10.4)
Distance: 2.4 miles round-trip
Duration: 2½ hours
Challenge: Easy–Moderate
Elevation Change: 940ft

Begin at the Compton Gap parking area and cross the road. This trail forks ahead, and you should explore both paths for different views of the peak. Look for the AT marker, and begin with the trail on the right. Along the way you'll encounter many unusual **rock formations**, including 'columnar jointings' (you'll have to hike it to see what we mean!), as well as unexposed rock face with hand and footholds to help navigate, especially around some slippery areas. Look for the large boulder and hop up for good views of Skyline Drive and Mt Marshall.

Backtrack to the fork and head the opposite direction along the crest. The trail makes a quick descent to an area where you can view the impressive Piedmont Plateau, Dickey Ridge and the town of Front Royal.

TRACES (MP 22.2)
Distance: 1.7 miles round-trip
Duration: 1½ hours
Challenge: Easy
Elevation Change: 335ft

One of the easiest and prettiest day hikes in the park, this is a good bet for small children (but no dogs). The 'traces' you'll pass include an old mountain settlement, as the trail winds through a cool, mature oak forest.

Start from the Mathews Arm Campground, where the trail quickly winds past pieces of former foundations and roads. Enveloped in a canopy of red oaks, the trail soon rises above the campground amphitheater.

Near the end of the trail, a solitary oak stands like a beacon, and there are points ahead where you can take in mountain vistas. Retrace your steps to the parking lot.

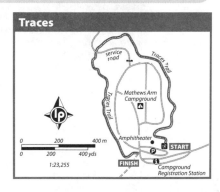

OLD RAG LOOP (MP 31.5)
Distance: 7.2-mile loop
Duration: 6–7 hours
Challenge: Moderate–Difficult
Elevation Change: 2380ft

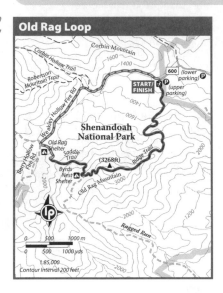

One of the park's most popular and challenging hikes, Old Rag Loop requires you to depart from Skyline Drive. To get to the trailhead, take US 211 east from the Thornton Gap Entrance Station for about 7 miles, then head south on US 522 for just under a mile. Make a right on VA 231 and another right onto VA 601. After about 4 miles, you'll arrive in the lower parking area. Head left on the road, following the sign 'Old Rag 0.8 mile.' After the last house, the road leads uphill to a second, smaller parking area that only has space for eight cars. The trailhead is to the left, along with some interpretive signs.

From here, head uphill into a **hemlock forest**, which will eventually give way to hardwoods. This is a gentle but persistent climb in the shade of tall trees. Early morning is the best time of day for bird-watching and animal sightings. When the path isn't too rocky, look up into the trees for bears, which sleep in the branches (if you follow the normal precautions of keeping a safe distance and not provoking the animals, you needn't worry – there haven't been any bear attacks here). About 45 minutes from the trailhead, a few trailside boulders offer limited views. Formed a billion years ago from molten rock under, the earth's crust, the 'Old Rag' granite that was thrust up to make this mountain has since been broken down by wind, water and temperature swings over many millennia, resulting in the great, rounded boulders and cracks you're climbing through today.

After a little more than an hour, the rock scrambling begins. There are a few more views of the ridge that you'll be scrambling on and to the rocky top of Old Rag itself.

This next section is only 0.6 mile long, but it will take you longer than any simple hike in the woods. About 90 minutes from the trailhead you'll negotiate a natural stairway between two giant boulders. At the two-hour mark, you'll arrive at the top of the first of two flat, moonscape mountaintops. There are excellent views from here; up to the left you can see the top of **Old Rag**.

Twenty minutes later comes the summit itself, marked on the trail with a cement trail marker. Scramble up the rocks past the trail to get to the precipitous viewpoint, which offers many comfortable resting places from which to contemplate the 360° panoramic view, one of only four in the park. Due west is Hawksbill, and to the right, below Bettys Rock, are the multiple falls of Whiteoak Canyon. A bit farther to the right is Stony Man, and Marys Rock is due north. Below is Weakley Hollow, where the return path travels. Back toward the crest of the Blue Ridge you can make out the large, green expanse of Big Meadows. To the southeast are the farmlands of Piedmont.

After filling your senses with the view from atop this rocky crag, continue on the blue-blazed trail down into the forest. This descent seems extremely tame after the boulder-dashing ascent. In 15 minutes you will arrive at a trail marker and **Byrds Nest Shelter**, an open-sided stone structure with a huge stone fireplace. It's for day use only, except in the case of extreme weather. Another half hour of descent on the Saddle Trail will bring you to **Old Rag Shelter**, on a little knoll in a clearing of green grass and ferns. From here the Saddle Trail doubles in width, evidence of its former use as a logging road.

The Post Office intersection, 10 minutes farther, features an interpretive sign explaining that this was once the hub of a small mountain community, which included several roads, a post office, a schoolhouse, a church and far fewer trees than there are today. From here turn right on Berry Hollow Fire Rd and then quickly right again onto Weakley Hollow Fire Rd. A few trails diverge from this road, but stick to Weakley Hollow Fire Rd for the next 2.5 miles, until you reach the upper parking area of Old Rag.

STONY MAN NATURE TRAIL (MP 41.7)
Distance: 1.4 miles round-trip
Duration: 1½ hours
Challenge: Easy
Elevation Change: 340ft

This self-guided nature walk, with a few rocky spots, takes you to the top of the park's second-highest mountain. Enter Skyland off Skyline Drive and park in the Stony Man parking area (which should also have brochures about the hike). Look for the cement post and follow the AT north for a little while. You'll soon reach a clearing; ahead, a fork leads to the **summit viewpoint**. (Incidentally, you've just reached the highest point in the park.) From the fork, either path is fine, since they both meet up at the viewpoint.

At the top, you'll see a handful of recognizable mountains such as Hawksbill, Massanutten, Bushytop and The Pinnacle, as well as the town of Luray, a portion of the Skyland complex and even a few stretches of Skyline Drive. If you're really lucky, you might spot a falcon, which are known to soar here, as well as the funky red berries of the mountain ash plant.

CEDAR RUN–WHITEOAK CANYON LOOP (MP 45.6)
Distance: 8.8-mile loop
Duration: 5–6 hours
Challenge: Difficult
Elevation Change: 2495ft

From the parking area at Hawksbill Gap, cross to the east side of Skyline Drive and look for the Cedar Run Trailhead. Descend into the forest on a blue-blazed trail. In a few hundred yards, a yellow-blazed horse trail enters from the right and then goes off to the left a short while later. Stay on the blue-blazed trail.

After 10 minutes (half a mile) the trail meets Cedar Run, which it follows for the next hour or more. In summer this narrow, little-used path is flanked by stinging nettles, so you must stay on the trail. The creek remains difficult to access until 25 minutes into the hike, when a big boulder affords a good resting place. A pool at the base of a **cascade** spreads a wide sheet of water across the rock face.

The next section of trail mostly descends, occasionally crossing the creek. About 70 minutes from the trailhead (2.5 miles), the trail crosses the creek past a metal post with a 'Leave no trace' message. Turn right after the crossing,

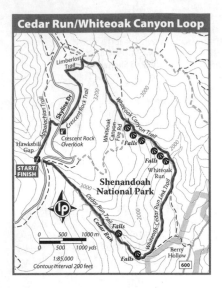

Cedar Run/Whiteoak Canyon Loop

Limberlost Trail
Skyline Dr.
3200
3000
Crescent Rock Trail
Appalachian Trail
Whiteoak Canyon Trail
3000
Crescent Rock Overlook
Whiteoak Canyon Fire Rd.
Falls
2000
Hawksbill Gap
START/FINISH
Falls
Whiteoak Run
Shenandoah National Park
3000
2000
Cedar Run Trail
Falls
Cedar Run & Cedar Run Link Trail
Cedar Run
Falls
Berry Hollow
Falls
600

0   500   1000 m
0   500   1000 yds
1:85,000
Contour interval 200 feet

continuing on the blue-blazed trail. After 10 more minutes (2.8 miles), veer left at the Y-intersection onto the Cedar Run Link Trail. (To the right is the continuation of the Cedar Run Trail, which leads to the Berry Hollow parking area on VA 600.) Cedar Run Link is a pleasant meander on a smooth dirt path through a hardwood forest with a few struggling hemlocks. Birdsong replaces the sound of the tumbling creek waters.

After 10 minutes you'll arrive at **Whiteoak Run** (a good swimming hole); the trail crosses the creek to a cement trail marker. You've come 3.6 miles. Turn left here to begin climbing upstream. Whiteoak Run is a more popular trail than Cedar Run, but due to its difficulty, there are relatively few hikers this far downstream. The forest here has some very large, old white oaks and hemlocks and a few large red cedars. It's lush and verdant along this narrow gorge, and the moisture seeps from the rock walls at all times of the year.

About 15 minutes from the trail marker, past some switchbacks, you'll cross the largest of the many tributary streams that flow into Whiteoak Run. In a few minutes you'll reach the first of six **waterfalls** in this gorge, just after a sign warning, 'Avoid poison ivy, stay on the trail.' Unfortunately, just after you pass the pool at the base of the falls, there's a fork in the trail with a well-used but unofficial trail going up steeply to the left. Take the right path, which ascends much more reasonably on a switchback. Twenty minutes later, after a steep climb over some rock faces, you'll reach a clearing where the trail levels out and a very inviting rock face offers a place to rest, with a big view of the east side of the park.

Another 15 minutes of climbing follow, and the trail emerges on a pool at the base of **Second Falls** (about 60ft high). If you haven't had a swim yet, this is the place to do it. First Falls, coming up, invariably attracts a lot of visitors, as most people only hike that far. Ten minutes from Second Falls, begin to climb a set of rock-and-cement steps; a further 10 minutes of climbing will bring you to the base of the longest waterfall, about 90ft high.

Veer left off the trail to see **First Falls** themselves and to swim in the pool at their base. To get to the top of First Falls, continue for another seven minutes or so on the trail. You'll come to an intersection with a horse trail, an old wagon road built by George Pollock (founder of Skyland Lodge) in the 1890s. Turn left at this intersection, and you'll see the top of First Falls. Veer right before reaching the creek to stay on the blue-blazed trail and cross the walking bridge. At the far end of the bridge is a trail marker. Turn right to continue upstream on the Whiteoak Canyon Trail, and enter a stretch of **old-growth hemlock**, the healthiest bunch in the park.

About 30 minutes from the bridge you'll reach the intersection with the Limberlost Trail. Turn left onto this well-manicured trail; it was recently the recipient of a grant to make it wheelchair-accessible. For 0.3 mile enjoy the gentle uphill climb on a wide, pebble-covered path with comfy wooden benches every few hundred yards. Turn left onto the Crescent Rock Trail, marked by a cement trail marker. Within 15 minutes you'll hit Skyline Drive at Milepost 45. Cross the road, veering right to enter the driveway of Crescent

Rock Overlook. Follow the driveway. Just before the parking lot, turn right onto the Bettys Rock Trail and proceed for only a few seconds before turning left downhill to reach the AT after 150 yards. Once on the AT, turn left, heading south on a descending path. At the next intersection, about 10 minutes later, turn left and walk less than a mile back to the Hawksbill Gap parking area.

HAWKSBILL SUMMIT (MP 45.6)
Distance: 1.7 miles
Duration: 2–3 hours
Challenge: Moderate
Elevation Change: 800ft

This tremendous climb to the park's highest peak offers an unforgettable picture of the mountain landscape. There are two options for this climb – either a 2.8-mile loop or 1.7-mile up-and-back. (This description follows the latter.)

Start at the Hawksbill Gap parking area and look for the Lower Hawksbill Trail, which leads into the woods. The steep ascent is lined with mountain ash and red spruce – beware of small, frequent rockslides along the jumbled path. When you encounter a cement post, you'll know you're close to the summit. Go right until you see a three-sided building, the **Byrds Nest Shelter 2** (no water or camping here). A little farther up is the **observation platform**, which offers breathtaking vistas in every possible direction of Browns Mountain, Stony Man and even the town of Luray twinkling in the distance. After taking a peek at the cool compass embedded in the cement post, retrace your steps to the parking lot.

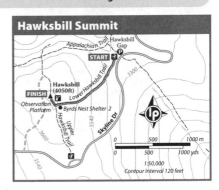

DARK HOLLOW FALLS (MP 50.7)
Distance: 1.4 miles round-trip
Duration: 1½ hours
Challenge: Moderate–Difficult
Elevation Change: 440ft

This small waterfall is close to Skyline Drive, but the rocky terrain makes for a tough hike in certain sections, and the return trip is all uphill. It's not unusual for hikers to suffer accidents here, so take extra caution when stepping over slippery rocks and make use of those handrails – they're there for a darn good reason!

Start at the Dark Hollow Falls parking area. Upon entering the forest, you'll encounter a small stream. You might wonder how such a small stream could turn into a powerful waterfall, but less than a mile ahead you'll see the 70ft **Dark Hollow Falls** pouring over a

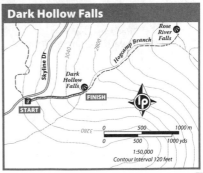

craggy ancient lava flow. Descend about 0.1 mile to the base of the falls and imagine what was racing through the mind of one of the forefathers – Thomas Jefferson was a frequent visitor to this area.

You can either hike farther down to see more small waterfalls and cascades created by Hogcamp Branch (which will eventually put you out at the Rose River Fire Rd) or take a deep breath and begin that arduous ascent back to the trailhead.

SOUTH RIVER FALLS (MP 62.8)
Distance: 2.2 miles round-trip
Duration: 2 to 3 hours
Challenge: Moderate
Elevation Change: 850ft

The third-highest waterfall in the park is also one of its most picturesque, and the phrase 'go jump in a lake' would be apropos here, as the base pool is an awesome swimming hole and fuel for the tough return climb.

From the water fountain at the South River picnic area, descend to a junction with the AT. A marker denotes distances to Milam and Swift Run Gaps, the former of which contains a vast orchard of apple trees. The trail is relatively wide and smooth, with a series of initial switchbacks, and you'll soon come to a clearing, where a wide swath of **wildflowers** offer an unexpected reward if you're hiking in June.

Just under a mile later, you'll hear water running beneath the rocks (even though you might not be able to see it) before you hit another series of switchbacks. At the mile mark, a glance straight ahead reveals nothing but sky, as the South River takes a quick, 83ft plunge. You can't see the falls very well yet, so continue ahead, past two trail markers, to a manmade **observation point** (park officials constructed a concrete wall along the ledge) and a bird's-eye view of the falls.

If you want to take that dip in the cool water, keep going (this will increase your hike to 4.4 miles) until the trail joins an old road; instead of taking the South River Falls Fire Rd, stay on the trail. The base of the stream is about three-quarters of a mile from here, and the trail gradually widens. Here's the slightly challenging part – you actually have to hike up a path that's steep at times and cross a jumble of slippery rocks to get to the **rocky beach** at the base pool. Retrace your steps back to the picnic area.

BLACKROCK SUMMIT (MP 84.8)
Distance: 1 mile loop
Duration: 1½ hours
Challenge: Easy
Elevation Change: 175ft

This nice loop climbs through an area of wartime lore – it's rumored that during the American Revolution, Virginia's great seal and state archives were hidden within Blackrock from the advancing British army. The area also boasts an interesting geologic past. Blackrock used to be a quartzite cliff, until the cliff broke off and became a heap of giant rocks below.

Start at the Blackrock Summit parking area, and cross the chain to join the Trayfoot Mountain Trail (an old fire road) for a short spell. Luckily, this trail is fairly level compared to other summit trails. When you reach the AT junction, take the AT south for about 0.4 mile. Soon the landscape opens up to reveal what looks like a pile of gray peanut brittle, and it's these boulders you'll have to scramble over in order to reach the **summit**, as the trail doesn't go that far.

An old fire tower marks the summit, but be extremely careful navigating these rocks. The reward is, naturally, one of the best views of the entire Shenandoah Valley. Don't be alarmed if you see black patches on the rocks – it's just a form of lichen called rock tripe. Be sure, though, to watch out for rattlesnakes, though you probably won't encounter any.

BACKCOUNTRY HIKES
Permit Information
An area is considered backcountry if it's more than 250 yards from any paved road and a half mile from any park facility other than trails, unpaved roads and trail shelters. Permits are free and required for all backcountry camping. They're available from the park entrances, ranger stations, visitor centers and park headquarters, by mail (see Information, p166) or by self-registration; if you haven't registered, you could be slapped with a hefty fine. Inside the park, permits are only issued between sunrise and one hour before sunset.

Bicycles and motor vehicles are prohibited on trails. And, importantly, carry out what you carry in.

Backcountry Camping
Certain rules apply: Campers have to set up out of sight of a road, trail, overlook, cabin or other campsite and at least 25 yards from any water source. No-camping areas include Limberlost, Hawksbill Summit, Whiteoak Canyon, Old Rag Summit, Big Meadows clearing and Rapidan Camp. Open fires are prohibited except in fireplaces or designated fire pits, so bring cold food or your own stove (the penalty for lighting fires can be as much as $5000). Campers are limited to two consecutive nights in a single location (within 250 yards) and 14 days in the same location in a calendar year. Overnight stays in shelters are prohibited. *Giardia* (a microscopic parasite that can cause nausea, diarrhea and fever) is a problem in some parts of the park, so bring your own water, or a suitable filter, or boil stream water.

MT MARSHALL TRAIL
Distance: 13.5 miles loop
Duration: 8 hours over two days
Challenge: Moderate–Difficult
Elevation Change: 2450ft

Actually a combination of three trails (the Appalachian, Bluff and Mt Marshall Trails), this hike circles the peaks of North and South Marshall Mountains. It's a moderate-to-strenuous trek that could be done in a day, but most people opt for an overnight excursion, staying in the Gravel Springs hut or in the surrounding camping area.

Day One
Start from the Jenkins Gap parking area off Skyline Drive (MP 12.4) and look for the AT marker. Head south on the AT, passing a small stream and then crossing over Skyline Drive (the first of several such crossings). The terrain is soft underfoot until you ascend North Marshall Mountain. Keep your eyes peeled for dainty white-tailed deer – you're almost guaranteed to see some as the trail leads through the Hogwallow Flat area. Bear droppings, as well as an occasional rattlesnake, are common, though few bears are actually spotted on this trail. Don't expect great views at the summit – trees obscure the sight

line, and you'll need to take one of the two (or both) spur roads past the mountain to see the horizon open up to vistas of Dickey Ridge, Stony Man Mountain, Hogback Mountain and slices of Skyline Drive. A bonus for spring hikers is the absolute explosion of wildflowers that will line your route like the yellow brick road.

After a steep descent and another crossing of Skyline Drive, continue south on the AT until you reach South Marshall Mountain. Again, find the spur trail on the descent for the best views.

Continue on the AT until the trail comes to Gravel Springs Gap. Here you'll find your bed for the night – the Gravel Springs hut is open to backcountry campers with permits only (and we're assuming you did the good- camper thing by getting yours). Otherwise, you'll have to pitch a tent on the surrounding land.

Before setting up camp for the night, make a run down to Big Devils Stairs and back. From the hut, take the relatively level Bluff Trail until you see a cement post. Make a right here to get to Big Devils Stairs, which is a strenuous descent and ascent to the edge of a canyon rim but well worth it for amazing views of the valley and water. Return to the Gravel Springs hut for the evening.

Day Two

The next day, retrace your steps along the Bluff Trail, veering left at the cement post (to Big Devils Stairs) to pick up the Mt Marshall Trail. It's a fairly tame hike up the trail, which crosses several pretty streams. Near the end, you'll descend an old fire road flanked by wild grape bushes. You'll emerge on Skyline Drive – walk north a few yards, past the Jenkins Gap Overlook, and back to the parking lot.

RIPRAP TRAIL
Distance: 9.3-mile loop
Duration: 11 hours over 2 days
Challenge: Moderate–Difficult
Elevation Change: 2000ft

Not only is this a fun trail to pronounce, it's one of the most enjoyable obstacle courses to scamper along. It's a 'wild' trail with a capital 'W,' where the mantra 'Lions and tigers and bears, oh my!' might loop through a hiker's mind. There's no chance of encountering lions and tigers here, but bears? Absolutely. Along with the Riprap Trail, hikers will trek along a portion of the AT, as well as the Wildcat Ridge Trail. If you have two cars, you might want to leave one at the Wildcat Ridge parking area in order to shorten the hike. As with the Mt Marshall Trail, this could be tackled in one day, but if had to choose just one overnight adventure in Shenandoah, this hike is the one. Pull those backpack straps tight and hold on.

Day One

Start at the Riprap Overlook on Skyline Drive (MP 90) and look for the concrete AT marker. Like a scene change in a movie, you're instantly thrust into the wilderness – literally. This section of Shenandoah National Park was incorporated under the National Wilderness Act, which aims to preserve the last standing areas of true wilderness that humans haven't permanently altered.

After half a mile, the trail forks. Take the left fork, which should be signed 'Riprap Trail' – the AT continues along the other fork to Loft Mountain. Just what the heck is a 'riprap' anyway? Along the trail, you'll encounter piles of rocks covered with lichen, and these are the aforementioned riprap.

As you ascend through Riprap Hollow, the hike is a picturesque jaunt through the silent woods, with blueberry bushes sprinkled along the path. You'll soon come upon the sparkling white quartzite of Chimney Rock and remnants of what used to be an iron bridge.

It's all downhill from here, on a steep descent over rocky boulders with some hopping across streams. But you'll be well rewarded for the strenuous effort. At the bottom you'll find what may be one of the most deserted and beautiful pools on the East Coast – a perfect spot for a solitary swim amid a canopy of lush hardwood and fragrant Catawba rhododendron with not a sunburned tourist in sight. Depending on the water level, a small cascade may pour into the pool like a perfect natural shower. Nearby is a small trail leading to the old Riprap Shelter, you're best off camping around this section for the evening.

Day Two
Get an early start and continue south along the Riprap Trail till you reach a cement marker indicating the start of the Wildcat Ridge Trail. You'll cross several streams on the ascent to Wildcat Ridge, where the sight line opens up through thinning trees. If you left a car at the Wildcat Ridge parking area, look for the AT marker and follow the right-hand path for about 10 minutes; it will dump you out at your car. Otherwise, continue along the AT toward the Riprap parking area by taking the left fork at the marker. The terrain isn't as wild here, with many breaks in the trees and fairly easy climbs. From the last marker it's just under 3 miles to the parking area, where civilization awaits with the click of the engine and a radio blast of tunes.

OTHER ACTIVITIES
Bicycling
Biking is only permitted on Skyline Drive and certain public roads. Cycling or mountain biking on backcountry trails and fire roads is not allowed. Normal cycling rules apply along Skyline Drive – use correct lighting at night, travel single file and keep to the right. Even though many bicyclists told us they were discouraged from riding Skyline Drive's narrow, sometimes blind-curve route, it remains a popular and challenging route for two-wheelers.

Bird & Wildlife Watching
More than 200 bird species have been spotted in the park, not to mention more than 40 species of mammals, 50 species of reptiles and amphibians, and 20 species of fish. In the park's Birds of Prey program (which departs from Skyland's amphitheater), winged predators such as owls and red-tailed hawks are described in detail. Rockfish Gap is a particularly good place to see hawks in flight.

Big Meadows is the best spot to view an interesting assortment of wildlife, from wild turkeys to white-tailed deer to loping bears lolling about in the fields.

Hang Gliding
There are only three authorized sites from which hang gliders can be launched: **Dickey Hill** (MP 6), **Hogback Mountain** (MP 20.5) and **Millers Head** (from Skyline Drive, turn into Skyland's south entrance at MP 42.5, pass the stables and keep left when the road forks; park at the top of the hill). If you're going to land on private property, you must obtain the owner's permission. Special-use permits are required in advance, and you must be rated at least Hang 3.

Contact the Superintendent at **park headquarters** (Shenandoah National Park, 3655 US 211E, Luray, VA 22835).

Horseback Riding

Riding is allowed on designated trails. **Skyland Stables** (☎ 540-999-2210; 1hr $20-22, 2.5hr Mon-Fri $42; ☯ May-Oct) offers guided rides along neighboring trails; children saddle up on ponies (15/30min $3/6).

Ranger Programs

Ranger programs are great for educating yourself and your family on the park's ecology, geology and any other '-ology' related to the national park system. Most programs, such as nature hikes and bird-watching trips, originate from Skyland and Big Meadows lodges. Topics range from historic homes to wildflower walks, and there's a **Junior Ranger Program** aimed at kids (see Kids' Activities, below).

Rock Climbing

Though it's still unregulated in the park, rock climbing has become increasingly popular; most climbers head to the areas around Little Stony Man Cliffs and Old Rag Mountain.

Skiing

You're allowed to cross-country ski on some trails and fire roads, as well as on the unplowed shoulder of Skyline Drive, but you must have your own equipment and appropriate clothing. (There are no equipment-rental facilities within the park.)

Swimming

Swimming is permitted in all park waters at your own risk.

Classes/Education

Shenandoah National Park's **Education Office** (☎ 540-999-3489; www.nps.gov/shen/seminars.htm; from $30) hosts **Field Seminars**, which educate people on the wilderness, flora and fauna, and history of the area, as well as basic camping and hiking skills. These classes are extremely popular, so it's best to register well in advance. Registration includes the park entrance fee, resource materials and tuition. The office also provides classes for families, tour groups and schoolchildren.

Kids' Activities

Kids seven and older can become Junior Rangers when they complete 15 activities, which earn them stickers, badges or patches. Purchase notebooks ($2.50) in any information center, where you can also rent Junior Ranger backpacks (which includes the notebook, field guides and binoculars) to assist the mission.

Besides letting them run loose on the more than 500 miles of trails, you can also put smiles on kids' faces with pony rides at Skyland Stables (see Horseback Riding, above).

SLEEPING
Camping

There are five major NPS campgrounds, almost all of which feature picnic tables, grills, stores, laundries and showers (except for Mathews Arm), but none have RV hookups. They're open on a first-come, first-served basis, except for Big Meadows and Dundo Group Campgrounds.

Big Meadows (MP 51.3; Map 7, p158; ☎ 800-365-CAMP; $19; ⏰ late May-Nov). Find the perfect spot among 217 sites and you might just snap a quick photo of a resident bear lumbering past your campfire. This campground tends to be crowded, especially during fall, but it's smack in the middle of Skyline Drive and a convenient base for all exploration.

Lewis Mountain (MP 57.5; Map 8, p159; ☎ 800-365-CAMP; $16; ⏰ Apr-Oct) The smallest campground (only 32 sites) is also the most intimate when it comes to getting close to Mother Nature.

Loft Mountain (MP 79.5; Map 8, p159; ☎ 800-365-CAMP; $16; ⏰ late May-Oct) This 'lofty' campground features some serious altitude on top of Big Flat Mountain. It's also the largest, so expect crowds.

Mathews Arm (MP 22.1; Map 7, p158; ☎ 800-999-3500; $16; ⏰ May-Oct) This campground doesn't have a store (there's one 2 miles south at Elkwallow), but does boast plenty of rushing water – Overall Run Falls, the highest waterfall in the park, is accessible from here.

Dundo Group Campground (MP 83.7; Map 8, p159; ☎ 800-365-CAMP; $32) Reservations are required for this group-only campground (minimum eight campers, maximum 20). There are seven large, primitive sites with water and pit toilets, and one wheelchair-accessible site.

Lodging

The park contains three lodges; contact **Aramark Virginia Skyline Company** (☎ 540-743-5108, 800-999-4714; www.visitshenandoah.com; PO Box 727NP, Luray, VA 22835). A few rooms in these facilities have TVs, but none come with phones. Both Skyland and Big Meadows include onsite restaurants, taprooms, gift shops and playgrounds. They're also the starting points for a few trails. No pets are allowed at any lodging facility. To the prices quoted below, add about $10 to $20 in October.

Skyland Lodge (MP 41.7; Map 7, p158; ☎ 800-999-4714; cabin r/lodge r/ste midweek $55-100/80-115/115-170, weekend $60-105/100-125/130-180; ⏰ early Apr-late Nov) Located at the highest point on the drive, Skyland Lodge is also one of the park highlights. Most of the rooms are motel-type units only a quick hike from the main lodge, but there are a few rustic cabins, and many of the accommodations offer magnificent views of the Shenandoah Valley.

Big Meadows Lodge (MP 51.3; Map 7, p158; ☎ 800-778-2851; main lodge/cabin r/lodge r/mini-ste/ste midweek $70-105/80-85/80-90/115/125, weekend $75-120/85-90/100-110/125/140; ⏰ mid-Apr-early Nov) The awesome main room inside the lodge is the perfect place to end a strenuous day, nestled beside the cozy stone fireplace playing board games or rocking in the line of chairs that overlook the valley. Rustic cabins are the way to go for their earthy silence – end cabins get you your own fireplace. Don't be surprised to see deer or a bear stroll by your steps. Some rooms have TVs, but none have phones.

Lewis Mountain (MP 57.5; Map 8, p159; ☎ 800-778-2851; tent/1r cabin/2r cabin midweek $25/65/90, weekend $25/70/95; ⏰ early May-early-Nov) Think of it as tent camping with a hard shell, plus a few modern conveniences thrown in, like heat and private bathrooms. Onsite showers, a coin-operated laundry and a small camp store, as well as an adjoining outdoor cooking area, round out this 'camping-with-a-net' experience.

PATC Cabins (PATC; ☎ 703-242-0693; www.patc.net/activities/cabins; 118 Park St SE, Vienna, VA 22180; cabin midweek/weekend $15-55/25-110) Roughing it with a few comforts is the best way to describe staying at these six fully enclosed cabins, which the Potomac Appalachian Trail Club has opened to the public (the remaining 22 are for members only). Each contains bunk beds, water and a stove and lies in a backcountry area of the park. The closest access points off Skyline Drive are **Range View** (MP 22.1), **Corbin** (MP 37.9), **Pocosin** (MP 59.5), **Rock Spring** (MP

81.1) and **Doyles River** (MP 81.1). **Jones Mountain** is the only one not accessible from Skyline Drive (it's in Criglersville, on County Rd 600).

No permits are required for overnight stays in the cabins, but reservations are necessary and they're available on a first-come, first-served basis. Some cabins can only be reached on foot. Check in and check out are at 3pm. Groups must include one person aged 21 or over. Make sure you bring your own flashlights. The PATC also offers seven three-sided trailside huts for AT hikers (p40). You can purchase a **handbook** (☎ 703-242-0693 ext 19; www.patc.net/store/PC280.htm; members/nonmembers $4.40/5.50), which lists all the PATC cabins and their amenities.

EATING

The aptly named **Panorama Restaurant** (Map 7, p158; ☎ 540-999-2265; MP 31.5; sandwiches $3.50-6, entrees from $8; ☺ 9am-5:30pm Apr-Nov) serves good, traditional Virginia country fare like fried chicken and country ham.

The dining rooms at **Skyland Lodge** (p183; ☺ late Mar-Dec) and **Big Meadows Lodge** (p183; ☺ May-Oct) offer sweeping views of the woods that far outweigh the rather pricey, bland fare. Unfortunately there's not much choice in these parts. Both serve medium-size breakfast, lunch and dinner menus; hours are extended at all park restaurants in peak season.

Wayside lunch counters and snack bars at **Elkwallow**, **Big Meadows**, **Lewis Mountain** and **Loft Mountain** serve distinctly ordinary snacks and lunches.

ENTERTAINMENT

At Skyland and Big Meadows lodges you can take in plays or campfire programs in the amphitheaters, while the restaurants offer live music and showcase local talent (including cloggers!). On most Fridays from June to September, Skyland hosts the **Shenandoah Jubilee Music Show** (adult/child $12/6). Both lodges contain a pub/bar area where you can grab a drink. Apart from telling spooky tales around your campfire, all other entertainment options lie outside the park.

INTERNET ACCESS

You'll find no WiFi here! If you really need to be wired, try the **Samuels Public Library** (☎ 540-635-3153; 538 Villa Ave) in Front Royal, or if you're staying at Big Meadows, sign up at the front desk for free limited Internet access.

LOST & FOUND

Ranger stations, entrance stations and visitor centers handle lost and found items. If you leave the park before realizing you forgot something, contact the **Shenandoah National Park Communications Center** (☎ 540-999-3422; Rte 4, Box 348, Luray, VA 22835).

MEDICAL SERVICES & EMERGENCIES

There are no medical facilities within the park. The nearest hospitals are in Front Royal, Luray, Harrisonburg and the **Augusta Medical Center** (☎ 540-332-4000, off I-64 in Fishersville; ☺ 24hr emergency treatment facilities), midway between Staunton and Waynesboro. In an emergency, call ☎ 800-732-0911.

MONEY

Stock up on cash before entering the park, as there are only two ATMs, at Skyland and Big Meadows.

POSTAL SERVICE

Drop mail in the gift shops at Elkwallow, Panorama, Skyland, Big Meadows, Lewis Mountain and Loft Mountain.

SHOWERS & LAUNDRY

You'll find coin-operated showers and laundry facilities near the campgrounds at Big Meadows, Lewis Mountain and Loft Mountain.

TELEPHONES

Pay phones are available at entrance stations, waysides, visitor centers, Skyland Lodge (MP 41.7), Big Meadows Campground (MP 51.3), Lewis Mountain (MP 57.5) and park headquarters (at US 211).

TRASH & RECYCLING

Look for trash bins and recycling containers at visitor centers, campgrounds, park stores and restaurants. Please make sure to carry everything out – plastic bags hang around for 10 to 20 years!

AROUND SHENANDOAH

FRONT ROYAL
Map 9, p160 / ☎540 / pop 13,800 / elevation 567ft

This strollable town at the northern end of Shenandoah National Park and Skyline Drive is a perfect base from which to explore the park. Originally called LeHew Town, a stopover on an important packhorse route, Front Royal was dubbed 'Helltown' in the mid-18th century, thanks to its raucous reputation. It featured prominently in the battles of the Civil War and served as a base for infamous Confederate spy Belle Boyd. Today, Front Royal is an important commercial center, and each May it hosts the **Virginia Mushroom Festival** for fun guys and gals who like fungi. You'll find a well-preserved historic district along Chester St.

Visit the **Front Royal–Warren County Visitor Center** (☎ 540-635-5788 or 800-338-2576; www.ci.front-royal.va.us; 414 E Main St; ☺ 9am-5pm) in the old Southern Railroad train depot.

Sights

BELLE BOYD COTTAGE
This **cottage** (☎ 540-636-1446; 101 Chester St; adult/child $2/1; ☺ 9:30am-4pm Mon-Fri, noon-4pm Sat) was the onetime home of Confederate spy Belle Boyd, who lived here with relatives. On one occasion, through a small hole in a closet floor, Belle overheard a Union general discussing plans with his officers. She wrote the details down in cipher and rode for 15 miles to pass the information to Stonewall Jackson's Confederate troops. The Confederates then moved on Front Royal and captured the town – albeit only for a week. Tours last a half hour.

WARREN RIFLES CONFEDERATE MUSEUM
Another place with a Civil War theme is this small **museum** (☎ 540-636-6982; 95 Chester St; adult/child $4/free; ☺ 9am-4pm Mon-Sat, noon-4pm Sun Apr 15-Nov 1), which attempts to make saints of other members of the Confederacy.

OASIS WINERY
A number of vineyards dot the landscape near Front Royal. This 75-acre **vineyard** (☎ 540-635-7627; www.oasiswine.com; 14141 Hume Rd; tour $5; ☺ 10am-5pm Mon-Fri, to 6pm Sat & Sun), off Rte 635 in Hume, faces the Blue Ridge Mountains. Known internationally for its sparkling wines, it's open for tours and tastings.

Activities

CANOEING, RAFTING & TUBING
The **Downriver Canoe Company** (☎ 800-338-1963; www.downriver.com), **Front Royal Canoe Company** (800-270-8808; www.frontroyalcanoe.com) and **Shenandoah River Outfitters** (☎ 800-622-6632; www.shenandoahriver.com), all near Front Royal, offer a number of trips, from a 3-mile taste of white water to ultra-serious trips of 120 miles and longer. A 3-mile trip costs $35 to $40 per canoe; a day trip runs about $59; a three-day trip is $137 (there are midweek discounts). Tubing costs about $18 per tube.

These outfitters operate from March to November. To get there, follow US 340 south from Front Royal to Bentonville. (If you're coming from Skyline Drive, at MP 20, follow US 211 west for 8 miles, and then head north on US 340 – from there, it's 14 miles to Bentonville.) Call for specific directions.

HORSEBACK RIDING

The 4200-acre **Marriott Ranch** (☎ 540-364-3741; www.marriottranch.com; 5305 Marriott Lane; 1hr ride weekdays/weekends $32/35), in nearby Hume, offers short and extended trail rides near Front Royal.

HOT AIR BALLOONING

Blue Ridge Hot Air Balloons (☎ 540-622-6325 or 877-743-3247; www.rideair.com; 552 Milldale Hollow Rd; 1hr ride $175 per person) offers groovy balloon rides year-round; you'll feel as if you can reach out and touch the peaks of the Blue Ridge. It's best to call a few weeks in advance, especially during leaf-peeping season.

Sleeping & Eating

Front Royal/Washington DC West KOA Kampground (☎ 540-635-2741 or 888-204-4803; 1370 N Shenandoah Ave; 2-person site/Kamping Kabin $30-35/50-57) It may advertise that it has a 'Civil War nearby,' but you shouldn't hear the guns these days. Instead, this compact campground offers good shady sites, electricity/water hookups, a

---

WHAT LIES BENEATH: VIRGINIA CAVERNS

Particular to the Shenandoah Valley are a handful of 'cavernous' attractions: chilly caves with bizarre stalactites and stalagmites, dizzying light displays and crazy rock formations that look like pipe organs, Japanese gardens and even bacon strips. Though some of these establishments push the line when it comes to tackiness and political correctness, they are nevertheless a wild way to see Virginia's rocky underbelly.

At the northern tip of Skyline Drive in Front Royal, **Skyline Caverns** (☎ 800-296-4545; www.skylinecaverns.com; US 340; adult/child 7-13 $14/7, train ride $3; ☉ Mon-Fri 9am-5pm, 9am-6pm Sat & Sun) boasts rare, white-spiked anthodites (quill-like crystals that resemble Fourth of July parade sparklers) and a 37ft rainbow wall. A preachy light show, though, overshadows whatever spiritual feelings the caverns may inspire.

Endless Caverns (☎ 800-544-2283, 540-896-2283; www.endlesscaverns.com; I-81 exit 264; adult/child 4-12 $14/6; ☉ 9am-5pm, to 6pm in summer) is an ooh- and ahh-inspiring cave where a fossilized woolly mammoth tooth was found and where virgin passageways and rooms are still being discovered today. A tour of **Shenandoah Caverns** (☎ 540-477-3115; www.shenandoahcaverns.com; I-81 exit 269; adult/child 6-14 $17.50/7; ☉ 9am-5pm, to 6pm in summer), near Monticello, begins in the only cavern elevator and leads to the odd 'bacon strip' and 'Scottish castle' formations. An antique window-display exhibit features fantastical, nostalgic window dressings from prominent US stores.

Grand Caverns (☎ 888-430-2283; I-81 exit 235; adult/child 3-12 $16/9; ☉ 9am-4:30pm Mon-Fri, to 5pm Sat & Sun), the nation's oldest show cave, is steeped in Civil War history and features enormous stalagmites with rippling flowstone (rounded calcium deposits formed from minerals in constantly flowing water). At **Crystal Caverns** (☎ 540-465-5884; www.wayside-ofva.com/crystalcaverns; I-81 exit 298; adult/child $10/8, includes admission to adjacent Stonewall Jackson Museum; ☉ 9am-5pm), guides in period costume lead lantern-lit tours and relate tales of Civil War skirmishes above.

The granddaddy of all Virginia cave systems is **Luray Caverns** (☎ 540-743-6551; www.luraycaverns.com; I-81 exit 264; adult/child 7-13 $18/8; ☉ 9am-6pm, to 7pm in summer). See p190 for a full listing.

pool, a playground, recreation room and even Wi-Fi Internet access ($6 for 12 hours).

Killahevlin (☎ 540-636-7335 or 800-847-6132; www.vairish.com; 1401 N Royal Ave; r/ste $145-185/245) At this indulgent, Irish-inspired retreat atop a Civil War encampment (the highest point in Front Royal), guests are pampered at every moment. Something will feel good, whether it's the complimentary in-room champagne or the scent of freshly baked cookies or the breathtaking mountain vistas from the cozy gazebos. Sure, it's pricey, but creature comforts include unlimited Irish lager on tap in the onsite pub!

Chester House (☎ 540-635-3937 or 800-621-0441; www.chesterhouse.com; 43 Chester St; d/cottage $120-150/225) This pretty Georgian home is only a short stroll from town and the visitor center. Sink into the massive beds either in the main house or the romantic cottage that overlooks the boxwood garden. Hopefully, you'll get to enjoy the owner's famous mile-high popovers for breakfast.

Main Street Mill & Tavern (☎ 540-636-3123; 500 E Main St) A barnlike place a block from the visitor center, this restaurant serves huge sandwiches and big Southern dinners with all the trimmings.

Apple House (☎ 540-636-6329; Rte 55E, Linden) Diner food never tasted better than at this reliable standby, featuring an unusual menu of barbecue, country fare and donuts.

14th Street Bistro (☎ 540-636-8400; 101 W 14th St; ☽ lunch 11:30am-2:30pm, dinner 5-9pm Mon-Thu, 5-10pm Fri & Sat, 5-8pm Sun) Trade those hiking boots for sensible shoes at this deliciously upscale French-American bistro. A full bar and dancing round out the experience.

HARRISONBURG

☎ 540 / pop 41,000 / elevation 1352ft

First settled in 1739, this market city has become an agricultural center (beef, dairy and poultry) and a college town, home to James Madison University and Eastern Mennonite College; just south of town is Bridgewater Community College.

You will probably see the incongruous sight of distinctively dressed Mennonites in horse-drawn buggies going about their simple lives in the bustling commercial center of town.

The **Harrisonburg–Rockingham County CVB** (☎ 540-434-2319; www.hrcvb.org; 10 E Gay St) provides tourist information. **Shenandoah Valley Regional Airport** (☎ 540-234-8304; www.flyshd.com), 10 miles south of Harrisonburg at Weyers Cave, is served by US Airways Express and charter planes. Most people traveling in this part of the Shenandoah do so by car.

Sleeping & Eating

Harrisonburg–New Market KOA Kampground (☎ 540-896-8929; site/Kamping Kabin $20-22/40) Sites come with full hookups at this campground near George Washington National Forest. To get there from Harrisonburg, take Rte 11 north for 9 miles and turn east onto County Rd 608, following that for 3.2 miles.

Joshua Wilton House (☎ 540-434-4464; 412 S Main St; d $115-130) This delightful, late 19th century house close to downtown features a sunroom on the back patio, an upscale restaurant and an adjacent café that serves good, moderately priced dinners. The rooms are tastefully furnished with antiques.

Health Trek Deli (☎ 540-433-2359; 451 University Blvd; ☽ 9am-6pm Mon-Sat) Inside Kate's Natural Products, this deli serves just about the only decent, inexpensive vegetarian fare in town.

Blue Stone Inn Restaurant (☎ 540-434-0535; 9107 N Valley Pike; ☽ 4:30-8:30pm Tue-Sat) Open for more than 50 years, the Blue Stone Inn doesn't appear to have changed much. The dining room has a wealth of trophies (animal and fish) mounted on the walls; the ceiling's light fixtures are made from antlers. Large portions of good steak and seafood are the house specialties, and the small space fills up quickly. To get there, take exit 251 off I-81.

AROUND HARRISONBURG

Nestled in a beautiful part of the Shenandoah Valley, Harrisonburg is close to a number of interesting towns and attractions.

Natural Chimneys Regional Park

The Shenandoah Valley was once the floor of a great inland sea. Eons ago, as the sea receded, natural forces sculpted the Natural Chimneys, towers of solid rock that loom as much as 120ft above the surrounding pastoral terrain. Viewed from one angle, they resemble enormous chimneys; from another, they take on the appearance of a ruined castle or temple. Perhaps their castlelike appearance has something to do with the fact that the site hosts the annual **Jousting Tournament** on the third Saturday of August. Dating from 1821, this tournament is the oldest continuously held sporting event in North America.

The **Natural Chimneys Regional Park Campground** (☎ 540-350-2510; tent site/RV site $20/27, day use per person $4, per car $8) is open to visitors for day (9am to dusk) and overnight use. The campground features 120 sites with electric/water hookups, hiking and biking trails, picnic shelters, a pool, a store, hot showers, laundry, playgrounds and self-guided tours (the facilities are limited from December through February). The grounds also include a **visitor center** (☉ 9am-5pm Apr-Oct).

Massanutten Resort

This is one of Virginia's best all-season resorts, with an eye-popping list of activities for adults and kids alike.

Best known for its **skiing facilities** (☎ 800-207-6277; www.massresort.com; all-day lift ticket midweek adult/child 6-12/child under 6 $35/30/free, ski rentals $20/16/16, snowboarding $42/37/NA; ☉ 9am 10pm Dec–mid-Mar), the resort boasts a vertical drop of 1110ft (the highest in Virginia) and 14 slopes (including the 3400ft Diamond Jim and 4100ft ParaDice), all of which are lit at night. There is one quad chairlift, and the field has 100% snowmaking capacity.

A lot of ski racing happens here, and there's a PSIA ski school and SKIwee program. The mid-Atlantic snowboard series takes place in early February. The tubing park is extremely popular and usually sells out – call a day in advance ($16 for two hours).

Hot weather means pools, a skate park, tennis courts and canoe/kayak rentals. A sprawling indoor/outdoor water park with a lazy river, slides and a wave pool was due to debut in summer 2005 (call for prices).

After a hard day hiking on the trails or just keeping up with the kids, adults enjoy a little pampering at the onsite **spa** (☎ 540-289-4040) – ask for the 'Royal Treatment' ($100 for 50 minutes), complete with two massage therapists for twice the indulgence

Accommodations range from basic hotel rooms to spacious condos with fireplaces and decks.

To get to Massanutten from Staunton, take I-81 north to exit 247A in Harrisonburg. Head east on US 33 for 10 miles to County Rd 644; the entrance is on the left.

Grand Caverns Regional Park

In Augusta County near the appropriately named town of Grottoes, these **caverns** (☎ 540-249-5705; adult/child 4-12 $16/9; ☉ 9am-5pm Apr-Oct) contain one of the largest underground rooms in the East, the, Cathedral Hall (70ft high and 280ft long). There is some underground graffiti as well, creatively referred to as 'historic signatures' (instead of 'aged vandalism'). Jefferson rode on horseback from Monticello to see the caverns, and Stonewall Jackson let his troops sleep here after the Battle of Port Republic. (For more, see What Lies Beneath: Virginia Canyons, p187.)

To get there from I-81, take exit 235 to Rte 256. This meets US 340 at Grottoes; head south on US 340. Turn right on Dogwood Ave and proceed for about 1000ft. Make a right onto Grand Caverns Dr and look for the signs.

A few miles north of Grottoes, just off US 340, is **Port Republic**, site of one of the last battles of Jackson's 1862 Shenandoah Valley campaign.

LURAY

Map 10, p160 / ☎ 540 / pop 5000 / elevation 789ft

This small town has the good fortune of being situated astride two great wilderness areas – Massanutten Mountain (in George Washington National Forest, p229) and Shenandoah National Park. The **Luray–Page County Chamber of Commerce Visitor Center** (☎ 540-743-3915 or 888-743-3915; www.luraypage.com; 46 E Main St; �)9am-5pm) is smack in the center of town.

For the kids, the small but entertaining **Luray Zoo** (☎ 540-743-4113; 1087 US 211W; adult/child 3-12 $7/5; �) 10am-5pm) features a large reptile collection, a petting zoo and an amphitheater with live educational shows.

Luray Caverns

These **caverns** (☎ 540-743-6551; www.luraycaverns.com; adult/senior/child 7-13 $18/16/8; �) 9am-4pm Nov 1-Apr 4, to 6pm Apr 5-Jun 14 & Sep 4-Oct 31, to 7pm Jun 15-Sep 3) are the largest and most popular in the eastern US. Much of their popularity has to do with a most unnatural feature, a stalactite organ, feted as a 'stalacpipe,' which is played on all tours. In addition, the caverns boast crystal-clear pools, monumental columns and walkways; outside, you'll find an antique carriage, car and coach museum. The caverns lie 9 miles west of Luray on US 211 (10 minutes from Skyline Drive). Also see What Lies Beneath: Virginia's Caverns, p187.

Sleeping & Eating

Luray Caverns offers two lodging options: **Motel East** and **Motel West** (☎ 888-941-4531; www.luraycaverns.com; 831 W Main St; d Sun-Thu/Fri & Sat/holidays & Oct weekends $65/80/86), both with panoramic views of the Blue Ridge Mountains.

Yogi Bear's Jellystone Park (☎ 540-743-4002; www.campluray.com; site/deluxe site/cabin $25-29/25-33/35-135 Mar 26-May 27 & Sep 6-30, $34/41/35-135 May 28-Sep 5; �) Mar-Nov; ☒) The 400ft waterslide, miniature golf course and three swimming pools make this campground stand out in the Yogi Bear chain. Convenient to Shenandoah National Park, it's 3 miles east of Luray on US 211.

Woodruff Inns (☎ 540-743-1494; www.woodruffinns.com; 330 Mechanic St; d $149-289) This charming collection of properties ranges from riverfront cabins to elegant B&Bs. The Victorian Inn throws a lavish high tea, while the Woodruff House offers indulgence in the form of an outdoor spa and Jacuzzi (which is lit by candles at night!).

Jordan Hollow Farm Inn (☎ 888-418-7000, 540-778-2285; www.jordanhollow.com; 326 Hawksbill Park Rd, Stanley; d $133-190) The gourmet breakfasts are legendary at this restored colonial horse farm. Some rooms open onto a pristinely manicured garden, while several suites contain Jacuzzi tubs. The farm also has a bar, restaurant and stables. It's 6 miles south of Luray in Stanley (just off US 340 on County Rd 624).

Parkhurst Restaurant (☎ 540-743-6009; 2547 US 211W; �) dinner) Close to Luray Caverns, this pleasant redbrick place serves American and Continental fare in an enclosed verandah with views of the surrounding mountains.

Farmhouse Restaurant (☎ 888-418-2210; 326 Hawksbill Park Rd; ◐ dinner & Sun brunch) In this restored Colonial farmhouse, eat like the forefathers did – with a few exceptions like indoor plumbing and electricity, of course. Traditional American cuisine paired with local wines is a revolutionary combination indeed. The restaurant is part of the Jordan Hollow Farm Inn.

STAUNTON

☎ 540 / pop 24,000 / elevation 1402ft

Staunton – pronounced *stan*-tun (and don't forget it!) – is another old Virginia town that exudes history. There has long been a pathway through this area, originally traversed by Native Americans as they moved up and down the Shenandoah Valley. In 1732 the family of Scotch-Irish immigrant John Lewis built a homestead here, 2 miles east of present-day Staunton.

Once the settlers came in force, Staunton became the government seat of huge Augusta County, named after the then princess of Wales. (In 1738 the county included modern-day West Virginia, Ohio, Kentucky, Illinois, Indiana and the Pittsburgh area of Pennsylvania.) During the Revolutionary War, the parish church was briefly (for 17 days in June 1781) the capital of Virginia, as Thomas Jefferson and the General Assembly moved here to evade the British Redcoats.

During the Civil War, the Virginia School for the Deaf & Blind was turned into a military hospital and remained as such for the duration. In 1862 Stonewall Jackson, ostensibly leading his men out of the valley to Richmond, took them back over the Blue Ridge Mountains into Staunton by train – probably the world's first use of the railway as a military tactic.

And the historical claims to fame kept on coming: Staunton was also the birthplace of US president Thomas Woodrow Wilson (1856) and the site of a huge party in 1922, when the president returned home.

Because the town has weathered the ravages of history so well (it was untouched during the Civil War), today Staunton boasts a fine collection of immaculately preserved Victorian buildings. If you stop here, you'll be rewarded with engrossing, albeit quite hilly, walks.

Staunton lies off I-81 (or off US 250, 11 miles west of the southern end of Skyline Drive).

Information

Stop by the **Staunton Visitor Center** (☎ 540-332-3971; ◐ 9:30am-5:30pm Nov-Mar, 9am-6:30pm Apr-Oct) at the New Street Garage or the small **information center** (☎ 540-332-3972; ◐ 9am-5pm) at the Museum of American Frontier Culture (p192).

Sights

HISTORIC DISTRICTS

There are five historical districts in town, all easily accessible on foot. **Gospel Hill**, near the corner of Beverley and Coalter Sts, got its name in the late 1790s, when religious meetings were held here. Today it's an area of shady streets and elegant homes. The **North End**, an older neighborhood adjoining Mary Baldwin College (founded in 1842), contains lots of historical buildings and steep hills. **Newtown** is the oldest residential area and includes the city's first black church. **Downtown** is a compact area west of Gospel Hill; it exudes 19th century charm. Most of the buildings date from 1860 to 1920, Staunton's boom period.

The **Wharf** historical district dates from the era when the Virginia Central Railroad hit town in 1854. The railroad transformed the sleepy rural village into an important commercial center. Warehouses sprang up around the train depot and supplied everything from fresh produce to wagons and harnesses.

If you get tired traversing the San Francisco-esque hills, hop the free **trolley** that runs through downtown.

WOODROW WILSON BIRTHPLACE & MUSEUM

Thomas Woodrow Wilson was the 28th president of the US (1913-21) and the eighth Virginia-born president. This stately Greek Revival house, built in 1846 and occupied by Wilson's Presbyterian minister father beginning in 1855, has been restored to the splendid condition it was in when Wilson was born here in 1856.

The **museum** (☎ 540-885-0897; www.woodrowwilson.org; 18-24 N Coalter St; adult/student/child 6-12 $8/5/3; ☺ 10am-5pm Mon-Sat, noon-5pm Sun Mar-Oct, 10am-4pm Mon-Sat, noon-4pm Sun Nov-Feb) features seven exhibition galleries that outline the accomplishments of Wilson, probably the first of the true international American statesmen. Wilson's presidential limousine, a 1919 Pierce-Arrow sedan, is on display. Winter opening hours may vary. There's a gift shop in the gardens and free parking.

MUSEUM OF AMERICAN FRONTIER CULTURE

At this wonderful folk **museum** (☎ 540-332-7850; www.frontiermuseum.org; adult/senior/student/child 6-12 $10/9.50/9/6; ☺ 9am-5pm mid-Mar–Nov, 10am-4pm Dec–mid-Mar), staff in period costume organize demonstrations of daily and seasonal activities on 18th and 19th century farmsteads, such as tending livestock, planting and doing domestic chores. The museum lies on the old 'Warriors Path,' used by Indians traveling up and down the valley. This path later evolved into County Wagon Rd, used by settlers traveling from Pennsylvania to Georgia. To get here, take exit 222 off I-81 to US 250.

BLACKFRIARS PLAYHOUSE

Staunton's intimate, 300-seat **theater-in-the-round** (☎ 540-851-1733; www.ishakespeare.com; 35 S New St; tickets $18-28) provides the perfect venue in which to see rousing plays from the grand Bard. The theater's authentic reproduction of an Elizabethan indoor theater extends to the hard audience benches – bring a cushion or rent one ($2) and your tush will thank you, especially during longer plays.

Sleeping

Shenandoah KOA Kampground (☎ 540-248-2746; www.koakampgrounds.com; site/Kamping Kabin $27-29/46; ☺ Mar 15-Nov 1) A great selection of shaded campsites surrounding a large lake, tons of kids activities, a game room, indoor hot tubs and satellite TV – is this camping? The stellar location close to Skyline Drive also makes for a great, inexpensive family sleepover.

Walnut Hills Campground (☎ 540-337-3920; www.walnuthillscampground.com; 484 Walnut Hills Rd; site $21, Kamping Kabin/cottage weekday $29/69, weekend $44/84; ☺ year-round; 🐾) This campground and kiddie fun park wrapped into one features a lake, swimming pools, hayrides, a game room and playground. Live music and dancing on weekends allow everyone to indulge the kid inside. The level RV sites come with electric/water/sewer hookups, and the facilities also include a store, laundry and free showers.

Thornrose House at Gypsy Hill (☎ 540-885-7026; www.thornrosehouse.com; 531 Thornrose Ave; d $75-95) Enjoy morning coffee on the wraparound verandah of this Georgian Revival brick home across the street from a lovely park. The rooms (infant- and smoke-free) have private baths and air-conditioning and are furnished with antiques. Afternoon snacks are served in the elegant parlor.

Belle Grae Inn (☎ 540-886-5151; www.bellegrae.com; 515 W Frederick St; d Mon-Fri $109-149, Sat & Sun $149-179) A romantic old place, this inn is comprised of closely grouped, carefully restored original Victorian residences, each with decorated guestrooms and suites. It is restricted to adults and well-behaved youth 14 or older, and no pets are allowed.

Eating

Rowe's Family Restaurant (☎ 540-886-1833; 74 Rowe Rd; dishes under $15), just off I-81 exit 222, is one of the state's best restaurants, serving inexpensive, tasty meals. All the homespun Virginia staples are here, including mincemeat pies, Virginia ham dishes, succulent potato soup, breaded catfish and Southern fried chicken – and did we mention the bottomless cups of coffee and waitstaff fresh from the 1950s?

Pampered Palate Café (☎ 540-886-9463; 26-28 E Beverley St; dishes $5-20; ⏰ breakfast & lunch Mon-Sat) This European-style nook is an especially good choice for vegetarians, with a wide range of fresh-produce sandwiches, strong coffees and local wines.

Wrights Dairy Rite Inc (☎ 540-886-0435; 346 Greenville Ave; dishes under $15) This drive-in restaurant is a local institution; it's offered curb service since 1952 and even appeared on a Statler Brothers' album cover (Don and Harold often pull in for a meal).

Shorty's Diner (☎ 540-885-8861; 1013 Richmond Ave; dishes $5-15; ⏰ 7am-9pm Sun-Thu, to 10pm Fri & Sat) Bottomless sweet tea and cakes and pies bigger than a breadbox make for good Southern eats at this spot with checkerboard floors.

McCormick's (☎ 540-885-3111; 41 N Augusta St; dishes $10-20; ⏰ dinner) It's not quite fine dining, but the food is good and the place boasts a casual atmosphere, great prime rib and, occasionally, live entertainment. Come Wednesdays for all-you-can-eat crab legs!

Depot Grille (☎ 540-885-7332; 42 Middlebrook Ave; dishes $6-20) The 40ft Victorian oak bar takes center stage; there you can enjoy a large selection of beers. Order at the bar or enjoy creative entrées in oak booths made from old wooden pews. Activities for the kids make this spot, housed inside an old freight depot, very family-friendly.

Mill Street Grill (☎ 540-886-0656; 1 Mill St; ⏰ dinner & Sun brunch) Another modern restaurant occupying an industrial building (this one a converted gristmill), the Mill Street Grill is known for killer barbecue and melt-off-the-bone ribs doused with tongue-burning Cajun spices. For late-night entertainment, try the adjacent tavern, with pool tables, a good selection of beers and a colorful crowd.

RAMSEY'S DRAFT WILDERNESS AREA ?

A beautiful, quiet and moody place, this section of the George Washington & Jefferson National Forests is a pure wilderness area designated by Congress in 1980 to preserve a deeply wooded valley with the last remaining tracts of virgin forest in Virginia. Some hemlock stands here have never seen an ax or chainsaw – one fallen tree had its rings measured and was estimated to be more than 450 years old.

At the Ramsey's Draft picnic area, interpretive signs relate the first battle of Stonewall Jackson's 1862 Valley campaign. There are Confederate breastworks nearby.

Hikers are in for a special treat, as the wilderness lives up to its name, remaining blissfully uncrowded, and all trails reveal a unique view of the forest. Whether it's the quiet trickle of Ramsey's Draft along the Ramsey's Draft Trail, the grandiose vistas of the surrounding mountains from the Shenandoah Mountain Trail, or the most popular and rewarding White Oak

Trail (a 32-mile trek), hikers in this area will encounter solitude not found elsewhere in Shenandoah or along the Parkway.

There is a sad footnote to the story of this wilderness area: Recent tests confirm the presence of the destructive woolly adelgid among the giant hemlocks. If you want to experience these towering beauties, hike through soon; hemlocks infested with the adelgid face a 100% mortality rate and will be gone very soon.

Mountain bikes are not permitted, but hunting is at certain times, so always wear bright clothing.

This area is an excellent location for cross-country skiing – especially for novices, thanks to the relatively level terrain. Anglers enjoy the fishing here, with native brook and rainbow trout, smallmouth and largemouth bass, bluegill and catfish along 300 miles of waterways.

Primitive camping is allowed in most of the forest (no permit required), and though campfires are technically legal, it's recommended that campers instead carry in backpacker stoves, in order to protect the unspoiled land. For information, including trail maps, check with the **USDA Forest Service Headquarters** (Deerfield Ranger District; ☎ 540-885-8028; www.patc.net/history/archive/ramseys. html; 2314 West Beverley St, Staunton) and ranger offices.

To get to Ramsey's Draft from Staunton, take Rte 250 west (it is well signed).

WAYNESBORO
Map 11, p161 / ☎ 540 / pop 20,000 / elevation 1300ft
Settled in 1797 by Irish and German immigrants and named for Revolutionary War hero General 'Mad' Anthony Wayne, Waynesboro offers a few sights to see, but the town is best known as the place where Skyline Drive and the Blue Ridge Parkway meet – convenient place to fuel up, chow down and get a good night's sleep before journeying forth. It lies 8 miles east of the I-81/I-64 junction.

For more information on attractions, contact the **Waynesboro Tourism Office** (☎ 540-942-6644; 301 W Main St; ☉ 8am-5pm Mon-Fri). There is a **visitor center** (☎ 540-943-5187; ☉ 10am-6pm Mon-Sat) at Afton Mountain (exit 99 off I-64).

The **P Buckley Moss Museum** (☎ 540-949-6473; 150 P Buckley Moss Dr; admission free; ☉ 10am-6pm Mon-Sat, 12:30-5:30pm Sun) is a fine arts museum dedicated to Moss, very much a 'people's artist,' whose subject matter includes the Amish and Mennonite communities. There are also four galleries in the **Shenandoah Valley Art Center** (☎ 540-942-7662; 600 W Main St; admission free; ☉ 10am-4pm Tue-Sat, 2-4pm Sun).

Sleeping & Eating
Shenandoah Acres Resort (☎ 540-337-1911; www.shenacres.com; County Rd 660; site/camper cabin/cottage summer $22/50/107; ☉ May-Sept; 🖳) Miniature golf, playground equipment in the water, basketball, volleyball and other pursuits will keep kids easily amused. Go to the website to view your sleeping arrangement in advance. You can camp here or stay in one of the cottages, which are available year-round. The **swimming area** (adult/child 6-11 weekdays $7.25/5, weekends $9.25/5.75) is open to the public.

Waynesboro North 340 Campground (☎ 540-943-9573; US 340; 2-person site $18-21; 🖳) Most sites come with electricity and water at this campground, 5 miles north of Waynesboro off I-64 exit 94.

Afton House (☎ 877-214-8133; www.aftonhouse.com; r/cottage $85-95/300-400; 🖳) The original inn served as an 1860s summer resort, but burned down in 1963. Fortunately, the present B&B is just as charming and close to the Parkway. From I-64, take exit 99 (Afton Waynesboro), then US 250 east to Rte 6 east. Follow Rte 6 less than a half mile to Afton House.

Iris Inn (☎ 888-585-9018; www.irisinn.com; 191 Chinquapin Dr; d Sun-Thu/Fri & Sat $95-105/105-125) This modern mountain retreat draws guests with its spacious great room and roaring fireplace for those chilly evenings. Take in vast views of the Shenandoah Valley from the lookout tower. There is a room equipped for disabled guests.

Weasie's Kitchen (☎ 540-943-0500; 130 E Broad St; dishes under $10) Come here for inexpensive lunches and dinners and rib-sticking breakfasts that are served all day.

Capt'n Sam's Landing (☎ 540-943-3416; US 250W; dishes under $15) A lively bar in this slow neck of the woods, Capt'n Sam's offers good local seafood dishes.

'Wow, what a view!' you'll find yourself uttering at every eye-opening curve. Photos in books just don't do this ribbon in the sky justice.

EXPERIENCING THE
BLUE RIDGE PARKWAY

The drive north-south climbs from serene canopied forests, to hilly open meadows and farmland, to alpine swathes of spruce and pine layered like a great green blanket someone shook out and placed on a larger-than-life bas relief map. The grand Blue Ridge Parkway, one of America's most popular road trips, traverses the southern Appalachian ridge from Virginia's Shenandoah National Park at Mile 0 to North Carolina's Great Smoky Mountains National Park at Mile 469. Wildflowers bloom in spring, and fall colors are spectacular. High-quality National Park Service campgrounds and visitor centers are open May to October. And though the Parkway is the main attraction, don't miss the quaint towns and historic sites that lie just off this majestic ribbon.

WHEN YOU ARRIVE

There is no entrance fee for the Parkway; visitors come via car and bicycle.

The Parkway is open 24 hours year-round, though most lodges and facilities close during the winter – except for **Peaks of Otter Lodge** (p209) and the campgrounds at **Linville Falls** (p226) and **Otter Creek** (p209) – and snow and ice force certain sections of the Parkway in higher elevations to be gated shut. Elevations change dramatically, from 600 to 6000ft above sea level, so weather sometimes shuts down certain stretches of the road. Winter sees the most closures, with frequent roadway freezing. Though the Parkway doesn't close for fog, it can make for a treacherous journey through these misty mountains, so use extra caution. Call for **road conditions** (☎ 828-298-0398).

ORIENTATION
Entrances

The Parkway winds through two states for 469 curvy miles: Virginia for 217 miles and North Carolina for 252 miles. Though there are no entrance stations where you have to stop and pay a fee, you could say there are two 'official' Parkway entrances: the north end off I-64 east of **Waynesboro** (p194) and the south end off NC 441 in the **Cherokee Indian Reservation** (p219). Otherwise, the Parkway is intersected by numerous state roads and interstates, making for easy access at many junctions.

Major Roads

Unlike Shenandoah, where only one road traverses the park and only four other roads provide access, the Blue Ridge Parkway intersects numerous state roads and interstates, allowing easy access from several points in Virginia and North Carolina. In Virginia, I-77 intersects at Milepost (MP) 200, just south of Fancy Gap; US 58 intersects at Meadows of Dan; and US 220 intersects at Roanoke Mountain. In North Carolina, US 21 intersects at MP 229, before Brinegar Cabin; US 221 intersects at Blowing Rock and Linville Falls; and I-40 and I-26 intersect near Asheville.

There's controversy over the construction of a new road, I-73, which will cross the Parkway at Roanoke, Virginia, and extend to North Carolina. Environmental groups are concerned that this new route will damage the ecosystem of the Parkway and the surrounding land and will open the area up to developers. As of publication, there's been no groundbreaking on the project.

INFORMATION

Since there are no entrance stations per se, visitors can pick up free information at any of the 12 visitor centers along the Parkway: **Humpback Rocks** (MP 5.8), **James River** (MP 63.6), **Peaks of Otter** (MP 86) and **Rocky Knob** (MP 169) in Virginia; and **Cumberland Knob** (MP 217.5), **Moses H Cone Memorial Park** (MP 294.1), **Linn Cove Viaduct** (MP 304.6), **Linville Falls** (MP 316.4), **Museum of North Carolina Minerals** (MP 331), **Craggy Gardens** (MP 364.6), **Folk Art Center** (MP 382), and **Waterrock Knob** (MP 451.2) in North Carolina.

POLICIES & REGULATIONS

Travelers are urged to call ☎ 800-PARKWATCH (727-5928) to report any accidents, emergencies, fires or crimes.

Wildlife

Don't feed the wildlife. Not only does it teach animals the bad habit of seeking food from noisy humans, but it's just plain dumb. You could jeopardize your life by luring a cute bear cub closer – Mama's right around the corner, and you can guarantee she's got her eyes on you. Plus, get caught handing out treats, you'll pay a hefty fine.

Food Storage

Lions, tigers and bears, oh my! Well, you shouldn't see any of the first two (unless safely behind bars at the Mill Mountain Zoo, p231), but you're almost guaranteed a glimpse of at least one of the third. Bears are hungry animals, and if you've got a stash of Krispy Kreme doughnuts triple-sealed in Ziploc bags and hidden under clothes in the 'safe' corner of your tent, they'll find 'em. Assuming you don't want bears

TOP FIVE

- ✔ Admiring the ethereal, 360-degree views from mist-shrouded **Craggy Gardens** (p218)
- ✔ Enjoying crisp apples, hayrides and twangy bluegrass jams at historic **Altapass Orchard** (p216)
- ✔ Taking a moonlight walk to the **Cone family graveyard** (p212) by lantern light.
- ✔ Experiencing the thrilling rush of a waterfall hike, particularly **Crabtree Falls** (p221) and **Linville Falls** (p221)
- ✔ Attending a live broadcast of *Blue Ridge Backroads*, an old-time bluegrass radio show, at the **Rex Theater** (p232) in Galax

PIT STOPS

The scenery may be breathtaking, but there will probably come a point in your 469-mile road trip when no sight is more beauteous than a roadside restroom. Here's a handy list of facilities for those much-needed bathroom breaks:

Humpback Rocks	MP 5.8	EB Jeffress Park	MP 272
Otter Creek	MP 60.9	Moses H Cone Memorial Park	MP 294.1
James River	MP 63.6	Julian Price Memorial Park	MP 297.1
Peaks of Otter	MP 86	Linn Cove Viaduct	MP 304.6
Roanoke Mountain	MP 120.4	Linville Falls Recreation Area	MP 316.4
Smart View	MP 154.5	Museum of North Carolina Minerals	MP 331
Rocky Knob	MP 169	Crabtree Meadows Recreation Area	MP 339.5
Mabry Mill	MP 176.1	Craggy Gardens Recreation Area	MP 364.6
Groundhog Mountain	MP 189	Folk Art Center	MP 382
Cumberland Knob	MP 217.5	Mt Pisgah	MP 408.8
Doughton Park	MP 241.1	Waterrock Knob	MP 451.2
Northwest Trading Post	MP 258.7		

nosing around your campsite, you must adhere to a few food storage regulations: put all food in park-approved bearproof canisters and/or use a storage pole – provided at backcountry camp huts – to hang food at least 10ft off the ground and 4ft from a tree trunk.

Camping & Campfires

Only camp in designated areas (the Parkway has nine campgrounds, see p209 and p226). Campsites are assigned on a first-come, first-served basis, though at Linville Falls and Price Park in North Carolina, travelers can make advance **reservations** (☎ 877-444-6777; www.reserveusa.com). All NPS campgrounds provide at least one wheelchair-accessible site. Stays are limited to 21 days in any campground between May and October, and checkout is at noon. Quiet hours run from 10pm to 6am. All campgrounds offer sanitary dump stations, ranger programs and access to hiking trails. Each loop has a common comfort station with running water.

Limited backcountry camping is available at Basin Cove in **Doughton Park** (☎ 336-372-8568) and Rock Castle Gorge in the **Rocky Knob District** (☎ 540-745-9660). Permits must be requested in advance. Check with a park ranger to learn about access to neighboring US Forest Service backcountry areas along the Parkway.

Regulations forbid backcountry campfires – campers must use a backcountry stove. In campgrounds, fires are permitted only in designated fire pits.

Fishing

The Parkway is ideal for fishing, with 13 artificial lakes and more than 100 miles of stocked streams curving around the mountains. A license is required. In Virginia, nonresidents pay $6 for a five-day pass or $30 for annual pass; in North Carolina, the fees for nonresidents are $10 for a day pass, $15 for three days or $50 annually. Those under 16 fish for free. Only one license is required to fish both Virginia and North Carolina waters along the Parkway.

Fishing is allowed from one half hour before sunrise to one half hour after sunset, and only single-hook artificial lures are allowed. Most anglers use the catch-and-release method, though it's not required.

The following are classified as 'special waters': Abbott Lake, Little Stoney Creek and Otter Lake in Virginia; Doughton Park's Basin Creek and tributaries, Boone Fork, Cold Prong Branch, Laurel Creek, Sims Creek and Camp Creek in North Carolina. Insects, worms, live or dead fish or fish parts and other organic bait are prohibited in the special waters.

Boating

Boats without motors and/or sails are permitted only on **Price Lake** (MP 295) in Julian Price Memorial Park – there's a ramp behind the parking area, and visitors can also rent boats. Otherwise, national forests like **Mt Pisgah** (p239) and recreation areas like **Lake Powhattan** (p218) and **Cave Mountain** (p202) allow nonmotorized boating in their waters.

GETTING AROUND
Car & Motorcycle

The speed limit is 45mph, dropping to 25mph in certain congested areas. Cars are permitted to pull over anywhere along the Parkway, as long as the vehicle does not touch the pavement, but you must notify a ranger if leaving your car overnight. Motorcycles are allowed, but must keep their headlights on in North Carolina by law. Drivers should note that the North Carolina section of the Parkway has 26 tunnels (Virginia has one), and headlights are required when passing through.

Bicycle

The Parkway is a great route for avid bicyclists, especially with its low speed limit and absence of loud, commercial vehicles. However, it was primarily designed for motorized travel, and several developed areas are spaced too far apart for comfortable travel by bicycle, particularly campgrounds. Cyclists should then seek shelter and facilities off the Parkway, but be warned that roads leaving the Parkway can be quite steep (particularly around Floyd, Virginia and NC 80 in North Carolina).

Endurance and preparation are key, as traveling the length of the Parkway involves an elevation change of more than 48,000ft (equivalent to roughly 9 vertical miles), with the lowest point at 600ft and the highest at 6000ft.

Bicycles are not permitted on trails or walkways. Riders should travel single file (except when passing or turning left) and well to the right-hand side of the road. Bikes should be equipped with a white light or reflector visible from at least 500ft in the front and a red light or reflector visible from at least 200ft in the rear during periods of low visibility, between the hours of sunset and sunrise, or when traveling through a tunnel. You must maintain (and not exceed) a speed that's consistent with weather conditions and other traffic.

To make sure your bike trip is as safe as possible, wear a bicycle helmet at all times, carry a first-aid and tire repair kit, wear breathable, high-visibility clothes in layers, pack extra water and high-energy snacks, and avoid the Parkway during foggy conditions. For information before your trip, or to check current weather conditions, contact the **Superintendent's Office** (☎ 828-298-0398; Blue Ridge Parkway, 199 Hemphill Knob Rd, Asheville, NC 28803).

Some final words of caution: seriously consider using a flashlight in the Parkway's 27 tunnels, as some of them have severe curves and are pitch black (tunnels are not illuminated). Also, use extra caution when leaving the Parkway for local towns. Because the road lies along a ridge, the exits are downhill trips at a steep grade on winding roads.

Bus

There is no bus service to the Parkway. **Greyhound** (☎ 800-229-9424; www.greyhound
.com) serves the following towns, in order from north to south: Charlottesville,
Waynesboro, Staunton, Buena Vista, Lynchburg, Roanoke, Hillsville, Galax,
Boone and Asheville. A typical fare from Washington, DC, to Waynesboro,
Virginia (the start of the Parkway), is $40; the trip takes four hours and 45
minutes.

Shuttles

At Peaks of Otter, a small **bus** (adult/child $3.75/2.25 ; ☺ May-Oct) shuttles visitors to
the Sharp Top summit; crowds are crazy in summer.

Organized Tours

Carolina Tailwinds (☎ 888-251-3206; www.carolinatailwinds.com; PO Box 24716, Winston-Salem, NC
27114-4716; ☺ Jun-Sep) offers an exhilarating overnight Blue Ridge **bike tour** ($825-
925 for 4 days/3 nights, $80 bike rental) that canvasses the nooks and crannies of North
Carolina's northwestern mountains. Meals, lodging, snacks, maps and route
guides, van support and transportation back to the starting point are included
in the package price, as is a ride from the Greensboro airport.

High Mountain Expeditions (☎ 800-262-9036; www.highmountainexpeditions.com; PO Box
1299, Blowing Rock, NC 28605; ☺ year-round) runs overnight hiking and rafting trips
on the Nolichucky and Watauga rivers.

The excellent mountain biking guides at **Backcountry Outdoors** (☎ 704-883-9453;
www.backcountryoutdoors.com; 18 Pisgah Hwy, Pisgah Forest, NC 28768) give personal tours of
the rugged mountains.

Queen's Trading Post & Outfitters (☎ 704-497-4453; US 441N, Cherokee, NC 28719) offers mountain biking and hiking trips, as well as bike rentals and camping
equipment.

VIRGINIA

Map 12, p162

The Blue Ridge Parkway stretches for 209 country miles in Virginia, passing
fantastic recreational lakes, world-class bluegrass venues and the vibrant city
of Roanoke. It may not boast the same caliber of alpine vistas as the North
Carolina portion does, but don't knock the bucolic farmland, which suddenly
opens to a panoramic spread that shutterbugs clamor for.

It would take about five hours to drive this section of the Parkway without
stopping, from Humpback Rocks to Cumberland Knob, but who wants to do
that? This is a 'scenic' drive, so allow plenty of time for stopping at overlooks
and snapping that perfect Kodak moment.

Humpback Rocks (MP 5.8)

Humpback Rocks is the first visitor center on the Parkway, with a small exhibit on mountain life in the 19th century and an overworked air-condition-
ing system that keeps the place just above freezing. An easy, self-guided trail
(complete with a brochure detailing the surrounding geology and plant life)
leaves from the visitor center.

For a more moderate hike and access to the Appalachian Trail (AT), stop
at MP 6 and head 1 mile straight up to the smooth, rounded peaks (hence
the name) of Humpback Rocks, where you'll see a hazy, 360-degree view of
the Rockfish and Shenandoah Valleys below. The path is quick and steep, but
allow about an hour if you're a novice climber.

MOUNTAIN FARM

A scaled-back version of Williamsburg, Virginia, the **Mountain Farm** (☎ 540-377-2377), part of the Humpback Rocks complex, is a reconstructed farmstead featuring a trail past stone buildings that hold interactive demonstrations in summer (other months the trail is self-guided). Kids will especially enjoy climbing, scrambling and poking around the chicken coop, log cabin and honey tree while learning about quilting, basket-weaving and preparing homemade foods over an open-hearth fire – they'll also thank their lucky stars for microwaves.

Greenstone Trail (MP 8.8)

A short nature hike (0.2 mile) leaves from the Greenstone parking area and loops through an old oak and hickory forest, as well as greenstone rock formations, giving hikers a glimpse of the geology of the northern Blue Ridge Mountains.

Ravens Roost Overlook (MP 10.7)

Stop here for a sweeping vista of Torry Mountain and the Shenandoah Valley. This is also one of the Parkway's launch sites for hang gliding (p208).

Sherando Lake (MP 16)

At the foot of the Blue Ridge Mountains southeast of Staunton, the family-friendly **Sherando Recreation Area** (☎ 540-261-6105; 4 miles off parkway via VA 814; vehicle with 1/2/3+ people $4/6/8, bicycle $1; campsite $15-20; ☷ Apr 1-Oct 31; ☷) is part of the George Washington & Jefferson National Forest. The 24-acre lake boasts a small beach and bathhouse, a visitor center and an open-air, summer camp–like stone fireplace for spooky tales and perfect s'mores. The family campsites are available on a first-come, first-served basis. The **Cliff Trail** here takes hikers above the lake. You can also opt for a self-guided nature trail closer to the camping area.

Whetstone Ridge (MP 29)

If the term 'Grindstone Cowboy' leaps to mind when you're passing through here, it's probably because the name of this spot came from the sharpening stones used by mountain men near the ridge. Today you'll find a restaurant that specializes in hearty home cookin' and provides restrooms and a pay phone.

A tiny wooden marker denotes the entrance to the **Whetstone Ridge Trail**; from here South Mountain is 8 miles away and VA 603 is 11. Barren spots and tree skeletons remind hikers of a forest fire that consumed a section of the trail.

Indian Gap (47.5)

An easy 0.3-mile trail begins in the parking area and loops past the SUV-sized boulders at Indian Rocks. It's an excellent trail for young'uns (supervised, of course), featuring an abundance of nooks and crannies and even a cave.

James River & Otter Creek Recreation Area (MP 60.8)

A major transportation hub during the Civil War, the James River once contained a series of canal locks, which never really proved successful at taming the water. But it's the water today that lures travelers to its banks, with creek fishing (there's a wheelchair-accessible fishing pier at Otter Creek, MP 63) and riverside picnicking.

VISITOR CENTER (MP 63.6)

An exhibit on the restoration of one of the failed locks (Lock 7) is adjacent to the center. This center includes restrooms, a restaurant and gift shop, with water available onsite; there's also a nearby campground. Two trails leave from the parking lot. The easy 0.4-mile **James River Trail**, with a footbridge that crosses beneath the Parkway bridge, leads to an exhibit about the Kanawha Canal Locks. The moderate half-mile self-guided **Trail of Trees** nature hike features a breathtaking view of the James River.

Cave Mountain Lake Recreation Area

The **Cave Mountain Lake Recreation Area** (☎ 540-291-2188; entrance fee $5, campsite $15-20; ☾ May-early Nov) is an isolated paradise with a 7-acre lake surrounded by hardwoods and pines. There's swimming and fishing from the sandy beach and shores, plus shaded lakefront picnic areas and a few easy to moderate hiking trails. Hot showers are available at the bathhouse.

From the Parkway, take US 501/130 west at MP 70 (Petites Gap) and continue along US 130 at the split. About 3 miles later, turn left onto State Rd 759 and follow that 3 miles to State Rd 781. Turn right; the lake is 1.6 miles farther.

Peaks of Otter (MP 85.9)

A popular breather on the Parkway, Peaks of Otter is always packed with people. Rightly so, as three peaks form a striking triangle of mountains enclosing Abbott Lake: **Sharp Top Mountain** (3875ft), **Flat Top Mountain** (4001ft) and **Harkening Hill** (3372ft). Stone from Sharp Top was used in construction of the Washington Monument.

You can also stop here for restrooms, picnic areas, a gas station, campground and water, and hikers and campers can stock up at the camp store. The visitor center houses a district ranger station, and the shuttle to Sharp Top Mountain departs from here.

Sharp Top Trail (p206) is a strenuous 1.5-mile hike, one of the Parkway's busiest. Most tourists opt for the shuttle.

POLLY WOOD'S ORDINARY & JOHNSON FARM

Ever been unhappy with your hotel room? Take a peek at the **Ordinary**, along the north shore of Abbott Lake, and see how lucky you really are. Polly Wood was widowed in 1830, and as she couldn't sustain herself by farming the small tract of land her husband willed to her, she opened her 'ordinary' home as a travelers' inn.

Johnson Farm dates back to the late 1700s, but it wasn't until 1852 that John T and Mary Elizabeth Johnson moved in and raised a whopping 13 children within these walls. Future families would raise even more kids here, all of whom collectively cared for the land by farming and gardening. Today it's an interpretive farmstead with living-history demonstrations during warmer months, when visitors can help tend the garden, among other chores.

From the Peaks of Otter Visitor Center parking lot, an easy-to-moderate 2-mile trail parallels the lake at points and leads past both attractions. It's also part of two other trails: Harkening Hill and Elk Run Loop.

Roanoke Mountain (MP 120.3)

A quick, 10-minute jaunt on the **Roanoke Mountain Summit Trail** leads to a dramatic view of Roanoke and Mill Mountain. This overlook is another of the Parkway's launch sites for hang gliding (p208). Farther north, at MP 114, is the **Roanoke River Trail**, which affords stunning views of the river and the Niagara Hydroelectric dam.

Illuminated by its giant, mountaintop star, Roanoke is the largest city along the Parkway and is popular for its family-friendly attractions; see **Mill Mountain Zoo** (p231) and **Virginia's Explore Park** (p231).

Kelley Schoolhouse (MP 149)

What could you get for $15 in 1877? A tract of land, believe it or not. And that's just what the local government paid the Kelley family to build a one-room schoolhouse. **Kelley Schoolhouse** is the only remaining school building along the Parkway.

Smart View (MP 154.5)

Named for the beautiful vistas of the mountains and valleys ahead, this small recreation area includes an exhibit on the **Trail Cabin**. Early pioneers lived in this one-room cabin and sustained themselves on the surrounding land and freshwater spring. Today you'll find restrooms and picnic areas, as well as a few short trails good for stretching your legs.

Floyd County

Southeastern Virginia is synonymous with bluegrass, and Floyd County is the penultimate mecca of mountain music.

You haven't experienced bluegrass until you've visited the legendary **Floyd Country Store** (☎ 540-745-4563; www.floydcountrystore.com; 206 S Locust St). The **Friday Night Jamborees** (adult/child 16 and under $3/free; performances 🕑 6:30-11:30pm) draw record crowds – it's not unusual to see children clogging to frenetic banjo twangs alongside a blue-haired betty cutting a rug with a visiting city slicker. Saturdays feature more great music from local and national bands ($15), and in summer, musicians often spill into alleys, driveways and parking lots, making for a giant jam session.

Not far from the store is the **Jacksonville Center** (☎ 540-745-2784), a refurbished old barn that hosts musicians and festivals.

Held in late July or early August in Floyd, **FloydFest** (☎ 540-745-FEST; www.floydfest.com) is a new grassroots festival that showcases not just acclaimed mountain music, but a kaleidoscope of diverse rhythms from African to Zydeco.

At Tuggle Gap (MP 165.3), take Rte 8 and prepare for an extremely twisty descent from the Parkway to Floyd – don't blink.

Rocky Knob (MP 169)

This small visitor center has a pay phone, restrooms and a picnic area with a shelter. Two leg-stretching trails leave from the picnic area: the 1-mile **Rocky Knob Picnic Area Loop Trail** and the 3.1-mile **Black Ridge Trail**. The loop trail offers a gentle hike circling the picnic area through hemlocks and thickets of rhododenron.

The **campground** (p209) is 2 miles north at MP 167.1.

Mabry Mill (MP 176.2)

Built in 1910, this historic water-powered gristmill is now the most photographed sight along the Parkway. A short stroll from the restaurant and gift shop are several cabins which feature NPS demonstrations of blacksmithing, carving, weaving and other early pioneer jobs. There's even a whiskey still! The small restaurant serves the best buckwheat pancakes this side of the Appalachian Trail.

Meadows of Dan (MP 177)

Taking its name from the Old Testament, this farming community was a bustling epicenter of Appalachian life in the early 1900s. Mabry Mill served as a gathering place for the town, providing settlers with work as well as social release from their labor-intensive lives.

A nearby **campground** (p209) makes a good base for exploring Mabry Mill and the Floyd area.

Groundhog Mountain (MP 188.8)

At this well-shaded turnout with restrooms and picnic tables, you'll find displays of the three basic fence forms found along the Parkway: snake, post and rail, and buck. Strangely, a small cemetery occupies an island in the parking lot. From the lot, a quick trail leads to an observation tower with a good view of Groundhog.

Blue Ridge Music Center (MP 213)

One of the Parkway's most anticipated attractions, the new **music center** (Map 13; p163; ☎ 276-236-5309; www.blueridgemusiccenter.net) represents a collaboration between the NPS and the National Council for the Traditional Arts. It will be a major educational resource on the roots of local mountain music. As of this writing, only the amphitheater is open. It hosts the center's summer weekend concert series. Most concerts are free, although tickets to big-name bands start at $10. The center eventually plans to feature film screenings, a listening library, a museum and a system of trails designed to showcase the evolution of this old-timey art form.

DAY HIKES

In addition to the hikes listed here, there are many short leg-stretchers from numerous points along the Parkway.

WHITE ROCK FALLS (MP 19.9)
Distance: 1.8 miles one way
Duration: 2 hours
Challenge: Moderate
Elevation Change: 840ft

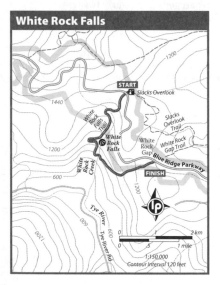

Named for the area's abundant quartz, White Rock Falls may not be the most spectacular waterfall on the Parkway, but getting to it makes for a pretty excursion through dense hemlocks. You'll also be rewarded with a crystal clear plunge pool. The south-north route, described below, is an easier hike than the reverse.

The trailhead starts at the **Slacks Overlook**, where you'll cross the road and walk about 50 yards. (Supposedly there's a wooden sign pointing to the trailhead, but it's easy to overlook, so keep a close eye out for the start of the trail.) Soon you'll come to the first of three crossings of White Rock Creek. Here the trail meanders along the creek until the trail takes a quick right and the creek plunges off to the side. **White Rock Creek Valley** comes into view before a switchback that takes you to a small outcropping. You can hear the falls from here, so push forward about 100 yards for the best view of the waterfall. As you get closer, the stony walls tower overhead, wrapping you in a cool rock enclave where the only sounds you hear are the rushing water and the odd robin call.

Head back out the way you came and continue on the trail as it makes a sharp right past more rocky switchbacks before coming to the falls pool, where a few toes have been known to sneak in for a dip. Past the pool are two more switchbacks. Beyond these, you'll cross the stream and head up through a thick pine forest. Look for the old wagon road and cross a few small bridges. As you ascend, you'll be able to see the Parkway. The hike ends at **White Rock Gap** (MP 18.5).

APPLE ORCHARD FALLS (MP 78.4)
Distance: 3.4 miles round-trip
Duration: 3–4 hours
Challenge: Difficult
Elevation Change: 1000ft

Apple Orchard is a bit of a misnomer, since there are no apple trees – instead you'll find stunted, gnarled oaks whose lumps resemble really ugly fruit. The highlight of the hike is a stunning 200ft waterfall. Plan your return trip for the early evening, when you can enjoy a similarly stunning sunset.

Look for the trailhead in the middle of the parking lot at the **Sunset Fields Overlook**. It starts immediately within the Jefferson National Forest and then passes over a section of the AT. A word of warning: the reason this hike is classified as strenuous is because of the 1000ft elevation change between the parking lot and the falls, so be prepared for steep climbs and descents.

Part of the trail follows a series of old logging roads dating from the early 1900s, when the Virginia Lumber & Extract Company owned them. Toward the end of the logging roads you'll pass a rock overhang, which is handy for shelter if necessary, and then approach the creek. From the wooden footbridge at the creek's edge you'll see the thunderous falls spilling above, but for the money view, you'll need to cross the creek and follow two switchbacks.

To make this a loop trail, look for the **Apple Spur Road**, about 0.8 mile from the Sunset Fields Overlook, and turn left onto the **Cornelius Creek Trail**; this will add another 2.9 miles to the hike.

FALLINGWATER CASCADES LOOP (MP 83.1)
Distance: 1.6-mile loop
Duration: 2 hours
Challenge: Moderate
Elevation Change: 260ft

Part of the Peaks of Otter system, this moderate trail winds through a piece of the George Washington & Jefferson National Forest. It's a pleasant, quiet hike past a series of tumbling cascades. Do this one in fall for the sheer crush of color.

Start at the **Fallingwater Cascades Overlook** and look for the stone staircase. The trail descends to Fallingwater Creek, which turns into a series of gentle cascades that create a nice soundtrack during the hike. Along the way the foliage varies from hemlocks to hardwoods to bushy rhododendron that grows so thick it appears to strangle the path. At the base of the falls is a small footbridge. Take it across the creek, then recross just below the falls, which empty spectacularly

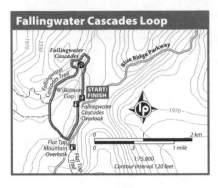

Fallingwater Cascades Loop

into **Wilkerson Gap**. Between the misty sprays and lush surroundings, snap that picture to send home.

Fallingwater is known for its unusual geologic formations and swathes of low vegetation, which together reveal the effects of weathering on the landscape. A few strategically placed benches let you study this phenomenon further.

As you climb out into a hardwood forest, the trail really opens up, offering scenic views of Harkening Hill Mountain. Soon you'll see a sign for **Flat Top Trail** – take that if you're up for an additional 4.5-mile journey to the Peaks of Otter picnic area. Otherwise, continue on the loop trail back to the overlook.

SHARP TOP (MP 85.9)
Distance: 1.6 miles round-trip
Duration: 2–3 hours
Challenge: Difficult
Elevation Change: 1400ft

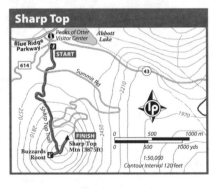

Sharp Top

One of the most commanding peaks in the Blue Ridge Mountains, Sharp Top is also one of the most recognized, thanks to its nearly perfect conical shape. Since the 19th century it has been a favorite picnic spot for locals, and it continues to grow in popularity – which isn't necessarily a good thing. The mountain can feel downright crowded on summer weekends, especially because there's a shuttle bus that brings a lot of visitors who wouldn't normally be inclined to hike both directions. The whole experience is a little like Disneyland: You have to brave the crowds at least once to say you've been there. But you won't be disappointed.

Begin at the camp store across the Parkway from the Peaks of Otter Visitor Center. The trail crosses the summit road (the shuttle bus route) and switchbacks sharply to a junction with a trail leading to **Buzzards Roost**. Above the junction is the steepest part, with a staircase embedded within the hulking rocks. Suddenly the glorious summit appears above a garden of giant boulders, at which point you're guaranteed to encounter other people. The summit itself offers incredible views of the town of Bedford to the east; the James River Valley, Harkening Hill and, the Alleghenies to the west; and the Parkway snaking north and south. The Peaks of Otter and Abbott Lake appear as specks far below.

On the **summit** you'll see a side path leading to the shuttle bus and a small shelter where you can hide away from bad weather or break for a quick snack. Either catch the bus here for the descent or return along the trail – walking on the summit road is prohibited.

The local equivalent of the 'Hollywood' sign, the city of Roanoke's famous star was built as a Christmas decoration in 1949. But folks loved it so much that it stuck around. This trail isn't exactly on the Parkway, but it's a fun hike up to the glowing landmark.

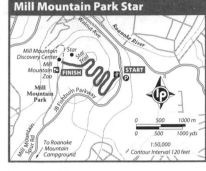

From the Roanoke Mountain Campground, head toward Roanoke Mountain on **Mill Mountain Spur Rd**. Go past the Mill Mountain Park entrance to a parking area on the right.

Cross the street and look for the clearly marked Star Trail at a flight of stairs. You'll climb about six switchbacks, but don't worry about the number – it sounds harder than it is. Numerous shaded benches line the trail, offering rest stops amid rows of pines, oaks and maples.

At the summit is a junction where you can turn back and retrace your steps. But that's not why you climbed up here in the first place. To get the most out of this trail, you'll have to do some fancy footwork. Head left toward the paved parking area, right along gravel, then back onto the paved surface to reach the giant neon star.

For an alternative view, hike to the **Mill Mountain Discovery Center** and take the trail across from the building. That way you can hike from the lower to the higher viewpoint, and then back down. If you're hiking with kids, you might want to take a detour at the Discovery Center or the **Mill Mountain Zoo** (p231).

BACKCOUNTRY HIKING & CAMPING

There are virtually no opportunities to backcountry camp along the Parkway, but you can do it anywhere within the adjacent national forests (see Pisgah National Forest, p239, and George Washington & Jefferson National Forests, p229), as well as along the AT. Permits for hiking and camping are required for the Parkway, but, they're free and available at ranger stations.

OTHER ACTIVITIES
Bicycling

Biking along the Parkway is enjoyable, but the elevation changes and strenuous rides require you to be in prime shape. It also helps if you're fearless: Since bikes aren't allowed on trails or walkways, cyclists must share the road with cars, requiring extra caution, especially in the tunnels. It's best to bring your own gear, as there are no convenient rentals on the Parkway (outside of major towns like Roanoke).

For more information, see Bicycle under Getting Around (p199).

Horseback Riding

Novices and pro riders alike should check out **Wintergreen Resort** (☎ 434-325-8260; $46 per person; ✆ 10:30am & 1:30pm weekdays, 9:30am, 11am, 2pm weekends Mar 13-Jun 7 & Sep 7-Nov 28; 9am, 10:30am & 4pm Tue-Sun Jun 8-Sep 6) for guided rides, pony rides ($14) and lessons ($37); fuel up on a gourmet, lakeside meal with the Sunset Dinner package ($85 per person) before riding off into the sunset. Hi-ho!

From the Parkway, take the Reeds Gap exit (between MP 13 and 14) and follow Rte 664 east about a mile, until you see the sign for Wintergreen.

Hang Gliding

The Blue Ridge Parkway offers two designated hang gliding areas: **Ravens Roost** (MP 11) and **Roanoke Mountain** (MP 120). Special permits are required and can be obtained at ranger stations. Gliders must be rated Hang 3 due to the steep terrain; Ravens Roost requires a Cliff Launch rating. Only two kites are permitted at a time at each site.

Skiing

High in the Blue Ridge just a few miles from the Parkway, **Wintergreen Resort** (☎ 434-325-2100; all-day lift ticket midweek adult/child 6-12/child under 6 $40/33/free; ski rentals $32/27/22; snowboarding $42/37/NA; ☉ Oct-Mar) is the state's oldest and 'the South's single best' (according to *Skiing* magazine). Of the 23 trails, about 20% are beginner, 42% intermediate, 21% advanced and 17% expert. A 1003ft vertical drop is served by double, triple, quad and two six-person high-speed chairlifts.

For family fun, or to satisfy that kid inside, hit the two **tubing runs** (☎ 434-325-2100). The 10-lane monster hill called **The Plunge** (2hr session midweek/weekend $18/22) is geared toward older thrill seekers (only recommended for ages six and up), while **The Slide** (2hr session $18; ☉ weekends & holidays only) caters to tamer snow bunnies, ages two and older.

Massanutten (p189) and Wintergreen have tapped into the burgeoning snowboarding craze. Eastern adherents of soft boots and radical boards ('shredders') have discovered the pleasures of these two places, and the dollar-wise resorts have accordingly added snowboard parks to their slopes. You get a free 90-minute lesson at Wintergreen when you rent a board. Snowboarders (lift rates are the same as the above) can catch some serious air in the terrain park, with fun boxes and rainbow and battleship rails.

Night skiing is offered from 5pm to 10pm Sunday through Thursday ($25/23) and 6pm to 11pm Friday, Saturday and holidays ($31/27).

Kids' Activities

Parents need not fear the dreaded phrase 'I'm bored' – there are endless options for fun along Virginia's stretch of the Parkway. The **Mill Mountain Zoo** (p231) is a small yet cool animal treehouse in the sky, and the sprawling **Virginia's Explore Park** (p231) is like a *Three Little Pigs* book come to life, with various buildings made of straw, wood and stronger stuff (Staunton's **Museum of American Frontier Culture** is similar; see p192). At **Mabry Mill** (p203), little ones follow along a path of living-history demonstrations, learning about everything from blacksmithing to carving – thankfully, the patient park service staff is happy to answer many questions.

For outdoor recreation, try tubing at ski resorts in winter and the sandy lakeside beaches at the **Cave Mountain Lake** (p202) and **Sherando** (p201) recreation areas in summer.

FESTIVALS & EVENTS

Most festivals and events revolve around bluegrass music and flower power. Two of the region's biggest events are **FloydFest** (p203) and the **Old Fiddler's Convention** (p232). And don't forget about leaf-peeping in fall – it's the most popular event, and it's free!

SLEEPING
Camping on the Parkway

Four of the Parkway's **campgrounds** (☎ 877-444-6777; www.reserveusa.com; campsite $14) are in Virginia: the year-round **Otter Creek** (MP 61) and the seasonal **Peaks of Otter** (MP 86), **Roanoke Mountain** (MP 120) and **Rocky Knob** (MP 167). Otter Creek is one of the loveliest, with many sites perched along gurgling streams. All campsites are on a first-come, first-served basis.

Meadows of Dan Campground (☎ 276-952-2292; 2182 Jeb Stuart Hwy; campsite/cabin $18/79-165; ⓨ year-round) This privately owned campground, just off the Parkway at MP 177.7 and US 58 west, boasts coveted showers, washers and dryers. Cozy cabins come outfitted with TVs, VCRs, refrigerators and microwaves – roughing it never felt so good.

Nearby Camping

Crabtree Falls Campground (☎ 540-377-2066; 11039 Crabtree Falls Hwy in Tyro; campsite/camping cabin $18/50) The heated bathhouse, waterfront tent sites, mega-cool playground, and Pac-Man arcade in the game room make for a winning combination. You need to bring your own linens for the rustic cabins, but there's a small camp store for replenishing your s'mores supply. From MP 27, take US 56 east 7 miles; the campground is on the right.

Lodging on the Parkway

Misty Rose Cottage (☎ 276-236-7658; www.pdbloghomes.com; MP 202-203; r $120 nightly) This cozy two-bedroom home is just a pebble's throw from the Parkway. It features a fully stocked kitchenette, a small hot tub on the screened-in back porch and comfy rocking chairs on the front porch – the perfect setting for a mountain sunset.

Peaks of Otter Lodge (☎ 800-542-5927; www.peaksofotter.com; MP 86; r weekday/weekend $63/69 Nov 1-Apr 30, $86 May 1-Sep 30) These motel-style rooms are nothing fancy (and they're sans TV or phone), but they do command a fantastic view of Abbott Lake and Sharp Top Mountain. The lodge includes a good restaurant.

Rocky Knob Cabins (☎ 276-952-2947; MP 174; cabin $57, extra person $8, rollaway bed $8, firewood $3.50; ⓨ late May-Oct 31) You'll find just a refrigerator, kitchenette and linens in these rustic yet cozy cabins close to the popular Mabry Mill. A bathhouse and comfort station are only a short, flashlight-guided trek away. There's a discount for multiple nights.

HI Blue Ridge Mountains (☎ 276-236-4962; MP 214.5; dm $17; ⓨ closed Jan; no credit cards) At MP 214, look for a gray iron pipe gate that marks the hidden entrance to this popular mountain hostel. Enjoy fantastic views and a toe-tapping music room. Guests are encouraged to bring musical instruments.

Nearby Lodging

Wintergreen Resort (☎ 800-266-2444; www.wintergreenresort.com; d summer/winter $154-181/126-199) This full-service resort features downhill **ski slopes** (opposite), restaurants, a bar, indoor and outdoor pools, tennis courts, 45 golf holes, hiking trails, a riding center, an exercise room and sauna, and 20-acre Lake Monocan for swimming and canoeing. A staff biologist organizes interpretive walks through the more than 6000 acres of protected forest. But all of this does not come cheap. A round of golf runs $90 on weekdays and $100 on weekends, and fees apply for tennis, the Wintergarden spa (but oh, so worth it), guided mountain bike trips and horseback riding. Bring lots of money!

To get here from the Parkway, take the Reeds Gap exit (between MP 13 and 14) and follow Rte 664 east about a mile, until you see the sign for Wintergreen.

continued on p211

EQUIPMENT & SUPPLIES

Camping supplies are sold at waysides, and there's a camp store at Loft Mountain. You can also stock up at supermarkets and retail chains like Wal-Mart and Target in major towns (see Waynesboro, p194; Roanoke, p230; and Galax, p231), as well as local supply shops.

INTERNET ACCESS

It's hard to hook up to web in this neck of the woods, but you should have luck at **public libraries** off the Parkway. **Wintergreen Resort** (☎ 800-266-2444) has Wi-Fi access.

LOST & FOUND

Park rangers and information centers handle lost and found items. If you leave the Parkway before realizing you forgot something, contact the **Blue Ridge Parkway Communications Center** (☎ 828-271-4779; 199 Hemphill Knob Rd, Asheville, NC 28803-8686).

MEDICAL SERVICES & EMERGENCIES

There are no medical facilities along the Parkway. The nearest hospitals are in Waynesboro and Roanoke. In an emergency, call ☎ 800-PARKWATCH (727-5928).

MONEY

Though there are a smattering of ATMs at restaurants (eg, Mabry Mill), it's best to stock up on cash before entering the Parkway.

POSTAL SERVICE

Drop off mail at information centers or in the surrounding towns.

SHOWERS & LAUNDRY

No public shower and laundry facilities are available along the Parkway, except inside private lodgings.

TELEPHONES

Pay phones are available at information centers, museums, restaurants and most lodge lobbies. Cell-phone service is spotty at best, so don't rely on that as your only means of communication.

TRASH & RECYCLING

Trashcans are abundant at all visitor centers, picnic areas and overlooks, but there are no official recycling facilities along the Parkway.

continued from p209

EATING

There aren't many restaurants along the Virginia stretch of the Parkway. Snacks are usually available at visitor centers and waysides, and there's more fare to choose from in surrounding towns.

The tasty, hearty breakfasts at **Mountain View Restaurant** (weekends only) in Fancy Gap draw plenty of repeat business – and they're a bargain, at under $10. The restaurant is just off the Parkway at MP 199 and the junction of US 52.

You'll find full-service restaurants at **Otter Creek** (MP 60.8; ☎ 434-299-5862), **Peaks of Otter Lodge** (MP 86; ☎ 800-542-5927) and **Mabry Mill** (MP 176.2; ☎ 276-952-2947), the latter of which reportedly has the best buckwheat pancakes on the Parkway.

NORTH CAROLINA

Map 13, p163

The Parkway stretches for 262 glorious miles in North Carolina, where the meadows give way to alpine vistas. Among the towering peaks, the North Carolina section can lay claim to impressive manmade structures around Grandfather Mountain, an assortment of talented craftspeople and their workshops, 26 beautiful arched tunnels and the gem city of Asheville, with all her Southern charm.

Cumberland Knob (MP 217.5)

This is where it all started. On September 11, 1935, the parkway groundbreaking was held at Cumberland Knob, and the information center remains one of the earliest standing structures along the road.

Pick up parkway maps, books and a small assortment of gifts at the **visitor center** (☎ 336-657-8161). Along with restrooms and a spacious picnic area, you'll find an old cemetery that reveals how short and hard life was in the mountains. A young mother, Rebecca Moxley, had asked to be buried beneath an apple tree, as she feared she wouldn't live much past the birth of her son. As predicted, she did indeed pass away after her son's birth and now rests here, among other family members.

Two trails depart from here: the easy half-mile **Cumberland Knob Trail** and the strenuous 2-mile **Gully Creek Trail**. The Cumberland loop is nothing spectacular, just a lazy-day hike up to a historic stone structure that has unfortunately succumbed to 21st century graffiti. The Gully Creek Trail, however, is a rewarding hike that skirts a refreshing mountain stream.

Several good roadside observation points lie to the south. At MP 232.5, pull into the **Stone Mountain Overlook** to examine the 500ft granite patch opposite, which looks like a bump on the head. It's a heavenly spot for a picnic. Three miles on, **Devil's Garden** is a gap between two crags; rattlesnakes and copperheads have made their home there.

Doughton Park (MP 238.5-244.7)

Originally called 'The Bluffs' (hence the name of the restaurants and lodging in these parts), this meadowy landscape was renamed in honor of Congressman Robert L Doughton, an avid Parkway supporter. Today it's known for its abundant wildlife – you may spy red and gray foxes, white-tailed deer and the occasional bobcat.

Within the park are several lodging options, including Bluffs Lodge and a campground (see Sleeping, p226).

Pick up maps and brochures and fuel up at the **Bluffs Gas Station** (MP 241).

BRINEGAR CABIN

Former home of local farmer Martin Brinegar, this wood cabin offers a glimpse into daily life in the early 1900s. Adjacent to the cabin is a vegetable garden, tended by the park service. Living-history demonstrations, including weaving on an old loom, are held in summer. Trailheads for the strenuous 4.2-mile **Cedar Ridge Trail** and moderate 7.5-mile **Bluff Mountain Trail** are in the parking lot.

Northwest Trading Post (MP 258.7)

A spacious **gift shop** (☎ 336-982-2543; ☾ 9am-5:30pm Apr 1-Oct 31) here sells home-made crafts from local artisans. All gifts marked with white tags are certified by the National Park Service as authentic Indian crafts. The facilities include restrooms.

Jumpinoff Rock (MP 260.3)

Starting from the parking area, the easy half-mile **Jumpinoff Rock Trail** skirts the valley and ends with a spectacular view atop sheer rock cliffs.

Cascades Overlook (MP 271.9)

A leisurely 30-minute hiking loop (0.6 mile) descends from this overlook through a hemlock forest to a spectacular 'cascading' waterfall. Another half-mile trail leads to **Cool Springs Baptist Church** and the **Jesse Brown Cabin** buildings. You'll also find restrooms and a shaded picnic area, with plenty of room for impromptu bluegrass performances – you might just see one if you stop.

EB Jeffress Park (MP 272)

Along a 2-mile stretch of the Parkway, this park features an overlook and a trail leading to a steep waterfall. It's named for EB Jeffress, a strong Parkway supporter who fought against making it a toll road. He was also the chairman of the North Carolina State Highway & Public Works Commission in 1933.

Daniel Boone's Trace (MP 285.1)

This tiny parking area sports a bronze plaque and historical marker where, local legend has it, Daniel Boone passed through on his way to Kentucky.

Moses H Cone Memorial Park (MP 294.1)

Another 2-mile stretch of the Parkway, this park takes its name from Moses Cone, the so-called Blue Denim King who owned a pants factory in Greensboro. The park includes the breathtaking **Flat Top Manor** and a crafts shop, as well as 25 miles of carriage trails that start from the visitor center parking lot and wind among wild blueberry thickets, wildflower meadows and hemlock forest.

VISITOR CENTER

Housed just inside Flat Top Manor, the visitor center boasts a comprehensive selection of reading material on the region, including cookbooks, bicycle trail guides, flora and fauna guides, and even ghost stories. Call or sign up for the free **tour** (☎ 828-295-3782; 30mins; ; ☾ 10am, 11am, 2pm, 3pm & 4pm weekends only Jun-Oct) of the manor house here and admire the unusual dormers, leaded-glass windows and stark white columns up close.

The center also offers Junior Ranger programs for kids on Sunday and free evening entertainment on Friday and Saturday, including a moonlight tour of the Cone graves, which lie about a mile away. Restrooms are a short walk from the center, but be forewarned that they close in the evening (at 6pm from November to April, 8pm otherwise).

Horseback riding (p224) is popular along the Cone trails.

FLAT TOP MANOR (CONE ESTATE MANSION HOUSE)

An imposing sight nestled into the mountainside, Flat Top Manor is a fine example of what Southern money was all about. A gleaming-white staircase leads to a circular porch, which wraps around the right side of the mansion. From the porch, a series of striking white columns supports the second-story verandah, while a knee-high white railing prefaces the beautiful view of the old carriage route and town of Blowing Rock below. The house is a hive of activity in summer, when hot hikers and equestrians come in off the nearby trails to sit on the porch and admire the panorama.

PARKWAY CRAFT CENTER

The **center** (☎ 828-295-7938; www.southernhighlandguild.org; ⊗ 9am-5pm Mar 15-Nov 30) is one of five shops run by the Southern Highlands Craft Guild, which showcases regional artists' work to educate the public about the area and its resources. You'll find unique pottery designs, intricate woodwork, hand-detailed jewelry and quilts among the treasures here. The goods might be a little pricey, but you're paying for the quality; check out the stained-glass sun-catchers for an inexpensive souvenir. The shop is inside Flat Top Manor, across from the visitor center.

Julian Price Memorial Park (MP 295.1) *107*

Perched at the base of Grandfather Mountain, this area sports an exciting assortment of wildlife species, plant life and water activities, as well as three trails for all difficulty levels. That also means it's a prime destination for families and college students (due to its proximity to Appalachian State University), especially in summer. Amid thickets of vivid wildflowers and rhododendron, see if you can spot the kooky jack'-o-lantern mushrooms that supposedly glow in the dark. The park is named for Julian Price, president of the Jefferson Pilot Standard Life Insurance company, which donated this land to the NPS upon Price's death.

The moderate 4.9-mile **Boone Fork Trail Loop** starts from the spacious picnic area by a meandering stream. Beginners enjoy a slight challenge with the 2.7-mile **Price Lake Loop Trail**, which circles the trout-stocked lake – it's best to bring a change of socks for this one, as the lakeside trail gets quite wet. The moderate **Green Knob Trail** (aka Lost Cove Ridge Trail) weaves through meadow, arriving at a rickety lookout tower. Restrooms are available, and leashed pets are allowed.

Price Lake is ahead, on the east side of the Parkway, and a small wooden platform juts over the water for a cool view. Farther south, on the west side of the road is the Parkway's largest **campground** (p226), which features a small registration center, a trash depot, clean water fill-up and public telephones.

On the east side of the road, the **Boone Fork Overlook** offers **canoe rentals** (1st hr/hr thereafter $6/4; ⊗ 8:30am-6pm; no credit cards), a small snack shop and a public boat ramp.

At the Boone Fork parking area (MP 300), you can access the **Tanawha Trail**, as well as the nine trails to Grandfather Mountain (permits are required – purchase them at Grandfather Mountain).

Linn Cove Viaduct (MP 304.6)

This manmade wonder provides spectacular views of Grandfather Mountain; it's considered the 'missing link' that finally made the Blue Ridge Parkway complete.

Due to the mountain's rugged nature, heavy equipment and crews would have irreversibly damaged the fragile ecosystem. Hugh Morton, a spunky conservationist, fought for years against the construction of the final segment of the Blue Ridge Parkway around Grandfather Mountain. Officials eventually decided the viaduct would utilize a 'progressive placement' of sections, essentially building each of the seven vertical piers on top of one another. Construction began in 1979 and lasted until 1983; the dedication and opening were held in 1987. Today visitors don't have to get off at Holloway Rd (US 221) to complete their journey, because the Parkway is one complete 469-mile road.

Grandfather Mountain (MP 305)

Scared of heights? Don't even attempt to enter this **privately run park** (☎ 800-468-7325; www.grandfather.com; adult/child 4-12/senior $12/6/11; ☺ 8am-6pm spring & fall, to 7pm summer, to 5pm winter) because the steep, twisty climb is a mile of hairpin turns with absolutely no guardrails. However, brave visitors are rewarded with camera-clicking panoramic shots of Linville Gorge and the mountain itself, especially from the famous Mile-High Swinging Bridge (a scene from *Forrest Gump* was filmed here).

While you're here, you can also spend time at seven enclosed wildlife habitats (otters, bears, etc), a nature museum, a rather tacky gift shop and a snack counter (skip the pizza). Shaded picnic areas are scattered throughout.

Give those calf muscles a workout on one of four trails. Beginners should stick to the relatively easy 0.4-mile **Woods Walk** or push themselves a little on the **Bridge Trail**, which skirts beneath the bridge and ventures toward stunning rock outcrops. The **Crest Trails** are the black diamonds of trails here and require strenuous exertion.

MILE-HIGH SWINGING BRIDGE

After driving straight up and climbing 50 steps, you've finally arrived at the highest point in North Carolina. Crossing the precarious bridge may be a bit nerve-wracking – what with children running willy-nilly between your legs as you take deep mountain gulps of air – but it's worth it, worth it, worth it! Just don't think about the infamous scene in *Indiana Jones & the Temple of Doom*. Thankfully, this bridge is metal, not wood and string, so the only falling objects are the occasional camera lens or perhaps someone's lunch.

If you can't face the walk, get a great view of the bridge and gorge below from the parking lot.

Linville Falls (MP 316.4)

Boasting the largest water volume of all Parkway falls, Linville Falls is arguably the most famous waterfall along the Blue Ridge – and the crowds prove it. Go on a weekday if possible.

The Linville River begins at Grandfather Mountain, descending 2000ft through the Catawba Valley and a rugged gorge etched over many years. The falls are divided by two sections that used to be the same length, before a portion of the upper falls collapsed into the lower one in 1900. It's now known as a 'double cascade' and features an unusual effect: water seems to disappear between the two sections. The lower section releases a tremendous misty spray down the gorge.

An access road leads about a mile and a half from the Parkway to Linville Falls and dead-ends at the visitor center.

VISITOR CENTER

This center may house the worst bathroom along the Parkway, but the staff couldn't be friendlier. A stream parallels the parking area, and shaded picnic tables dot the grass. The best waterfall hike is the 1.6-mile **Falls Trail**, which starts across the bridge just beyond the visitor center – judging from the

EXPERIENCING THE BLUE RIDGE PARKWAY

throngs of schoolchildren on the path, it's not a tough-guy trail. See Day Hikes for details of the strenuous **Linville Gorge Trail** (p221).

The Parkway's most popular **campground** (p226) is here, as are restrooms and water.

Linville Caverns

An underground labyrinth of odd-shaped rock formations, North Carolina's only **caverns** (☎ 800-419-0540; www.linvillecaverns.com; US 221S; adult/child 5-12/senior $5/3/4) make a great destination for kids. Let them explore the 'bat cave' while you learn the difference between a stalactite and stalagmite. Bring a warm, water-proof jacket, since the cave hovers around a chilly 52 degrees, with cold drips around every nook. Sure, it's a little hokey, but it's a lot of fun and one of the cheaper attractions around. It's also wheelchair accessible. Be forewarned that hours vary widely and heavy rain can close the caverns. Take the Linville Falls exit off the Parkway and follow US 221 south for about 5 miles (entrance is on the right).

Penland School of Crafts

Like a Salvador Dali painting come to life, this artists' educational retreat abounds with strange and beautiful works of art. Pupils study unique art forms like glassblowing, forged ironworking, bookmaking and even concrete jewelry and guitar making.

As the Industrial Revolution threatened to wipe out hand weaving on giant wooden looms, a woman known as Miss Lucy sought to preserve traditional methods and established the Penland Weavers in 1923. By 1929 word got out about this unique organization, and an official school was established for regional weavers. The artists' mediums grew broader over the years to include metals, glass and elements of the environment, and today the school enjoys an international reputation.

If you're serious about craftsmanship or perhaps curious how to make your own paper, consider taking a class. Programs usually last one to 2½ weeks, and tuition starts at $2936; scholarships are available.

If you don't have that much time, browse the masterpieces in the eclectic **crafts shop** (☎ 828-765-2359; www.penland.org; ☯ 10am-5pm Tue-Sat, from noon Sun), where prices range from a couple hundred dollars for a mouth-blown glass bowl to a buck for a handmade button.

Penland is a long, twisty drive from the Parkway, but it's worth it. From

GRAND CANYON OF THE SOUTH ✓

An amazing detour, **Wiseman's View** overlooks Hawksbill and Table Rock, as well as one of North America's wildest gorges. Peregrine falcons and golden eagles can often be seen soaring above these jagged, rocky cliffs.

Go at sunset to catch a glimpse of the mysterious Brown Mountain Lights, which flicker red and blue over Brown Mountain. Cherokee legends mention this phenomenon, and modern-day scientists have no explanation for it.

To reach Wiseman's View, get off the Parkway around Linville Falls (MP 317) and take the misleadingly named Kistler Memorial Hwy (actually a rough dirt road) until it turns into a gravel road, then proceed to the end.

the Parkway, take NC 226 toward Spruce Pine. Then take NC 19 south and look for a Texaco station on the left. Directly across from the station, make a right onto Penland Rd and follow it for 3 (long) miles. Cross the bridge and railroad tracks, and about a mile farther, bear left at the big curve and head all the way up the hill.

Altapass Orchard (MP 328.3)

So much more than your ordinary apple farm, this **orchard** (☎ 888-765-9531; www.altapassorchard.com; ☺ 10am-6pm Wed-Mon, closed Tue except May 21-Nov 1) thrives today despite the area's many near-death experiences.

The Clinchfield Railroad – an engineering marvel of its time, boasting 18 tunnels in a 13-mile stretch – developed this land in the late 1800s as a resort area for rail travelers, until a new highway bypassed the gap and turned the place into a ghost town. The railroad sold the land above its tracks to a former employee, who planted fruit trees and hired many out-of-work locals to tend them. But the vibrant orchard began to fade when construction of the Blue Ridge Parkway divided the property in half, despite protracted court battles.

Long dormant, this lush treasure turned overgrown mess found a savior in 1995, when Kit Trubey essentially prevented future development by purchasing more than 280 acres. Today Kit's brother and his wife own the orchard and have spearheaded a foundation to preserve mountain heritage.

An old-timey general store and occasional live bluegrass jams add to the atmosphere, as do hayrides, storytelling and butterfly tagging for the wee ones. How 'bout *them* apples?

Museum of North Carolina Minerals (MP 330.9)

Four hundred million years ago, a continental collision forced molten material down into the cracks of a dark rock known as gneiss, forming huge deposits of minerals.. Today quartz, feldspar, mica and gemstones abound in the southern Appalachians.

Unless you're a miner or geologist, this quirky **museum** (☎ 828-765-2761; ☺ 9am-5pm) may be your only opportunity to see the area's rich mineral resources in their pure forms, including copper, iron, quartz and mica. Ever wonder what a silica tetrahedron looks like? Here's your chance. Kids can poke around the hand-on exhibits, learning which minerals glow in the dark, working a morphing rock machine and seeing petrified wood up close.

The **Mitchell County Chamber of Commerce** (☎ 800-227-3912) operates a small information counter inside the museum.

Mt Mitchell State Park (MP 355)

The highest peak in the Black Mountains, as well as east of the Mississippi River, **Mt Mitchell** (6684ft) boasts an intriguing history that revolves around a mathematical controversy and an accidental death.

In the mid-1800s Grandfather Mountain was thought to be the highest peak in the southeastern US. But a science professor at the University of North Carolina, Elisha Mitchell, believed the Black Mountains were higher. He started measuring the Carolina and Black Mountains and found a peak with an elevation of 6672ft – 708ft higher than Grandfather.

However, a dispute arose in 1855 when Mitchell butted measuring sticks with US Senator Thomas Lanier Clingman, who claimed to have been the first to measure the highest peak in the Black Mountains. Mitchell, determined to verify his own measurements, embarked on a return trip to the Black Mountains in 1857 with his son, daughter and a servant. On Saturday, June 27, Mitchell said he was going to check on the Caney River settlement and that he would return on Monday. It was the last time his family would see him alive.

HOW THE BRITISH LOST AMERICA

Don't be surprised to see men in uniform here – Revolutionary War uniforms, that is. Located in Gillespie Gap, the Museum of North Carolina Minerals marks an important battle that changed the way Yanks would speak forever.

On September 29, 1780, hundreds of Patriot militiamen streamed through the pass (Gillespie Gap) on their way to a battle Thomas Jefferson declared would 'turn the tide of the Revolutionary War.' The Overmountain Men, as they were known, crossed the gap, splitting their numbers and making it across safely. At the time, British Major Patrick Ferguson (under Lord Cornwallis) was under orders to head for the Blue Ridge to suppress possible resistance from Western militia. On October 7, the Patriots killed Ferguson at the Battle of Kings Mountain and captured or killed his entire force of 1000 men. This devastating defeat ultimately destroyed Britain's hopes for a quick end to the war, and the battle would later be referred to as the 'first link in a chain of evils that led to the loss of America.'

It wasn't until Thursday that Mitchell was deemed missing. Upon retracing his steps, the search team reached a 40ft waterfall. It looked as if a piece of its dangerous precipice had been ripped away, and when the team peered over the waterfall into its deep pool, they saw Mitchell's body Originally buried in Asheville, his remains now lie atop the mountain on which he lost his life (near the foot of the observation tower). Named in his honor, Mt Mitchell became North Carolina's first state park in 1915.

As for Thomas Clingman, he settled for second place (see Clingmans Dome, p85).

Today the **park** (☎ 828-675-4611; www.ils.unc.edu/parkproject/visit/momi/info.html; Rte 5, Box 700, Burnsville, NC 28714; ☻ 8am-6pm Nov-Feb, to 7pm Mar & Oct, to 8pm April & Sept, to 9pm May-Aug) is a perpetually misty overlook with chilly temperatures, though rangers say it's the best place to watch a sunrise/sunset...that is, when you can actually see the sun.

Nine **tent sites** ($9/15 Nov 1-Apr 30/May 1-Oct 31) await brave, thick-skinned campers (no hot water or showers provided). Otherwise, make it a day trip and enjoy a mile-high picnic nestled up to fireplaces in the two shelters. Don't forget to grab a sweater or windproof jacket if jaunting up to the tower – temperatures can be 10 to 15 degrees cooler than on the Parkway, and winds have been clocked at 100mph. Restrooms are available.

OBSERVATION TOWER
Feeling lightheaded? It's no wonder – you're 1¼ miles above sea level here. Despite the lofty perch, though, you'll be hard pressed to see much; mist obscures the view 90% of the time. However, at the first sign of the sun peeking through, make a run for the space-agey tower for a spectacular, 85-mile panorama and linger for the legendary sunset.

EXHIBIT HALL
Near the summit, this **hall** (☻ 10am-6pm May-Oct, weather permitting) presents dioramas and topographic maps, a reproduction of Elisha Mitchell's cabin and a life-size model of 'Big Tom,' a legendary bear hunter in these parts who led the search for Mitchell upon his disappearance. There's also an interactive weather station where you can plug in your vitals and read about the weather conditions on your birth date.

Craggy Gardens (MP 364.6)

A great place to marvel at wildflowers is the **Craggy Gardens Trail** (MP 364.5). Look for Indian pipe, bee balm, spiderwort, Turk's cap lily, jewelweed, fire pink, dodder and dozens of other varieties – all in a hundred different colors. Other good hikes range from half-mile strolls to 4-mile adventures. Breathtaking vistas await.

The visitor center here is arguably the Parkway's best, thanks to its sprawling view of the mountains, valley, wildflowers and tunnels. There's always a crowd on both sides of the parking lot snapping photos of the incredible panoramic vistas, so be careful when passing through. Restrooms are available.

Folk Art Center (MP 382)

Part of the Southern Highlands Craft Guild, the **center** (☎ 828-298-7928; 🕑 9am-6pm Apr-Dec, to 5pm Jan-Mar) contains a permanent and rotating exhibit gallery that showcases unique local craftsmanship. An adjacent building, which will house more interpretive exhibits is under construction and scheduled for completion by 2007.

The term 'gift shop' seems inadequate to describe the long gallery of beautiful crafts for sale. Intricate jewelry using gems mined from local quarries, complex woven baskets, detailed patchwork quilts, silky scarves and smooth wooden carvings merely scratch the surface of what's available here. If you're interested in seeing how these unique gifts take shape, ask about the live demonstrations (such as broom-making) in the lobby.

There's also a small, NPS-staffed information center here. Consider buying a bluegrass CD to keep you in the mood as you travel along the Parkway. Recommended artists include Doc Watson, David Holt or Ralph Stanley (of The Clinch Mountain Boys, whose music was featured in the movie *O Brother, Where Art Thou?*).

Blue Ridge Parkway Headquarters (MP 382)

Tucked off a side road from the Parkway, the **headquarters** (☎ 828-298-0398; www.nps.gov/blri; 199 Hemphill Knob Rd, Asheville, NC 28803; 🕑 8am-4:30pm Mon-Fri) is primarily an administrative office, and the reception desk is unmanned. There are a few maps and brochures if you're in dire need, but you'd be better off browsing the plethora of pamphlets at the Folk Art Center. The Mountain-to-Sea Trail starts from the parking lot.

Lake Powhatan Recreation Area

Go jump in a lake – better yet, take your pick from 13 of 'em at **Lake Powhatan** (☎ 828-670-5627; 375 Wesley Branch Rd; 🕑 mid-Mar–late-Oct). Families and single travelers alike will love this bustling outdoor playground with ample fishing, mountain biking, swimming and hiking. It's a favorite with mountain bikers for its exciting network of single-track and forest road trails, as well as with anglers for its abundant rainbow and brown trout. Varied hiking trails, ranging from the **Mountains-to-Sea Trail** to an old route toward the Biltmore Estate, challenge and entertain hikers along the border of Mt Pisgah National Forest. You *will* see bears here – some trails pass through a bear sanctuary, and researchers collect data in the area.

At MP 393.7, take NC 191 west to Bent Creek Branch Rd (NC 3480) and follow signs to the rec area.

There's also a pretty **campground** (p226) here with showers.

Mt Pisgah (MP 407.6)

Originally part of George Vanderbilt's 100,000-acre estate, this area allegedly took its name from a biblical reference; some thought the mountain over-looked a sprawling land of milk and honey. And the view is heavenly, espe-cially from the observation deck of George's old hunting lodge, the modern **Mt Pisgah Inn** (p226), one of the few restaurants where what you see out the window is just as appealing as what you see on your plate.

Across from the inn you'll find a large **campground** (p226), a camping supply store and restrooms. And, lo and behold, there's even **internet access** ($2/20min) in the inn's lobby.

Looking Glass Rock Overlook (MP 417)

You'll be lucky to pass through here just after a rainstorm, when the sun shines on the wet rock and produces a mesmerizing, mirror-like effect. It's one of the most striking views on the Parkway, as visitors gawk at the largest mass of granite in the eastern US.

Devils Courthouse (MP 422.4)

A Cherokee legend claims that the devil holds court up in the caves you can see from this overlook – hence the sinister name. And some say that the craggy summit looks downright menacing. Regardless, it's a magnificent vista, and a lovely short hike yields even better, 360-degree views of the devilish formations.

Richland Balsam (MP 431)

Look for shutterbugs snapping photos of the sign, which states that this is 'the highest point of the Parkway' (6047ft). A moderate, 1.5-mile self-guided nature hike from the overlook loops through a disappearing spruce and fir forest.

Waterrock Knob Visitor Center (MP 451.2)

Its ethereal location perched at the top of the mountain makes Waterrock one of the Parkway's most unique visitor centers. A half-mile hiking trail leads to the knob and 360-degree views of the Smoky Mountains – what the sign doesn't tell you is that it's a steep, rocky, uphill climb the entire way. Don't forget to pick up your certificate for climbing the knob – kids love this proof of their accomplishment.

See Day Hikes for details on the **Waterrock Knob Trail** (p224), which is the highest trail on the Parkway.

Qualla Boundary Cherokee Reservation

At **Soco Gap** (MP 456) the Parkway enters the Qualla Boundary Cherokee Reservation, lands held in federal trust by the Eastern Band of the Cherokee Indians. Soco Gap was known as the 'ambush place' (from the Cherokee word *ahaluna*) because it represented the entrance to Cherokee land from the north and east in the 1700s. In 1811 it was the scene of an auspicious council between Shawnee Chief Tecumseh and Cherokee Chief Junaluska, at which Junaluska refused a proposal that the two tribes combine forces to fight white settlers.

The Native Americans living here trace their lineage to about 1000 individu-als who eluded capture by federal agents during the forced relocation of the Cherokee to Oklahoma in 1838 (see Cherokee, p139, for more information). Today the Qualla Boundary Cherokee Reservation comprises 56,688 acres. Towns include Big Cove, Birdtown, Paint Town, Snowbird, Wolftown and Yellow Hill, but most visitors are satisfied to visit only Cherokee, the largest North Carolina gateway town to Great Smoky Mountains National Park.

NC 19 crosses the Parkway here; Cherokee lies 8 miles west, and Maggie Valley (p138) 3 miles east.

Lickstone Ridge Overlook (MP 459)

Atop Lickstone Ridge (5150ft), a broad, flattop mountain running roughly southwest, this overlook offers a panoramic view of most of the Qualla Boundary. **Lickstone Ridge Tunnel** distinguishes itself by making a 45-degree turn inside the mountain.

Big Witch Gap (MP 461)

The gap and **Big Witch Tunnel** are named for Cherokee medicine man Tskil-e-gwa, also known as 'Big Witch.' At the time of his death in 1897, Big Witch was the eldest man of the tribe and the only one who could remember the Creek War of 1812-14. A skilled medicine man and herbalist, he was also revered for knowing how to kill an eagle so that its feathers could be used for sacred ceremonies.

At **Big Witch Overlook** (4160ft) you'll find appealing picnic tables with an excellent view overlooking the Qualla Boundary.

End of the Blue Ridge Parkway

At MP 461.9, Blue Ridge Parkway ends at the junction with US 441, just south of the entrance to Great Smoky Mountains National Park (p78) and at the northern edge of the town of Cherokee (p139).

DAY HIKES

The North Carolina portion of the Parkway also offers a variety of trails.

BLUFF MOUNTAIN (MP244.7)
Distance: 7.5 miles one way
Duration: 6 hours
Challenge: Moderate
Elevation Change: 320ft

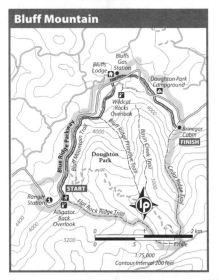

Bluff Mountain

This trail parallels the Parkway. With only moderate elevation changes, it's an excellent walk for beginners. Pack a picnic to enjoy at the shelter near trail's end.

Start at the **Alligator Back Overlook** in Doughton Park – the views from the overlook alone should pump you up for the hike to the summit. Descend the stone steps and turn left onto the trail. You'll soon encounter a series of switchbacks, and the climb turns steep, first through dense forest, spilling out onto bald cliffs. A view of Cove Creek Basin is visible from hereon clear days.

You'll pass through two fences – the first just before a right turn at a red blaze, the second on the way toward the mountain top, where you'll find an open shelter. If you packed your lunch, linger a little here, admiring the craggy peaks in the distance.

Pack up and continue along the ridgeline to **Brinegar Cabin** (MP 238.5), where you can explore the old farmstead and perhaps drop in on a living-history demonstration.

LINVILLE GORGE (MP 316.4)
Distance: 1.4 miles round-trip (2 miles if you take the Plunge Overlook detour; add .25 mile for the Duggers Creek loop)
Duration: 1–2 hours
Challenge: Difficult
Elevation Change: 1400ft

An unusual double cascade, **Linville Falls** is the most famous waterfall along the Parkway. From the Linville Falls Visitor Center, three trails branch out to different views of the falls. The trail detailed here is the most difficult but most rewarding – after all your work, you'll find yourself face to face with the gusher. The other two hikes are the moderate 1-mile **Duggers Creek Trail** and the easy 1.6-mile **Erwins View Trail** (aka Falls Trail).

Start at the visitor center and go through to the back, where you'll come to a bridge. From here the Duggers Creek Trail leads left, and you can take this for a pretty loop around the creek, complete with inspirational sayings on planks, slapped up on trailside trees. The trail rejoins the junction with the Gorge Trail, which bears right.

A gradual 0.3-mile ascent leads to the **Plunge Basin Overlook**. The overlook path veers right; follow it down steep stone steps to a small rocky alcove above the falls. You'll find a bench here to admire the falls and take a short rest before climbing back up to rejoin the Gorge Trail. Turn right and be careful on the steep descent – there are numerous slippery rocks but handrails are there to help right your footing.

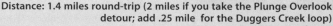

At the bottom, don't be fooled by what looks like a path to the left. Stay right and descend past a craggy overhang (which makes a good shelter, by the way) to a wet cliff. The gushing waters begin to roar here. Keep descending and be sure to bear right again until you reach the base. You've arrived when you can see thin rays of sunshine streaming through the canopy and piercing the blue water of the plunge pool – it's a true wilderness feeling. As tempting as the pool is, swimming is not allowed. On the way back, watch your footing here as you'll have to step over slippery rocks to negotiate the trail.

CRABTREE FALLS LOOP (MP 339.5)
Distance: 2.5-mile loop
Duration: 1½–2½ hours
Challenge: Difficult
Elevation Change: 600ft

The length of this journey, to see one of the prettiest waterfalls along the Parkway, will depend on whether you hike back after viewing the falls or continue on the loop. From the campground beside the **Crabtree Falls Visitor Center**, descend the wide path of primitive steps. At the bottom is a fork – go right to reach the falls.

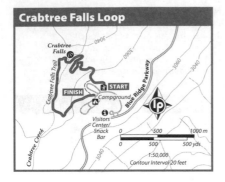

Crabtree Falls Loop

Crabtree Falls · Crabtree Falls Trail · FINISH · START · Campground · Blue Ridge Parkway · Visitors Center/Snack Bar · Crabtree Creek

0   500   1000 m
0   500   500 yds
1:50,000
Contour Interval 20 feet

On your steep descent, you'll likely see many **colorful salamanders** enjoying the many wet-weather springs. The trail is slippery in places, with standing water hiding sharp rocks, and it is cut around extremely rocky ground. There are three steep and narrow stone staircases; the first takes an angled curve to the bottom, and the next two are slippery and steeper. Fortunately, a few benches help ease the pain.

The loud rush of the falls signals your approach. Just past a treacherous, narrow section, cascading water roars off the 60ft cliff en route to the rocks below. A small wooden bridge provides the best picture-taking opportunities, with a built-in bench where you can rest and admire. Cross the bridge for the rest of the 1.6-mile loop, which levels out after a short, strenuous climb, then meanders across **Crabtree Creek** and into the parking area.

TANAWHA (MP 303)
Distance: 13.5 miles one way
Duration: One day
Challenge: Easy–Moderate (Difficult near Rough Ridge)
Elevation Change: 900ft

The newest and most expensive trail along the Blue Ridge Parkway does lay claim to unbeatable views. Perched along Grandfather Mountain's southeastern slope, the terrain shelters a fragile ecosystem of rare plants – which explains the arched bridges and walkways (many flown in via helicopter), that allow hikers to enjoy the natural beauty without disturbing future growth.

Though the trail has many entry points off the Parkway, the hike is described here in its entirety, from the Beacon Heights parking area to the Boone Fork Overlook. This route runs south-north, as it's a more moderate climb on that route.

Access the trail from the Beacon Heights parking area just before the Linn Cove Viaduct. You'll hike a set of steep stone steps beneath the Linn Cove Viaduct and past a giant boulder wall, while cars whoosh over the bridge. Catch your breath as the trail levels out and moves into a shady grove of trees. Nearby Wilson Creek gurgles as the path moves through a clearing sprinkled with more boulders, then climbs sharply to the best section of the hike, **Rough Ridge**. Here a 200ft wooden boardwalk leads not over dunes, but wild mountain heather and rare sand myrtle. The 360-degree view from 6000ft is breathtaking, especially of the Linn Cove Viaduct. Get the camera out: to the south is the Wilson Creek Basin, to the right is the Black Mountain Range and directly behind you is towering Grandfather Mountain.

From the boardwalk you'll head toward **Raven Rock** through a forest of dense trees, from spruce to oak. The trail soon opens up to an area reminiscent of Ireland's craggy landscape, with a rock garden of boulders that jut up from the earth. Continue through rhododendron patches to the junction of the **Daniel Boone Scout Trail** (one of the Grandfather Mountain trails – hiking it requires a permit and fee, as it's on private land). On the way to Boone Fork Creek the terrain can be a bit soggy, so step lightly. The trail passes more thick walls of

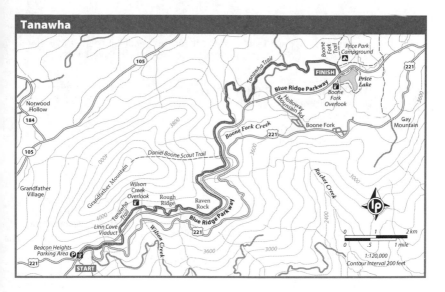

Tanawha

rhododendron and trickling cascades until it meets up with a logging road and moves through another hardwood forest. Here's where you're most likely to hear the frequent zoom of a motorcycle, among other sounds of the Parkway. However, the trail ahead holds more delights, such as apple orchards and blankets of wildflowers, as it changes from forest to field. Soon it meets up with Boone Fork Rd and ends at the campground.

WATERFALLS IN GRAVEYARD FIELDS (MP 418.8)
Distance: 0.8 mile round-trip
Duration: 45 minutes
Challenge: Moderate
Elevation Change: 340ft

There's nothing spooky about hiking in Graveyard Fields, though the crowds can be a bit scary. If you don't mind a few staircases, the only thing that'll jump out at you are three spectacular waterfalls.

The first thing you'll notice in the parking lot is a burned area of foliage below the overlook. In 1975 a massive fire raged through this valley, surprising more than 200 trout fishermen. They survived by jumping into the Yellowstone Prong of the Pigeon River and waiting underwater, taking small gulps of air amid the flames. When it was all over, the area's burnt-out stumps left a landscape resembling a field of tombstones, hence the name.

Start by descending the stone steps at the Graveyard Fields Overlook down through a thick spread of rhododendron and cross a small streambed. The path can be a bit muddy due to heavy traffic and/or recent rainfall. **Yellowstone Falls** is the first you'll encounter, just after crossing the Yellowstone Prong. A few steps below the wooden observation platform you'll feel the mist from the falls. From here, you can return to the parking lot or stay straight for a moderate 3.2-mile hike to **Upper Yellowstone Falls**. As you hike away from the river, the trail climbs a little here, past more picture-worthy clusters of rhododendrons. You'll know you're getting close when small stones turn to boulders and the sound of water grows louder.

Unique to this particular trail is the sheer number of wild berries (blueberry, blackberry and gooseberry); they make good snacks for hikers and deer.

WATERROCK KNOB (MP 451.2)
Distance: 0.5 mile round-trip
Duration: 1 hour
Challenge: Moderate–Difficult
Elevation Change: 410ft

This might be the hardest half mile you'll ever walk, but the extremely steep hike to the pedestrian overlook is absolutely worth the burn – and yes, there are plenty of benches along the way.

From the Waterrock Knob Visitor Center parking lot (an ethereal experience in itself when the fog rolls in), walk up the paved path (with handrail) until it ends on rocky ground. Soon you'll encounter a **tunnel of rhododendron**, and if you peer over the trail to the left, you may spot a bear hole. Keep your eyes open so the wildlife doesn't surprise you.

Push on until you hit the pedestrian overlook, about a quarter mile from the parking lot. Catch your breath and take a few snaps here before climbing farther, where it gets even rockier for a few hundred feet. Soon, the trail opens up, and the terrain looks meadowlike – despite the high altitude (6000ft). Speaking of which, you may be feeling lightheaded, as some hikers experience a bit of altitude sickness due to the sudden elevation gain.

At the **peak** you'll see views of the Great Smokies in Tennessee, as well as peaks in North Carolina, South Carolina and Georgia. You can even see the Ghost Town in the Sky amusement park down in Maggie Valley. A perfectly placed bench makes for a nice sunset perch. It's downhill all the way back... just watch out for those bears.

BACKCOUNTRY HIKING & CAMPING
Permits are free and must be requested in advance. Limited backcountry camping is available at Basin Cove in **Doughton Park** (☎ 336-372-8568) and Rock Castle Gorge in the **Rocky Knob District** (☎ 540-745-9660). Check with a park ranger to learn about access to neighboring US Forest Service backcountry areas along the Parkway.

OTHER ACTIVITIES
Horseback Riding
Reservations are encouraged for all rides.

Blowing Rock Equestrian Center (☎ 828-295-4700; 1500 Laurel Ave off NC 221; 1hr/2hr $35/50 adult and child over 9; ⏱ 9am, 11am, 1pm, 3pm, 5pm & 6:30pm) offers leisurely trail rides through hemlock forest and up to **Flat Top Manor** (p213).

Pisgah Forest Stables (☎ 828-883-8258; 1hr/2hr $25/50; ⏱ 10am, 11am, 12noon, 2pm, 3pm & 4pm), on NC 276 near Brevard, offers a chance to ride in Pisgah National Forest. Ask about the thee-hour waterfall tour ($85 per person).

You can come to **Clear Creek Ranch** (☎ 800-651-4510; 100 Clear Creek Dr, Burnsville; adult/ child 5-12/child 2-5 $205/135/40 daily, $1350/850/250 weekly; ⏱ Apr 1-Dec) just for the day, but for the true *City Slickers*–type experience, wrangle a weekly stay for family-style eats, marshmallow roasts and nightly hootenannies by the river.

Rafting & Canoeing
High Mountain Expeditions (☎ 800-262-9036; www.highmountainexpeditions.com; Main St, Blow-

ing Rock; ☉ year-round), less than 2 miles from the parkway, offers a little bit of everything, from rides on frothy rapids (starting at $49/44 adult/child) to spelunking ($75 per person) to kayak rentals ($15 for four hours). Certain expeditions require a minimum of four people.

Ever been white-water 'canoeing'? **Wahoo's Whitewater Rafting & Canoe Outfitters** (☎ 800-444-RAFT; www.wahoosadventures.com; US 321, Boone, NC; ☉ year-round) can help you do it, along with lazy tubing, traditional canoeing (plus picnic lunches), swimming and braving Class V rapids.

Skiing

Appalachian Ski Mountain (☎ 800-322-2373 or 828-295-7828; www.appskimtn.com; all-day lift ticket midweek adult/child 6-12/child under 6 $26/18/free, ski rentals $12/9/9, snowboarding $22; ☉ ski season mid-Dec–mid-Mar) is the most family-oriented range around, with nine gentle downhills, snowboarding and an ice-skating rink. It's on US 221/331 between Boone and Blowing Rock.

Ski Beech (☎ 800-438-2093, 828-387-2011; www.skibeech.com; 1007 Beech Mountain Pkwy; all-day lift ticket midweek adult/child 5-12/child under 5 $28/21/free, ski rentals $19, snowboarding $25), not far from Boone in Beech Mountain, towers 5506ft above sea level and boasts an excellent outdoor ice-skating rink ($12 including rentals).

Sugar Mountain (☎ 800-784-2768; www.skisugar.com; all-day lift ticket midweek adult/child 5-11/child under 5 $26/21/free; ski rentals $12/8/8; snowboarding $22; tubing weekday/weekend $15/20; ☉ Oct-Mar), about 15 minutes from the town of Boone, is one of few Southeastern ski resorts to boast a vertical slope over 1000ft.

Classes/Education

Penland School of Crafts (p215) offers two-week classes on everything from glassblowing to weaving. The **Folk Art Center** (p218) presents free demonstrations of crafts such as broom-making.

Kids' Activities

Most visitor centers participate in the Junior Rangers program, in which children earn a badge and certificate for their exploration of the natural environment. Activities include wildlife observation and easy hikes. Kids can also participate in the Junior Geologist program at the Museum of North Carolina Minerals (p216).

Just outside Blowing Rock, **Tweetsie Railroad** (☎ 800-526-5740, 828-264-9061; www. tweetsie.com; adult/child 3-12 $25/18; ☉ 9am-6pm May 28-Aug 15, 9am-6pm Fri-Sun only Aug 20-Oct 31 & Apr 30-May 23) is a great, if somewhat hokey, family-oriented theme park. Wee cowpokes get a taste of the Wild West by helping the US Marshall fend off train robbers, sampling down-home grub and enjoying country fair rides and music. There are even a few modern arcade games to keep the tiny ones happy. From the Parkway, take the Boone exit at MP 291 and follow the signs (just listen for the 'tweet tweet' as you approach the park).

A favorite kid (or kid at heart) activity along the Parkway, **Sliding Rock** (☎ 828-877-3350; $1) is a must on hot summer days. It's exactly what the name implies – a naturally smooth 'sliding rock' that's been developed into a 60ft waterslide, plunging riders into a chilly 7ft pool. It's hard to resist the refreshment – even Lassie slid down once for her TV series. No tubes are needed here, but do your butt a favor and wear an old pair of jeans, as the surface is tough on swimsuits. Smaller children need to slide with mom or dad. Don't want to get wet? Check out the squeals of laughter from two observation decks. Sliding Rock is open year-round, but restrooms, changing rooms and lifeguards are open Memorial Day to Labor Day only. From the intersection of US 276 and US 64 in Pisgah Forest, drive about 8 miles north on US 276. You'll pass Looking Glass Falls on the right after 5 miles.

Watch for signs directing you to the Sliding Rock Recreation Area parking lot on the left.

Another family-friendly attraction is **Altapass Orchard** (p216), with its penny candy selection, hayrides, live music (kids are encouraged to get their mountain groove on) and apple pickin', naturally.

FESTIVALS & EVENTS

Claiming to be the 'world's largest Scottish clan gathering,' the **Grandfather Mountain Highland Games** (☎ 828-733-1333; www.grandfather.com) in early July is a three-day strongman contest that pits kilt against kilt. Careful of those strong winds.

SLEEPING
Camping on the Parkway

Along the North Carolina section of the Parkway, there are five official campgrounds: **Doughton Park** (MP 239.2), **Julian Price Memorial Park** (MP 296.9), **Linville Falls** (MP 316), **Crabtree Meadows** (MP 339.5) and **Mt Pisgah** (MP 408.8). They are open from May to October, except Linville Falls, which is open year-round. **Reservations** (☎ 877-444-6777; www.reserveusa.com) are accepted in advance for Linville Falls and Price Memorial Park only; all other sites are assigned on a first-come, first-served basis.

Campground fees are $14 for families or groups of two adults, plus $2 for each additional person over 18. There are no hookups or showers. Along the Parkway, you'll also find seven picnic grounds in developed areas, plus tables at some of the overlooks.

Nearby Camping

Bear Den Campground (☎ 828-765-2888; 600 Bear Den Mountain Rd, Spruce Pine; campsite/cabin $28-30/55-210; ☼ Mar 1-Nov 30, cabins year-round) One of the best campgrounds around for sheer fun, this one boasts a sandy beach with lake swimming and paddleboat and canoe rentals, a playground, a super-clean bathhouse with *hot* showers and miles of trails. Hit the ATM in the trading post for camp supplies and groceries. To get there, at MP 324.8, turn left onto Bear Den Mountain Rd.

Raccoon Holler (☎ 336-982-2706; 493 Raccoon Holler Rd, MP 257-258; site $17) Another quaint lakeside campground, Raccoon Holler features fishing, showers, laundry and a small camp store.

Grandfather Mountain Campground (☎ 800-788-CLUB; site/cabin $18/109) Just outside Boone, this makes a good base for exploring Blowing Rock, Boone and nearby children's attractions. To get there, turn onto NC 105 north at MP 305.1.

Lake Powhatan (☎ 877-444-6777; site $15; ☼ 7am-10pm campground gate mid-May–late Oct) A pretty campground with showers, this spot will put you in proximity to mountain biking, hiking and lake swimming. Weekends require a two-night minimum.

Lodging on the Parkway

Bluffs Lodge (☎ 336-372-4499; www.blueridgeresort.com; MP 241.1; s/d $79, extra person $8, rollaway bed $8; ☼ late May-Oct 31) There's a great open-air fireplace on the stone verandah, but otherwise it's no frills in these small, motel-style rooms with no TVs or phones.

Mt Pisgah Inn (☎ 828-235-8228; www.pisgahinn.com; s/d $80-90, extra person $8, rollaway bed $8; ☼ Mar 29-Nov 1) An extremely popular venue, the inn offers recently renovated rooms with balconies overlooking its famous namesake. And hey, it's one of the few places TV junkies can get their fix in the mountains.

Nearby Lodging

River House Inn (☎ 336-982-2109; www.riverhousenc.com; 1896 Old Field Creek Rd, Grassy Creek;

d $115-150) A delightful gem hidden off the Parkway (from MP 259), this inn overlooks the gentle New River. The main house has comfy porch rockers, an intimate bar and an award-winning restaurant. Guestrooms are scattered throughout quaint cottages, each with cozy gas fireplaces and huge Jacuzzi tubs (but no TVs, phones or keys!). The super-friendly staff makes you feel like one of the gang – have a chat with owner Gail Winston about her incredible life story.

Chetola Resort (Map 15, p164; ☎ 800-243-8652; www.chetola.com; N Main St, Blowing Rock; lodge r/condo $86-106/130-140 Jan-Apr, $131-141/170-195 May-Dec; 🏊) Don't let the term 'resort' deter you from missing this beautiful, affordable complex just a mile off the Parkway. Individual condos create a home-away-from-home atmosphere, and you'll be spoiled at the spa. It's a great place for families, with an indoor swimming pool, playground and sparkling lake where kids can hike or chase the geese. From here you can walk to downtown Blowing Rock.

Nu Wray Inn (☎ 828-628-2329; www.nu-wrayinn.com; Town Square, Burnsville; d $65-85 including breakfast) A multilevel Victorian mishmash, the Nu Wray is reminiscent of a traditional boarding house along a well-traveled route. Its seasoned past has fueled stories about guests' so-called 'sightings' of previous residents. The creaky front porch and second-floor verandah boast cozy rocking chairs and a perfect view of Burnsville's historic town square. All in all, it makes a good stopping-off point for those exploring Mt Mitchell.

Balsam Mountain Inn (☎ 800-224-9498 or 828-456-9498; www.balsaminn.com; d $125-175) A wonderful escape up a mountaintop drive, this luxurious inn hangs onto down-home charm: there's a lobby with a fireplace, clapboards, sprawling porches and a very good restaurant. Rooms come without phones or TVs, but the inn offers an alternative diversion: regular shows of Appalachian art. To get there, from MP 443 take US 74/23.

EATING

Try the buckwheat pancakes with cooked apples at **Bluffs Coffee Shop** (MP 241.1; ☎ 336-372-4744; ⌚ 7:30am-7:30pm; dishes $5-15). Just across the Parkway is the larger and slightly more expensive **Bluffs Restaurant** (☎ 336-372 4499; dishes $5-20), with more rib-sticking country fare. Pick up small sandwiches and homemade treats at the **Northwest Trading Post** (p212), or grab a healthy, premade meal to go at the **Crabtree Falls Visitor Center** (MP 339.5).

ENTERTAINMENT

The drive itself is the main entertainment along the Parkway, but it's also easy to come by live bluegrass performances anywhere, particularly at the **Blue Ridge Music Center** (p204) and **Altapass Orchard** (p216). Watch a flick in retro seating at the historic **Yancey Theatre** (☎ 877-678-3322; 119 W Main St; $5) in Burnsville.

EQUIPMENT & SUPPLIES

There are supermarkets and major retail chains in major towns like Boone, Blowing Rock, Asheville and Cherokee. **Footsloggers** (☎ 704-262-5111; 553 W King St) in Boone sells hiking and camping equipment.

INTERNET ACCESS

It's hard to hook up to the web in this neck of the woods, but there are a few places to hop online. **Chetola Resort** (p227) provides Wi-Fi access, while **Mt Pisgah Inn** (p226) offers a terminal for public use ($2 for 20 minutes). Otherwise, try **public libraries** off the Parkway.

LOST & FOUND

Park rangers and information centers handle lost and found items. If you leave the Parkway before realizing you forgot something, contact the **Blue Ridge Parkway Communications Center** (☎ 828-271-4779; 199 Hemphill Knob Rd, Asheville, NC 28803-8686).

MEDICAL SERVICES & EMERGENCIES

There are no medical facilities along the Parkway. The nearest hospitals are in Spruce Pine, Boone, Asheville and Cherokee. In an emergency, call ☎ 800-PARKWATCH (727-5928).

MONEY

Though you'll find a few ATMs at restaurants and lodging facilities and one at Grandfather Mountain, it's best to stock up on cash before entering the Parkway.

POSTAL SERVICE

Drop off mail at information centers or at post offices in surrounding towns.

SHOWERS & LAUNDRY

There are no public shower or laundry facilities along the Parkway (including campgrounds).

TELEPHONES

Pay phones are available at information centers, museums, restaurants and most lodge lobbies. Cell-phone service is spotty at best, so don't rely on that as your only means of communication.

TRASH & RECYCLING

Trashcans are abundant at all visitor centers, picnic areas and overlooks, but there are no official recycling facilities along the Parkway.

AROUND THE BLUE RIDGE PARKWAY

GEORGE WASHINGTON & JEFFERSON NATIONAL FORESTS

Combined in 1995, these wonderfully remote forests provide ample opportunity to enjoy natural beauty the way the forefathers intended. Together, they stretch northeast to southwest across Virginia, spilling slightly into West Virginia and Kentucky and comprising a jaw-dropping 1.8 million miles of public land, one of the largest tracts in the eastern United States. Fewer than 10 miles from Waynesboro, the districts are conveniently accessible.

The forests are divided into three parts: **Massanutten Mountain**, in the north between the north and south forks of the Shenandoah; **Jefferson National Forest**, which straddles the Blue Ridge Parkway between Charlottesville and Roanoke; and the larger **George Washington National Forest**, which skirts the West Virginia border and includes parts of the Shenandoah and Allegheny Mountains.

The US Department of Agriculture (USDA) Forest Service is the administrator of these national forests. The **Supervisor's Office** (☎ 540-265-5100; www.southernregion.fs.fed.us/gwj; 5162 Valleypointe Pkwy, Roanoke, VA 24019) is the main headquarters, where you can pick up good maps of the entire forest and detailed brochures. Other ranger district offices include the following:

G'NIGHT, JOHN BOY

Heading southeast toward the small town of Schuyler, you can almost hear the strains of 'G'night, John Boy' coming over Waltons' Mountain, a fictional setting based on the boyhood home of author Earl Hamner, who grew up in Schuyler. Though *The Waltons* wasn't filmed here, there's a small **museum** (☎ 434-831-2000; www.waltonmuseum. org; Rt 617, Schuyler VA; 🕙 10am-4pm Mar-Nov; $5 adults, $4 seniors, $2 children) with sets and memorabilia from the TV show, plus a 30-minute behind-the-scenes film of cast members.

Deerfield (☎ 540-885-8028), west of Staunton on Rte 254
Dry River (☎ 540-432-018), 112 North River Rd, Bridgewater
Glenwood/Pedlar (☎ 540-291-2188), 2424 Magnolia Ave, Buena Vista
James River (☎ 540-962-2214), 810-A Madison Ave, Covington
Lee (☎ 540-984-4101), 109 Molineu Rd, Edinburg
Massanutten Visitors Center (☎ 540-740-8310), New Market
Warm Springs (☎ 540-839-2521), Rte 220 south, Hot Springs

NATURAL BRIDGE

Though hardly the eighth wonder of the world, this bridge is a national historic landmark and one of the most spectacular sights of the Shenandoah Valley, a must-see for visitors to the region. The limestone arch, 215ft high and 90ft long, has been carved and shaped over the centuries by the seemingly lazy Cedar Creek, a tributary of the James River.

The Native American Monocan tribe worshipped the natural arch as the 'Bridge of God'; George Washington surveyed it for Lord Fairfax; Thomas Jefferson, impressed by its grandeur, purchased it at one stage; today it supports a portion of Rte 11.

Somehow, the beautiful, natural structure has been incorporated into a macabre complex known as the **Natural Bridge Inn & Conference Center** (☎ 800-533-

1410, 540-291-2121; ☯ 8am-dark), which includes an attached wax museum, nearby caverns and an unspooky monster museum – the only truly frightening thing here is the plethora of kitsch.

Attraction-wise, your best bet is to take in the Natural Bridge from below (adult/child $10/5), the only real photographic angle. From June to September, the bridge is lit up after dark, but unfortunately you can't enjoy the experience without being subject to a preachy, over-the-top sound-and-light presentation called *The Drama of Creation* (☯ 9 and 10pm). Only the impressive sight of the arch at night justifies the high admission.

If you're arriving from the south, you're probably just beginning to experience 'cavern fever.' It gets worse the farther north you travel up the valley. **Natural Bridge Caverns** (☎ 800-533-1410; www.naturalbridgeva.com) are the equivalent of 34 stories deep. And lurking some 347ft underground is the Natural Bridge ghost, supposedly a catacomb resident for more than 100 years.

If you dare venture into the kitsch sites, the **wax museum** (adult/child $8/5), **toy museum** (adult/child $8/5) and **monster museum** (adult/child $6/5) will probably delight kids for about five minutes. Combo tickets are available for most attractions. The best overlook, Pulpit Rock, has been closed to the public.

The Natural Bridge lies 20 miles south of Lexington, just off I-81 (take exit 180 onto Rte 11 or exit 175 onto Rte 130). The caverns lie to the east of Rte 11, a mile north of Natural Bridge village.

The most beautiful spot to camp near Natural Bridge is Cave Mountain Lake Recreation Area.

Natural Bridge KOA Kampground (☎ 540-291-2770; site/Kamping Kabin $19-22/34-45) Even though it has fewer amenities than its sister campground in neighboring Staunton, this is a clean and quiet facility close to many attractions. The campground sits at the junction of Rte 11 and I-81 (exits 180 northbound and 180B southbound).

Yogi Bear's Jellystone Park Camp Resort at Natural Bridge (☎ 800-258-9532; site/cabin $25/from $50; ⬛) A true breath of fresh air far (enough) away from the madding Natural Bridge crowds, this campground offers all the fun amenities associated with the chain, including a lake with swimming beach, tube rentals, basketball court and brand-new swimming pool. It's 5 miles from Natural Bridge. Take exit 180A off I-81 and follow Rte 130 east for 3 miles.

The Natural Bridge Inn & Conference Center and Stonewall Inn are operated by the **Natural Bridge of Virginia Resort** (☎ 800-533-1410; www.naturalbridgeva.com; hotel r/cottage $56-70/46 Jan 1-Mar 18 & Nov 7-Dec 31, $76-90/56 Mar 19-Jun 10, $76-110/60 Jun 11-Nov 6). Look for the reservations desk at the Natural Bridge ticket office.

The **Colonial Dining Room** (☎ 800-533-1410; Fri buffets $23.95, Thu buffets $17.95) at Natural Bridge doles out rib-sticking Southern buffet grub on Friday and Saturday night. Also check out the Wednesday grill night and the gi-normous farm-fresh breakfasts buffets (April to October only).

ROANOKE

Map 14, p164 / ☎ 540 / pop 95,000 / elevation 940ft

Illuminated by its giant mountainside star, Roanoke is the big city in these parts, with a compact set of attractions based around the great downtown **farmers market** (213 Market St; ☯ 7:30am-5pm Mon-Sat). For maps and local information, check out the **Roanoke Visitor Center** (☎ 540-342-6025, 800-635-5535; www.visitroanokeva.com; 101 Shenandoah Ave NE; ☯ 9am-5pm), in the Old Norfolk & Western railway station, and the **Blue Ridge Parkway Visitor Center** (☎ 540-427-5871; MP 115 off the Parkway; ☯ 9am-5pm May-Nov).

Center in the Square (☎ 540-342-5700; www.centerinthesquare.org; 1 Market Square; ☯ closed Mon) houses five downtown attractions, including a science museum, theater, planetarium, local history museum and free art museum that showcases the work of folk and local artists. The nearby **Virginia Museum of Transportation** (☎ 540-342-5670; www.vmt.org; 303 Norfolk Ave SW; adult/child 3-11 $7.40/5.25; ⊙ 11am-4pm Mon-Fri, 10am-5pm Sat, from 1pm Sun) will thrill kids and trainspotters alike with its locomotive garden, and the **Harrison Museum of African American Culture** (☎ 540-345-4818; 523 Harrison Ave; admission free; ⊙ 1-5pm Tue-Sun) chronicles the impact of black Americans on the history of the area.

The Roanoke Appalachian Trail Club organizes hikes, and the Blue Ridge Bicycle Club offers year-round rides; ask at the visitor center for contact information. There's cross-country skiing at **Mountain Lake** (☎ 540-626 7121).

Downtown's **Hotel Roanoke** (☎ 540-985-5900; www.hotelroanoke.com; 110 Shenandoah Ave NE; r from $84) has faithfully integrated 1882 features into an ultramodern convention hotel. Budget options include the **Sleep Inn Tanglewood** (☎ 540-772-1500; VA 419 at US 220; r from $65), southwest of town, and the **Roanoke Mountain Campground** (p209).

City Market houses local vendors that serve pizza, sushi, burritos and more, with counter seating. Neighboring restaurants and cafés offer more choices, including seafood and Brazilian and vegetarian cuisine. The beloved hole-in-the-wall **Texas Tavern** (114 W Church Ave) is a must if you can nab one of the few seats; the chili bowls ($3) are great.

Mill Mountain

Perched on this mountain near the parkway, **Mill Mountain Zoo** (☎ 540-343-3241; www.mmzoo.org; adult/child 3-12 $6.75/4.50; ⊙ 10am-4:30pm) and an adjacent wildflower garden are perfect for kids – the Zoo Choo train is $2 extra. Directly next door is the **Roanoke Star** and a breathtaking view of the city. **Virginia's Explore Park** (☎ 800-842-9163, 540-427-1800; www.explorepark.org; adult/child 3-11 $8/4.50; ⊙ 10am-5pm Wed-Sat Apr-Oct, from noon Sun) uses living-history demonstrations to depict three centuries of the area's past.

To get to Mill Mountain from downtown Roanoke, take Jefferson Ave south to Walnut. Turn left on Walnut, cross over a bridge and continue straight up the mountain. From the Parkway, look for signs for Roanoke Mountain Campground and Mill Mountain (at approximately MP 120.4) and take the Spur Rd up the mountain.

AROUND ROANOKE

Per capita, the tiny town of Bedford suffered the most casualties during WWII and hence was chosen to host an eerily moving tribute, the **National D-Day Memorial** (☎ 540-586-3329; www.dday.org; US 460 at US 122; $10/car; ⊙ 10am-5pm). Among its towering arch and English flower garden, bronze figures reenact the storming of the beach, complete with bursts of water symbolizing the hail of bullets the soldiers faced.

Twenty miles southeast of Roanoke, the **Booker T Washington National Monument** (☎ 540-721-2094; US 122; admission free; ⊙ 9am-5pm), is a recreated tobacco farm that honors the former slave who became an international and controversial African American leader.

Smith Mountain Lake State Park (☎ 540-297-6066; www.dcr.state.va.us/parks/smithmtn.htm; 1235 State Park Rd), 25 miles southeast of Roanoake, contains the state's second-largest body of water and comes alive in summer with a plethora of biking, hiking and fishing activities, as well as cool **waterfront cabins** (☎ 800-933-7275; from $68).

GALAX

☎ 276 / pop 6900 / elevation 2382ft

On the cusp of Virginia and North Carolina, **Galax**, Virginia, is a classic slice of hometown America in the mountains. Dubbed the 'world's capital of bluegrass music,' it lives up to that nickname by hosting a slew of concerts throughout the year. In early August, the **Old Fiddler's Convention** (☎ 276-236-8541; www.oldfiddlersconvention.com; nightly/season ticket $5-10/30), Galax's biggest hootenanny, draws the best fiddlers in the country to jam with fellow dulcimer, banjo, mouth harp and bull fiddle players (think Woodstock with a major twang). The **campground** ($70/site) hosts players and listeners – what could be better than drifting off on a summer night to a bluegrass lullaby?

Pick up information at the **tourism office** (☎ 276-238-8130; www.ingalax.net; 111 E Grayson St).

The Smokehouse (☎ 276-236-1000; 101 N Main St; dishes under $10) is an award-winning barbecue joint across from the Rex Theater. Also try **Macado's** (☎ 276-236-0399; 201 N Main St; dishes under $15) for stuffed deli sandwiches.

The **Southwest Virginia Farmer's Market** (☎ 276-728-5540; US 58 at I-77) offers fresh fruits and homemade pies.

On Friday night the **Rex Theater** (☎ 276-238-8130; E Grayson St; 🕐 8-10pm; admission by donation) is the place to be for the *Blue Ridge Backroads* live broadcast of traditional bluegrass, one of only three live bluegrass radio shows in the country. If you can't make it to the theater, tune in on 98.1FM.

On Saturday night in summer, see more live bluegrass at the **Blue Ridge Music Center** (☎ 276-236-5309; www.blueridgemusiccenter.net; Blue Ridge Parkway MP 213; admission varies). The music starts at 7pm.

BOONE

☎ 828 / pop 13,500 / elevation 3266ft

Named the 'firefly capital of America,' this artists' colony boasts an electrifying assortment of outdoor activities, as well as a few kitschy attractions and even an old-fashioned drugstore counter. Pick up information at the **Convention & Visitors' Bureau** (☎ 800-852-9506; www.visitboonenc.com; 208 Howard St).

Try **Murphy's Restaurant** (☎ 828-264-5117; 747 W King St) for great beer specials, big burgers and burritos from $5 to $7. **Angelica's** (☎ 828-265-0809; 506 W King St) is a New Age veggie joint with a juice bar. Who would have reckoned on toasted seaweed sheets ($5 to $8) up here?

Horn in the West (☎ 828-264-2120; admission $15; 🕐 late Jun–mid-Aug) is a musical drama that attempts to 'relive the frontier days with Daniel Boone' at an amphitheater off Blowing Rock Rd.

More worthwhile that the town of Boone is a visit to **Mast General Store** (☎ 828-963-6511), on NC 194 in Valle Crucis, about 30 minutes' drive west of Boone. This quaint, old-fashioned place with a potbelly stove is just this side of contrived but stacked to the gills with everything from thick woolen socks to gout cures. Here you can pick up such mountain toys as the 'gee-haw whimmy diddle,' a stick with a propeller that spins when you rub the notches on the stick.

BLOWING ROCK

Map 15, p164 / ☎ 828 / pop 1500 / elevation 3579ft

Reminiscent of a quaint New England coastal town (minus the ocean), Blowing Rock is just a mile off the Parkway on US 321 south. Main St is a tightly packed, colorful corridor with flowery B&Bs, shops and open-air restaurants. The town makes for a charming sleepover, especially at the exciting **Chetola Resort** (p227). For maps and information, stop by the **visitor center** (☎ 800-295-7851; www.blowingrock.com; 132 Park St).

The **Appalachian Cultural Museum** (☎ 828-262-3117; University Hall Dr off Blowing Rock Rd; adult/child 10-18/senior $4/2/3.50; 🕐 closed Mon) is a serious attempt to present mountain life and history beyond hillbilly stereotypes. Housed in the Mystery Hill complex, it features some first-class exhibits and thoughtful interpretive material.

Don't waste your money on two Griswald-worthy tourist traps: The Blowing Rock and Mystery Hill. On US 321 south of town, **The Blowing Rock** (☎ 828-295-7111; www.theblowingrock.com; ⊙ daily Mar-Dec, weekend Jan & Feb) is a cliff with an unusual wind pattern that blows objects back at you. **Mystery Hill** (☎ 828-264-2792; 129 Mystery Hill Lane; www.mysteryhill-nc.com; adult/senior/child 5 & over $8/6/5; ⊙ 8am-8pm Jun-Aug, 9am-5pm Sep-May) is a slightly rundown house that claims to harbor strange energy patterns that defy the laws of physics. Neither attraction manages to impress adults, but hey, if it's a rainy day, the kids might think they're cool.

For information about outdoor adventures in Blowing Rock, see Other Activities (p224). Also see Kids' Activities (p223).

You can't go wrong with the overstuffed pot pies at **Six Pence Pub** (☎ 828-295-3155; 1121 Main St) or the massive burgers and spicy wings at **Cheeseburger Grill & Paradise Bar** (☎ 828-295-4858; US 221 at Main St). Save room for a Blowing Rock specialty – a scoop of rich homemade ice cream at **Kilwin's** (☎ 828-295-3088; 1087 Main St) and savor your cone on one of the park benches across the street.

ASHEVILLE
Map 6, p157 / ☎ 828 / pop 69,000 / elevation 2100ft

Asheville's boosters exhort you to refer to their exceedingly pleasant western North Carolina city as the 'Paris of the South.' Perhaps they've never seen the bright lights of Paris. Notwithstanding, their enthusiasm for Asheville's bohemian pleasures is not misplaced. By day the streets are filled with hipsters perusing used clothing shops or comparing tattoos; at night the sweet-smelling mountain air is graced with the sounds of musicians tuning their instruments as the many clubs and cafés open their doors to showcase the local music scene.

More than a century ago, millionaire George Vanderbilt raved that Asheville was the 'most beautiful land in the world.' Whatever your means, it's hard not to be impressed with this surprisingly liberal town, which retains a certain 1920s charm in a fabulous setting. Don't be surprised if you extend your stay, just as Vanderbilt did.

History
In the late 1700s Asheville was but a crossing of two Indian trails when homesteaders from Northern Ireland dubbed the valley 'Eden land.' A real estate broker developed the area, and tiny Asheville was founded in 1797 and named after North Carolina Governor Samuel Ashe. At first the town became not a resort but a stopover for cattle farmers driving their herds to market. Growth was slow in those early, mud-caked years.

Asheville remained a backwater until the railroad came to town in 1880. Virtually overnight the place was transformed, as trains chugged in thousands of tourists from the East Coast and beyond. One carriage carried 26-year-old George Vanderbilt, heir to a vast railway fortune, and the region's rugged beauty opened both his heart and wallet. Vanderbilt purchased 125,000 acres of land, stretching from Asheville to the present-day Pisgah National Forest, and in 1890 he asked Richard Morris Hunt to draw up plans for Biltmore Estate. Hundreds of artisans and builders from Europe would spend six years fashioning the interior and exterior of this grand chateau, the largest residence in the United States.

In recent years Asheville has regained much of its Jazz Age allure. Dozens of architectural gems have been restored, and the crisp mountain air now draws a varied crowd of bohemians, outdoors enthusiasts and retirees. Fortunately, mutual tolerance is in ample supply, and a good time is had by all.

Orientation

At the confluence of the Swannanoa and French Broad Rivers, Asheville sits in the middle of a loop formed by I-40 and I-240. The town is relatively compact and easy to negotiate on foot. The sprawling Biltmore Estate lies on its southern boundary.

Information

The **visitor center** (☎ 828-258-6101, 800-257-1300; 151 Haywood St; ☷ 8:30am-5:30pm Mon-Fri, 9am-5pm Sat & Sun) is at exit 4C off I-240.

Malaprop's Bookstore & Café (☎ 828-254-6734; 55 Haywood St; ☷ 9am-9pm Mon-Thu, until 10pm Fri & Sat, until 6pm Sun) is an excellent place to pick up regional maps and travel guides; join the cappuccino-sipping bohemians. Bring your laptop for free Wi-Fi access.

The main **post office** is at 33 Coxe Ave. The **public library** (☎ 828-251-4991; 67 Haywood Ave; ☷ 10am-8pm Mon-Thu, until 6pm Fri, until 5pm Sat) offers free Internet access.

The **Mission St Joseph's Hospital** (☎ 828-213-1111; 509 Biltmore Ave) has a 24-hour emergency ward, plus walk-in care services from noon to 10pm. Adjacent to Days Inn, **Midtown Family Medicine & Urgent Care** (☎ 828-232-1555; 120B Patton Ave; ☷ 11am-5pm Mon-Fri, 10am-2pm Sun) is a drop-in clinic for non–life-threatening emergencies.

The *Asheville Citizen-Times* (www.citizen-times.com) is the biggest daily newspaper in western North Carolina. *The Mountain Xpress* (www.mountainxpress.com), a free independent weekly paper available in local bars and restaurants, is the place to look for nightlife and entertainment listings.

Sights

BILTMORE ESTATE

With 250 rooms, the gorgeous, sprawling **Biltmore Estate** (☎ 828-255-1333, 800-624-1575; www.biltmore.com; adult/child $39/20; ☷ 9am-4pm Jan-Mar, 8:30am-5pm Apr-Dec) is overwhelmingly sumptuous in scale and decoration. Built for the filthy-rich Vanderbilt family as a holiday home, the 1895 mansion is styled after a French chateau. George Vanderbilt quaintly referred to the charming behemoth as his 'cottage.' Many visitors recognize the grounds from the late, great Peter Seller's film *Being There*. Author Henry James complained during a 1905 visit that his bedroom was at least a half mile from the library. Be sure to save time for the cavernous basement, which housed the bowling alley, swimming pool, kitchen and servants' quarters.

Plan to spend quite a few hours viewing the estate to justify the hefty admission price. The Biltmore's **winery** (free with general admission ticket) offers tastings and sales. Mid-priced meals are available at several venues, and the gift shop is the size of a small supermarket.

THOMAS WOLFE MEMORIAL

This local literary landmark is an early-1900s boardinghouse that provided the setting for Wolfe's epic autobiographical novel *Look Homeward, Angel*. The author described the rambling clapboard structure as an 'old dilapidated house with 18 or 20 drafty, high-ceilinged rooms.' The 1929 novel was peppered with sometimes unflattering local color, and its references incensed so many locals that the public library banned it for seven years. In 1998 an arson attack unleashed an enormously destructive blaze that devoured many original artifacts and caused widespread damage. Following a costly renovation effort, 2004 marked the grand reopening of the house as a museum and **visitor center** (☎ 828-253-8304; 52 N Market St; adult/student $1/50¢; ⊙ 9am-5pm Tue-Sat, 1-5pm Sun).

BOTANICAL GARDENS ✓

On a 10-acre site north of downtown, the **Botanical Gardens** (☎ 828-252-5190; www.ashevillebotanicalgardens.org; 151 Weaver Blvd; admission free; ⊙ dawn-dusk) offer a year-round show of blossoms, buds, fruits or leaves, depending on the season. The displays of Appalachian plants and flowers are a botanist's dream, but anyone will enjoy a stroll on shady, leaf-covered paths beneath giant sycamores and along babbling brooks. There's a Garden for the Blind with labels in Braille. From downtown, take Merrimon Ave (US 25) north for approximately 1.5 miles to Weaver Blvd and turn left. The entrance to the gardens is ahead on the right. (Alternatively, take Broadway north and turn right on Weaver Blvd.)

Activities

Asheville is a heaven on earth for outdoor activity enthusiasts.

Scale the heights at the full-service **ClimbMax Indoor Climbing Center** (☎ 828-252-9996; 43 Wall St; indoor bouldering/rope climbing $8.50/12.50; ⊙ 3:30pm-10pm Tue & Thu, noon-10pm Wed & Fri, 10am-10pm Sat, 1-6pm Sun), or head to the hills on a rock-climbing excursion with an expert guide (from $165).

An excellent operation, **Bio-Wheels** (☎ 888-881-2453, 828-232-0300; www.biowheels.com; 76 Biltmore Ave; tours half/full day $85-150/140-250; ⊙ 10am-6:30pm Mon-Sat, 1-5pm Sun) is the best regional provider for outdoor cycling activities. In addition to rentals, sales and service, Bio-Wheels offers guided excursions, including leisurely sunset rides along the Blue Ridge Parkway and mountain bike tours, such as the intermediate-level Epic Backwoods Ride. Tours are priced according to group size.

Going underground is the only way to see what's underneath that mountain. The unique **Inner Mountain Caving Explorations** (☎ 866-444-7935; www.innermtnexplorer.com; 85 Ed DeBruhl Hill Rd, Alexander) leads expeditions to underground lakes, rivers and waterfalls. Each trip is fully outfitted with safety gear, but you must bring good hiking boots and appropriate clothing for cool temperatures. Trips range from a three-hour subterranean stroll tailored to beginners ($58) to the six-hour Adventurer trip ($95) for folks who live to wallow in the mud; there's even an overnight trip ($190). It's enough to make any neophyte spelunker test the echo with a lusty shout of 'Cowabunga!' Inner Mountain is in Alexander, 12 miles southeast of Asheville. From I-240, take exit 4A and follow US 19-23 north toward Weaverville for approximately 8 miles. Take the Marshall exit onto US 25-70 North, drive 3.8 miles and turn left onto Lower Flat Creek Rd. Go 500ft and turn right onto Snelson Rd; after 0.8 mile, turn left onto Ed DeBruhl Hill Rd and turn into the first drive on the left.

Black Dome Mountain Sports (☎ 828-251-2001; 140 Tunnel Rd; ⊙ 10am-8pm Mon-Sat, 1-5pm Sun) is the best-stocked outdoor supply store in the region, selling everything from technical climbing gear to polypropylene underwear.

Sleeping

Prices listed reflect summer high-season rates; rates in Asheville fluctuate depending on season, availability and day of the week. Note that prices really jump in October, the height of the leaf-peeping season.

BUDGET & CAMPING

Chain motels cluster north of downtown along Merrimon Ave, with rates averaging $50 to $60. East on Tunnel Rd at I-240 exit 6 are several independent places such as the nondescript **Blue Ridge Motor Lodge** (☎ 828-254-0805; 60 Tunnel Rd;

r $40-60; (P) (🍴)). For local color, try the **Mountaineer Inn** (☎ 828-254-5331, 800-255-4080; 155 Tunnel Rd; r from $45; (P) (🍴) (📶)), with its towering neon hillbilly sign and cedar-walled rooms.

Days Inn Downtown (☎ 828-254-9661; 120 Patton Ave; weekdays/weekends $72/78; (P) (🍴) (💻) (📶)) The cheapest downtown option features unexceptional rooms in a building that would benefit from a top-to-bottom update. The location, however, is plum. Pets are welcome for a $15 fee.

Bear Creek Campground (☎ 828-253-0798, 81 S Bear Creek Rd; campsite with/without electricity $28/25, RV site $31; (🕐) year-round) Right next to the Biltmore Estate, this campground offers full facilities (clubhouse, laundry, pool, etc), RV sites with hookups and nice tent sites. If you're going westbound on I-40, take exit 47 and proceed from the signal to the campground; eastbound, take exit 47, turn right at the signal, then left on S Bear Creek Rd.

Asheville East KOA Kampground (☎ 800-562-5907, 828-686-3121; 102 US 70E, Swannanoa; suite with kitchen $110, rustic cabin $45-60, RV site $27-30; (P) (📶)) Ten miles east of town, this campground offers a range of accommodations, from tent sites to suites. Take I-40 exit 59, drive north one block to the signal, turn right on US 70 and go 2 miles.

MID-RANGE

The **Renaissance Asheville Hotel** (☎ 828-252-8211, fax 828-236-9616; 1 Thomas Wolfe Plaza; high/low season $139/105; (P) (🍴) (💻) (📶)) This 12-story downtown high-rise with excellent mountain views offers singles and doubles in Marriott-style luxury. A standard buffet breakfast is included in the price. The hotel houses a large fitness center.

Forest Manor Inn (☎ 828-274-3531; www.forestmanorinn.com; 866 Hendersonville Rd; r $89-169; (P) (🍴) (📶)) Near the Biltmore Estate, this charming and immaculate 21-unit motel sits on 4 acres of landscaped, wooded grounds adjacent to the good-quality Wildflower Restaurant. Complimentary continental breakfast is provided.

DoubleTree Biltmore Hotel (☎ 828-274-1800; www.biltmoreinns.com; 115 Hendersonville Rd; s/d $119/179; (P) (🍴) (💻) (📶)) This comfortable, 160-room hotel features a pretty setting and a long list of amenities, including a gym, spa and laundry service.

TOP END

Grove Park Inn Resort (☎ 828-252-2711, 800-438-5800; www.groveparkinn.com; 290 Macon Ave; r from $209; (P) (🍴) (🍴) (💻) (📶)) Fancy as all get-out, this excellent hotel occupies a classic Arts and Crafts building built in 1913. It's famous for its 510 gorgeous rooms and also boasts a fitness center, tennis courts, spa and four restaurants. Prices – always high – fluctuate wildly, depending on the season. To get there, from I-240 take exit 5B (Charlotte St) and drive north about 1.3 miles. Turn right on Macon Ave and continue 0.8 mile to the inn.

Inn on Biltmore Estate (☎ 828-225-1660, 800-922-0084; 1 Antler Hill Rd; r $259-2000; (P) (🍴) (🍴) (💻) (📶)) A stunning option on Vanderbilt's property, this world-class resort rests its reputation on meticulous attention to detail. Expect to be pampered with fluffy robes and warmed slippers, turndown service and chocolates on your pillow (if this is their idea of seduction, it works!). The service and atmosphere are surprisingly down-to-earth and casual. Many rooms feature gorgeous view of the Great Smokies, marble counters and separate tubs and showers. Don't miss the wonderful breakfast buffet on the terrace overlooking the mountains and the Biltmore Estate.

B&BS

Asheville is justifiably famous for its B&Bs; many housed in impressive Jazz Age houses. The **Asheville Bed & Breakfast Association** (☎ 828-252-0200, 877 262-6867;

www.ashevillebba.com) handles bookings for 21 area B&Bs, from Victorian mansions to mountain retreats.

Eating

For a small city, Asheville has an astonishingly good cuisine scene. Loosen your belt and linger over something delicious.

Thibodaux Jones Kitchen & Meantime Lounge (☎ 828-225-3065; 48 Biltmore Ave; dishes $8-20; ☼ dinner 5-10 pm Tue-Sat, lounge 5pm-close Mon-Sat) The Creole-inspired kitchen of this lively place sends out delicious dishes inspired by hot New Orleans jazz. Don't miss the New Orleans–style barbecue shrimp, sautéed in a spicy sherry and garlic herb sauce. There's live music Thursday to Sunday.

Café Soleil (☎ 828-650-1140; 62 N Lexington Ave; dishes $3-10; ☼ 11:30am-10pm Tues-Wed, 11:30am-1:30am Thu-Sat, 10am-3pm Sun) This classy, cozy creperie serves 'em savory and sweet in a pleasant dining room painted in sunbaked hues. Excellent soups and salads and a great wine list make this one of Asheville's most enjoyable restaurants. Friday and Saturday evenings feature live music – klezmer, gypsy and jazz.

Blue Moon Bakery (☎ 828-252-6060; 60 Biltmore Ave; lunch $4-7; ☼ 7:30am-4pm) This co-operatively run bakery serves wholesome, well-conceived sandwiches: try the Mango Magic with smoked turkey, Swiss cheese and piquant mango chutney. Also tempting are the fresh salads and soups.

Tupelo Honey Café (☎ 828-255-4863; 12 College St; breakfast $6-13, dinner $8-12; ☼ 9am-3pm Tue-Thu, 9am-3pm & 5pm-3am Fri & Sat, 9am-3pm Sun) This pleasant eatery extols the virtues of 'Southern home cooking with an uptown twist.' The amazing breakfasts include a standout called Eggs Crawley: two seared crab cakes topped with poached eggs and hollandaise. It's richer than Vanderbilt.

Doc Chey's Noodle House (☎ 828-252-8220; 37 Biltmore Ave; noodle bowls & rice plates $6-8; ☼ 11:30am-10pm Sun-Thu, 11:30am-11pm Sat) A cheerful interior with bright red walls and vibrant decor is the perfect complement for the steaming bowls of tasty noodles that emerge from the kitchen.

Barley's Taproom (☎ 828-255-0504; 42 Biltmore Ave; pizzas $12-15; ☼ 11:30am-2am Mon-Sat, noon-midnight Sun) This cavernous place is famous for beer and music, but the taproom also serves uncommonly good bar food, including pizzas, sandwiches and calzones. Come for live music four nights a week, generally on Sunday, Tuesday, Thursday and sometimes Saturday.

Max & Rosie's (☎ 828-254-5352; 52 N Lexington Ave; lunch $4-7; ☼ 11am-5pm Mon-Sat) For your health, this little place serves well-priced veggie burgers, pitas, salads, fresh-squeezed fruit juices and tonics.

Rio Burrito (☎ 828-253-2422; 11 Broadway; burritos $4.50-6; ☼ 11:30am-7:30pm Tue-Sat) This nouveau burrito joint rolls 'em California-style (that is to say, hot and hefty). If it suits your temperament, try the 'nerve gas' salsa, made from sweet potatoes, peaches and in-house smoked habañero peppers.

French Broad Food Co-op (☎ 828-255-7650; 90 Biltmore Ave; ☼ 9am-9pm Mon-Sat, noon-8pm Sun) This sweet-smelling grocery store sells organic produce and bulk and natural foods. Vegetarians may want to stock up here before heading west to Great Smoky.

Drinking & Entertainment

Asheville has a rich music scene and plenty of good bars. To see what's on, pick up a copy of the free alternative weekly *Mountain Xpress* or the *Smoky Mountain News*.

Vincent's Ear (☎ 828-259-9119; 68-B N Lexington Ave) This amiable, darkened hovel serves coffee and light meals by day, beer in the afternoon and earsplitting live music at night.

The Orange Peel Social Aid & Pleasure Club (☎ 828-225-5851; www.theorangepeel.net; 101 N

Biltmore Ave) Quality funk, punk and alt-country acts do their thing at this most excellent music hall.

Smokey After Dark (☎ 828-253-2155; 18 Broadway) This gay bar still retains the ambience of its roadhouse origins. It's got pool tables and people in-the-know.

Fine Arts Theatre (☎ 828-232-1536; 36 Biltmore Ave) The latest art house films are screened here.

Bean Streets Coffeehouse (☎ 828-255-8180; 3 Broadway) This well-loved coffeehouse with free Wi-Fi access is a great place to hang out, despite the occasional open-mic poetry readings.

Shopping

Mast General Store (☎ 828-232-1883; 15 Biltmore Ave; ☺ 10am-6pm Mon-Thu, 10am-9pm Fri-Sat, noon-5pm Sun) A satellite of the well-known general store, this downtown emporium recalls the halcyon days of the American department store. Downstairs is a complete outfitters department that sells hiking and camping gear, boots and casual footwear.

Getting There & Away

On I-26 15 miles from downtown, **Asheville Regional Airport** (☎ 828-684-2226; www.flyavl.com) is served by Continental Airlines, Delta Air Lines, Northwest Airlines and US Airways.

Greyhound (☎ 828-253-8451; www.greyhound.com; 2 Tunnel Rd) operates several buses daily to Knoxville, Tennessee ($27, two hours), and one to Atlanta, Georgia ($38, from seven hours).

Getting Around

Asheville Transit (☎ 828-253-5691; www.ashevilletransit.com; 60 W Haywood St; fares adult/senior 75/35¢) provides limited local bus service.

Three public parking garages serve downtown; parking is free for the first hour and 50¢ an hour thereafter.

HOT SPRINGS

☎ 828 / pop 645 / elevation 1330ft

This bucolic little town 40 minutes north of Asheville is a wonderful place to relax and soak up the scenery while also soaking yourself. In 1788 explorers discovered the hot springs that earned the town its name (although the Cherokee had been savvy to their existence for centuries).

Buncombe Turnpike – the South's first superhighway – was completed in 1828. Connecting Tennessee and Kentucky to the East Coast, this road brought farmers and thousands of horses, cattle and other livestock through town (though only the farmers were allowed to take in the springs). James Patton of Asheville bought the springs in 1831 and by 1837 had built the 350-room Warm Springs Hotel, which featured 13 tall columns commemorating the first colonies. Due to its size and grandeur, it was called Patton's White House. It burned to the ground in 1920.

Today, Hot Springs is a quiet place, save for the contented sighs of pleasure floating on the breeze from the direction of the spa. The town also has several charming B&Bs and a good restaurant or two. Visit Hot Springs' **website** (www.hotspringsnc.org) to learn more.

Hot Springs Spa & Campground (☎ 828-622-7676; 315 Bridge St; regular/riverside/deluxe campsite $10/20/25, cabins from $40; ☺ 9am-11pm) Pamper your weary traveler's bones at this backwoods spa 35 miles northwest of Asheville. Curative mineral baths in secluded outdoor settings start at $10 per hour; well-priced massage ($55 per hour) is also available. The campground is a pleasant, sprawling affair on the banks of the French Broad River. In addition to campsites, you'll find a variety of cabins ranging from basic to splendid.

Held annually in mid-June, the **Bluff Mountain Festival** (☎ 828-689-5507; www. main.nc.us/bluff; admission free) showcases some of the region's best traditional and bluegrass music. Attendees camp at the Hot Springs Campground and soak at the spa, enjoying great music and a nightly square dance. It's a hoot!

French Broad Rafting Expeditions (☎ 800-570-7238; www.frenchbroadrafting.com; US 25-70) offers morning, afternoon and evening sunset trips on the beautiful French Broad River, with both calm-water (adult/child $30/25) and white-water (adult/child $68/61) rafting trips. A shorter white-water route is offered at a savings (adult/child $45/39).

GETTING THERE & AWAY

From Asheville, take US 19-23 north from I-240, following signs to Mars Hill and Weaverville. Follow US 25-70 past Marshall and continue on the two-lane road as the highway takes a left turn over Laurel River toward Hot Springs and Newport.

PISGAH NATIONAL FOREST

South of Asheville, the Blue Ridge Parkway winds into the **Pisgah National Forest**. Railway magnate George Vanderbilt's purchase of 125,000 acres included Mt Pisgah (5749ft), at MP 408.6. A good 1.5-mile trail leads to the summit from the **Pisgah Inn** (p226) parking lot. The mountain takes its name from a smaller mountain near the Dead Sea in Jordan.

Several minor sights beckon visitors to the forest south of Mt Pisgah. At MP 412, the **Cold Mountain Overlook** affords a view of the 6030ft peak popularized in Charles Frazier's Civil War–era novel. The fact that no scenes were actually shot here for the movie still rubs locals the wrong way. Near the same spot you'll see a turnoff for US 276 east, which leads to the **Cradle of Forestry in America** (☎ 828-877-3130; adult/child 4-17 $5/2.50; ☾ mid-Apr–early Nov), the country's first forestry school (founded in 1898 by Vanderbilt). It's a good spot to take kids, with live demonstrations of basket weaving (among other things) and a short film. Guided tours through the surrounding woods are more interesting for grown-ups. At MP 412, take US 276 toward Brevard about 4 miles and follow signs for the Cradle.

North Carolina contains no less than 300 waterfalls, and this region is renowned for them. About a mile southeast of the forestry school on US 276, **Looking Glass Falls** is a 30ft-wide watery curtain that cascades 60ft into a ridiculously clear pool, accessible by a short set of steps.

Straddling the South Carolina border southwest of the forest, the magnificent cascades of **Whitewater Falls** are definitely worth a detour. The two-tiered falls tumble 411ft down a craggy mass; they're higher than Niagara Falls (but quite a bit narrower). From Brevard, take US 64 southwest for about 23 miles to NC 281 and turn south.

GEORGE GRANT, COURTESY OF NATIONAL PARK SERVICE

It's widely known that these mountains are old; what's less well known is that the southern Appalachians were once among the highest mountains on earth.

HISTORY

They date back perhaps 200 million years to a time when supercontinents collided, pushing the earth's crust upward to form high, craggy peaks. The softly smoothed mountains we enjoy today were sculpted over eons by abundant rain and erosion.

The glaciers that scoured much of North America never quite made it to the Smokies. Consequently, many species of flora and fauna that were displaced from their northern homes found refuge here. Moreover, the plants that thrive here are closely related to many species found across the Pacific, attesting to the ancient migration of flora from Asia via the Bering Strait land bridge.

Humans, too, made the journey. The first settlers in the southern mountains were aboriginal Native Americans who traced their lineage to the people who had crossed from Asia to North America as early as 50,000BC.

GREAT SMOKY MOUNTAINS NATIONAL PARK

Archaeologists conjecture that the first clans to put down roots in the Smokies arrived at least 11,000 years ago. The tribe known today as the Cherokee are believed to have been a breakaway clan of itinerant Iroquois who had foraged and hunted ever southward, eventually settling in the verdant, game-rich forests of the southern Appalachians. At one time their domain stretched all the way from northern Kentucky to South Carolina.

Oral tradition, handed down by generations of shamans, tells the story a different way: The ancient Cherokee traveled 'a long way' from 'a cold place.' In Cherokee terms the Iroquois are their 'uncle,' the Creeks and Chickasaw their 'elder brothers,' and they are the 'uncle' of the Choctaw.

The Cherokee people were comprised of seven distinct clans. Its towns constituted a confederacy of red (war) and white (peace) communities. The chiefs of the red towns answered to a supreme war chief, while the officials of the white towns were subordinate to the supreme peace chief. In general, the Cherokee lived in small, agriculture-based villages, favoring fertile river bottoms to high country. Their towns of log and mud cabins were centrally arranged around a public square and the council house. This large, seven-sided domed building was the heart and soul of the community, a place where civic meetings and religious ceremonies were conducted. It was here, also, where the sacred fire burned.

Searching for gold in 1540, Spanish explorer Hernando de Soto and a party of 600 soldiers passed through Cherokee territory. After this first encounter with Europeans, the Cherokee way of life would never be the same. As the legend goes, when de Soto asked the chiefs where the gold was, they pointed to the far western horizon, indicating that copious amounts of the stuff were waiting beyond the furthest mountain. This ploy worked but once.

Like many tribes, the Cherokee were a warrior culture and at various times battled the Americans, British, French and Spanish while simultaneously battling other Mississippi Valley tribes, such as the Creek, Iroquois, Seneca, Shawnee, Chickasaw and Catabwa. Wars mainly revolved around the struggle for land, a struggle the Cherokee ultimately lost against the relentless waves of new settlers.

Even so, the Cherokee readily embraced the weapons and tools brought by the European interlopers. In the early 1800s the Cherokee Nation adopted a written legal code and constitution and soon after elected a supreme court. The best-known Cherokee from this period is Sequoyah, who created an alphabet and system for writing the Cherokee language. Sequoyah's alphabet was composed of 86 characters. Within two years nearly all the Cherokee could read and write their language.

In spite of these advances, the fate of the Cherokee was already sealed. The infamous and tragic Trail of Tears in 1838 and 1839 represented the final defeat. Andrew Jackson's Indian removal policy forced 15,000 Cherokee off their bountiful ancient lands to the barren desolation of an Oklahoma reservation. More than 4000 Cherokee died from starvation, disease or utter exhaustion during this relocation at gunpoint. For some riveting and poetic reading on this sad part of American history, see John Ehle's *Trail of Tears: The Rise & Fall of the Cherokee Nation*.

Cherokee Indian Fair, 1937.

Sequoyah, holding a copy of the Cherokee alphabet.

GREAT SMOKY TIMELINE

7000BC–1540AD Native Americans inhabit southern Appalachia. Cherokee lands cover a large portion of what is now the southeastern United States.

1540 Searching for gold, Hernando de Soto and 600 Spanish soldiers arrive in the Great Smokies. Here they find the Cherokee, a branch of the Iroquois Nation.

1750 A smallpox epidemic kills roughly half the Cherokee people.

Late 1700s The last wild elk in the Great Smokies is killed by a hunter.

1795 The Hughes and Mingus families claim homesteads by the Oconaluftee River near modern-day Cherokee.

1814 The Caldwell family clears the first homestead in Cataloochee Valley.

1819 After decades of incursions and resistance, the Cherokee relinquish claim to the last of their lands in the Smoky Mountains.

1821 Families begin settling in Cades Cove.

1827 The Cherokee Nation – with a constitution and code of law – is established. The South's first superhighway, the Buncombe Turnpike, is completed, connecting South Carolina to Tennessee and passing through Asheville.

1830 Cades Cove population swells to 271.

1838–1839 Fifteen thousand Cherokees are forcibly moved from the southeastern US to the Oklahoma Territory along the Trail of Tears. About 1000 flee into the mountains, hiding out in the lands between Newfound Gap and Mt Guyot.

1850 Cades Cove population is 685.

1861–1865 The Civil War divides the allegiances of those in the Great Smoky Mountains. A majority oppose seceding from the Union. Soldiers from both sides of the conflict often raid farms and homesteads for food, livestock and supplies.

1870 Cable Mill is built in Cades Cove.

1886 Mingus Mill is built in Oconaluftee Valley.

1889 The Eastern Band of the Cherokee – those who avoided relocation to Oklahoma – gain charter to the 56,000-acre Qualla Boundary Cherokee Reservation, along the southern border of what is now Great Smoky Mountains National Park.

1900 Cades Cove population reaches 1250.

About 1000 Cherokee managed to avoid this disaster, either on legal grounds or because they managed to escape the great roundup by hiding out deep in the Smoky Mountains. The leftover band of North Carolina Cherokee struggled for years for official acknowledgment. During the Civil War some fought with the Confederacy.

In 1866 the state of North Carolina finally recognized the remaining Cherokee as permanent residents. In 1868 the first council of the Eastern Cherokee

GREAT SMOKY TIMELINE

1913 Horace Kephart publishes *Our Southern Highlanders*, a widely read biography about the people of the southern Appalachians. Kephart's work plays a vital role in the eventual formation of Great Smoky Mountains National Park.

1903–1933 Lumber companies begin operations throughout the Smokies. Railroads extend deep into the mountains, making timber readily available. By 1934 two-thirds of what is now Great Smoky Mountains National Park is logged.

1933–1942 At the behest of President Franklin Roosevelt, the Civilian Conservation Corps (CCC) reforest clear-cut lands, restore historic structures, build hundreds of miles of roads and trails and make countless other improvements to what will become the national park.

1934 Great Smoky Mountains National Park is established.

1938 The last tree felled by a logger is cut near Townsend. Parkland shows the ravages of clear-cut logging. Streams are filled with silt; some are devoid of life. Deer, bear and other wild game have nearly been hunted out of existence.

1940 The CCC completes Newfound Gap Rd, and hundreds of cars travel up the dirt motorway to Newfound Gap to witness Roosevelt's dedication ceremony.

1950 The first performance of the historical drama *Unto These Hills* is staged at the outdoor Mountainside Theatre in Cherokee.

1983 Following 50 years of protection, fertile soil and substantial annual rainfall have spurred large-scale regeneration, returning the forests and mountains within the 800-square-mile park to a pristine state reminiscent of pre-Columbian America. This phenomenal biodiversity earns the park a World Heritage Site designation.

1985 The National Park Service reintroduces the peregrine falcon into the park.

1988 Great Smoky is designated an International Biosphere Reserve.

2001 The National Park Service reintroduces elk into Cataloochee Valley.

2005 With nearly 10 million annual visitors, Great Smoky is America's most-visited national park.

was held, and Flying Squirrel was chosen as chief. The group became incorporated in 1889 as the Eastern Band of Cherokee Indians.

With the advent of the timber industry in the region, the Cherokee turned to logging to prop up their economy, and the forests that had sustained them for so long were largely denuded. But the opening of Great Smoky Mountains National Park in 1940 changed all that. As hundreds of thousands of visitors descended on the region, the Cherokee tried their hand at tourism. The

Archery contest, Cherokee Indian Fair, 1937.

Cherokee Historical Association was organized in 1948 and two years later premiered its outdoor drama, *Unto These Hills*. In 1952 the association opened the Oconaluftee Indian Village. Today tourism is the primary industry in the Qualla Boundary area, providing jobs for some 65 percent of the local population. The Eastern Band of the Cherokee now numbers nearly 10,000, most of whom live on the reservation.

A HEADY BREW OF SETTLERS

The first Europeans to arrive in the Blue Ridge were English, Irish, Scotch-Irish, Welsh, Dutch, German Protestants and Protestant French Huguenots. While each immigrant group had specific motivations for leaving Europe, they shared a fervent desire for religious and economic freedom and self-determination in the New World.

Those who put down roots in the southern Appalachians in the late 18th century found a fertile but isolated wilderness. As more and more immigrants arrived, they found the choicest lands already claimed and had to make do with the steep slopes and remote hollers (hollows) that earlier arrivals had rejected. Regional biographer Horace Kephart described the cultural isolation of these early settlers in his landmark 1913 tome, *Our Southern Highlanders*:

> Conceive a shipload of emigrants cast away on some unknown island, far from the regular track of vessels, and left there for five or six generations, unaided and untroubled by the growth of civilization. Among the descendants of such a company we would expect to find customs and ideas unaltered from the time of their forefathers. And that is just what we do find today among our castaways in the sea of mountains. Time has lingered in Appalachia. The mountain folk still live in the eighteenth century. The progress of mankind from that age to this is no heritage of theirs.

In retrospect, Kephart's evocative consideration was perhaps a mite overstated. While the mountain people were indeed isolated, their lives where indelibly shaped by political and economic forces of the world at large.

Completed in 1827, the Buncombe Turnpike brought goods – and even the region's first wave of tourists – to the region. Connecting South Carolina to Tennessee, the toll road transformed Asheville, North Carolina, from a lonely backwater into a thriving supply center for travelers. While plenty of livestock drovers, gold prospectors and itinerant families plied the roadway, it was hogs that created the biggest traffic jams. One year, more than 150,000 porkers were recorded passing through Asheville – enough to earn the town the unfortunate moniker Hogtown (an epithet that Asheville wasn't able to shake until George Vanderbilt arrived decades later to change the tenor of the place). Restaurants and inns opened along the turnpike, many with special holding pens for livestock, and Hot Springs, North Carolina, became the region's first tourist attraction. As always, travelers carried with them news, goods and ideas from other territories.

In the mid-1850s the communities of southern Appalachia began to shake the mantle of 'frontier outpost' in favor of the small-town solidity that characterized other rural areas of the young nation. In the Great Smokies, Cades Cove, Cataloochee, Greenbrier and many other small bastions of civilization prospered as the fertile, loamy soil proved well suited to cultivation. Schools, shops and churches – the benchmarks of any healthy community – brought a steadfast sense of civic pride and continuity. Between 1830 and 1850 the population in Cades Cove surged from 44 households and 271 residents to a whopping 70 households and 451 residents.

Family of George H Caldwell of Cataloochee, 1902.

Life in Cades Cove was not easy; all who lived there depended on subsistence farming to survive. Most arrived from Virginia or central North Carolina with a single wagon or packhorse, carrying nothing but simple tools, clothing and a few treasured items. They cleared the forests and built cabins, barns and fences from the felled trees. Each family had to provide nearly all the food for itself and its livestock. Every member who could walk was ceaselessly involved in the cultivation and preservation of food, from the earliest days of the spring planting to the final days of the autumn harvest. In winter families made do with stored grains, canned vegetables and dried meat. Few goods were available to buy, and settlers rarely used currency anyway. Most transactions were conducted by the well established rules of the barter system.

The most important regional crops were those that put bread on the table. Farmers cultivated wheat, rye, barley and oats, but the most important crop of all was corn. Cornbread, corn mush, spoon bread or hoecakes were served at nearly every meal. But turning harvested corn into a meal required ingenuity, and the settlers provided such by devising gristmills that harnessed the region's most plentiful source of power: the water surging down from every mountain. Almost immediately upon arrival, settlers in Cades Cove began building water-powered mills on nearly every large

Little Greenbrier School, 1936.

creek in the area. Today two of these mills remain in Great Smoky: Mingus Mill, near the Oconaluftee Visitor Center, and Cable Mill in Cades Cove. At both places, you can hear the creaking gears and humming millstones even today, as millers continue to grind grain in the time-honored fashion.

THE RAVAGES OF WAR

During the Civil War, despite living well within the boundaries of the Confederacy, most residents of southern Appalachia held pro-Union views. The reasons for this political perspective are complex. Many residents were descended from patriots who had fought for American independence from the British, and they could not support the geographic division of the United States. Few farms in the region were large enough to support slavery, and therefore mountain people were not inclined to shed blood defending the institution. Moreover, the people here shared a common resentment of the powerful slaveholders of the lowlands, whose political clout resulted in self-serving laws that did not favor the mountain dwellers.

While the Blue Ridge held considerable strategic importance to the Confederacy, and many large-scale confrontations between the two armies erupted in Virginia's Shenandoah and Luray Valleys, inhabitants of the Great Smokies mainly had to contend with skirmishes between Confederate militia and Yankee raiders. Particularly irksome was the rise of terrorism by 'bushwhackers,' lawless men who claimed to be serving the interests of the Union through the pillaging of private homes and farms. As the Civil War entered its fourth year, lawlessness descended on the mountains and random murders became commonplace. As one Confederate officer reported to the North Carolina governor, the 'bushwhackers' would 'enter houses violently, breaking open every door and helping themselves to what suited their various fancies – not provisions only, but everything, from horses down to ladies' breast pins.'

While this sort of senseless violence waned at the end of the war, the region continued to suffer the effects of economic deprivation. Many men never returned, and many who did make it home found their mountain farms destroyed and their families suffering. Economic recovery was slow in coming, but the resilient mountain people ultimately found the means to survive by relying once again on the bountiful natural resources of the mountains and valleys.

Stills confiscated within the park by park rangers, 1935.

LEE EXLINE, COURTESY OF NATIONAL PARK SERVICE

MOONSHINE RIVER

Before the Civil War, the federal and state governments meddled little in the affairs of people living in the Smokies, but after Reconstruction, new taxes and demands on the region's natural resources were the source of much consternation on the part of the mountain folk. The matter that riled people the most, however, concerned a particular practice that had flourished in the hollers and coves since the earliest settlers brought in their first crop of corn. We're speaking, of course, about 'the ancient art of the hills,' the distilling of moonshine whiskey.

When the federal government first announced that Americans producing homemade liquor were subject to taxation, the people of the Blue Ridge were incensed and refused to pay. In turn, the government sent armed agents into the mountains to enforce compliance, spurring many violent episodes. The moonshiners – many of who had learned the craft directly from their Scotch-Irish forebears – considered whiskey distillation a cultural birthright and vowed to protect the activity by concealing their stills ever deeper in the backcountry.

In their flagrant defiance of the federal government, moonshiners became folk heroes. In the days before Prohibition, Horace Kephart wrote:

The little moonshiner...fights fair, according to his code, and single-handedly against tremendous odds.... There is nothing between him and the whole power of the Federal Government, except his own wits and a well-worn Winchester or muzzle loader.... This man is usually a good enough citizen in other ways, of decent standing in his own community, and a right good fellow toward all of the world, save revenue officers.

At the stroke of midnight on January 17, 1920, evangelist Billy Sunday celebrated the beginning of Prohibition with a sermon predicting that, with the eradication of liquor, 'The slums will soon be only a memory. We will turn our prisons into factories and our jails into storehouses and corn-cribs.... Hell will be forever for rent.' This was naught but wishful thinking: In the year 1925 alone, Prohibition agents seized nearly 30,000 stills and arrested more than 76,000 people! Prior to Prohibition, Blue Ridge moonshiners distributed their product mainly to friends and neighbors, but now, in response to the burning national demand for white lightning, they increased production and initiated many eager young scofflaws into the brotherhood. Put into the awkward position of enforcing a reviled law, many local sheriffs refused to arrest moonshiners. After all, some of them were kin.

WHITE LIGHTNING: THE PROS & CONS

'Here's to Old Corn Likker,
Whitens the teeth,
Perfumes the breath.
And makes childbirth a pleasure.'
–North Carolina folk saying

When you absorb a deep swig of it, you have all the sensations of having swallowed a lighted kerosene lamp.
– Irwin S Cobb

THE FORESTS FELLED

As the 19th century came to a close, much of the Great Smokies remained heavily forested despite two centuries of settlement. This was about to change. The expansive forests of the northeast, from Maine to Ohio, had been heavily logged for centuries and were largely denuded. Formerly discouraged by inaccessible terrain, the logging companies took new inspiration from the advent of industrial railroading and began to look greedily upon the old-growth stands of virgin forest that blanketed the southern mountains. As companies snapped up cheap land in the Smokies and railroad beds reached deep into the mountains, logging began in earnest.

In 1903 Little River Lumber Company built a high-capacity sawmill at Tuckaleechee and changed the name of the town to Townsend. Over the next 30 years one of the greatest remaining virgin forests on earth would

Load of logs at Elkmont, 1925.

be cut down to the nubbin and hauled away. Only the trunks of the trees were taken; everything else was left to dry in the sun. Oftentimes, heavy equipment would spark fires that set the mountains ablaze for months. When the rains came, they brought great floods and winds, which scoured the land into bare

A young hunter poses next to a fresh-cut chestnut stump during the early days of logging, 1906.

cliffs and gullies. Once bountiful cropland and forests were gutted and desecrated.

To be sure, the arrival of large-scale logging provided many jobs and eased the economic deprivation of the region. As the forces of industrialization changed the rural landscape across America, many communities once and for all abandoned subsistence farming as a means of survival. The forests and farmlands were no longer able to provide for swelling populations, and in the end people desperate to make a living turned to selling the forest itself. By 1930 only the most remote and inaccessible regions of the Great Smokies remained unlogged.

THE NATIONAL PARK CURE

Even as the lumber trains carted off the forest, on their return they brought something new: tourists. In 1904 one prominent visitor, Horace Kephart, took up residence in Bryson City, North Carolina. He arrived to a largely primeval wilderness, but over the next 27 years until his death, he would witness the wholesale destruction that logging wrought on his beloved mountains. Joining with a group of prominent, forward-thinking Knoxvillians, Kephart devoted his remaining years to saving the desecrated landscape by promoting the 'national park idea.' The federal government, wanting to replicate the popular success of the western national parks, was receptive to

HILLBILLY BLUES

While Horace Kephart's *Our Southern Highlanders* is still considered a classic for its fascinating attention to the daily lives and folklore of the mountain people, others decry it as an early source of negative 'hillbilly' stereotypes. Widely embraced by popular culture, the hillbilly stereotype would later be gleefully enacted in television shows such as *The Beverly Hillbillies* and *The Dukes of Hazzard* and in films like *Deliverance*. With but a few exceptions, Hollywood's lazy habit has been to depict the men of the southern mountains as thick-headed, with proclivities for alcoholism and indolence. In turn, women have been commonly portrayed as wild and hopelessly naïve. In the Burt Reynolds film *Deliverance* the hillbilly stereotype reaches its apotheosis. The film's most notorious line – 'Squeal like a pig!' – was uttered by a vile mountain man in an act of unspeakable violence; soon the phrase entered the popular lexicon as a joke about loathsome redneck behavior. As the hillbilly stereotype began to take on a menacing veneer in popular culture, the proud heritage of the Appalachian people was due for an image makeover.

As a visitor to Great Smoky Mountains National Park, you will have an opportunity to see firsthand the stuff that mountain people are truly made of. As you learn their stories and visit their churches, schoolhouses, homes and mills, you'll likely agree that the designation 'hillbilly' does not do justice to the grit, intelligence and resourcefulness of 'our southern highlanders.'

the idea. The first hurdle was fundraising, as the government declined to contribute funds for land acquisition. Private citizens and the states of North Carolina and Tennessee contributed, but it was the $5 million contribution by John D Rockefeller Jr that sealed the deal.

Still, the park idea had plenty of detractors, not the least of whom were the people whose small farms lay within the proposed boundaries. Initially, officials promised these families that their homes and communities would not be affected by the creation of the park. But as the park dream became a reality, most residents were evicted under the authority of 'eminent domain,' much as the Cherokee had been ousted from the region a century before. They were compensated for their land, however, and many moved into surrounding communities, ultimately setting up businesses that catered to the new influx of tourists.

In 1934 an act of Congress created Great Smoky Mountains National Park. It would be another six years, however, before the park welcomed visitors. In the interim the Civilian Conservation Corps (CCC), a work program ordered by President Franklin Roosevelt and directed by the US Army, built trails, roads, bridges, campsites and visitor centers. On September 2, 1940, Roosevelt himself presided over the park's first traffic jam as he led a caravan of cars to the heights of Newfound Gap, where he officially dedicated the park.

GREAT SMOKY TODAY

By any measure Great Smoky Mountains National Park has been one of the great success stories of the National Park Service. Today nearly 10 million annual visitors enjoy Great Smoky, making it the most-visited national park in the US. This piece of trivia, however, is by no means the true measure of the park's worth. Great Smoky's early superintendents were faced with managing land that had been despoiled by logging and had become a hostile environment for a great number of native species. Anyone who has walked one of the park's trails into the unbelievably lush and fertile backcountry – or read about the successful reintroduction of elk, peregrine falcons or river otters – soon realizes that nature has reclaimed and restored these lands to a state approaching the primeval.

This is not to say that Great Smoky doesn't continue to face daunting challenges, such as air pollution, traffic congestion and the continued destruction of high-elevation forests by persistent pests. However, the park has largely lived up to its mission to provide enlightened stewardship of our treasured national lands.

FOR FUTURE GENERATIONS

In his eloquent farewell letter, the first director of the National Park Service expressed his hopes for future generations of National Park Service personnel:

Oppose with all your strength and power all proposals to penetrate your wilderness regions with motorways and other symbols of modern mechanization. Keep large sections of primitive country free from the influence of destructive civilization. Keep these bits of primitive America for those who seek peace and rest in the silent places; keep them for the hardy climbers of the crags and peaks; keep them for the horseman and the pack train; keep them for the scientist and student of nature; keep them for all who would use their minds and hearts to know what God had created. Remember, once opened, they can never be wholly restored to primeval charm and grandeur.

– Horace M Albright

SHENANDOAH NATIONAL PARK

The roots of Shenandoah National Park's humble beginnings stretch long and deep, like the old-growth forests and clear mountain streams running through the park today. Creation of the park wasn't without controversy, but it provided a much-needed boost to the Virginia economy and to the mission of environmental conservationists. Shenandoah remains one of the prettiest national parks in the country.

EARLY INHABITANTS

Native Americans, especially of the Monocan and Manahoac tribes, were undoubtedly Shenandoah's earliest inhabitants, arriving some 11,000 years ago. According to one curious theory, Big Meadows was formed when Indian tribes set fire to clear the land, fostering berry growth and encouraging wild game to wander through in the early hours near dawn. Grazing bison and elk kept the meadow clear until the arrival of the Europeans, who then used the land for their cattle, and many of the Native Americans' primitive trails became well-trodden routes later traveled by Europeans during their 200-year settlement of the area.

The area played host to its earliest 'hiker' as far back as the late 1600s. German physician John Lederer, looking for a passage to the Indian Ocean, made several explorations of the Shenandoah Valley, in what is now the cen-

Road constuction courtesy of the Civilian Conservation Corps, 1935.

tral section of Shenandoah National Park. Though he was unsuccessful in his quest, Lederer's fluency in Indian languages and customs allowed him to travel unscathed through the Virginia mountains; he made friends and bartered with native tribes as he went. Lederer's maps and journals were later published in London in 1672.

Further exploration of the valley took place throughout the 1700s, as settlers established working mountain communities. The scarcity of available land in the valley forced many early settlers into the mountains, where they used natural earth and water resources to create small industries like gristmills, quarries and forges. Churches and schoolhouses weren't far behind, and though conditions were harsh for most of the year, these mountain folk established their own identity apart from settlers at lower elevations.

The Civil War overwhelmed the Shenandoah Valley; more than 300 skirmishes took place in the area, especially during Confederate General Stonewall Jackson's crucial Valley Campaign of 1862. Battles raged in Front Royal, as well as in neighboring Winchester (which changed hands more than 70 times during the war), in New Market and along a corridor that parallels present-day Skyline Drive. Though no battles were formally fought within the boundaries of today's national park, Union and Confederate armies used the thick forests and canopies, the area's agricultural bounty and the mountaintop views of the valley below to assist in fighting the war.

The war destroyed farms in the Shenandoah Valley, and after the fighting stopped, many families moved to higher ground to make their living. The population in the mountains reached its peak in 1900, but as Shenandoah National Park became a reality, the rural community shrunk to a mere 500 families, many of whom had no choice but to sell their land to the government and relocate to the valley below. Remnants of several homesteads have been preserved and are still visible today along Skyline Drive (Brinegar, Corbin and Nicholson Cabins, for example).

SHENANDOAH BECOMES A NATIONAL PARK

Though the idea to create a national park in southern Appalachia was proposed in the early 1900s, it wasn't until 1926 that Congress authorized the establishment of Shenandoah National Park, with the unusual stipulation that land couldn't be purchased by the government; instead, private donations and so-called condemnation laws provided the government with a backhanded way to get its hands on land that was judged to be 'condemned' (always a questionable verdict, in those times).

Foundation of the park stirred enormous controversy among local landowners and families who didn't want their way of life disrupted by tourists or

SHENANDOAH TIMELINE

1750 Settlers move into the hollows of the Shenandoah Valley.

1888 The development of what ultimately becomes Skyland Resort begins; the early camp promotes nature adventures in the area.

1924 Shenandoah Valley Inc is established to push for creation of a national park in the Shenandoah region.

1925 The new Shenandoah National Park Association begins to raise funds and collect donated lands for the proposed national park.

1926 US Congress authorizes the creation of a 521,000-acre Shenandoah National Park.

1927 Just established, the Potomac Appalachian Trail Club (PATC) promotes the Appalachian Trail (AT) and the future national park.

1931 Construction of Skyline Drive begins.

1932 The park's acreage is reduced to 160,000.

1933 The Civilian Conservation Corps (CCC) arrives and helps to build park facilities.

1935 US Congress officially opens Shenandoah National Park in December; in January 1936 the official dedication ceremony takes place at Big Meadows.

1935–1938 Resettlement occurs around the boundaries of Skyline Drive.

1964 US Congress signs the Wilderness Act, protecting some portions of Shenandoah from the impact of activities like hunting.

1996 Tropical Storm Fran pummels a section of the park, creating devastating mudslides that destroy part of the forest.

2003 Shenandoah National Park gets its mug on a specialty license plate.

2004 An unusually active hurricane season sends several storms inland, damaging small sections of the park. A renovation project begins to turn the Panorama building into a visitor education center.

CCC enrollee wearing standard-issue work uniform, ca 1935.

their unspoiled land ruined by urbanization. Many were forced to sell at ridiculously cheap prices. In 1931, upon orders by the US Department of Agriculture's Bureau of Public Roads, surveyors plotted the area stretching between the Blue Ridge Mountains and President Herbert Hoover's mountain fishing camp. Ultimately Congress would order construction of what would be a 'skyline drive' along the spine of the Blue Ridge Mountains.

Construction of this mountain road began in 1931. A small portion of Skyline Drive officially opened on October 22, 1932, while the final section was completed on August 29, 1939, at a hefty final price tag of $5 million. During the Great Depression the CCC played a major role in building the road and overlooks, as well as the public facilities and signage that remain today throughout the park. Shenandoah National Park was established in December 1935, and President Roosevelt officially dedicated the park the following year.

In September 1997 Shenandoah National Park's Skyline Drive earned an illustrious place on the National Register of Historic Places, thanks to its 400-plus structures dating from the 1930s.

Today the park encompasses more than 196,000 acres, nearly 80,000 of which fall under the National Wilderness Preservation System. It welcomes more than 1.5 million visitors annually, who come either for the brilliant fall colors, quiet winter solitude, spring wildflower fields or cooling waterfall mist on a hot summer day.

THE FIRST RESORT

In an area known for its abundance of copper, timber and charcoal, the Stony Man Mountain Tract drew investors from cities like Boston and Washington, DC. One such group, which included George Pollock, purchased almost 5500 acres of land in order to establish a copper mine.

On a visit to the Stony Man Mountain Tract, Pollock's son, George Freeman Pollock, returned with visions of a grand resort in the wild mountains. Sensing a moneymaking idea, dad backed his son, and in 1888 the junior Pollock began fundraising. In 1893 George Freeman Pollock suffered several big blows, including the death of his father and, with it, the loss of financial support to fund his resort. But he didn't give up. The following year Pollock threw a grand camping party at Stony Man Camp, inviting friends, family and neighbors to experience nature up close and at its most wild – only 14 people made that initial trip.

But, between 1900 and 1920 Pollock built up the resort, adding a dining hall, tennis courts, a bathhouse, a recreational hall, bungalows and even a gas plant to power the facilities until electricity arrived in 1920. In 1937, after the opening of Shenandoah National Park, the Virginia Sky-Line Company renamed the camp Skyland and assumed operations of the resort. Under new management, Skyland Resort opened in 1939, and guests paid $9.50 a week for a true mountain lodging and dining experience – today's travelers will unfortunately have to dig a little deeper in their wallets to stay here (p183).

CCC AS S.O.S

With more than 13.5 million Americans out of work following the Great Depression, President Roosevelt's ambitious public works project couldn't have come at a better time for the young men of the rural Virginia mountains. The Civilian Conservation Corps (CCC) gave unmarried boys ages 18 to 25 the best opportunity to earn money for their families. Boys could join organized work camps where clothes, room and board were paid for by the government. They earned $30 a month – $25 of which went to the boys' families. The young men of the CCC could also take classes while learning skills on the job.

Of the half million boys in the CCC across the country, more than 100,000 were assigned work in Virginia's forests, parks and historic sites, including Shenandoah National Park. Not only are most facilities still standing, but much of the park signage is a visual testament to these young men and their arduous work.

THE BLUE RIDGE PARKWAY

Another ambitious CCC project, the Blue Ridge Parkway was originally conceived as merely a pastoral link between Shenandoah and Great Smoky Mountains National Parks. But after Franklin Roosevelt visited the brand-new Shenandoah National Park, it wasn't hard to persuade him to initiate an ambitious new construction project connecting two treasured national parks. Today the road's 469 miles are a living museum of master craftsmanship, engineering marvels and restored homesteads, not to mention one heck of a scenic drive.

Planning a grand Blue Ridge Parkway was no easy feat, requiring a visionary who could seamlessly blend modern technology and unspoiled environment. That person was landscape architect Stanley Abbot, a young Cornell graduate with a not-so-shabby résumé; his previous projects included Central Park and the lawn at Biltmore Estate.

Everyone agreed that the Parkway should glide through southern Virginia, but where to go from there caused a bitter debate between Tennessee and North Carolina, with both states coveting the enormous economic gains the roadway would bring. Ultimately North Carolina won: Interior Secretary Harold Ickes decided that the existence of two national forests in that state (Mt Pisgah and Nantahala) would make for an easier established route. Plus, North Carolina was just more darn scenic than its neighbor – a sentiment highly contested by Tennessee.

It took two years to design the twisting roadway, as Abbott's visions of a smooth, paved surface and unobtrusive visitor facilities beside centuries-old farmland and homesteads slowly became a reality. Construction began in 1935, and a series of CCC camps created numerous job opportunities for the poor Appalachian communities. Harsh weather conditions, a lack of naps, laborious work and a scarcity of machinery took a toll on CCC workers, many of whom were nonetheless grateful to be employed during tough economic times. Men hollowed out tunnels with bare hands and lifted heavy rock on their backs, which made for many painstaking days. The detailed stonemasonry on tunnel entrances and overlook walls is a testament to their fierce perseverance.

After the CCC disbanded in 1942, leaving the Parkway with a significantly decreased workforce, construction was sporadic at best. World War II slowed the project even more.

In 1967 only a 7.5-mile section of missing pavement at Grandfather Mountain stood in the way of the Parkway being one continuous road. Drivers could travel the Parkway but had to be diverted 14 miles around the mountain. Grandfather Mountain presented a series of problems; few could agree on how to create a route without disturbing the natural environment, and the government and the owner of the mountain clashed over property rights. Eventually, construction of a sweeping, double S-curve bridge, hugging the rugged mountainside at milepost 304, was completed in 1983. The impressive Linn Cove Viaduct, considered a great engineering feat, became known as the 'missing link' and today remains one of the most photogenic spots along the Parkway.

After 52 years of on-again, off-again construction, the Parkway officially opened September 11, 1987, as one contiguous road. With no commercial vehicles or signage allowed, the Parkway allows visitors to enjoy the unspoiled environment the way nature intended (albeit in a car). Stanley Abbott would surely be amazed at the stunning popularity of this 'mere link,' which is one of the country's most traveled and best-loved routes.

The geology of the Blue Ridge Province is complex, old and hidden under a cloak of verdant vegetation.

GEOLOGY

The true lay of the land is hard to read, and the geologic story has had to be assembled with bits and pieces of clues. This is a region where billion-year-old rocks were crumpled into a tightly folded fist by the collision of North America and Africa about 200 million years ago. Rock formations and individual rocks themselves record the impact of this collision in their mangled strata. In cross section the mountains look something like a bookshelf that has been crushed from above, leaving vertical or near-vertical layers crumpled into an indecipherable mess – except that in this case the layers were lying horizontally and the crushing pressure came from the side as the edge of the continent was shoved 160 miles westward.

THE BLUE RIDGE PROVINCE

Geologists collectively refer to the mountain ranges that stretch from Newfoundland to Alabama as the Blue Ridge Province, named for its characteristic bluish haze. Within the Blue Ridge Province, the scenic Blue Ridge Parkway connects Shenandoah and Great Smoky Mountains National Parks. West of the province, beyond a wide trough known as the Great Valley, stretches the Ridge and Valley Province, characterized by a dramatic landscape of parallel ridges and valleys. To the east lies the Piedmont Province, with its low rolling landscape. Together these three geologic provinces (plus another further west, known as the Appalachian Plateaus) form the **Appalachian Mountains**.

Rising as high as 4000ft in the Shenandoah region and topping 6000ft in the Smokies, the mountains of the Blue Ridge Province may receive more than 100 inches of precipitation a year. Thousands of miles of streams create a highly dissected landscape with many hidden hollows that reveal something of the nature of the underlying rocks. Streams west of the main ridgelines follow a 'trellis drainage' pattern, in which roughly parallel streams cut gorges in soft layers of rock that are sandwiched between more resistant layers. To the east, rocks of uniform hardness force streams to meander across the landscape, creating a 'dendritic drainage' pattern, with forks like tree branches.

The intense pressure that crumpled this landscape into a convoluted series of folds also created deep cracks, or **faults**, that run throughout the region.

FOOL'S GOLD

One of the Great Smoky Mountains' most distinctive rock formations is the **Anakeesta Formation**, named after the Anakeesta Ridge. Old timers referred to it as 'slaterock.' Glowing with a rusty or dark slatelike color, these rocks originated from metamorphosed silt and mud that accumulated in the Lapetus Sea, an ancient precursor of the Atlantic Ocean. Structurally, they are composed of thin layers of shale that break easily and are dangerous to climb on. The Anakeesta Formation is magnificently exposed at the Chimney Tops, where a trail from Newfound Gap Rd ascends 2 miles to the top of vertically aligned layers of slate.

You may notice a musty, sulfurlike smell around these rocks. The Anakeesta Formation is rich in sulfide-bearing minerals, including pyrite ('fools gold'). Leaching out in water, these minerals create sulfuric acids that can harm plants and animals downstream. In 1963 Anakeesta stones were inadvertently used on a local road for fill, and the acid runoff killed all the fish for 3 miles downstream.

Faults continue to shape these mountains, as internal forces within the crust are relieved along fault lines. This combination of powerful pressures and faults has created a landscape of rock formations that overlap each other like shingles on a roof, often with older layers thrust atop younger ones. In several places the older, uppermost rocks have eroded away, opening windows down onto younger rocks below. These unique pockets are known as **coves**, which tend to have deep, fertile soils resulting from the breakdown of limestone within the younger rocks.

Many of the formations in the Blue Ridge Province are composed of very old **metamorphic rocks**, meaning that they initially formed as one type of rock and were then transformed by intense heat and/or pressure into another type of rock. Some of these original rocks were volcanic (igneous) in nature, while others began as layers of accumulated sediments. **Metamorphosed sedimentary rocks** are the dominant rock types in Great Smoky Mountains National Park, while Shenandoah National Park is characterized by outcroppings of **metamorphosed igneous rocks**. The differing geology is due to the regional trend of older rocks to the east and younger to the west, arranged in tilted folds along a series of fault lines. Though not a perfect explanation, one way to think of the arrangement is that the old foundation, which was uplifted in Shenandoah, subsequently eroded and accumulated in the basin that became the Great Smoky Mountains to the west.

To better understand this complex saga, pick up copies of *A Roadside Guide to the Geology of Great Smoky Mountains National Park* by Harry Moore and *Geology of the Shenandoah National Park, Virginia* by Thomas Gathright.

EVOLUTION OF A LANDSCAPE

At first glance the Appalachian Mountains look like a homogenous line on a map, but they are actually composed of very different types of rocks of varying ages. Sections of the range were uplifted by different forces and at different times. The geologic stories of Great Smoky Mountains and Shenandoah National Parks are related but dramatically different.

The oldest known rocks in the region – **basement rocks** of granite, gneiss and schist – formed under intense pressure and heat more than a billion years ago. These were deep igneous rocks that required more than 300 million years of uplift and erosion before reaching the Earth's surface. Scarcely revealed in the southeast corner of Great Smoky Mountains National Park, these ancient rocks form the bulk of the Blue Ridge in Shenandoah National Park. Examples in Shenandoah include the whitish granite boulders of Old Rag Mountain and the greenish or bluish-gray Pedlar Formation at the Marys Rock Tunnel parking overlook.

Rocks that form the hills in Great Smoky Mountains National Park represent the next stage in the geologic storyline. Between one billion and 600 million years ago, a massive quantity of pebbles, sand and mud eroded from elevated landmasses into a relatively shallow ocean. Up to 50,000ft of sediments accumulated, until tremendous pressure, combined with the chemical action of saltwater, cemented the sediment into rocks. These mineralized layers are now known collectively as the **Ocoee Supergroup**, which includes diverse subgroupings. For example, the Great Smoky Group of pebbly conglomerates forms the bulk of the Great Smokies; these rocks appear along the highway from Sugarlands to Newfound Gap and on to Smokemont. For a completely different kind of rock, check out the rust-colored, thinly layered slate of the **Anakeesta Formation** along the Alum Cave Trail. And ledges of highly erosion-resistant **Thunderhead Sandstone** are visible at Laurel Falls and at many other falls in the park.

During the same time period, basement rock around Shenandoah National Park was releasing lava flows and ash through cracks in the ancient hills. All but the very highest peaks were eventually submerged in about 2000ft of

A ROCK PRIMER

Based on their origins and structure, rocks fall into one of three classes: sedimentary, igneous or metamorphic.

Sedimentary rocks originate as vast accumulations of sediments and particles that become cemented together. Sediments can be transported by streams or by wind and are deposited in layers that preserve many features showing how they were deposited (though in the Appalachians, these layers have become contorted and twisted almost beyond recognition). Sedimentary rocks are the dominant rocks of the Great Smoky Mountains, but because nearly all of them have undergone some metamorphosis over the millennia, the line between sedimentary and metamorphic rock is somewhat blurred. Unaltered sedimentary limestone and shale are present in Cades Cove.

Igneous rocks arise from molten magma that has either cooled underground or erupted to the surface as lava or volcanic ash. These rocks are rare in the Great Smokies but widespread in the Blue Ridge Mountains. Volcanic rocks interspersed with sedimentary rocks cap most of the higher peaks along the northern and central portion of Skyline Drive.

Metamorphic rocks are those that start out as either sedimentary or igneous rocks and then transform under intense heat or pressure into other rock types. Due to the great age of the rocks in the Appalachian region, metamorphic rocks are widespread, particularly in the Smokies. Their hard, crystalline structure makes them resistant to erosion. Examples include gneiss, schist and granite.

volcanic material. This congregation of a dozen or more flows is called the **Catoctin Formation**. From a high point like the crest of Stony Man, you can see the lava flows as a series of benches stepping down toward Skyland Lodge. About 80 percent of these rocks consist of dark green (or even purplish) **greenstones**, which now form many of the park's higher ridges. More or less vertical bands of greenstone indicate places where the basement rock split apart 700 million years ago and allowed lava to flow upward. The Ridge Trail to the summit of Old Rag follows one of these bands for a stretch, and because the band of greenstone erodes faster than the surrounding granite walls, the process creates a hallway-like cavity through the center of the harder rock.

WATERFALLS

Despite the Appalachian Mountains' great age and the astonishing power of streams to cut through rock, one band of rocks has proven remarkably resilient to these forces. Almost as if baffled by the anomaly, streams must flow over the top of **Thunderhead Sandstone** rather than digging down into it. In the process, however, they create some of the most beautiful features in Great Smoky Mountains National Park – its many diverse waterfalls. Nearly every waterfall in the park results from water cascading over a band of Thunderhead Sandstone as it rushes down a canyon.

Popular falls include Laurel Falls, Ramsey Cascades, Grotto Falls and the Place of a Thousand Drips. Each is a unique expression of land giving shape to water.

As the period of volcanic activity came to a close, the region experienced a gentle downwarping, or sinking, of the Earth's crust over the course of 150 million years (from about 600 million to 450 million years ago). From the east, the edges of a Cambrian sea advanced westward. Sandy beaches and silty ocean bottoms covered much of the landscape and left a new generation of sedimentary deposits. Accumulations of **limestone** and **dolomite** up to 12,000ft thick now underlie the Shenandoah Valley, while other such deposits appear around Chilhowee Mountain in Great Smoky Mountains National Park.

About 450 million years ago, continental plates began to converge into a supercontinent called Pangea. The ancient proto-Atlantic Ocean (the Iapetus Sea) was squeezed out by the collision. This slow moving but extremely powerful collision crumpled the leading edge of the North American continent 160 miles inward, collapsing dozens of layers of older, horizontally arranged rocks into an unbelievable mess. Shifting in a northwesterly direction, rock layers jackknifed and stacked up like shingles on a roof, with older layers slid atop younger ones.

The curve of the Appalachian Mountains appears to mimic the bulge of western Africa, the landmass that would have collided with North America at the time. However, no remnants of the African landmass have been discovered in the Appalachian region. An alternate theory suggests that instead of a direct collision, Africa may have pushed a piece of smaller land (a 'terrane') into North America.

THE MODERN LANDSCAPE

About 200 million years ago, the movement of the continental plates shifted, and Africa split from North America. This opened the gulf that widened into the Atlantic Ocean, and the Appalachian Mountains began to transform into the mountains we see today. This final period was one of gentle uplift and constant **erosion**. Over millions of years the chewing of streams has worn these mountains down and carved deep valleys and rugged slopes. Although metamorphosed rocks are very durable and erosion-resistant, the Appalachians are so old (about 500 million years old, compared to the 50-million-year-old Himalayas or the two-million-year-old Sierra Nevada) that they have had plenty of time to be rounded into what topographers call a 'subdued' landscape.

Weathering probably reached its peak during the Pleistocene period, when a cold, wet climate produced rainfall and repeated freeze-thaw cycles. Fortunately for the plants and animals of this region, Pleistocene glaciers never extended this far south, though their impacts were still felt. Several times over a two-million-year span, high peaks and ridges endured periods of alpine tundra conditions. Freezes and thaws split rock formations, leveraged huge boulders from the ground and pushed soils down slope. Boulders that were rolled downhill during the Pleistocene now display jackets of lichen and are such a prominent landscape feature that they've earned themselves an affectionate local nickname: 'graybacks.'

When the Pleistocene finally came to a close about 10,000 years ago, the warming climate softened up slopes and released another pulse of eroded materials. **Landslides**, often triggered by rainstorms, continue sporadically to this day, occasionally closing roads and trails.

As the climate warmed, vegetation also reclaimed the hills, densely cloaking all but the most rugged outcrops. This thin layer of life obscures the geology of the Appalachian Mountains and makes interpreting the story of the rocks difficult and speculative. Visitors will see few of the clues geologists rely on to understand this landscape, but everyone can appreciate the splendor of these amazing old hills.

The ancient landscapes of the Appalachian Mountains are home to a nearly unparalleled diversity of life, including more types of deciduous trees, salamanders, darters and shrews than any other region in North America.

ECOSYSTEM

At the southern end of the mountain chain, centered on Great Smoky Mountains National Park, this diversity reaches its apex. Species found here today took refuge in these hills when Pleistocene glaciers wiped out their populations elsewhere. The combination of intricately divided landscape and favorable climate continues to foster and protect the evolution of even more new species. A park-wide inventory of plants and animals in the Great Smokies could catalog as many as 100,000 species – an astonishing number by any standard.

The deciduous forests that comprise much of Great Smoky Mountains and Shenandoah National Parks and line the Blue Ridge Parkway were once part of a vast wilderness that covered most of the eastern US. Bears, wolves, elk, bison and billions of passenger pigeons roamed these virgin forests at will. With few exceptions these animals are no longer present, and most of the trees have been cut. Great Smoky Mountains National Park's 500,000 acres protect the largest remaining tract of these mighty forests and offer the best chance of survival for many species.

Paralleling the Atlantic Ocean and stretching from Canada south into Alabama, the Appalachian Mountains are a complex of scattered peaks and ridges that define the elevated axis of eastern North America. Of this group, the prominent, easternmost ridge (known as the Blue Ridge) looms largest in the popular imagination and garners the most attention from visitors to the national parks and the Blue Ridge Parkway. Peaks in the central Appalachian region (including Shenandoah National Park) top out around 4000ft, while those in the southern part of the range extend over 6000ft, just high enough to support plant communities that have a lot in common with Canadian boreal forests.

This remarkably diverse landscape is described in many excellent books, but three deserve special mention for the broad overviews they provide: *Great Smoky Mountains National Park: A Natural History Guide* by Rose Houk; *Hollows, Peepers & Highlanders: An Appalachian Mountain Ecology* by George Constantz; and *Mountains of the Heart: A Natural History of the Appalachians* by Scott Weidensaul.

LIFE ZONES

Although much of this region has been broadly classified as 'eastern deciduous forest,' there are still distinct forest types that visitors can readily recognize. With more than 100 species of trees, however, the forest more often feels like a multifaceted, ever-changing mosaic of trees that defies description.

At one time the dominant forest cover in this region was oak-chestnut forest, but with the demise of chestnut trees due to an introduced fungal disease, hickories have filled the niche to produce the widespread **oak-hickory forest**. Covering many mid-elevation slopes up to 4500ft, these forests are dominated by various species of oaks, along with a variety of hickories, pines and other trees.

On lower and drier southwest-facing slopes, **pines** of several species take over as the major tree. These forests depend on frequent fires to keep plentiful oak seedlings in check, so after decades of fire suppression the parks reintroduced prescribed fires in the 1990s. Controlled burns keep plant communities healthy and vigorous and protect endangered species like the red-cockaded woodpecker.

Sheltered areas with deep, moist soils give rise to **cove hardwood forests**, the richest temperate forests anywhere in the world outside of China. Harboring about twice as many plant species as neighboring forests, cove hardwoods also protect the largest and most impressive trees found in the parks. The many species of trees include beech, buckeye, birch, tulip tree, maple, magnolia and hemlock. On wetter, north-facing slopes or along streams, hemlocks may become so dominant they form a distinct **hemlock forest**.

At elevations from 4000 to 5000ft, deciduous trees form a band of cold-tolerant trees around the highest peaks. Beeches, birches and buckeyes characterize northern hardwood forests, which are especially prominent around mountain gaps. These trees may mingle with spruce and fir and often take over where spruce-fir forests are disturbed.

Spruce-fir forests are remnants from the Pleistocene era, when glaciers pushed these forests down from Canada. After the glaciers melted, spruce-fir forests moved back north to Canada, though in places they retreated up slope to find refuge on Appalachia's highest and coldest peaks. Today they form fragile 'sky islands,' separated from each other and from Canadian forests by many miles, offering refuge to such northern species as red crossbills and golden-crowned kinglets.

Also scattered across a few ridgetops are mysterious habitats known as 'balds.' No one has come up with a convincing explanation for these unexpected open spaces in the midst of vast forests. **Grassy balds** are simply meadows of mountain grasses, often surrounded by hawthorn and huckleberry bushes. Now that cattle are no longer grazed in the parks, grassy balds are in danger of being overgrown by invading shrubs, and in several locations they are being preserved with prescribed burns. **Heath balds** (known locally as 'hells' or 'slicks') consist of low dense shrubs like rhododendron, myrtle and azalea. Pruned to a uniform height by strong winds, these shrubs weave their branches into impenetrable thickets.

Streams

The 2000 miles of streams in Great Smoky Mountains National Park, and countless other streams around the region, deserve special mention because they are a unique and beautiful treasure. Nearly every visitor will hike to a waterfall or admire a stretch of sparkling waters during their time in the parks, and given the estimated 890 billion gallons of annual rainfall on just the Smokies alone, water would be hard to miss here.

But these waters do more than create scenic vistas or carve hollows winding through the hills; they're also home to one of the most diverse **fish** populations in the entire US. Many of these fish species live in single drainages and nowhere else in the world. Even if you don't see any of the nearly 100 fish species, you can admire the nuptial flights of **mayflies**, which last for only a single day, or gaze in fascination at the elegant skating of **water striders** as they dart like kinetic toys across quiet pools. **Belted kingfishers** fly along streams with hoarse rattling calls as they hunt for the 90-odd fish they need every day to feed their growing families. You might even be lucky enough to spot the region's most spectacular amphibian, the **hellbender**. More than 2ft long and covered with enormous folds of loose skin, these unsightly creatures have an oddly flattened head.

Otters were reintroduced to the Great Smoky Mountains in 1986, and today more than a hundred individuals roam the park's many streams in search of their favorite prey. Prime otter foods include the 3-

Otter

to 4-inch-long crayfish that frequently nibble on waders' toes. Another otter delicacy is the park's most abundant fish, a small minnow known as a 'stoneroller.' Found in streams at altitudes up to 3000ft, stonerollers outweigh and outnumber all other fish combined.

Brook trout formerly occupied 425 miles of streams in the Great Smokies, but logging, overfishing and introduced exotic trout greatly diminished their populations. Speckled with blue halos around red dots, these gorgeous fish have earned the nickname 'speckled trout,' or 'spec' for short. Unfortunately, they've retreated to a scant 123 miles of streams, while introduced rainbow trout commandeer more than 800 miles. Park managers are now trying to manage streams for the specs.

Brook trout

The paths that water takes over the landscape are perhaps the best way to understand the region's underlying geology. On alternating soft and hard layers, streams (better known by their colorful local names – branches, prongs and forks) carve distinctive parallel drainages that follow lines of soft rock. Over uniformly hard crystalline rocks, small streams coalesce into progressively larger streams as if flowing from the tips of a tree's branches down toward its trunk. And nearly all of the parks' characteristic waterfalls mark places where streams must flow over the top of highly resistant sandstone layers.

LIFE THROUGH THE SEASONS

Whether you're coming for the annual Spring Wildflower Pilgrimage or to see autumn colors, seasonal changes in the Appalachians are one of the main draws for visitors to the region, and each season offers something special.

Winters are surprisingly mild, especially at lower elevations, though the highest peaks usually wear a blanket of snow. Flowers may bloom in January and frogs emerge in February, but March is the rainiest month, and unpredictable freezes strike any time. Some early wildflowers poke out in March, but when spring finally arrives in April, the effect can be mind-boggling. Wildflowers erupt in stupendous variety and profusion, colorful warblers flit through the trees and waterfalls flow with great force and beauty.

Wildflowers bloom with such intensity because they must race to complete their life cycle before the forest canopy fills out with leaves in May and June. Emerging leaves create a wall of green that virtually shuts out sunlight until October. But even as the forest closes in, the floral display shifts to the open balds, where purple-pink catawba rhododendron bloom profusely from early to mid-June, while brilliant flame azaleas draw visitors like honeybees to Gregory Bald in late June.

The hazy, warm days of summer make an ideal time to retreat to the region's cool streams, or to enjoy firefly displays at night. Thunderstorms may arise on hot, sunny afternoons, and bullfrogs can be heard croaking around still waters.

September marks the beginning of the mighty hawk migrations that funnel along the region's ridgetops. This is also the season of ripening huckleberries, spawning brook trout and colorful sumac leaves. Preparing for hibernation, bears roam the hills in the ceaseless search for food. By October the main pulse of songbirds and hawks have left the region, and the hills take on the flaming red and orange of turning leaves. These colors reach their peak during the last two weeks of the month. In November snows return to the highest elevations, and many animals enter their winter sleep.

ANIMALS GREAT & SMALL

A remarkable range of animals find their homes here, and most are relatively easy to observe. Campers are likely to hear skunks, opossums and bears snuffling around camp at night. Streamside hikers can count on seeing beaver, muskrat and otter. Cades Cove in Great Smoky Mountains National Park is considered to be one of the best all-around wildlife-viewing sites, with great chances to watch deer and foxes.

Black bear

Bird-watching is a particularly rewarding exercise, as the region hosts more than 300 recorded species. The parks' large stands of healthy forest support such birds as vireos, warblers and tanagers, whose populations are declining sharply in other regions. Migrating hawks draw people from all over the world to the Blue Ridge – it's possible to spot several thousand in a single day in late September, when migration is in full swing.

Large Mammals

Although bear and deer are particularly abundant, this region also once supported extensive populations of elk, wolves, bison

BEARS IN THE SMOKIES

No other animal has come to symbolize the Appalachian Mountains quite like the **black bear**. This is especially true in Great Smoky Mountains National Park, where the population of 1500 to 2000 bears ranks as the densest in the world – a crowded two bears per square mile – so your chances of seeing black bears are very high!

Hungry bears emerge from hibernation in spring, but find little to eat at first. Much of their diet consists of squawroot, grasses, leaves and stems. Mother bears with new cubs are under a lot of pressure to find food and may be particularly irritable. It's extremely dangerous to annoy a bear at any time, but it's an especially bad idea to come between a mother and her cubs. No matter how slow and lumbering a bear looks, they are astonishingly fast and agile animals if the need arises.

When fruits and berries come into season, bears have a lot more food choices, and they begin to fatten up in preparation for the next winter's hibernation. A bountiful acorn and nut crop allows bears to pack on a good 3 to 5 pounds a day in extra weight, but some years the crops fail and bears must comb the woods night and day in search of other foods. Always keep your food supplies safely stored and your campsites clean, or you might become an unfortunate participant in a 'bear incident.' Bear feeding is prohibited and carries a hefty fine, and if you tempt a bear into a confrontation over food, the bear will likely have to be 'disposed.'

and other large mammals. Some of these are being reintroduced with mixed results. Elk are likely to do well in their new home, for example, but wolf reintroduction was not a success.

BLACK BEARS

Black bears are so widespread and common in the mountains that they have become a popular symbol for Great Smoky Mountains National Park. Only scarcely encountered when the park was set aside in 1934, they have rebounded so well that more than 1500 now roam the park – the densest population in North America.

White-tailed deer

WHITE-TAILED DEER

After a sharp decline in the early 1900s due to hunting, logging and disease, **white-tailed deer** numbers quickly rebounded, and today deer are very common around open areas. In fall, males sport large antler racks and spar with each other. By June females give birth to several white-spotted fawns. In summer, herds of males, females and youngsters gather to feed in meadows.

ELK

At one time the most widespread game animal in North America, **elk** were hunted to extinction in the Appalachians by the mid-1800s. They're now being reintroduced in small numbers. A calf born in 2001 is the first hopeful sign that this charismatic species may roam these woods once again. Listen in September and you may hear the male's eerie bugling calls echo through the woods. You'll know you've spotted an elk if you see an extremely large, dark deer that appears to be wearing a blackish hood. Elk are best observed i early evening, when they leave dense forests to graz in open meadows.

Elk

RIVER OTTERS

Like the elk, the **river otter** was hunted into oblivion by the 1920s. In 1986 a reintroduction effort began in earnest in Great Smoky Mountains National Park, and now these beguiling river dwellers can be seen in and along Abrams Creek, Little River, Hazel Creek, Fontana Lake and Lake Cheoah.

River otter

COYOTES & FOXES

Of the four species of undomesticated dogs, only coyotes and foxes live in the region, although wolves were briefly reintroduced in the 1990s. **Coyotes** are western animals that have been expanding their range eastward. A sighting in 1982 proves they have recently reached Great Smoky Mountains National Park. Adaptable carnivores with wide-ranging appetites, red and gray foxes live at lower elevations and are common around open areas. **Red foxes** are so successful that they have

Red fox

the largest range of any other land mammal except humans, while **gray foxes** are very nimble climbers that readily hunt in trees as well as on the ground.

Small Mammals

Small mammals are much more abundant than their larger cousins, and you may spot many types of squirrels, chipmunks and small carnivores on any given day. Watch for them around campsites, on picnic grounds, along trails or at roadside stops.

SQUIRRELS & WOODCHUCKS

Red squirrels (known locally as 'mountain boomers') are active throughout the year, though in winter they may retreat for periods of time into bulky nests of bark and other plant materials. Their preferred foods are conifer seeds, and in preparation for winter they hoard huge numbers of cones in a single large cache.

Red squirrel

Also common are the paler **gray squirrels** of low elevation forests. Once dependent on chestnuts for most of their diet, gray squirrels now rely on unpredictable supplies of acorns, so their populations fluctuate according to the acorn crop. Gray squirrels also harvest hickories and walnuts, burying seeds individually throughout the forest and relocating them later by smell.

Few people see nocturnal **flying squirrels**, though they are as common as their daytime cousins. These squirrels don't actually fly; rather, they glide between perches on outstretched skin flaps. If you're standing close by, you may hear a soft plop as one lands on a tree trunk.

Parklike openings and cleared roadsides are home to **woodchucks**, or 'groundhogs,' stocky rodents that usually weight about 10lb. In popular legend, when this ground-dweller emerges from its burrow on Groundhog Day in February, its shadow (or lack thereof) allegedly determines how much longer winter will last. In truth, woodchucks have better things to do, like eat lots of grass all summer long so they can sleep soundly through those cold winter days.

RACCOONS

Raccoon

In suburban neighborhoods, **raccoons** can become persistent pests, but in a natural setting they are playful and intelligent denizens of streamside habitats. In their native surroundings they feast on all kinds of tasty plants and animals, from ripe berries to crayfish and clams. When raccoons leave their dens in late spring, you may be treated to the unforgettable sight of small, gangly youngsters falling over each other as they try to keep up with their mother.

SKUNKS

Two species of skunk dwell in Appalachia, where they find ideal habitat among the old fields and farms scattered throughout the region. **Spotted skunks**, the smaller of the two varieties, hide out in the jumbled rocks at the bases of cliffs, while the more common, housecat-sized **striped skunks** favor brushy areas near meadows. Both species are primarily nocturnal and feed on a variety of grubs, eggs, berries and rodents. Because they readily spray antagonists with noxious fluid from musk glands at the base of their tails, they are not animals to play around with.

Birds

In a word, Appalachian birds are colorful. This is especially true of the migratory songbirds that arrive en masse each spring, though even resident species like eastern screech owls and chickadees add an undeniable charm to these verdant hills.

SMALL BIRDS

Considered by many observers to be *the* birds of deciduous forests, **red-eyed vireos** have sadly declined over much of their range. It seems that only in the protected forests of large parks have their numbers remained strong. Like other neotropical migrants (songbirds that migrate to and from the tropics each year), these boisterous vireos make an appearance each April. There's no missing their arrival, because these loud, persistent singers seem to break all records by singing from dawn to dusk (one was recorded singing more than 22,000 songs in a single day).

Red-eyed vireo

Among other common deciduous forest birds are secretive **ovenbirds**, which stay largely hidden on the darkened forest floor. Streaky underneath, but with an orange-crowned head, ovenbirds announce their presence with a loud *teach, teach, teach* song as they walk along wagging their tails and poking into leaf litter for snails and insects. Their curious name comes from the shape of their nests, which have arched tops and look like Dutch ovens.

Many visitors look forward to hearing the distinctive song of **black-throated green warblers** as these birds hunt for insects in the forest canopy. You're far more likely to hear the bird's *zee, zee, zee, zoo, zay* song than to see one, though if lucky, you might spot this small warbler's attractive yellow face and black bib. They seem to favor conifer trees and can sometimes be seen darting out to catch insects in flight.

Given the number of flowering plants in the Appalachian Mountains, it's no surprise that many visitors see **ruby-throated hummingbirds**. Only adult males have the characteristic red throat, which might appear blackish in anything but full sunlight. Females perch on pea-sized eggs in their nests, largely hidden in shrubs and smaller trees. Hummingbirds can be found at all elevations from April to October.

Perhaps the region's most charismatic birds are the cocky and noisy **blue jays**. Whether snooping into the business of other animals or hoping to glean crumbs from a picnic table, blue jays signal their moods by raising their jaunty crests and peering around with inquisitive eyes.

They feed mainly on nuts and in fall spend much of their time collecting acorns and other nuts to store for winter.

Small cousins of the jay, **chickadees** have a similar curiosity and strident attitude. You'll frequently hear their *chick-a-dee* calls ringing through wooded areas. Two species of nearly identical appearance make their home in the region, but most visitors are content to identify each as simply chickadees. In winter months, chickadees are some of the most active and lively of all birds.

Chickadee

The park also sustains many species of thick-billed, seed-eating birds, including ubiquitous and colorful **northern cardinals**. Common residents below 3500ft, these brilliant scarlet birds frequent roadsides, meadow fringes and yards. They have little fear of humans and are one of the most frequently observed birds at birdfeeders. Cardinals sing most of the year, and both males and females produce strong whistled songs.

Weighing in at but a few ounces each, tiny **northern saw-whet owls** are the smallest owls in eastern North America. They hunt almost exclusively at night, dining on a diet of deer mice, voles, shrews and occasionally small songbirds. If you're lucky, you'll hear them after dark from early March to June at elevations of 4500ft or higher. Seeing one, however, is another story. Most birders consider observing the saw-whet owl a once-in-a-lifetime experience.

If you ever need to open a pinecone, find the nearest **red crossbill**. The crossed mandibles of this bird's bill and its flexible tongue are singularly suited to the task. This sparrow-sized, brick-red bird can be spotted almost anywhere in the parks, as long as there are pine trees about.

LARGE BIRDS

Whether they're soaring over open countryside or gathering around carrion, vultures are a most distinctive sight. Large black birds with bare-skinned heads, these scavengers are misunderstood and sometimes feared. In fact, they play an important ecological role by consuming dead animals and keeping the forests clean. **Turkey vultures**, with red-skinned heads, have an astonishing sense of smell and are quick to locate carrion. Black-skinned **black vultures** don't have much of a sense of smell, so instead they watch turkey vultures and swoop in to take their food.

Peregrine falcon

Common summer nesters, **broad-winged hawks** stage one of the foremost migration spectacles in North America in late September, when tens of thousands swoop down the ridges of the Appalachian Mountains en route to South America. Apparently the north-south alignment of these parallel ridges acts like a superhighway for migrating hawks. Countless park visitors climb to high peaks to glimpse this great migration – a vast improvement over the time when hunters used to climb these same peaks to shoot passing hawks for sport.

Long endangered **peregrine falcons** are staging a comeback. Distinguished by their blackish helmets and impressive size, these princely raptors are once again breeding at higher elevations in Great Smoky, nesting on high cliffs and preying on other birds in mid-flight. Watch for them soaring in the sky over the ridges around Newfound Gap Rd, from the Alum Cave Trail and along the AT near Newfound Gap.

It's said that the Cherokee considered **wild turkeys** to be cowardly and stupid birds and would not hunt them for fear these characteristics might be contagious. The polygamous turkeys are frequently sighted in the open fields of Cades Cove and Cataloochee, where males strut with fanned tails in hopes of attracting a harem.

Along roadsides in the early morning you might spot brown camouflaged **ruffed grouses** as they strut through the low grasses. You might also startle one of these birds on a hike, though it is more likely that they will startle you when they explode from the ground at your very feet. Listen carefully in the woods during the early spring mating season for a distant 'drumming' as males beat their wings to attract females.

Two species characterize the owls of this region. The reddish-hued **eastern screech owls** live in woodlands below 4000ft, where their mournful, quavering whistles have been known to raise a few goose bumps. An imitation of their call can elicit responses from several different owls at once. By day screech owls take refuge in tree cavities, and when disturbed, they peer forth with an annoyed, sleepy expression. Twice as large, and with broad, dark-eyed stares, **barred owls** can often be heard in high-elevation forests. Their distinctive call is a loudly hooted *who-cooks-for-YOU? Who-cooks-for-YOU-all?* Both species prey on mice and other rodents.

Ruffed grouse

Amphibians & Reptiles

Amphibians and reptiles seldom garner the attention they deserve, but a surprising number of beautiful and unique species call this area home. In fact, the Appalachian Mountains rank as the foremost site in the world for salamander diversity, with more than 30 species. And new species are still being discovered.

AMPHIBIANS

The majority of the region's salamanders belong to a group known as 'lungless salamanders,' because they lack lungs and breathe through their skin. This odd adaptation requires constant moisture, and the salamanders find an ideal home in the water-saturated Appalachian Mountains. Limited by steep terrain, these salamanders have rapidly evolved into highly localized forms. For instance, **Shenandoah salamanders** have only been found on three mountaintops, where they survive along isolated talus slopes completely surrounded by an abundant competitor, the **red-backed salamander**. These particular mountaintop habitats, which originated in the Pleistocene era, are being buried beneath accumulating soil, and their disappearance threatens the Shenandoah salamander.

Likewise, **Jordan's salamanders** exist nowhere else in the world except the Great Smokies, though they're very common within a limited range above 3000ft. This endemic species is in the process of separating into a series of geographically isolated populations that may one day become entirely new species.

Birds avoid the Jordan's salamander due to its noxious skin secretions, and **imitator salamanders** mimic its coloration with great success. Even professional herpetologists have difficulty distinguishing these two species, and birds simply leave imitators alone rather than run the risk of making a mistake.

Unquestionably the region's most unusual salamanders, **hellbenders** look something like prehistoric socks that have been left underwater too long. More than 2ft long, they are little more than loose folds of brown skin hanging over a long slender form. Completely aquatic but lacking gills, hellbenders breathe through these folds of skin. Though the stuff of legend, they are seldom encountered, because they burrow in the clay bottoms of large streams.

Due to the general absence of ponds and swamps, not many frogs live in this mountainous region, but those that do are an attractive lot. First to emerge in early spring, while snow still lies on the ground, are black-masked **wood frogs**. They are explosive breeders, which means their entire breeding season is condensed into just a few nights, with most of the calling and courting occurring on a single night. Their calls have been likened to the weak cackling of ducks. Wood frogs breed in temporary waters so fish won't eat their tadpoles, but this means that the larvae need a head start in order to metamorphose before the waters evaporate. Adult wood frogs have the remarkable ability to survive when even two-thirds of their body fluids freeze; they rely on anaerobic metabolism to stay alive when their hearts can no longer beat.

In March and April the popular **spring peepers** announce the arrival of spring with deafening choruses. Brownish, and marked with a crisp X mark on their backs, these are the frogs that enliven many childhood memories in the Appalachians. The peeper's call is a high-pitched *peep* repeated once every second. After the breeding season, peepers retreat to moist woodlands, where they can be seen hopping around on rainy summer days.

Languid summer nights in these parts are filled with the deep *jug-o-rum* calls of **bullfrogs**, giant green frogs that make their homes in permanent still waters. Here their larvae grow so large that they take several years to transform into frogs. The 6-inch-long adults are voracious predators that eat every moving animal they can fit into their mouths, including ducklings, snakes and small mammals.

LIZARDS & TURTLES

Due to the moist environment of the Appalachian Mountains, lizards play a minor ecological role. The region's superabundant salamanders have claimed most of this niche, though a few hardy lizard species survive, including widespread **northern fence lizards**. The only lizards in the region with dark chevrons on their backs, they're better known for their bluish bellies, which inspire their common nickname, 'bluebellies.'

Turtles fare much better, though all species except one are aquatic and rarely observed by visitors. Land-loving **eastern box turtles**, with radiating yellow stars on their domed backs, are a favorite sight as they stomp along woodland trails. While box turtles prefer woodlands with openings where they can bask in the sun, they readily retreat to the shelter of bushes. Sunny days from April to October find them active in woodlands below 4000ft. On the first freezing day in October, they quickly burrow down into the leaf litter – if they hesitate, they risk being caught above ground, unable to burrow into frozen soils.

SNAKES

Snakes deserve special mention simply because two poisonous species garner a lot of attention. **Northern copperheads** bite far more people than any other snake, but surprisingly they've rarely killed anyone. In fact, toxins in their venom are relatively weak and not deadly to healthy adults because they are designed to kill nothing more than small rodents and lizards. Copperheads rely on their fabulous camouflage, waiting in ambush up to several days at a time until a small animal wanders by. They mate at night and have two breeding seasons – one in April and May, the other in September and October – so each female's eggs includes the sperm of two separate males. In October they ascend to south-facing hilltops to hibernate in rocky crevices.

While not as aggressive, **timber rattlesnakes** have large fangs and potentially deadly venom. Their bites must be treated in a hospital or might prove lethal. Heavy-bodied and up to 5ft long, these snakes readily announce their presence with a loud buzzing rattle. Avoid them if possible. Park regulations strictly forbid killing these animals.

Timber rattlesnake

Other Creatures

You'll not soon forget your first encounter with a brilliant green **luna moth**. A delicate, 5- to 7-inch-long creature with swallowlike wings, the luna moth flies on warm spring nights. During their two-week lifespan, adult moths eat no food and live only to mate. To help in this task, male luna moths have huge feathery antennae that track down the scent of females. Larvae feed on hickory and sweet gum leaves.

If you don't see a luna moth, perhaps you'll witness a nocturnal display of **fireflies**. Male fireflies fly around to attract mates by emitting light from specialized tissues at the tip of their abdomens. Females waiting on the ground respond with their own light flashes, and each species has developed unique signaling codes between the sexes. So far so good, except that the females of some species are predatory and trick males into approaching by imitating the appropriate female light patterns. These mimics then kill and eat their prey. Competition for mates is so intense that males also trick each other with their own devious counter-flashing. What seems at first glimpse like a fantastic light show is actually a life-or-death drama.

On one level, the backbone of the aquatic food chain in the Appalachian Mountains is the lowly **crayfish**. Nicknamed the 'river lobster' by some, crayfish can be seen walking on stream bottoms, especially at night. Three to 4 inches long, they fall prey to frogs, fish, raccoons, otters and other animals. Female crayfish carry about 200 eggs beneath their tails through the winter, protecting them until they're ready to hatch in May.

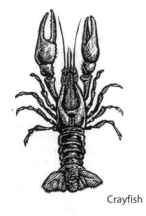

Crayfish

ECOSYSTEM

271

Water striders are the most commonly seen stream insects, and many visitors are curious about these weird-looking creatures that skate effortlessly over the surfaces of pools. Riding on a film of surface tension, water striders detect the vibrations of other insects that fall helplessly on the water surface; they then swoop in to grab the victim with their front legs. Striders also communicate with each other by tapping out messages on the water's surface. If you watch carefully, you will see how these insects constantly interact with each other and dart over to check out every object that falls on the surface of the water.

PLANT LIFE

The deciduous forests of eastern North America are home to a fantastic assemblage of plants, including more than 100 species of trees in Great Smoky Mountains National Park alone. Steep elevation gradients in the Appalachian Mountains produce a rich diversity of habitats, including dry, south-facing hillsides; cold, wet ravines; grassy balds; and foggy, high-mountain conifer forests. In a single day, by hiking from a low valley to the crest of the Smokies, you can experience the same transition of species and habitats found on a journey from Georgia to Maine.

These forests also claim a fascinating connection with the forests of eastern Asia. If you were to journey to forests in China, you'd be hard-pressed to distinguish them from those in the Appalachians. In fact, the regions share 50 genera of plants found nowhere else in the world. These are remnants of an ancient and widespread forest that has long since disappeared elsewhere in the Northern Hemisphere.

If nothing else, the forests of the Appalachians are incredibly rich. You will notice this fact right away in the melee of wildflowers and overwhelming diversity of tree species, but you might not realize just how productive these forests can be. Despite the complete loss of the region's most important tree, the American chestnut, an astonishing amount of nutrients still goes into the soil each year. During a good year, oaks can produce several million acorns (about 12 tons!) for each acre. In Great Smoky Mountains National Park about 500,000 tons of leaves fall to the ground each autumn, providing nutrients that nourish the ecosystem the rest of the year.

Trees

Without a doubt, trees are the dominant feature of the Appalachian Mountains, and for many people they are the main reason to visit the area. Not only do the trees here show a striking display of color, but few other places in the eastern US are home to so many giant old trees. The national champion trees – the largest known living individuals – of seventeen species live in Great Smoky Mountains National Park (though the actual count changes whenever new champions are discovered or old ones pass away).

As days grow shorter in early fall, sugars accumulate in tree leaves and break down into compounds that create flamboyant reds and oranges. For a few weeks in mid-October the hills blaze with these brilliant colors before the leaves begin to fall.

Though it's often difficult to pick out specific trees amid this lush panorama, you shouldn't have any trouble noticing what might be the most abundant hardwood in the region. Even though **tulip trees** have thrived here for more than 50 million years, most individuals today are mere youngsters that have reclaimed old homesteads and cleared areas. Because they provide a popular building wood, many larger tulip trees were cut long ago. Unmistakably straight and tall, tulip trees produce 2-inch yellow flowers in May.

White basswoods are abundant in cove hardwood forests. Their shimmering heart-shaped leaves take on a silvery appearance in the wind due to their reflective hairy undersurfaces. In May the tree sports wonderful, creamy-yellow flowers that attract many honeybees, which turn the flowers' nectar into a prized honey.

Among the most beloved trees are **flowering dogwoods**, whose vibrant white floral displays are honored by regional festivals each spring. Easily identified by their opposite leaves (which sprout in pairs along the stem) and uniquely checked bark, dogwoods brighten woodlands below 3000ft. They sport conspicuous four-petal 'flowers' – actually white-colored leaves that spotlight a tight cluster of flowers at their center.

Mingled in a variety of forests, widespread **yellow birches** and **American beeches** sometimes pair up in high-mountain gaps to create their own distinct habitat. Birches bear characteristic shiny, paper-thin bark that effectively repels water in drenching rains. They frequently stand on stilt-like roots; this occurs when seedlings germinate on old logs and grow into trees as the logs decay. Beeches can be recognized by the crinkled brown leaves that remain on their branches all winter. Relished by countless forest animals, their spiny-husked fruits (beechnuts) open after the first frost.

Two other trees of the high mountains thrive only in limited areas but still play an important ecological role. **Red spruces** and **Fraser firs** are remnants of an ancient Canadian boreal forest that migrated south to avoid Pleistocene glaciers. Today they survive on just a handful of cold mountaintops where they provide homes for a unique community of life, including rare salamanders and mammals and birds at the very southern limits of their ranges. Spruce cones hang from their branches and have spiny needles that are more or less rounded, while fir cones stand upright on the uppermost branches and their needles are flattened.

Other resident conifers include **eastern hemlocks,** found on moist slopes and ravines up to 4500ft. Known for their flat needles (arranged loosely compared to the densely layered needles of firs) and small, egg-shaped cones, hemlocks are important trees because they provide cooling shade along many streams. The half dozen or so species of **pines** in the area are major components of dry forests at lower elevations. Their needles grow in groups of two, three or five, and their cones are large and woodlike (as opposed to green and succulent). Pines rarely grow well in shade, so they rely on frequent wildfires to keep the forest open and help their seeds sprout.

A number of different oaks grow amid the pines, though they can also grow in moist habitats and are thus more widespread. **Scarlet oaks**, with deeply cut, angular leaves, often appear with pines. Remarkably fast-growing, the tree takes its name from the magnificent color its leaves turn in autumn, in stark contrast to pines' dark green foliage. **Northern red oaks** prefer moister sites and are very common up to 6000ft. These are perhaps the region's largest oaks, with individuals that reach 100ft tall and 15ft in circumference.

Shrubs

Shrubs seem to attain their greatest prominence around mountain balds, where they sometimes form impenetrable thickets, hunkered together against the wind. Showiest of all are the famed **catawba rhododendrons**, whose peak bloom in Great Smoky Mountains National Park is among visitors' foremost attractions. Along Newfound Gap Rd in early June, the displays of purple-pink flowers can be phenomenal. When not in bloom, identify them by their long, leathery evergreen leaves.

Characteristic shrubs of the heath balds include **mountain laurel**, a beautiful and abundant plant with pink, candy-striped flowers. Mountain laurels also grow on dry, south-facing slopes and in the pine-oak forests at lower elevations. They have slightly shorter leaves than rhododendrons, though both plants grow to about 10ft tall.

The intensely orange flowers of **flame azaleas** have made Gregory Bald in Great Smoky Mountains National Park a favorite destination. A variety of rhododendron, the azalea is a widespread plant that blooms from late April through July.

Flame azalea

With the end of cattle grazing, grassy balds are now being invaded by spiny-branched **hawthorns**. Abloom with white flowers in early spring, hawthorns are best recognized by their small, red, crabapple-like fruit, which appear in summer.

Common in open woods and disturbed areas are sprawling vines of **poison ivy**, a plant that every visitor should learn to recognize because even casual contact can cause a severe inflammation and rash. Watch for its clusters of three large leaves and clumps of small, whitish flowers. In late summer the leaves often turn shades of red, as if warning you to steer clear. Though closely related to poison ivy, the region's **sumac** species lack toxic oils. To identify them, look for narrow leaflets arranged in long opposite rows and clusters of bright red berries in summer.

Perhaps because there are so many streams in the Appalachian Mountains, **streamside spicebushes** have become some of the region's most abundant shrubs. Their bright yellow blossoms add a lively air in early spring, before other flowers emerge. Bruised leaves emit a potent lemon scent from the resins that also make this plant hard to digest for all animals, except caterpillars of the spicebush swallowtail. The large red berries, however, are rich in fat and eagerly eaten by many birds.

Wildflowers

After fall colors, many visitors rank wildflowers as the region's second-best attraction. April's Spring Wildflower Pilgrimage in Great Smoky Mountains National Park is a guaranteed traffic jam, but it's still worth every minor inconvenience.

Poison ivy

Well before trees begin to bud, a distinct group of 'prevernal' wildflowers make their appearance on the forest floor. These plants characteristically have white, bowl-shaped flowers that track the sun's movement in order to warm their sexual organs and create an enticing spa for pollinating insects. Some plants even burn sugars to generate their own heat and then melt through the snow to get an early jump on the season!

Bloodroots are among the very first flowers to bloom each spring, their long white petals forming an attractive halo around the flower's golden center. The red sap in the plant's roots is toxic but has important medicinal qualities.

Yellow-flowered **trout-lilies** are also early risers. Mottled like a trout (hence the name), this familiar wildflower often grows in large patches amid moist woodlands. Its main pollinators are the large bees that wear their own fuzzy jackets to stay warm on cold days of early spring. Queen bumblebees will mix the pollen and nectar of these lilies to feed growing larvae in their new colonies.

After an initial pulse of wildflowers in March, the main wildflower display picks up full steam by mid-April. There are so many popular flowers it's hard to pick any favorites, but everyone asks about the well-named **Jack-in-the-pulpits**. Unlike any other flower you've ever seen, the flowering structure of this 2ft tall plant consists of a brown central column ('Jack') covered by a vividly striped hood. The flowers themselves are tiny and clustered at the base of the central column. Each plant is either male or female and can switch sex from year to year. Its scent lures small fungus gnats into the flowers, and once inside, the gnats are forced deeper by downward-pointing hairs. While the gnats can eventually escape male flowers (albeit thoroughly dusted with pollen), once inside female flowers, they are trapped until they die.

More than a dozen trillium species thrive in the region, ranging from maroon wake robins to lemon-scented yellow trilliums to big-flowered white trilliums. Glorious **painted trilliums** produce some of the most beautiful flowers of all. Distinctive red bases mark each petal of its large white flowers; the plant also features three spreading leaves.

Pink lady's slippers are prized discoveries anywhere they're found – look for a tall stalk rising from two large, bright green leaves. The flower consists of an oddly inflated pouch (the 'slipper') that nods elegantly over the plant's leaves. Its sweet smell attracts large solitary bees, which are coaxed into the flower by inward-pointing hairs. Like other orchids, this plant produces thousands of dustlike seeds that float long distances on the wind.

In a forest of marvelously designed and strangely shaped flowers, simple **squawroots** poke out of the ground with no leaves and little fanfare. Looking like an elongated, yellowish pinecone, this parasitic plant steals all of its energy from the root systems of neighboring oaks. When bears emerge from hibernation, however, this humble plant is one of the main foods they feast on to rebuild their atrophied muscles.

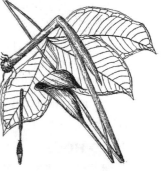

Jack-in-the-pulpit

STRESSES ON THE SYSTEM

Early settlers' journals and accounts are filled with awed descriptions of the vast wilderness that once covered eastern North America. Cathedral-like forests of massive trees stretched to every horizon, abundant animal life filled the woods and the skies were darkened for hours at a time by passing flocks of billions of passenger pigeons. The Appalachian Mountains were a magnificent national treasure that was plundered within an incredibly short period of time. Today the last vestiges of these great wild places hold on in Great Smoky Mountains National Park, Shenandoah National Park and a handful of other protected places.

Plant Diseases & Pests

In a region that was logged, overhunted, overfished, farmed and mined, the single most devastating blow came from a plant disease that spread like lightning in the early 1900s. Up till then, American chestnuts dominated eastern deciduous forests. Each fall these huge trees produced an unbelievable abundance of nuts that sustained enormous numbers of passenger pigeons, bears, deer and many other animals. Chestnuts were also the lifeblood of rural farmers and small towns throughout the region.

Accidentally introduced in a shipment of nursery plants from Asia, the microscopic **chestnut blight fungus** utterly destroyed one of North America's most important trees within decades. Decaying chestnut stumps still produce hopeful sprouts to this day, but the disease lurks in the wings and attacks them before they grow large enough to reproduce. In chestnuts' absence, oaks and other trees filled the niche, but unfortunately their seed crops are episodic and can't sustain all the animals that feed on nuts each fall. Introduced hogs cause further damage because they eat so many of the already limited nuts.

Introduced plant diseases and pests continue to wreak havoc on Appalachian forests. Three examples highlight the damage.

First arriving on the scene in 1963, the European **balsam woolly adelgid** has already turned mountaintops into ghost forests by killing nearly every single Fraser fir. Mature seed-producing trees are virtually extinct, and so many dead trees litter the ground that a single hot fire could kill all remaining fir seeds in

WILD HOGS

When 100 hogs escaped from a North Carolina game preserve in 1920, the face of the Appalachians was forever changed. Now rated as the number one wildlife pest, these 125lb creatures mow through forest habitats like unstoppable rototillers. Quick and evasive, hogs are fast learners that have proven extremely difficult to eradicate. They have few predators and their numbers can grow very quickly because they give birth to large litters and can breed any month of the year.

Every habitat has suffered great harm as herds of hogs tear up the soil and cause erosion along streams. Native wildflowers, salamanders, insects and small animals are all dramatically impacted by the activities of hogs. And in the fall, each hog eats half a ton of acorns and nuts, taking these important foods away from hungry bears, deer and other animals that need these nuts for their winter survival.

In a desperate attempt to moderate these impacts, park managers try to keep hog populations in check, though the hogs may never be completely eliminated. Park visitors will certainly see damage caused by wild hogs, and hikers may even hear the rush of a startled hog fleeing into the dense forest.

the soil. The loss of firs in the spruce-fir forest is leading to devastating, and still poorly understood, consequences. Already, breeding birds in these forests have declined 37 percent, and scientists anticipate many local extinctions.

While the balsam adelgid is attacking a tree with an extremely limited range, a **hemlock woolly adelgid** from Asia is now killing the widespread eastern hemlock so quickly that this important tree could go extinct. Millions of adelgids may infest a single tree, covering it so completely that the tree appears dusted with snow, and little can be done to save the tree. Hemlocks play a critical ecological role, providing homes to numerous species and covering entire hillsides on moist slopes. Their canopy provides cooling shade for countless creeks, keeping aquatic ecosystems healthy and vibrant. The loss of this species would have incalculable impacts, but we might soon find out what this future looks like.

Finally, there is the moth from Europe and Asia with a hunger for oaks. Introduced in 1869, the **gypsy moth** has swept over the eastern forests like a tidal wave. During a gypsy moth outbreak, one can actually hear the forest rustle with the sound of chewing caterpillars, and their dung pellets fall to the ground like a soft rain. Since oaks comprise about 75 percent of the region's trees, their loss would be highly significant.

Animals at Risk

Animals have fared poorly as well. Many of the region's large mammals were hunted to extinction within decades of settlement. Long gone are the original woodland bison, elk, wolf, mountain lion and fisher. However, there is always a chance that animals can be reintroduced, and several efforts have been made on their behalf. Wolves were reintroduced temporarily in the 1990s, river otters and elk have been successfully reintroduced and coyotes have introduced themselves. Black bears have also happily reestablished themselves in the region. Peregrine falcons are once again nesting here after an absence of 50 years, while native brook trout are making a minor but determined last stand against exotic trout that have taken over the lowland streams.

Amphibians are also under close scrutiny, especially since the region's many endemic salamanders may prove excellent barometers of environmental health. With their thin, moist skin, amphibians are particularly vulnerable to pollution and other environmental changes. One study found that wood frog populations in the Smokies declined 50 percent over five years, certainly a cause for concern.

Neotropical migrant birds have also gotten a lot of publicity. Since 1978 more than 70 percent of these species have declined in the eastern US, while the total number of migrating birds has declined 50 percent. Forest fragmentation is proving to be a primary reason for these declines, another reason why large protected forests like those in Great Smoky Mountains National Park are so critical. In fact, songbirds whose numbers are declining elsewhere are still holding strong in the parks.

Poachers & Pollution

But even national park boundaries don't stop poachers intent on profiting from the abundant resources. With wild ginseng fetching up to $365 per pound on the black market, and a gallon of gallbladder bile from black bears going for $3000, there's constant temptation to break the law. An estimated 11,000 ginseng roots have been poached from Great Smoky Mountains National Park in the past decade, and about 40,000 black bears are illegally killed in the United States each year. Undercover sting operations are getting a handle on this trafficking, but much more work needs to be done.

Another problem that doesn't respect park boundaries is the growing threat of air pollution and acid rain. Since 1948 average visibility in the southern Appalachians has dropped 80 percent, plummeting from 93 miles to 22 miles, as the air gets progressively hazier. Pollutants don't merely impact scenic vistas – several dozen plant species are exhibiting conspicuous signs of ozone damage to their leaves. Some forests are starting to resemble ghost towns, while in others the rates of tree growth are dropping dramatically. Acid rain also sterilizes the soil and streams, slowly and insidiously.

Despite the many impacts and threats, Great Smoky Mountains and Shenandoah National Parks and the Blue Ridge Parkway offer an opportunity to turn the tide. Here visitors can see for themselves the vitality of these animal and plant communities and advocate for their future protection. Here, as nowhere else, many species have their best chance to establish healthy, wild populations. Here the echoes of a great wilderness still ring strong and give us hope for the future.

APPENDIX

Great Smoky Mountains National Park

GENERAL PARK INFORMATION

Great Smoky Mountains National Park ☎ 865-436-1200 (road information ext 631, weather forecast ext 630); www.nps.gov/grsm
Backcountry Office ☎ 865-436-1297. Backcountry questions but not reservations
Backcountry Reservations ☎ 865-436-1231
Park Dispatch ☎ 865-436-9171. Response unit for auto failure

ACCOMMODATIONS

GREAT SMOKY MOUNTAINS NATIONAL PARK

Campground Reservations ☎ 800-365-2267; www.reservations.nps.gov. Elkmont, Smokemont and Cades Cove Campgrounds only
LeConte Lodge ☎ 865-429-5704, fax 865-774-0045; www.leconte-lodge.com; mailing address: 250 Apple Valley Rd, Sevierville, TN 37862

IN TENNESSEE

Tennessee Tourism ☎ 615-471-2159; www.tnvacation.com
Cosby/Newport ☎ 423-623-7201; www.cockecounty.com
Gatlinburg ☎ 800-267-7088; www.gatlinburg.com
Pigeon Forge ☎ 800-251-9100; www.mypigeonforge.com
Sevierville ☎ 865-453-6411; www.seviervillechamber.com
Townsend ☎ 800-525-6834; www.smokymountains.org

IN NORTH CAROLINA

North Carolina Tourism ☎ 800-VISIT-NC; www.visitnc.com
Asheville ☎ 800-257-1300; www.exploreasheville.com
Bryson City ☎ 800-867-9246; www.greatsmokies.com
Cherokee ☎ 800-438-1601; www.cherokee-nc.com
Fontana ☎ 800-849-2258
Maggie Valley ☎ 800-624-4431; www.maggievalley.org

TRANSPORTATION

AIRPORTS
Asheville Regional Airport ☎ 828-684-2226; www.flyavl.com; I-26, 15 miles from downtown Asheville
McGhee Tyson Airport ☎ 865-342-3000; www.tys.org; 2055 Alcoa Hwy, Knoxville, TN

BUSES
Asheville Greyhound ☎ 828-253-8451; 2 Tunnel Rd, Asheville, NC
Knoxville Greyhound ☎ 865-522-5144; 100 E Magnolia Ave, Knoxville, TN

HIKER SHUTTLES
The Hike Inn ☎ 828-479-3677; 3204 Fontana Rd, Fontana, NC
Mountain Mama's ☎ 828-486-5995; Waterville Rd, Hartford, TN
Standing Bear Farm ☎ 423-487-0014; 4255 Green Corner Rd, Hartford, TN
A Walk in the Woods ☎ 865-436-8283; 4413 E Scenic Dr, Gatlinburg, TN

TROLLEYS
Gatlinburg Trolley ☎ 865-436-3897. Service from Gatlinburg to Sugarlands Visitor Center, Laurel Falls and Elkmont Campground

ACTIVITIES

CYCLING
Bio-Wheels ☎ 828-236-2453 or 888-881-2453; 76 Biltmore Ave, Asheville, NC
Cades Cove Bicycle Rentals ☎ 865-448-9034; Cades Cove Campground
Cycle Quest ☎ 865-429-5558; 3406 Teaster Lane; Pigeon Forge, TN
Nantahala Outdoor Center ☎ 828-488-2446 or 800-232-7238; 13077 NC 19W, Bryson City, NC
Shifting Gears ☎ 865-908-1999; 636 Middle Creek Rd; Sevierville, TN

FISHING
CCS Fishing Outfitters ☎ 828-497-1555; 626 Tsali Blvd/US 441, Cherokee, NC
Little River Outfitters ☎ 865-448-9459; 7807 E Lamar Alexander Pkwy, Townsend, TN
Rocky Top Outfitters ☎ 865-429-3474; 3361 Parkway, Pigeon Forge, TN
Smoky Mountain Angler ☎ 865-436-8746; www.smokymountainangler.com; 376 E Parkway, Gatlinburg, TN

HIKING & CAMPING
Coleman Retail Store ☎ 865-908-3777; 2655 Teaster Lane, Belz Factory Outlet World, Pigeon Forge, TN
The Day Hiker ☎ 865-430-0970; 634 Parkway, Ste 1, Gatlinburg, TN
The Happy Hiker ☎ 865-436-6000 or 800-445-3701; 905 River Rd, Ste 5, Gatlinburg, TN
A Walk in the Woods ☎ 865-436-8283; www.awalkinthewoods.com; 4413 E Scenic Dr, Gatlinburg, TN

HORSEBACK RIDING
Cades Cove Riding Stables ☎ 865-448-6286; Cades Cove Loop Rd
Next to Heaven Stables ☎ 864-448-9150; US 321/Wears Valley Rd, Townsend, TN
Smokemont Riding Stables ☎ 828-497-2373; Smokemont Campground
Smoky Mountain Riding Stables ☎ 865-436-5634; US 321 near Gatlinburg, TN

WHITE-WATER RAFTING
5 Rivers Adventures ☎ 888-297-9059; Hartford Rd, Hartford, TN
Nantahala Outdoor Center ☎ 800-232-7238; www.noc.com; 13077 NC 19W, 13 miles from Bryson City, NC
Ocoee Adventure Center ☎ 888-723-8622; US 64, Ducktown, TN
Ocoee Rafting Center ☎ 800-251-4800; US 64, Ducktown, TN
Ocoee Whitewater Center ☎ 423-496-5197; 3970 US 64, Ducktown, TN

Paddle Inn Rafting ☎ 828-488-9651; 14611 NC 19W, 14 miles from Bryson City, NC
Smoky Mountain Outdoors ☎ 423-487-5290; Hartford Rd, Hartford, TN
Wildwater Ltd Rafting ☎ 800-451-9972; NC 19W, 12 miles from Bryson City, NC
Wildwater Rafting ☎ 800-451-9972; US 64, Ducktown, TN

TOUR OPERATORS
Little River Outfitters ☎ 865-448-9459; 7807 E Lamar Alexander Pkwy, Townsend, TN. Fishing excursions
Smoky Mountain Angler ☎ 865-436-8746; www.smokymountainangler.com; 376 E Parkway, Gatlinburg, TN. Fishing excursions
A Walk in the Woods ☎ 865-436-8283; www.awalkinthewoods.com; 4413 E Scenic Dr, Gatlinburg, TN. Guided hiking tours

USEFUL ORGANIZATIONS
Friends of the Smokies ☎ 865-453-2428; www.friendsofthesmokies.org
Great Smoky Mountains Association ☎ 888-898-9102; www.smokiesstore.org
Great Smoky Mountains Institute at Tremont ☎ 865-448-6709; www.gsmit.org
Smoky Mountains Field School ☎ 865-974-1000; www.outreach.utk.edu/smoky

MAPS
Great Smoky Mountains National Park, National Geographic/Trails Illustrated
North Carolina Atlas & Gazeteer, Tennessee Atlas & Gazeteer; DeLorme
Great Smoky Mountains Association ☎ 888-898-9102; www.smokiesstore.org. GSMA publishes inexpensive specialty maps.
Harpers Ferry Center www.nps.gov/hfc/carto. This site offers downloads of national park maps.
USGS Map Index ☎ 888-ASK-USGS (275-8747); http://geography.usgs.gov

BOOKS
FOLKLORE & FOLKLIFE
Cades Cove: The Life & Death of a Southern Appalachian Community, 1818-1937 by Durwood Dunn. University of Tennessee Press, 1988.
Blue Ridge Folklife by Ted Olson. University Press of Mississippi, 1998.
Folk Medicine in Southern Appalachia by Anthony Cavender. University of North Carolina Press, 2003.
Food & Recipes of the Smokies by Rose Houk. Great Smoky Mountains Association, 1996.
Mountain Spirits by Joseph Earl Dabney. Bright Mountain Books, 1974.
Our Southern Highlanders by Horace Kephardt. University of Tennessee Press, 1976.
Trail of Tears: The Rise & Fall of the Cherokee Nation by John Ehle. Anchor Books, 1988.
The Wild East: A Biography of the Great Smoky Mountains by Margaret Lynn Brown. University Press of Florida, 2000.

ECOLOGY
Great Smoky Mountains: A Visitor's Companion by George Wuerthner. Stackpole Books, 2003.
Great Smoky Mountains National Park: A Natural History Guide by Rose Houk. Houghton Mifflin, 2003.
Hollows, Peepers & Highlanders: An Appalachian Mountain Ecology by George Constantz. West Virginia University, 2004.
Mountains of the Heart: A Natural History of the Appalachians by Scott Weidensaul. Fulcrum Publishing, 2000.
A Natural History of Mt. Le Conte by Kenneth Wise and Ron Peterson. University of Tennessee Press, 1998.

ACTIVITIES
Day Hikes of the Smokies by Carson Brewer. Great Smoky Mountains Association, 2002.
The Fly Fisherman's Guide to the Great Smoky Mountains National Park by H Lea Lawrence. Cumberland House Publishing, 1998.

Hiking Great Smoky Mountains National Park by Kevin Adams. Falcon, 2003.
Hiking Trails of the Smokies by Carson Brewer et al. Great Smoky Mountains Association, 2003.
The New Appalachian Trail by Edward B Garvey. Menasha Ridge Press, 1997.
The Thru-Hiker's Handbook by Dan Wingfoot Bruce. Center for Appalachian Trail Studies, 2002.
Walking the Appalachian Trail by Larry Luxenberg. Stackpole Books, 1994.
A Walk in the Woods: Rediscovering America on the Appalachian Trail by Bill Bryson. Broadway Books, 1999.

Shenandoah National Park

GENERAL PARK INFORMATION
Shenandoah National Park ☎ 540-999-3500; www.nps.gov/shen
Dickey Ridge Visitor Center ☎ 540-635-3566
Harry F Byrd Jr Visitor Center ☎ 540-999-3283

ACCOMMODATIONS
Camping Reservations ☎ 800-365-CAMP
Big Meadows Lodge ☎ 800-778-2851
Lewis Mountain ☎ 800-778-2851
Mathews Arm Campground ☎ 800-999-3500
PATC Cabins ☎ 703-242-0693
Skyland Lodge ☎ 800-999-4714

TRANSPORTATION
Amtrak ☎ 800-USA-RAIL; www.amtrak.com
City Cab ☎ 540-886-3471 (Waynesboro – southern end of Skyline Drive)
Greyhound ☎ 800-229-9424; www.greyhound.com
Plaza Cab ☎ 540-622-8020 (Front Royal – northern end of Skyline Drive)
Shenandoah Valley Regional Airport ☎ 540-234-8304; www.flyshd.com

ACTIVITIES
CANOEING
Downriver Canoe Co ☎ 800-338-1963; www.downriver.com; 884 Indian Hollow Rd, Bentonville, VA
Front Royal Canoe Co ☎ 800-270-8808; www.frontroyalcanoe.com; Rte 340, Front Royal, VA
Shenandoah River Outfitters ☎ 800-622-6632; www.shenandoahriver.com; 6502 S Page Valley Rd, Luray, VA

HANG-GLIDING
Permits Write to: Shenandoah National Park, 3655 US 211E, Luray, VA 22835

HORSEBACK RIDING
Marriott Ranch ☎ 540-364-3741
Skyland Stables ☎ 540-999-2210

HOT AIR BALLOONING
Blue Ridge Hot Air Balloons ☎ 877-RIDE-AIR or 540-622-6325; www.rideair.com

TOUR OPERATORS
Wayfaring Travelers ☎ 410-666-7456; 27 Sunnyview Dr, Phoenix, MD 21131

USEFUL ORGANIZATIONS
Shenandoah National Park Association ☎ 540-999-3582

Virginia State Parks www.dcr.state.va.us/parks
Virginia Tourism ☎ 800-847-4882; www.virginia.org

MAPS
Shenandoah National Park Topo Map, National Geographic/Trails Illustrated
PATC ☎ 703-242-0693; www.patc.net
TopoZone www.topozone.com
TrailRegistry www.trailregistry.com

BOOKS
Hiking Shenandoah National Park by Bert and Jane Gildart. The Globe Pequot Press, 1998, updated 2000.
In the Light of the Mountain Moon: An Illustrated History of Skyland by Reed L Engle. SNPA, 2003.
Shenandoah Impressions by Pat and Chuck Blackley. Farcountry Press, 2003.
Short Hikes in Shenandoah National Park, by Joanne Amberson. SNPA, revised edition 2002.
We Can Take It: A Short History of the CCC by Ray Hoyt. American Book Company, 1935, reprinted 2000.

Blue Ridge Parkway
GENERAL PARK INFORMATION
Blue Ridge Parkway ☎ 828 298 0398; www.nps.gov/blri
Road Conditions ☎ 828-298-0398
Emergencies ☎ 800-732-0911 or 800-PARKWATCH

ACCOMMODATIONS
Camping Reservations ☎ 877-444-6777; www.reserveusa.com
Bear Den Campground ☎ 828-765-2888
Grandfather Mountain Campground ☎ 800-788-CLUB
Lake Powhatan Campground ☎ 877-444-6777
Meadows of Dan Campground ☎ 276-952-2292
Balsam Mountain Inn ☎ 800-224-9498; www.balsaminn.com
Bluffs Lodge ☎ 336-372-4499; www.blueridgeresort.com
Chetola Resort ☎ 800-CHETOLA; www.chetola.com
HI Blue Ridge Mountains ☎ 276-236-4962
Misty Rose Cottage ☎ 276-236-7658; www.pdbloghomes.com
Mt Pisgah Inn ☎ 828-235-8228; www.pisgahinn.com
Nu Wray Inn ☎ 828-628-2329; www.nuwrayinn.com
Peaks of Otter Lodge ☎ 800-542-5927; www.peaksofotter.com
Raccoon Holler ☎ 336-982-2706
River House Inn ☎ 336-982-2109; www.riverhousenc.com
Rocky Knob Cabins ☎ 276-952-2947
Wintergreen Resort ☎ 800-266-2444; www.wintergreenresort.com

TRANSPORTATION
Greyhound ☎ 800-229-9424; www.greyhound.com
Amtrak ☎ 800-USA-RAIL; www.amtrak.com

ACTIVITIES
HANG GLIDING
Permits Write to: Blue Ridge Parkway, 199 Hemphill Knob Rd, Asheville, NC 28803-8686.

HORSEBACK RIDING
Blowing Rock Equestrian Center ☎ 828-295-4700; 1500 Laurel Ave, Blowing Rock, NC
Clear Creek Ranch ☎ 800-651-4510; 100 Clear Creek Dr, Burnsville, NC
Pisgah Forest Stables ☎ 828-883-8258; NC 276 near Brevard, NC
Wintergreen Resort ☎ 434-325-8260

SKIING
Appalachian Ski Mountain ☎ 800-322-2373; US 221 btwn Boone & Blowing Rock
Massanutten Resort ☎ 800-207-6277
Ski Beech ☎ 800-438-2093; 1007 Beech Mountain Pkwy, NC
Sugar Mountain ☎ 800-784-2768
Wintergreen Resort ☎ 434-325-2100

SWIMMING & WATER SPORTS
Cave Mountain Lake Recreation Area ☎ 540-291-2188
High Mountain Expeditions ☎ 800-262-9036; Main St, Blowing Rock, NC
Lake Powhatan Recreation Area ☎ 828-670-5627; 375 Wesley Branch Rd, Asheville, NC
Sherando Lake ☎ 540-261-6105
Sliding Rock ☎ 828-877-3350
Smith Mountain Lake State Park ☎ 540-297-6066
Wahoo's Whitewater Rafting & Canoe Outfitters ☎ 800-444-RAFT

TOUR OPERATORS
Backcountry Outdoors ☎ 704-883-WILD; 18 Pisgah Hwy, Pisgah Forest, NC
Carolina Tailwinds ☎ 888-251-3206; www.carolinatailwinds.com
High Mountain Expeditions ☎ 800-262-9036
Queen's Trading Post & Outfitters ☎ 704-497-HIKE; US 441, Cherokee, NC

USEFUL ORGANIZATIONS
Blue Ridge Parkway Association www.blueridgeparkway.org
Blue Ridge Parkway Foundation ☎ 336-721-0260; www.brpfoundation.org
George Washington & Jefferson National Forest ☎ 540-265-5100; www.southernregion.fs.fed.us/gwj
North Carolina State Parks www.ncsparks.net
North Carolina Tourism ☎ 800-VISIT-NC; www.visitnc.com
Pisgah National Forest www.cs.unca.edu/nfsnc
Virginia State Parks www.dcr.state.va.us/parks
Virginia Tourism ☎ 800-847-4882; www.virginia.org

MAPS
Pisgah Ranger District, National Geographic/Trails Illustrated
PATC ☎ 703-242-0693; www.patc.net
TopoZone www.topozone.com
TrailRegistry www.trailregistry.com

BOOKS
The Blue Ridge Parkway by Harley E Jolley. University of Tennessee, 1969.
Hiking in the USA by Marisa Gierlich et al. Lonely Planet Publications, 2000.
Waterfalls of the Blue Ridge by Nicole Blouin and Steve and Marilou Wier Bordonaro. The Globe Pequot Press, 1994.
Wildflowers of the Blue Ridge Parkway by J Anthony Alderman. University of North Carolina Press, 1997.

BEHIND THE SCENES

THIS BOOK

This first edition of *Great Smoky Mountains & Shenandoah National Parks* was researched and written by Michael Read, Loretta Chilcoat and David Lukas. Coordinating author Michael Read researched and wrote the Great Smoky Mountains National Park chapter, as well as the Introduction and the majority of Highlights, Itineraries, Activities, Planning, History and the Appendix. Loretta Chilcoat researched and wrote the Shenandoah National Park and Blue Ridge Parkway chapters, as well as contributing to Itineraries, Activities, Planning, History and the Appendix. David Lukas researched and wrote the Geology and Ecosystem chapters.

SEND US YOUR FEEDBACK

We love to hear from travelers – your comments keep us on our toes and help make our books better. Our well-traveled team reads every word on what you loved or loathed about this book. Although we cannot reply individually to postal submissions, we always guarantee that your feedback goes straight to the appropriate authors, in time for the next edition. Each person who sends us information is thanked in the next edition – and the most useful submissions are rewarded with a free book.

To send us your updates – and find out about LP events, newsletters and travel news – visit our award-winning website: www.lonelyplanet.com.

Note: We may edit, reproduce and incorporate your comments in Lonely Planet products such as guidebooks, websites and digital products, so let us know if you don't want your comments reproduced or your name acknowledged. For a copy of our privacy policy, email privacy@lonelyplanet.com.au.

THE LONELY PLANET STORY

The story begins with a classic travel adventure: Tony and Maureen Wheeler's 1972 journey across Europe and Asia to Australia. There was no useful information about the overland trail then, so Tony and Maureen published the first Lonely Planet guidebook to meet a growing need.

From a kitchen table, Lonely Planet has grown to become the largest independent travel publisher in the world, with offices in Melbourne (Australia), Oakland (USA) and London (UK).

Today Lonely Planet guidebooks cover the globe. There is an ever-growing list of books and information in a variety of media. Some things haven't changed. The main aim is still to make it possible for adventurous travelers to get out there – to explore and better understand the world.

At Lonely Planet we believe travelers can make a positive contribution to the countries they visit – if they respect their host communities and spend their money wisely. Since 1986 a percentage of the income from each book has been donated to aid projects and human rights campaigns, and, more recently, to wildlife conservation.

CREDITS

Great Smoky Mountains & Shenandoah National Parks was commissioned, developed and produced in Lonely Planet's Oakland office by Kathleen Munnelly, who also served as project manager. Designer manager Candice Jacobus designed the cover, color pages and template for the series and the title. She also oversaw layout done by Hayley Tsang. Cartographer Bart Wright created the maps, and Valerie Sinzdak was the editor. David Lauterborn proofed, Jennye Garibaldi helped research illustrations and Ken DellaPenta compiled the index. Regional Publishing Manager David Zingarelli guided the project.

ACKNOWLEDGEMENTS

Many thanks to Great Smoky Mountains National Park for the use of its historic photos, and especially to Librarian Annette Hartigan, who was so helpful in providing them.

Thanks also to the National Park Service for additional historic and contemporary photos.

Brook trout (p263) illustration courtesy US Fish & Wildlife Service/artist Duane Raver.

White-tailed deer (p265) illustration courtesy US Fish & Wildlife Service/ artist Tom Kelley.

Red-eyed vireo (p267), Elk (p265), Otter (p262), River otter (p265), Red squirrel (p266) and Chickadee (p268) illustrations courtesy US Fish & Wildlife Service/artist Bob Hines.

Flame azaleas (p274), Poison ivy (p274) and Jack-in-the-pulpit (p275) illustrations courtesy USDA-NRCS PLANTS Database / Britton, NL, and A Brown. 1913. *Illustrated flora of the northern states and Canada. Vol. 1: 442.*

INDEX

N

O

CLIMATE CHARTS

Asheville 2100ft (640m)
Average Max/Min

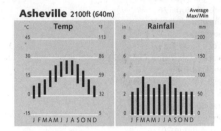

Gatlinburg 1340ft (408m)
Average Max/Min

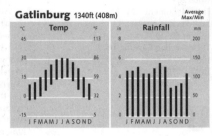

Luray 789ft (241m)
Average Max/Min

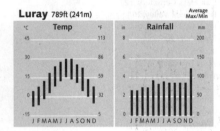

Clingmans Dome 6643ft (2025m)
Average Max/Min

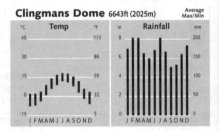

LONELY PLANET OFFICES

Australia
Locked Bag 1, Footscray, Victoria 3011
☎ 03 8379 8000 fax 03 8379 8111
talk2us@lonelyplanet.com.au

USA
150 Linden Street, Oakland, California 94607
☎ 510 893 8555, Toll Free 800 275 8555
fax 510 893 8572
info@lonelyplanet.com

UK
72–82 Rosebery Ave, Clerkenwell,
London, EC1R 4RW
☎ 020 7841 9000 fax 020 7841 9001
go@lonelyplanet.co.uk

www.lonelyplanet.com
Lonely Planet Images:
www.lonelyplanetimages.com